Problems of Religious Luck

Problems of Religious Luck

Assessing the Limits of Reasonable Religious Disagreement

Guy Axtell

LEXINGTON BOOKS
Lanham • Boulder • New York • London

Published by Lexington Books
An imprint of The Rowman & Littlefield Publishing Group, Inc.
4501 Forbes Boulevard, Suite 200, Lanham, Maryland 20706
www.rowman.com

6 Tinworth Street, London SE11 5AL, United Kingdom

British Library Cataloguing in Publication Information Available

Library of Congress Cataloging-in-Publication Data Is Available

ISBN 978-1-4985-5017-8 (cloth: alk. paper)
ISBN 978-1-4985-5018-5 (electronic)

∞™ The paper used in this publication meets the minimum requirements of American National Standard for Information Sciences—Permanence of Paper for Printed Library Materials, ANSI/NISO Z39.48-1992.

Printed in the United States of America

Contents

Acknowledgments

I have many persons to thank for opportunities to present ideas in this book, and for discussion and helpful comments along the way. The project began under sabbatical leave support in Fall 2016 from Radford University. I thank staff and other fellows at IASH, Duncan Pritchard, Matthew Chrisman, Alistair Isaac, David Ward, and other University of Edinburgh PPL faculty. Also to J. Adam Carter, University of Glasgow and the EIDYN Center; and to Jesús Navarro, Kegan Shaw, Harvey Siegel, Lee Whittington, and other members of the Epistemology Reading Group.

Special thanks also go to Scott Aikin, Lenn Goodman, Lucius Outlaw (Jr.), and Robert Talisse at Vanderbilt; Roger Ames and Peter Hershock at the East–West Center; Ron Bontekoe and Chun-Ying Cheng at University of Hawaii; Henrik Rydenfelt and Sami Pihlström at the Nordic Pragmatist Network. My warmest thanks to Heather Battaly, John Bishop, Ian Church, Catherine Elgin, Jacob Goodson, Robert Hartman, Phil Olson, Walter Sinnott-Armstrong, and Wesley J. Wildman; finally to Paul Thomas and my fellow RU faculty, and to Virginia Tech, Wake Forest, and UNC Chappell Hill philosophy departments. Katelyn Dobbins provided invaluable research assistance during Summer, 2018. Dedicated in memory of formative conversations with a good friend, Louis Pojman.

Part I

RELIGIOUS COGNITION AND PHILOSOPHY OF LUCK

Since opinions formed from experience, relative to the same class of objects, are the only rule by which persons of sound understanding are governed in their conduct, why should the philosophers be proscribed from supporting conjectures upon a similar basis, provided they attribute to them no greater certainty than is warranted by the number, the consistency, and the accuracy of actual observations?

–Marquis de Condorcet[1]

NOTE

1. Condorcet, "*Sketch for a Historical Picture of the Progress of the Human Mind: Library of Ideas*" [1794], Tenth Epoch.

Chapter 1

Kinds of Religious Luck

A Working Taxonomy

MULTI-SIDED INTEREST IN PROBLEMS
OF RELIGIOUS LUCK

To speak of *religious luck* certainly sounds odd to the ear. But then, so too "my faith holds value in God's plan, while yours does not." This chapter will argue that these two concerns—with the concept of religious luck and with asymmetric or sharply differential ascriptions of religious value—are inextricably connected. There is a strong tendency among testimonial faith-traditions to invoke asymmetric explanations of the religious value or salvific status of the home religion vis-à-vis all others. Philosophy of luck and risk will be presented in this book as aiding our understanding of what is going on, at least logically and psychologically, when persons, theologies, or purported revelations ascribe various kinds of religiously relevant traits to insiders and outsiders of a faith tradition in sharply asymmetric fashion. In particular, the connections between "religious luck" and "inductive epistemic risk," this book will argue, allow researchers to cross disciplinary boundaries in new ways.[1]

My thesis more carefully stated is that philosophers, theologians, and the numerous parties contributing to or drawing from the cognitive science of religion (CSR) will mutually benefit from a focus on concerns that arise with asymmetric attributions of religious value. They will benefit in particular from a focus on what we will describe as the *New Problem* of religious luck, which is concerned with asymmetric trait attributions in connection with a broader study of *inductive risk*, or the epistemic risk of "getting it wrong" in an inductive context. As contemporary philosophers like Heather Douglas understand and apply it, "inductive risk is the risk of error in accepting or rejecting hypotheses."[2]

3

We will return to develop the connections between luck and risk, as these connections will be important in later chapters. But for qualification, a thesis about "what is going on" in the case of sharply asymmetric attributions of religious value is not necessarily reductionistic. It is not an attempt at a sweeping error theory about religious belief or an attempt to "debunk" it all as unreasonable.³ Moral, theological, social scientific, and epistemological perspectives must all hold place in philosophy of luck, and our approach will be one that *invites* rather than closes off comparison of these perspectives. Theists and naturalists often share recognition of common factors—for instance evolutionary, psychological, and sociological factors—that arouse religious faith tendencies, while disagreeing about whether any combination of naturalistically understood proximate and distal factors are their *sufficient* explanation.⁴ For most theologians the efficacy of factors of nature and nurture in the development of a religious worldview is in turn explainable teleologically in terms of divine will, ultimate plan, and gifts to the faithful. We will not find it necessary to either endorse or deny such a realism about final causes. Rather, we will present the severity of problems of luck, of the manner in which luck-related problems can be "aggravated," as an indication of the need for researchers to much more carefully take notice of the plurality of existing *conceptions of faith*. William Lad Sessions articulates this key point when he writes, "Mostly unrecognized, [there is a] kind of diversity in faith. Different people think of faith so differently as to be using different *conceptions* of faith; they have different views as to what it is to have [or not to have] faith, what the essential features of faith are, what faith consists in, what faith is."⁵

Each of the ways in which a particular conception or model⁶ of faith may aggravate problems of luck will be shown to provide grounds for censure, but this critical side of the book's project is not directed against theistic belief per se. Rather it will be directed toward the reasonableness of different responses to religious multiplicity, and will be developed with the overarching aim of aiding our comparative understanding of religious fundamentalism.

Although there has been little written to date that speaks directly to problems of religious luck, certain aspects of them described in other terms have a long and voluminous history. The first section of this chapter introduces the existing literature that explicitly utilizes the concept; it also provides initial examples of the wide variety of perspectives from which the family of religious luck–related problems can been addressed. Following a brief methodological aside in the second section, the longer third section sets out a taxonomy of kinds of religious luck, encompassing kinds that interconnect primarily with the literature on *moral* luck, and other kinds that interconnect primarily with the literature on *epistemic* luck. These sections also provide examples of how theological positions can differ markedly in the extent to which they "lean on luck," or in other words, aggravate or exacerbate luck-related worries of one specific kind or another. While moral, epistemic, and theological consid-erations might all be raised in regard to specific problems of luck, we will later argue that they are never entirely disconnected. An initial indication of this interrelation among luck-related problems, which I hope to convince the reader are a needed focus today, is how they are described in the literature in overlapping ways: intra-religiously, inter-religiously, and counter-religiously. Let us start with an example of each of these three ways of addressing problems of religious luck, letting these examples introduce issues we can later develop in more depth.

One of the first attempts to connect philosophical discussions of luck with issues in philosophy of religion and theology was a 1994 paper by Linda Zag-zebski, "Religious Luck." Like many others, Zagzebski finds it troubling that people might be the proper objects of moral evaluation, including praise and blame, and reward and punishment, because of something that is partly due to luck, and to that degree outside of their control. Unlike some who deny the phenomenon of moral luck, Zagzebski believes that these problems do exist and, writing as a Christian philosopher, "that they exist for Christian moral practice and Christian moral theories as well." The author's focus is explicitly intra-religious in that her topic "is a problem internal to the concepts of moral responsibility, reward, and punishment as understood by the Christian." Zagzebski's central thesis is that Christianity has at least two core traditional teachings, those of eternal heaven and hell and of grace, that potentially "magnify the problem of luck to infinity."[7] Thus she finds it useful to engage philosophy of luck from the direction of moral theory, through drawing upon previous work on moral luck by Joel Feinberg and Thomas Nagel.

Taking discussion in a comparative direction, Jewish philosopher Charlotte Katzoff (2000), in "Religious Luck and Religious Virtue," compares the role of luck in two accounts of divine election, that of Paul and of Rabbi Judah Loeb. Katzoff agrees that God conferring religious value/status on persons without necessary reference to efforts or deeds is "perplexing." But she argues that Paul's account, *more* than Rabbi Judah's, suffers from concerns Zagzebski raises about the concept of grace. To say that the greatest religious virtues are infused by grace meant to Paul that faith, by its very nature, is not under the control of its possessor.[8] In emphasizing that God's plans are para-mount and may be indifferent to human will and exertion, Paul presents the virtues as "divine gifts, fortuitous, accidental, as it were." Katzoff is keen to point out how this impedes the attribution of religious value to the individual on the basis of those virtues. But she argues that this worry is at least lessened on an account like Rabbi Judah's, where the virtues adhere essentially to the character of the individual.[9]

What we called a contra-religious or skeptical focus includes certain prob-lems of luck discussed not just within theological circles, but as challenges to the coherence of divine attributes or to the reasonableness of beliefs or attitudes of a certain kind. Some of these challenges involve primarily moral luck concerns, while others lead us into connections with epistemic luck. "Counter-religious" can mean here that a writer raises de facto or de jure objections. A de facto challenge presents reasons for thinking that a particular religious claim must be false, or that the claim is only erroneously understood as a cognitive claim at all. A de jure challenge presents reasons for thinking that a certain specified range of beliefs or attitudes is morally and/or episte-mologically unjustified, unreasonable, or irresponsible.[10] De jure challenges will mainly be our focus in this book, so let us note that the "target" of criti-cism for these arguments is some normative standings like reasonable, ratio-nal, justified, warranted, and so on.

With a focus on epistemic luck, John Stuart Mill writes,

> The world, to each individual, means the part of it with which he comes in con-tact; his party, his sect, his church, his class of society. . . . It never troubles him that mere accident has decided which of these numerous worlds is the object of his reliance, and that the same causes which make him a Churchman in Lon-don, would have made him a Buddhist or a Confucian in Pekin[g]. . . . Nor is his faith in this collective authority at all shaken by his being aware that other ages, countries, sects, churches, classes, and parties have thought, and even now think, the exact reverse.[11]

There is an implicit luck-related de jure argument in this passage high-lighting the strong contingency of certain kinds of belief on people's found epistemic location—their family or culture, or their time in history. The contingency of belief "never troubles him," but Mill's perspective is that it *should*. Depending on how one interprets it, Mill's argument may suggest a sweeping sort of debunking argument of all "nurtured" beliefs, or it may sug-gest only the appropriateness of epistemic humility, and a de jure challenge to those who hold their beliefs in a certain, for example, unreflective or, again, absolutistic *way*.[12]

We will later look closer at other more carefully formulated demographic contingency arguments. Given only this passage, it is hard to say just what Mill's argument is exactly, and also whether and why variance with what we can call *epistemic location* should be thought *more* troubling for the well-foundedness of religious beliefs than for other nurtured beliefs he mentions, such as party (political orientation) and class. At this point it is enough to take note of these broader concerns about relationships between domains, and to initially take Mill's example of the London "Churchman" as raising a religious epistemic luck–related problem. But to anticipate just a little, we can say that especially strong epistemic luck–related worries arise for theologies which claim that God saves only those who adhere to one particular religious identity, or who assent to one particular religious creed among the many. Thus R. J. Hartman (2014) refers to those who assert religion-specific doxastic requirements on one's salvation as raising "the soteriological problem of geographic luck." For if this purported saving knowledge is not uniformly distributed, then as a condition of salvation it appears one must be environmentally lucky; otherwise that religious identity will not plausibly even be what William James referred to as a "live option" for them. This suggests to me that we should best interpret contingency arguments as challenging certain uncritical or dogmatic *ways* that we might hold our nurtured beliefs, rather than as intending to undercut the justification for whole *domains* of belief on account of their being more deeply conditioned than others by one's epistemic location.

Our next step will be to set in place a functional taxonomy of different kinds of religious luck, so that we can set the New Problem and the chapters of part II against this background. But to summarize this introductory section, problems of religious luck are common ground for theologians and philosophers of religion, though individual thinkers will approach them in substantially different ways. They may be debated as problems of theological adequacy either intra-religiously or inter-religiously. They may also be posed as challenges to particular teachings, to particular conceptions of faith, or to the very coherence of divine attributes.

ACCOUNTS OF AND KINDS OF LUCK: A METHODOLOGICAL PRIMER

Thomas Nagel (1979) adopted a *lack-of-control* account of luck when developing the concept of moral luck. The lack-of-control account takes moral luck to be implicit in moral evaluation to the extent that a person's degree of moral responsibility for an act or for a personal trait is held to go beyond the degree to which he or she controls it.[13] Nagel writes, "Where a significant aspect of what someone does depends on factors beyond his control, yet we continue to treat him in that respect as an object of moral judgment, it can be called moral luck."[14] More formally, Nagel articulates the problem of moral luck in terms of violation of the *Control Principle* and *Control Principle–Corollary*.

(CP) We are morally assessable only to the extent that what we are assessed for depends on factors under our control.

(CP-Corollary) Two people ought not to be morally assessed differently if the only other differences between them are due to factors beyond their control.

Philosophers of luck today utilize more accounts than lack of control, which Zagzebski's and Katzoff's initial forays into problems of religious luck generally followed. While control theory has been the most common approach in work on moral luck, Nicholas Rescher's book *Luck* (2001) employs a probabilistic account, and the study of epistemic luck typically employs one or another variant of a modal account.[15] Duncan Pritchard writes that at least for the kinds of luck at issue in epistemic evaluation, "the degree of luck involved varies in line with the modal closeness of the world in which the target event doesn't obtain (but where the initial conditions for that event are kept fixed). We would thus have a continuum picture of the luckiness of an event, from very lucky to not (or hardly) lucky at all."[16]

Some ethicists have been tempted to deny moral luck in order to affirm human moral autonomy and culpability for wrongdoing. Luck cannot affect praiseworthiness and blameworthiness. The interest dependence of attributions of luck—the sense in which an event might be improbable, yet not lucky or unlucky if nobody's interest were promoted by it—is also handled in a number of different ways by philosophers of luck. A philosophy of luck such as ours that ranges over several domains need not be given to any one account. It can draw from extant accounts but can also invite new ones. Luck *attributions* and luck-leaning *explanations* can also be studied psychologically, and as with some other "folk" concepts, attributions and explanations that appeal to luck might be challenged by an error theory. We can return to these points later, but in a review article on recent work on moral luck, Dana Nelkin counters attempts to dismiss the concept of moral luck: "It seems that there are countless cases in which the objects of our moral assessments do depend on factors beyond agents' control. Even though 'moral luck' seems to be an oxymoron, everyday judgments suggest that there is a phenomenon of moral luck after all."[17] And in a recent book *In Defense of Moral Luck,* Robert J. Hartman (2017) argues that "We have good evidence for the claim that resultant, circumstantial, and constitutive moral luck exist. Because the kinds of resultant, circumstantial, and constitutive luck that can affect praiseworthiness and blameworthiness are very common, we also have very good evidence that moral luck is everywhere."

Social psychological studies of moral judgment show that people's actual moral judgments are sensitive to the relationship between culpability and lack of control. As these authors acknowledge, folk psychological fact of this sort does not settle the philosophical issue, though they do bear strongly upon it. Excuse conditions for moral culpability are also a normative concern, but culpability attributions and whether people assign vice traits and culpability as readily to themselves as they do to others, or instead tend to appeal to bad luck (not bad character), to explain one's own wrongdoings, are aspects of moral judgment that moral psychology can study. So Hartman writes, the "*luck-free intuition*, that is, the principle-level intuition that luck is irrelevant to praiseworthiness and blameworthiness," is rebutted, but puzzles remain.[18] Even so, the concept of moral luck, its defenders would say, has practical, reformatory potential: it allows us to compare theory with practice, or with what moral psychology shows us about how we make moral judgments. The concept serves philosophy by allowing us to ask if one or more of these control principles are perhaps violated by an ascription of moral culpability to an agent/group for a particular action or practice. If so, the question remains whether to retract the culpability judgment or to qualify the principle itself.

One question that is background to our taxonomic project is whether religious luck is only a combination of moral and epistemic luck, or its own kind. But another is whether *any* concept of luck is philosophically viable and useful, in ethics, epistemology, or science, for that matter. Hales and Johnson (2014) and Ballantyne (2014) go the other way on this question and are critical of "philosophy of luck" generally.[19] So both supporters and critics of philosophy of luck appeal to psychological studies, and to the empirical adequacy of their own view vis-à-vis its distractors who they see as not understanding the implications of folk psychology.

Methodologically our taxonomic approach allows us to avoid the extremes of the debate between those who treat luck as objective and those like the above authors who see it as a cognitive illusion. We will treat religious luck as a unique animal, while also pointing out numerous connections with more established literatures on moral and epistemic luck. Our use of the concept of religious luck is primarily *diagnostic*, and what is meant by the diagnostic usefulness of the concept will emerge by degrees through the course of the book. I will take it that the value of the concept of religious luck must be demonstrated, not assumed. In later chapters we will attempt to demonstrate it through a) the genuineness of the *problems* it allows us to articulate and illuminate, b) the fruitfulness of the new diagnostic *questions* it helps generate, and c) the *broad-based discussion* about these problems and questions it invites. As mentioned earlier, luck and risk are closely connected concepts on the present account, so our translation of problems of religious luck into more formal and experimentally approachable terms of inductively risky habits of inference in later chapters should further support the philosophical worth of both concepts.

We have seen how the extant literature on religious luck has emerged mostly out of application to previous theological and philosophical work on moral luck. Theologians and religious philosophers, rather than secular philosophers, have to date done most of this application of philosophy of luck. But whether religious luck is the same as or different from a combination of moral and epistemic luck can largely remain an open question here. Note also that I will use "kinds" loosely to cover kinds and types. But if we more strictly employed a kind/type distinction, we would say that moral, epistemic, and religious luck are main kinds of luck, while the six members of our taxonomy are different types or sorts of *religious* luck that should, as a minimum, be distinguished.

A WORKING TAXONOMY

Earlier writers have referred to "religious" (Zagzebski), "salvific" (Davison 1999), and "soteriological" luck (Anderson 2011). Using "religious" as the unifying term, this section aims at a more detailed and comprehensive taxonomy. Although we are focusing on distinguishing different kinds of religious luck rather than on articulating the ins and outs of specific theological debates, we should note as background that there has been lively debate especially among Christian thinkers involving soteriology (the doctrine of salvation), and the *soteriological problem of evil*. David Myers describes the latter problem this way: "According to orthodox Christianity, salvation depends on faith in Christ. If, however, God eternally punishes those who die ignorant of Christ, it appears that we have special instance of the problem of evil: the punishment of the religiously innocent. This is called the soteriological problem of evil."[20]

As we will see, proponents of a doctrine of Hell need an account of how the condemning the apparently morally innocent is compatible with God's love and God's justice. The problem has non-Christian application also, as it seems to be an especially strong problem at least for exclusivists about salvation (salvific exclusivists). But we will concern ourselves with purely theological debates only as far as necessary to show a context in the literature for each particular kind of religious luck, and for the asymmetric trait-ascriptions with which each kind might be associated.

Philosophical theologians have written on problems of religious luck from a variety of theological perspectives: Catholic, Jewish, Open theist, Skeptical theist, Reformed, and Molinist. Their treatments, like Zagzebski's and Katzoff's, involve highlighted differences between traditionalists about binary, eternal, retributive hell (Craig 1989; Davison 1999), and between univeralists and annihilationists, for whom God's justice must be primarily restorative rather than punitive (Jones 2007; Buckareff and Plug 2009; Sider 2002). Other contributors we will discuss draw attention to problems of luck in connection with the teaching of predetermination, divine foreknowledge, the contingency of one's access to putative saving knowledge, and the extent of responsibility one plausibly bears for what religious beliefs one does or does not have. Although these problems are not usually seen as a connected, they are ones to which our taxonomic approach I believe aids understanding.

Our taxonomy may turn out to be far from complete, but one reason for us to begin with a taxonomy is a practical one: Serious philosophic interest in the concepts of moral and of epistemic luck only took off *after* comprehensive taxonomies for those kinds of luck were introduced, yet no such comprehensive taxonomy has been attempted for the concept of religious luck. Another reason for our taxonomy is to provide some overview of the theoretical problems and diagnostic questions illuminated by the concept of religious luck, and to familiarize readers further with the extant literature. Thirdly, laying out the taxonomy will provide opportunity to further identify specific problems and related debates that each kind of religious luck is associated with. One thing to keep in mind, though, is that kinds of religious luck, like kinds of luck better recognized in the literature, are *compoundable*: while the kinds are themselves distinct, there may well be more than one kind of luck in play in any particular described case.

Resultant Luck we can define as the (bad/good) luck of being harmed or benefited in consequence of an event, action, or decision/judgment, under conditions of close gaps among persons. When the harm or benefit involves the judgment or interventions of a supernatural being, we can call this resultant *religious* luck.

We can all imagine everyday cases where people miss or make some fairly arbitrary, random, or gradational "cut-off." The cut-off for college admission was a SAT score of 1200, and you got denied or accepted by scoring one point below or above that designated score. The talk show is giving a special travel gift you very much want to the first 100 lucky callers, and although you have no idea how quickly people will call, you are caller 101, or 100. Analogous questions surround what in the theological literature is called the *problem of close gaps.* From God's perspective, is there always a sharp line between the moral and the immoral, or between the faithful and faithless? How can God be fair in regard to judgments meted out if, as seems highly plausible, there must be close gaps between many people's on-balance moral character?

> *Chris is impacted negatively (positively) by resultant religious luck if Chris is close-gapped with others in terms of moral or religious qualities, but suffers (benefits) greatly through God's judgment of her relative to her close-gapped peers.*

Divine judgment under conditions of close moral gaps between people raises moral concerns about God's justice. The problem of close gaps raises at least three distinct moral objections about proportionality for soteriologies of divine judgment. These are: a) objections to the morality of divine *punishment,* b) objections to theologies that teach of *binary* heaven/hell, and c) objections to theologies that teach of *eternal* hell. It would be all the more lucky for you to benefit from a close-gaps comparison with me, or me with you, when the differences in our respective post-mortem existence are describable as reward for one of us and punishment for the other, and/or when the judgment settles a condition that each of us will necessarily remain in *eternally.*

Criterial Religious Luck overlaps with resultant religious luck. Criterial luck we can define as suffering harms or enjoying benefits through being judged, rewarded, or punished on a basis 1) which is not principled in such a way that it will be consistently employed across like cases (call this CRL_1), or 2) which the persons judged do not have a clear conception of (call this CRL_2), or 3) which the persons judged might not even be aware that they are subjected to (call this CRL_3). When this regards a purported divine judgment of souls, it is criterial *religious* luck.

> *Chris is impacted by criterial religious luck if Chris suffers (benefits) from a divine judgment made on the basis of criteria that is 1) whimsical, or not consistently employed across like cases (CRL_1), 2) not clear to Chris (CRL_2), or 3) not known at all to Chris (CRL_3).*

One difficulty in conceptualizing criterial luck is that it is difficult to distinguish absolutely between a person being constituted as certain way and the world into which we are thrown being constituted a certain way. We are already impacted by religious luck if, according to one's theology, the afterlife is bifurcated between heaven and hell, in contrast to ones where the distinction is between heavenly reward and mere annihilation, or where universal salvation/liberation is envisioned. Assuming semblance of human free will, God risks us much more in the former, which is what Zagzebski indicates in saying that the doctrine of eternal hell magnifies the problem of luck "to infinity." Immanuel Kant relatedly wrote,

> From the most ancient times there have been two systems concerning the future eternity: one of them is the *monistic* view of eternity, which grants all . . . eternal blessedness; the other is the dualistic view, in which *some* are chosen for blessedness, but all *others* are condemned to eternal damnation. . . . One could ask, why were the few, indeed, why . . . was a single person created if their only reason for being was to be lost for eternity, which is even worse than simply not to exist?[21]

Kant's distinction between "systems concerning the future eternity" leads him to a quite widely flung moral objection to a theological bifurcation between eternal reward and eternal suffering. His opinion seems to be that the damned would judge it "worse than simply not to exist" if they must exist as eternal beings into a dualistic system. In other words, the damned would count themselves unlucky to have been born at all. Annhilationist and universalist soteriologies, which Kant places under the monistic view of eternity, appear much less susceptible to these problems than are soteriologies of eternal hell. While the difference in value of finding myself born into a monistic or dualist afterlife would seem to be net neutral for those who are in either scenario heaven-bound, it is an infinite disvalue for the unsaved to find themselves in binary, heaven-or-hell afterlife. Whatever else one may say of them, they are so risked by their creator that they will not simply die (annihilate) when they die.

We will treat *individual* character or constitution, in contrast to humanity generally, under *constitutive luck,* below. But one of the many connecting issues between the world-side and the agent-side of the soteriological problem of evil is the diversity among conceptions of God's sovereignty/ providence. Criterial religious luck appears most challenging for theologies on which salvation is held to be unmerited, and wholly a gift, *sola dei gloria.* These theologies are arguably dependent upon conceptions of divine "power" and "kingship" long abandoned in social and institutional arrangements. Consider that for kings and tyrants of ancient times, the more willful or whimsical the ruler's decrees, the more "powerful" he was often perceived to be, and perhaps the more secure his reign. Consenting to issue only edicts that follow criteria of any sort beyond his own self-serving purposes might well have been interpreted as a weakness, and a limitation of "real" power. In the writings of Calvin every act of faith on the part of a person is due to some special divine gratuitous act. Election was "founded on his gratuitous mercy, totally irrespective of human merit . . . [and for those God condemns] the gate of life is closed by a just and irreprehensible, but incomprehensible judgment."[22] So there appear to be contemporary theologies which reject *all* moral determinability of criteria for the God-chosen traits of the elect and the percentage of saved versus damned individuals God creates. God's justice is reduced to whatever God chooses to do, just as moral goodness reduces to the duty to follow God's commands. The moral and theological adequacy concerns, however, are that divine sovereignty, so understood, partakes of such a "whimsical" model.[23]

Zagzebski seems to acknowledge this criterial concern as part of the problem of religious luck when she writes, "Christian moral theory replaces the concept of moral wrongdoing by the concept of sin, an offense against God, and the concept of an abstract state of moral worth which may or may not be determinable is replaced by the concept of one's moral state as judged by God. And presumably that *should* be determinable."[24] Theologies whose conception of sovereignty runs in the opposite direction, protecting God's "power" against genuinely *moral* criteria for election, arguably raise especially strong concern that they place God's creatures under a burden of religious luck of the criterial kind.

Problems of criterial luck are exacerbated not only in a criteria-free conception of God's sovereignty or power (suggesting CRL$_1$), but also the penchant of apologists to draw an ad hoc distinction between all the things they claim we can know about divine will and plan, and where, as skeptical theists say, we must just accept that God's will and plan are beyond human knowledge or comprehension. In the present analysis of religious luck this puts at least some sub-kinds of criterial religious luck on the *aleatory* side of the aleatory/epistemic distinction. This is to say that to the extent that a theology holds that God does not reveal his criteria, or that he makes salvation an unearned gift after rendering us equally unable to merit it, renders divine judgment from the human perspective more akin to genuine randomness *in the world* than to a problem of personal ignorance due only to contingent factors that one might overcome through effort to improve one's understanding.[25] For under these conditions, it just cannot *be* understood.

Perhaps few theologies are open to this particular problem of luck. Many theists presume that a just and loving God would want his creatures to understand clearly what is demanded for salvation, would want its expectations of humans to conform with human perspectives on doxastic and moral responsibility, and would want humans to have at least some amount of control in being able to welcome or resist grace. But where a theological conception of divine sovereignty submits grace and/or divine judgment of humans to criterial luck, this threatens to undermine each of these expectations. Inculpable ignorance can defeat one's opportunity to develop the religious value God seeks in people as their highest good. It can defeat one's prospects for heaven, and in a binary afterlife that means saddling them with hell.[26]

Escapist and universalist soteriologies, in which there are post-mortem opportunities for persons to morally reform or to be "converted" to the saving faith, aim to redress moral objections to binary eternal heaven and hell.[27] They also aim to address luck-related objections to the particularist tendency to attribute all religious value to one's home religion. But such revisions are seen as radical by others, in part because they push toward if not entail salvific inclusivism *rather than* exclusivism. To give just one specific example of such an exchange, Linda Zagzebski as we saw took quite seriously the need for Christian theology to be revised to address problems of religious luck, and she commented on several possible ways to do so, including dismissing eternal hell as inconsistent with divine attributes. But Scott Davison (1999) rejects every one of her five avenues of revision, for what he sees as their lack of orthodoxy and/or Biblical backing.

Theologies that allow *anonymous participation* in saving grace have not only a post-mortem but also a counter-factual, or middle-knowledge, version.

Since one need not have converted to the home religion during their actual lifetime, these accounts address moral objections to overt particularism about religious value, and invite religious inclusivism. The Catholic Catechism clearly states an inclusivist doctrine of implicit faith. Persons who, "through no fault of their own, do not know the Gospel of Christ or his Church, but who nevertheless seek God with a sincere heart, and, moved by grace, try in their actions to do his will as they know it through the dictates of their conscience—those too may achieve eternal salvation."[28]

While many others besides Catholics accept this view, five-point Calvinists and some self-described Molinists like William Lane Craig are among those who adhere instead to teachings of limited atonement, explicit doctrinal assent, and what has come to be called the *strong view* of hell.[29] For Molinists, named after the sixteenth-century Jesuit theologian, Luis de Molina, God has *middle-knowledge, or knowledge of* "counterfactuals of creaturely freedom," and this knowledge of what people would have done under different conditions of life played an integral role in his choosing a particular world to create. It also plays a role in divine judgment of each individual person's moral or religious worth. It is easy to see how middle-knowledge could support escapism and salvific inclusivism, since presumably many, many more would have converted had they been exposed to the putative saving faith; or they would not have done so many sinful things had they better moral luck in their life circumstances than to be battle-born, or born impoverished, etc. Indeed, David Hunt (1991) rejects Molinism for the very reason that he sees it as inconsistent with the exclusivity of salvation through Christ, adding that evangelical activity is rendered futile if God's judgment of the individual includes counter-factual knowledge of what the individual would have done under different life circumstances. But this is what he takes Molinism to *logically* imply. In fact, Craig holds (1991, 1995) that Molinism remains consistent both with Christian salvific exclusivism and with the teaching of binary eternal heaven and hell.[30] How he upholds this view, and why he thinks it is consistent with God's benevolence, is interesting from the point of view of our study. Here is the essential twist in Craig's Molinist response to the soteriological problem of evil:

> God in His providence has so arranged the world that as the Christian gospel went out from first century Palestine, all who would respond freely to it if they heard it did hear it, and all who do not hear it are persons who would not have accepted it if they had heard it. In this way, Christian exclusivism may be seen to be compatible with the existence of an omnipotent and omnibenevolent God.[31]

So actual conversion to Christianity seems still to be required for salvation, if only because "rejecting God" or "not responding freely" to his call is reducible for the Christian exclusivist to rejecting or even simply not being in position to be exposed to the Christian bible's claim of Christ as savior. I take Craig as maintaining that all actual non-Christians are damned, and maintaining it on the basis of a metaphysical guarantee that their *being* non-converts is proof positive that they are (unluckily) constituted such that they would "reject" God under counter-factual circumstances also.

One problem with this is that if you actually surveyed all the people who Craig takes as pre-ordained for damnation (but who are at least decent enough in this world to stop and take part in a survey) very few if any of them would recognize themselves as fitting Craig's description of them as "individuals who would have rejected His grace under any circumstances." Notably, this includes homosexuals, since this same strategy in defense of orthodoxy is indicated in Craig's treatment of the damnation of homosexuals, regardless of whether they are inside or outside the church.[32] The moral bad luck that has to be ascribed to those homosexuals in the face of scientific evidence of its largely biological basis also has to be rationalized in a theology of predetermination.

What I think Craig's unique apologetic "fix" suggests that should be of interest to philosophers and psychologists is that a common yet deeply flawed way of avoiding future cognitive dissonance (or simply reasoned arguments that challenge one's assumptions), is to *adjust just those states that conflict with one's biases, leaving the latter intact.*[33] While we cannot pursue it further here, there may be clear evidence to support this charge: Craig's Molinist account and his critic Hunt's evangelical account both still lean heavily on implicit appeals to religious luck, only they each appeal to a different *type* of luck. This leads us to introduce another type with many instances.[34]

Constitutive Religious Luck is the term we can use to describe religious analogues of bad/good luck in being the kind of person one is. One's personal constitution may include both contingent (e.g., inclinations, abilities, and temperament) and necessary features as a member of one's species. Moral theorists recognize a kind of (bad/good) luck that affects persons by manner of what inborn morally relevant capacities they lack or have (inborn inheritances), or by what disadvantageous or advantageous social groupings they are born into (cultural inheritances). When this involves being ascribed religiously relevant traits we can term it constitutive *religious* luck. Constitutive religious luck attributions will especially signify attributions of having or lacking religious value for reasons of inborn traits or inherited social standings.

> *Chris is constitutively religiously unlucky (lucky) when Chris's value in God's judgment or in any theological system is affected negatively (positively) by her inborn traits or inherited social standing.*

Reality is in some Hebrew scripture presented in just such a flip-sided way: "The lot is cast into the lap, but its every decision is from the LORD" (*Proverbs* 16: 33). *Sola dei Gloria*, as one of the five points of Calvinism, holds that *all* freedom, all power, and credit for achievement is attributable to God's unbridlable will, with *no* credit for achievement rightly going to the human. The relationship of this final cause explanation with proximate human agency explanation is unclear. The human actor still makes what appear to be choices, but is in reality a kind of stage actor to the extent that meticulous providence ensures that so-called natural or efficient causes of events are also just part of God's sustaining will in each temporal moment. But these metaphysical views are further moralized when the assertion of human responsibility for achievements is *therefore* taken as sinful self-pride, offending both theological truth *and* moral virtue. Here we find perhaps the strongest expression of religious luck as a raw "fact" dominating all of human existence. If it is presumptuous to claim to know or to hope to entreat God's will, the unfolding events of one's life cannot be understood, but only accepted as the good or bad luck, including religious luck, that God has willed for them.

Problems of constitutive religious luck are not restricted to any one family of religions. As suggested earlier, a comparative dimension to these problems should increase the utility of appeals to religious luck as a focus of scholarly study; this seems especially so with constitutive religious luck. In South Asian karmic religions (bad/good) karma is claimed to accrue to an individual as a result of past actions through previous incarnations. Its forward-looking sense provides a more just world than is experienced over the course of one lifetime, and is connected with the long-term religious goal of universal liberation/enlightenment. But the more so as the concept or "law" of karma is appealed to in its backward-looking sense to explain and justify what an individual experiences as their found social conditions, such karmic explanations are examples of *constitutive* religious luck attributions.

Although the caste system in India is on a path to being deinstitutionalized today through a widespread "cast out caste" movement, the privilege or servility that comes from high/low birth are rationalized by the Law of Karma in traditional Hindu thought—so are the lack of social mobility and economic opportunities experienced by *shudras,* and especially by those born into classification as "spiritually polluted" *untouchables*. Deep concern with the potentially *post hoc* and surreptitious nature of appeals to people's accrued karma to explain social inequities or to justify caste duties is reflected in the Buddhist critique of Hinduism. Both groups take the concept of karma as offering a way to understand suffering vis-à-vis the religious goal of liberation (*moksa*; *nirvana*). But Buddhists reject caste and repudiate its justification in terms of a law of karma.

In Abrahamic religions, predetermination teachings are one natural focus for ascriptions of differential religious value that appeal to constitutive luck. Predetermination makes it perplexing to understand how anyone can be deserving of damnation on account of his or her having a fixed or settled character that rejects God. For in a predetermined world, it would appear that people receive their fixed character when placed among the elect or the damned, rather than being saved or damned *because* of their fixed character. But this means that in a religiously deterministic world, it is always God or gods who do the "fixing."[35] So in general the more a religious worldview devolves toward fatalism in the form of "meticulous providence," the less that human will *can* matter, and the more the person comes to resemble an actor on a stage playing out a pre-set cosmic script for the pleasure of its author. To the degree that having or lacking purportedly religiously disvalued or valued traits is outside of people's control, but matters to them, it is bad/ good luck from a methodologically neutral perspective, and regardless of how deterministic the theological explanation might be, that ascribes these traits to people. Indeed, the more deterministic or even fatalistic is the given explanation on the theological side, the more will the good/bad constitutive endowment appear beyond human control from a neutral or uncommitted perspective. For a philosophy of religious luck these are not always mutually negating explanations, but are better seen as co-existing "flip-side" religiously committed and religiously neutral perspectives on the same subject matter: this is why it is often better to speak of religious trait *ascription*.

Describing what is often called the *problem of freedom and grace*, Sessions writes, "On the one hand faith is solely a divine gift—both the act of faith and the capacity for faith are God's new and special creation. On the other hand, faith is a responsible human act of affirmation." The tension between these two demands is seen as especially strong for conceptions of faith on which if we were genuinely creditable for anything, human humility would be overstepped and God's glory would be diminished. Particular teachings such as Calvin's doctrine of double predestination—the idea that God has chosen some to be saved and others to be damned—appear especially prone to problems of constitutive luck. For, on such a view, as Sessions puts it, "God eternally ordains not only election but also reprobation; humans do not even have the power to frustrate God by rejecting his offer of mercy; rejection as well as acceptance is foreordained."[36]

Einstein famously resisted certain implications of quantum mechanics by insisting that God does not play dice with the laws of the physical universe. Many scientists think Einstein was mistaken in this claim, even as metaphor. Some theologians we have seen aim to resist a conception of a divine creator who plays dice with eternal souls. Faith to them in a sense means trust that God *would not* play dice with souls, or set up conditions collectively detriment of his creations. But with soteriological teachings that are especially embroiled in problems of religious luck, it appears that God indeed plays dice. Soteriologies of reprobation and of limited atonement have accordingly both received much criticism as exacerbating, or aggravating, moral luck concerns. Many have found it perplexing how God could judge as immoral or unfaithful the character of the reprobate—those predetermined from the beginning of time for damnation. One may distinguish God's judgment of the dead from God's reprobating before creation, but it is difficult to make logical sense of the idea that there could as yet be any vicious or virtuous types of character in existence when God is reprobating. The concept of constitutive religious luck, I hope the reader will see, at least sharpens this problem, and throws a critical light on the asymmetrical religious trait-ascriptions (as lost or saved, outside or inside of God's truth and God's grace, etc.), which the accepted theological explanation might motivate.

The Christian interpretation of the narrative of *Genesis* and humankind's separation from God and expulsion from the Garden, arguably explains the human condition in terms of a kind of bad constitutive luck.[37] The influential Augustinian view of the fallen state of humanity inherited from *original sin* aims to establish certain negative views about our basic constitution. Here the human condition is theologically characterized in terms of effects outside of our control.[38]

Relatedly, another teaching that invites analysis in terms of its dependence upon constitutive religious luck is the *sensus divinitatis*. In Calvinist thought, this is conceived of as a sense or faculty that theologically explains the felt certitude and reliable etiology of theistic belief among believers, and among others the otherwise perplexing *lack* of belief. Damage to the functioning of this organ of divine perception is typically given theological explanation in terms of the effects of sin. Paralleling asymmetric attribution of a properly working *sensus divinitatis* is attribution of "work of the Holy Spirit" irresistibly infusing specifically Christian beliefs into some individuals but not into others. The asymmetric explanation here is one luck-related issue, but the main point is that claims concerning *infused* beliefs at either the general theistic or the religion-specific level carry the sense of being irresistible and hence outside of one's will or control. Due to their passivity and attendant externalist religious epistemology, infused beliefs have the logical character of *constitutive* trait ascriptions.[39]

Character epistemologists hold that there is an *ability constraint* on knowledge. Knowing has to be substantially creditable to an ability or competence of the agent. Kegan Shaw notes,

> This looks to be in considerable tension, though, with putative *faith-based* knowledge. For at least on the Christian conception, when you believe something truly

on the basis of faith this *isn't* because of anything you're competent to do. Rather, faith-based beliefs are entirely a product of divine agency.

Shaw finds that "there was no accounting for this even on a weakened conception of the ability constraint, so long as we were restricted to a kind of 'internalism' about cognitive processing." But like Alvin Plantinga he takes an externalist approach to Christian apologetics. Utilizing work on extended knowledge, he proposes that this tension is satisfactorily overcome by conceiving of faith,

> as a form of extended knowledge by virtue of its being produced by an *extended cognitive ability*. The idea is that people who know things on the basis of faith believe truly as they do on account of a cognitive ability of theirs that actually *consists* in the activity of the Holy Spirit in conjunction with the deliverances of Scripture.[40]

Here the Bible gets a remake as an extended part of its reader's mind and a *living* conduit to religious knowledge, much, perhaps, as the Sikh primary sacred text the Adi Granth is referred to as by adherents of the Guru Granth Sahib because the book itself is understood as the "living guru" for that faith tradition. In both cases the human authorship of scripture is entirely closed off from view, and its infallibility guaranteed by its either actually *being* the supernatural deity itself or, going the other way that puts it on a better par with extended epistemology, its being akin to perfectly reliable fact-stating dictionary or computer. As innovative as Shaw's suggested application of extended epistemology to religious apologetics may be, critics will doubt that it does anything to improve rational support or warrant for faith-based belief. One faith tradition appears able to claim this status of their sacred text no less than another, and Great Pumpkinites arguably can as well. Like more standard Calvinist appeal to a *sensus divinitatis*, this externalist account of religious knowledge clearly aggravates problems of constitutive religious luck.

Finally, in a more general sense the problem of the "hiddenness of God" raises concerns about constitutive luck. All separation from God is suffering or evil from the theological point of view, meaning that a just god would want a personal reciprocal relationship to obtain between itself and every person capable of it. "Non-culpable non-belief" thus seems incompatible with the conditions necessary for human–divine reciprocity; but under conditions of a hidden God we must predict there will be non-believers through no moral fault of their own. So argues J. L. Schellenberg (1997 & 2007), who develops the hiddenness problem and its implication of non-resistant non-believers as grounds for a de facto challenge to the existence of God.[41] Assuming monotheism, non-culpable non-believers suffer from bad religious luck in that they are so constituted, or so situated, etc., that through no necessary moral or intellectual fault they remain unable to know God, or to respond to grace. For some theologies the problem of divine hiddenness is exacerbated by what we can call the *Doxastic Component Problem*: the problem of why a just God would, as they insist, require a theistic or creed-specific cognitive component as a condition of heaven, and exclude or damn those who fail to meet it.

Even putting this aside, the problem of non-culpable non-belief leads to recognition of substantial differences in people's intellectual temperament which come to the fore under conditions of what philosophers of religion call *religious ambiguity*.[42] Might not people of different intellectual temperaments achieve virtue in somewhat different ways? Contemporary psychology seems to confirm how "good people can disagree about religion and politics," as Jonathan Haidt's (2012) work on philosophy and moral psychology argues. John Stuart Mill says that as we evaluate one another's "experiments of living . . . free scope should be given to varieties of character."[43] This does not mean virtuous versus vicious character, but more simply varieties of personal–emotional temperament. It sounds counter-intuitive to hold that God does otherwise, by favoring in divine judgment one particular inborn temperament among the many.[44] But salvific exclusivists seem to be saddled with this assumption.

To be under conditions of ambiguity is for theory selection to be underdetermined by the facts that they purport to explain. A god who places people in richly ambiguous epistemic circumstances, and endows them with naturally occurring basic differences in individual temperament, is a god who logically should give wide scope on matters of belief or non-belief. If instead God is claimed to reserve election only to those of one select temperament—the Jamesian tender-minded rather than tough-minded thinkers, for example—this would seem to burden God with *confusing* temperament with moral character.[45] If God's judgment is supposed to be characterological in a sense connecting judgment with religious and moral *virtue*, then how does it work that judging *character* ignores what we know can be profound differences in temperament *among the virtuous*? A model of saving faith such as this clearly exacerbates problems of *constitutive religious luck*.

Thus far we have primarily been talking about problems of religious luck that motivate *moral* objections: objections to a conception of Godhead, the afterlife, etc., on the basis of just and proportional punishment, fair access, and reasonable accommodation of different intellectual temperaments. But belief-acquisition and maintenance are of course also *epistemic* matters, matters involving the study of our cognitive faculties and abilities, and the limits of the conditions under which we reliably and responsibly employ them. In order to explore the fuller significance of problems of religious luck for philosophy of religion we now need to migrate to issues of epistemology, including the issue of the epistemic significance of disagreement.[46]

Duncan Pritchard holds that externalist (including mixed) epistemologies try to preclude instances of coming to have a true belief through a process dependent on *veritic luck* from counting as instances of knowing.[47] Epistemologists may seek to do this by way of an ability condition on knowledge, a modal safety condition, and so on (see Pritchard 2015; 2005; Coffman 2015; Engel, 2017; 1992). Debate is ongoing as to how many and what type of conditions are needed to preclude veritic luck, but it is generally conceded to split into two distinct subtypes: *intervening* luck and *environmental* luck, which both need to be accounted for in an adequate analysis of knowing.[48] These two kinds of epistemic luck will occupy us soon, but first let me introduce a type of epistemic luck that has only recently been given explicit treatment in the literature.

Propositional Religious Luck will be our term for religious analogues of the form of malign epistemic luck that Bondy and Pritchard (2016) term *propositional luck*. They understand propositional luck as impacting the agent in a malign way when he or she has good evidence available for a belief, yet does not believe *on the basis of* the good available evidence. "In a wide range of cases where S believes for bad reasons but has good reasons available, S is just lucky to have good reasons available, because it could easily have been the case that S would have held the same belief in the same way but lacked good reasons for it."[49] Applying this to religious belief,

> *Chris's belief that* p *is impacted by propositional religious luck if Chris has a purportedly true religious belief, and possesses purportedly rationally sufficient epistemic reasons for* p, *but Chris or the model of faith she endorses disclaims that her belief that* p *is inferentially based on those good reasons, and instead claims its basis to be a non-ratiocinative but reliably truth-apt belief-forming process of supernatural origin.*

Note that Bondy and Pritchard treat propositional luck as a malign form of epistemic luck *in addition* to veritic luck. While that may be contentious, there do appear to be religious analogues of the more everyday examples of propositional luck that they discuss. A theology may invite problems of propositional religious luck where, for instance, there is reportedly no shortage of available good epistemic reasons to accept monotheism and even specifically Christian belief, yet the guiding model of faith prescribed as Christian orthodoxy a) *describes* faith-based belief as the causal effect of the work of the Holy Spirit on an individual *rather than* any process of ratiocination and b) *prescribes* viewing propositional assent based in reasons and evidence as contrary to genuine faith, because tentative or only accepted *contingently* upon evidence presently had, or that might be overturned. They arguably have application especially to models of faith that prescribe that the teachings of the home religion should not be believed on the basis of reasons *at all.* Clearly, the self-attribution of anti-evidential "knowledge" is shown to be exceptionally risky. This can go unnoticed when it is rationalized through an externalizing *disownership* of the belief-forming process, a topic of special importance that we will take up later.[50]

So while of course I would not burden Bondy and Pritchard with subscribing to my way of applying propositional luck to religious belief, I suggest Alvin Plantinga and his A/C (Aquinas/Calvin), and Reformed epistemology more generally, provide a prime example of how propositional and doxastic justification are explicitly thought of as coming apart, but also of how this may have the unwanted consequence of exposing the account of warranted religious belief to problems of religious propositional luck. For in Plantinga's model of warranted Christian belief, grounding belief in good reasons is devalued in favor of viewing genuine faith as the reliable and irresistible work of God or God's emissary, not mediated by ratiocination like everyday beliefs, and not improved by efforts at natural theology or other forms of reasoned argument and inference.[51] At the least, Reformed epistemologists need a sound philosophical account of why propositional luck is not malign epistemic luck, after all.[52]

Intervening Veritic Religious Luck is the religious analogue for the kind of malign luck that Gettier-style cases are closely associated with in contemporary epistemology. In such cases the agent acquires a true belief, but we are not inclined to credit the agent for their true belief because intervening luck undermined the safety of his success. This intervening luck comes "betwixt the person and the world."[53]

> *Chris is impacted by intervening veritic religious luck if her having a purportedly true religious belief that* p *is not saliently creditable to her as a responsible epistemic agent, but rather to the intervention of a supernatural agent.*

I argue that at least some defenses of religious exclusivism can be described, by close attention to their formal logical structure, as plying or "leaning" on asymmetric attributions of this intervening kind of epistemic luck. A prime example is Paul J. Griffiths's use of Karl Barth's theology as his paradigm example of how best to articulate the grounds for Christian salvific exclusivism. Although neither Barth nor Griffiths is thinking in terms of these epistemological concepts, their apologetic, I argue, formally parallels a Gettier case. For according to Griffiths's reading of Barth,

1. Religion is part of culture, and every theist is roughly equally subjectively justified on historical, philosophical, and phenomenological grounds in accepting the divine authority of their home religion's scriptures, sacred narratives, prophets, etc.

2. But God views all religions that have ever existed as "nothing more than idolatry, something to be judged and rejected."
3. Yet in a turn of events more fortuitous for some than for others, God *intervenes*: The Christian religion is "chosen by God as the locus of revelation. . . . God transforms an idol into a means of salvation, but without God's free choice to do so, it would remain an idol."[54]

This exclusivist argument could formally run the same way whether it is the Christian or simply the "home" religion posited as uniquely favored of God. While *ex hypothesi* the agent's epistemic justification in believing the Christian or any other purported testimonial tradition is defeated through the first, bad luck event of how God initially views their value, the subsequent intervention by God coming betwixt the agent and the world results in the Christian (but none other) having a *true* belief about the divine authority of their scriptures. But isn't intervening luck as described in Gettier cases of just this kind? If so, the example generalizes, and this strongly suggests that any apologist's re-description of the case as one merely of benign evidential luck is epistemologically flawed. In both this Christian exclusivist and any standard Gettier case we witness a clear disconnect between the agent's intellectual *efforts* and the *success* of her belief. The agent's coming to hold a true belief or system of beliefs is something the cognitive abilities of the agent in the end had little to do with. It is not explained as merit or cognitive achievement on her part, but instead as felix culpa—truth attained (only) through a "fortunate fault"!

Barth's interesting faith-based assertion in (3) instills a form of religious fideism, something we will explore further in coming chapters as we connect strong fideism to violations of inductive norms on the one hand, and to religious fundamentalism on the other. But whatever description it is given, the Barthian claim in (3) is a clear example of asymmetric religious-status attributions that raise worries about "leaning on" luck. Still more troubling is that the specific *type* of epistemic luck Barth's explanatory narrative invokes is widely regarded by philosophers and lay audiences alike as *malign* epistemic luck in the sense of being *knowledge-precluding*.[55]

Let us note here that theorists widely distinguish between *Soteriological exclusivism*, or exclusivism about salvation (or liberation, depending on what the religious aim is taken to be), and *Doctrinal exclusivism*, or exclusivism about purported religious truth.[56] Griffiths in his book does note and reject moral objections to soteriological exclusivism,[57] the view that salvation (or its equivalent) is available only to adherents of one's home religion. But interestingly, he articulates this Barthian apologetic without noting any such logical or *epistemic* concern as its formal structuring along lines of a Gettier case.

Environmental Veritic Religious Luck will be our religious analogue of the kind of malign epistemic luck that operates in Fake Barn cases. Environmental luck is characterized by getting something right through a process of belief formation that in the agent's epistemic situation is an unsafe and/or insensitive process.

> *Chris's belief that* p *is impacted by environmental veritic religious luck if she is lucky to have acquired a true rather than false belief, given the lack of modal safety in her epistemic situation, of the doxastic strategy through which her belief was acquired.*

Summarizing the epistemological lessons he draws from the much-discussed Barney in Fake Barn County case, Pritchard writes,

> Cases like that of "Barney" illustrate that there is a type of knowledge-undermining epistemic luck, what we might call environmental epistemic luck—which is distinct from the sort of epistemic luck in play in standard Gettier-style cases. . . . In cases of environmental epistemic luck like that involving Barney, luck of this intervening sort is absent—Barney really does get to see the barn and forms a true belief on this basis—although the epistemically inhospitable nature of the environment ensures that his belief is nevertheless only true as a matter of luck such that he lacks knowledge.[58]

A majority of philosophers think that the agent does not know in the barn case, despite the belief arising from the usually reliable faculty of sight, under normal-enough visual conditions. In standard Barney cases, Barney is unaware, when he assents to "That is a barn," that he is in Fake Barn County. Let's call this basic scenario an *unenlightened Barney* case: one where Barney has no recognition that he is under conditions that may make his forming a visual belief unreliable, that is, that by relying upon sight-from-the-roadside alone he might easily have gotten a false rather than true belief. Then it was to no credit of his own that he happened in fact to be looking at one of the few non-fake barns when he assented to the proposition. He would have formed the same belief even if it was false, and given his method, this was far more likely the outcome of applying this method where and when he did. In normal environments visual identification of barns for people with decent eyesight like Barney is a safe method of settling belief; it is just that Barney is not in appropriate conditions for the doxastic method he employs. This invites readers to think about how Barney's doxastic method should change were he enlightened—that is to say, privy to the knowledge that many visually indistinguishable fake barns dotted his local epistemic environment. What is not normal is the inductive context of Barney's inference from his visual perception at a distance, to a belief that there is a barn by the wayside.

It seems easy to construct *testimonial transmission* cases that are strongly analogous to fake barn cases. All unenlightened Barney does, after all, is see the one barn within eyesight, and say, "That's a real barn." So arguably we have merely to swap out "the one real barn" for the exclusivist notion of "the one true theology," and "perceived by eyesight from a distance" for "believed on the basis of the purported special revelation dominant at one's epistemic location." Now, to the extent it is agreed that one would more often get false than true beliefs by this process of belief-acquisition, we again have a luckily true belief, (by hypothesis) a true religious belief, but one generated on an unsafe basis. If this is correct, it is not difficult to construct *religious* or more simply testimonial environmental luck cases: cases like that of Barney, who purportedly acquires a true belief, but given the mis-fit between his actual epistemic environment and the doxastic method he employs, could easily have acquired a false belief instead of a true one.

Problems of environmental religious luck are especially important because they engage religious diversity. These problems are most problematic for theological methods that too easily discount the epistemic significance of disagreement, or that treat testimonial transmission in epistemologically unsound ways. The malign character of environmental luck could have broad implications for religious epistemology, or what, following Alvin Goldman and Dominic Marbaniang, we will refer to as *religious epistemics*.[59] But no such claim is needed for the purpose of setting up our taxonomy. A more circumspect conclusion is that since environmental luck connects closely both with uptake in testimonial traditions, problems of veritic epistemic religious luck are especially strong for salvific exclusivists: those who believe that God places a religion-specific creedal requirement on salvation.

With six kinds of religious luck now introduced, our working taxonomy is basically complete. With environmental religious luck, however, we have not yet introduced specific examples from extant theological debate. The problem here is simply that most any attribution of true belief or knowledge on the basis of testimonial transfer under conditions of chronic peer disagreement is potentially an example. This makes evident that the significance of religious disagreement cannot be dispensed with by implicit appeal to the benign nature of evidential good luck. There is nothing in thinking that one's religious belief is true that guarantees the evidence or belief-forming process by which one acquired it is not impacted by malign luck. It is part of my thesis that the relationship between simple (benign) evidential luck and evidential luck as compounded by (malign) environmental luck, is vitally important for religious epistemics, but not well-understood or even well acknowledged in the literature. But we need to slow down here and proceed cautiously with respect to the appropriate criteria for malign luck, especially with regard to testimonial evidence.

So in order to clarify our taxonomy by showing how evidential and environmental luck are to be distinguished, it will aid us to make a sizable digression in the next section. We will try to fill out the claim just made, that it is not difficult to construct *testimonial environmental luck* cases, where our intuitions about epistemic status basically parallel those we report about Barney cases.[60] If my "Tess case" is at all successful, it will indeed suggest real-world correlates with problems of contrariety among and between faith-traditions based on different putative special revelations. But I caution the reader that the case is not intended as an argument for any fully *general* claim about religious testimonial reception and transfer. As inductive risk-focused, I take it to be neutral as between some of the debates in social/collective epistemology and in epistemology of testimony more specifically. Environmental luck, when it affects an agent's epistemic situation, on the present view *compounds* evidential luck, and this indicates a more contextual, and likely complex, relationship than one where we naively conceive the two kinds of luck to be mutually exclusive, such that any particular testimonial case is always *simply* an instance of a benign or a malign type of epistemic luck.

A Tess Case of Testimonial Environmental Veritic Luck

Imagine Tess, a good friend of Barney, traveling to visit relatives in Land of Lakes County. In the base case, this is Tess's first visit, and she does not know that many others refer to this county as "Fake News County." Scattered about on corners of the town and the whole county are brightly colored metal or plastic, free publication newsstands, each advertising its wares in its small front window. Sometimes there were several such boxes at the same corner, but most often just one. Tess, who knew none of this, is met by her Uncle Sal at the train station, and before they get to his ride they pass a corner outside the station with a blue metal newsstand. Tess's uncle goes to the box and gets them each a copy. "Blue-box publications. Yes, this one you can trust!" says Sal, and to emphasize his point he flips the paper over and taps the large printed warning on its back page: "Remember, trust only the news from this box! All of the other boxes contain fake news."

Tess finds this a bit quizzical, in part because she has not encountered other boxes; but they have much to talk about, and the conversation quickly takes another direction. But that night when she retires to the guest bedroom, she finds the paper on her dresser, and reads it in bed. It contains many tales about the county and its founding citizens that Tess finds quite moving and even profound. Although there were seemingly fantastical elements to these stories, and some of them drew strong moral lessons that clearly went beyond factual information, Tess remembers her uncle's assurance of the paper's trustworthiness, and she accepts the content of the paper pretty much at face value.

While being driven back to the station after her pleasant weekend visit, Tess notices for the first time a different colored news box, then another, then another. Indeed walking into the station she comes upon a veritable array of such boxes in a row. Having been so enamored of the first, Tess starts walking up to a yellow plastic one to get an issue of it for some reading on the way home. Picking it up, she is surprised to see the same strong warning against trusting other papers that Sal had called attention to on her blue-box paper. But immediately Sal stops her, saying, "All these other boxes are from different publishers, and they give only fake news. Return them. They are worthless—only trust the papers in a blue-box. They tell you all you need to know."

It saddens Tess a bit that she will not get more such stories, but out of respect for her uncle she puts it back and refrains from gathering more papers. On the train, though, she pulls out her blue-box paper and reads it again. It is growing on her, and when she tells her sister about her trip, what she relates as factual about the history of Land of Lakes County and its founding citizens is what she took up from reading her blue-box paper.

Now we can imagine multiple variations on this base Tess case. Perhaps she learns that had she listened to Sal's neighbor, she would have been introduced only to red-box papers, and been told that *that* was the one reliable or authoritative testimonial source. Perhaps all the people in Sal's family trust the blue-box paper, but most people in the county trust the yellow, or vice versa.[61] How would these specific variations affect epistemic evaluation of Tess and other Fake News County residents? And how in general, we really want to know, does their gaining etiological information/evidence impact the epistemological well-foundedness of their beliefs and the plausibility of their alethic claims?

Epistemologists refer to an agent's epistemic environment as "hostile" to their inquiries if it is an environment unsafe for the doxastic method employed. So let me just go on to describe the epistemic environment as "beguiling" if the agent's target belief, even if true, was acquired or maintained in a manner insensitive to defeaters she has for that belief. At least in modal accounts of epistemic luck/risk, which appear to be the most sophisticated and well suited to the project of the analysis of knowing, features of safety and sensitivity failure are mainly what distinguish mere evidential luck from a condition where that is *compounded* by environmental luck.

Although it is testimonial transmission rather than visual perception that is the source of belief in Tess cases, they are environmental luck cases if Tess was veritically lucky (i.e., lucky that she came to acquire a true rather than false belief) given the doxastic method she employed in her specific epistemic environment. I hold that these conditions of environmental veritic luck are fulfilled in the Tess case and that her beliefs fail to be knowledge even if there was one wholly true newsboy, and it was the one she invested authority in. True, this argument requires interpretations of modal closeness and of relevant similarity of basis, but these seem to be met in our case. There is a good deal of social epistemology that our Tess cases presuppose, but certainly also much that they ignore. But short of some kind of dogmatism/phenomenal foundationalism or other way to pre-emptively privilege Uncle Sal's exclusive testimonial trust in blue-box publications, I do not see other ways to pry the Barney and Tess cases apart. Nor should we think that affirming the impact of malign luck on Tess, as on Barney, implies or makes plausible some much broader skepticism about testimonial knowledge or reliable testimonial transfer. How lacking, at the time of acquisition, then later gaining etiological information affects the well-foundedness of a person's testimonial, and especially their culturally nurtured beliefs, will be addressed in some depth in later chapters. But our account will aim to show why it is wrong to construe safety, sensitivity, and proper basing concerns as inviting the "broad parity" response: the gambit that to be skeptical about the epistemic status of Tess's testimonial beliefs, we would end up having to be skeptical about *all* testimonial beliefs, or all inductive knowledge, or radically skeptical in general.[62]

An epistemic environment unsafe for the doxastic method an agent employs is a key characteristic that distinguishes mere evidential luck (acquiring veritical evidence) from a condition where that is compounded by environmental luck. Barney's method of coming to believe "That is a red barn" is unsafe, because he could have easily gotten it wrong in his driving environment, trusting only to his eyesight from the roadway. Barney's belief is also insensitive since he would have formed the belief, "There is a barn," even if what he was looking at was one of the many beguiling facades in his vicinity. Analogously, I argue that Tess's method of coming to believe that blue-box papers describe the true history of Land of Lakes County is unsafe, because too easily could she have gotten it wrong applying this strategy in her news-reporting environment.

Tess's belief is apparently also *insensitive,* because if we just change the case to say that the publisher was not reliable, we have to think that Tess would have still believed that it was. If she would trust the news of just the first box she came to, when it might be a small and/or unrepresentative sample, or if she would trust it when uniquely recommended by one among many disagreeing residents, or when uniquely recommended by someone who is considered a kinsman, then Tess would believe the same thing even were its stories fictional rather than reliably historical. Indeed, there are relevant differences between Barney's and Tess's epistemic situations, but I would argue that the most epistemically significant ones show Tess to be *more* impacted by veritic luck than Barney. Barney at least starts from the generalization that what looks to the eye like a red barn probably is a barn, which in most cases is a strong generalization; it was quite unusually bad epistemic luck that this is not a sound premise for Barney to rely on this particular day, or in this particular geographic vicinity. But Tess, once her attempt to widen her evidence and improve her epistemic situation by reading from non-blue-box papers is cut short by her uncle, does not have such a generalization as part of her doxastic strategy. The less sensitive to genuinely epistemic factors is her way of forming her belief, the more subject to trait-based overdetermination it is. An example is the emotional connection Tess found in the blue-box publications, a factor which we might infer heightened her adoption of them despite her concern about contrariety of content across the different newsstands. We do not find this in the Barney case.

Another example of why someone's belief in the reliability of one or another of the publishers must be seen as the product of a highly risky doxastic strategy, is the relationship between the testimonies that the papers provide about the history of the county: *the contrariety of content itself.* Our inductive risk account shows as epistemically significant not just the *diversity* of beliefs in a domain, but *contrariety* of those beliefs. Part of the intuition that there are propositional defeaters to Tess's personal justification for her testimonial beliefs is that the base case describes significant contrariety of content to the publications. Further, it describes what we will term *symmetrical contrariety*, in that each publisher claims all other publishers' publications are untrustworthy. Now had there not been such actual or reported contrariety to their contents, would Tess's beliefs, if we assume them true, be less impacted by malign environmental luck?

If the answer to this question is "Yes," as I want to argue that it is, then why do epistemologists of testimony seem so often ignore such factors, and think only in terms of the reliability of the single testimonial chain that an agent "trusts"? Why is "actual trust plus posited truth" supposed to be a defeater for the importance of testimonial diversity, and not "testimony diversity with symmetrical contrariety" a defeater for rational trust and the right to claim truth? Consider that the former direction relies on subjective factors, trust being a partly affective psychological state, and posited truth something projected rather than logically inferred from that state of trust. The alternative I am suggesting, where special factors of contrariety are central to epistemic assessment rather than peripheral to it, depends on objective factors, because diversity or contrariety is a fact, and the question of the safety of one's doxastic strategy, given a sufficiently well-described strategy and epistemic situation, is also an objective question. Ultimately, our inductive risk account argues for the claim that the epistemic status of belief is challenged not just by symmetrical contrariety, but more especially by *polarized and polemical contrariety*.

Speaking of variations among Tess cases that perhaps illumine Tess's challenging epistemic environment further, note that Barney cases typically start with an objective or external posit: There are exactly so many real barns—typically one, but it could just be a low percentage that is posited as objective fact. Call this armchair style of case "truth from on high." Truth from on high is easy with perceptual cases, but more difficult with testimonial claims, especially when those claims are within domains of controversial views. Some philosophers argue that we should regard assertions in all areas of controversial views as only "minimally truth-apt," something that would argue against the practice of relying on the simplifying device of positing truth from on high. Regardless, contrariety is something largely lacking is perceptual cases, and this is partly why I think Barney cases are not paradigmatic of, and do not aid philosophers in analyzing, environmental luck. But is this positing of "one true publication" (analogous to "one true barn") from on high *necessary* for assessing whether or not our Tess cases are instances of environmental veritic luck? Surely not. There is no reason why there has to be an objective fact-stater. All of the elements to determine objective defeaters to Barney's personal justification are already present without such a fact-stater if we know that the environment is *hostile* or *beguiling*. Very easily, using that method, could Barney have acquired a false rather than true belief, and very easily would he have believed "that is a red barn," when it is not.[63]

So with Barney cases it is typically posited from an objective perspective that Barney *in fact* saw the only genuine barn (or one of the few) in Fake Barn County. The assumption I think is largely superfluous, except where we specifically want to compare an objectively determinable alethic status (the one true barn, or one of the few in the environment) and the doxastic method (believing as real what you first see as a barn given normal perceptual and conceptual conditions). You can posit truth with testimonial cases also, if you stick to clearly empirical matters, but the epistemologically interesting cases, I am suggesting, may be ones where testimony is transmitted to an agent in what she either does or does not know is in a context of standing disagreement—or indeed ones where there is no assumption of an objective way of verifying which *if any* of these testimonies are true.[64]

Positing truth in testimonial cases also makes sense if what is testified to is a verifiable empirical claim. But if it is not, saying that Tess *did* see the one reliable paper makes the case more rather than less artificial.[65] What is more interesting may be a version where Tess does collect several papers and compares their contents herself. She might then improve her epistemic situation by virtue of the comparison this allows her. Yet what if she had no independent way to compare the reliability of their authors/publishers? Don't norms of inductive reasoning imply that Tess should become *less* sure about the truth of her earlier belief the more that people like Sal and his neighbors each recommended a *different* paper as the only reliable one? Or the more she herself discovers that these papers make conflicting factual claim, or that each asserts all other publishers to be biased and factually unreliable?

Compare versions of Tess as released from the bias of first-acquaintance, to *enlightened Barney*, who knew or suspected ahead of time that he was about to enter an area where fake barns abound. Presumably, enlightened Barney, when he glanced out his car window at a barn-shape, would positively resist believing "That is a barn," even though it very much looked like one to him. He arguably would only be doxastically responsible if he took his knowledge of his risky context into account, and deferred to inductive norms. Insofar as he knew a) that there was a quite significant chance of coming upon a fake barn, b) that he had no special expertise to tell fake from real barns by eyesight from the road, and c) that first-acquaintance might bias him to judge quickly of the first-sighted barn, the most reasonable thing for Barney to do seems to be to *resist* positively affirming, "That is a barn." Unless he wants to get out of his car and go kick it, or wait till he has acquired more of a comparison base, what he ought to do as a responsible epistemic agent involves acknowledging the limits of his vision-at-a-distance as a method for forming true beliefs. It is given to him, in other words, not by how real that roadside barn seems to him, but by his inductive context and the norms that attend cogent inductive inference. These are points that do not change just because it is posited from on high that "in fact it was the one real barn in the county that Barney happened to see."

Now note that while my Tess cases are intended to *suggest* authority assumption in religious testimonial traditions, whether and under what conditions an agent can gain safe testimonial belief from unsafe testimony is today debated.[66] My primary concern here is with establishing 1) that there *can be* testimonial environmental luck cases; 2) there also *can be* religious environmental luck cases if they are religious-belief cases that fit within the basic epistemic conditions for testimonial environmental luck; and 3) so this type of luck should be acknowledged whenever what is debated is the epistemic significance of disagreement, or limits of reasonable disagreement. It is not as if someone in a situation where only a rare few news sources is reliable could not come to know one particular source to be reliable. But modal closeness is not some matter of mere ratio of reliable to unreliable sources in one's environment. Also, the further information Tess might gain that would enlighten her about her epistemic situation is also etiological information she needs to digest, etiological information about just how unaware of the full context she previously was. To work herself out of her situation of malign luck, the evidence she needs must be reasonably *independent* of the initial beliefs she formed about the sole reliability of blue-box newsstands. It needs to corroborate or falsify the earlier belief, as independently as possible. But there are more problems in trying to fulfill requirements of an independence principle with some types of belief than with others. With strictly empirical beliefs it is typically not so difficult, but with nurtured beliefs and beliefs supported by the testimony of purported authorities or experts, it can be very difficult indeed. We will more directly discuss the possibility and desirability of meeting an independence principle in such cases in the next chapter.

The Tess case contributes to an account of well- and ill-founded nurtured belief that we can term our *inductive risk-focused account*, because it is focused upon doxastic strategies involving low and high degrees of *inductive risk*: the moral and epistemic risk of "getting it wrong" in an inductive context of inquiry. While I do take environmental epistemic luck to be malign, which is to say undercutting of positive epistemic status, there is a minority of epistemologists who hold that Barney does know in the classic Barn Façade County case. Acknowledging these different intuitions, I would argue that those who take that view are making the serious error of *conflating brute and inductive knowledge*. The very point of Barney cases and other environmental luck cases is that our epistemic environment is properly a major concern with inductive, or any sort of reflective knowing, as opposed to what in the literature is called brute or animal knowing.[67]

We can reserve talking more about what constitutes an inductive context of inquiry until later, but note that analyzing any testimonial cases that aim to parallel the Barney eyesight case do not *depend* on testimonial knowledge being inductive or inferential: we can precede neutrally with respect to debates between reductionists and anti-reductionists. In the primary sense, what characterizes environmental veritic luck as malign is simply the presence of potential *defeaters to justification* (such as the presence of fake barns indistinguishable without special means). It is this that transforms a person's context into an inductive one, so that, again, characterizing Barney as having a justified *visual* belief misses the need for the agent to know of and to weigh the impact of such potential defeaters to his personal justification. But if (as I do think) testimonial uptake indeed *is* inferential, then as will be elaborated in part II, this further substantiates logical connections between belief-acquisition through home religion testimonial authority assumption and high "inductive risk."

Perhaps the most interesting conclusion that might be drawn from the preceding discussion is that the positive epistemic status of beliefs based on testimonial transmissions is not guaranteed, *even if* it is maintained that the particular testimonial chain involved in the target beliefs to be analyzed is a trustworthy testimonial chain. It is not guaranteed any more than is Barney's true belief that he sees a barn has positive epistemic status. That depends not just on the object, and his process, but upon a third factor that situates his inference in an inductive context. In a simple, non-fake barn county scenario Barney's belief would certainly seem to have positive epistemic status, but this is far more problematic in Barn Façade County. For here, whether recognized or not, Tess, like Barney, is in an epistemic environment in which there are defeaters to personal justification. From both internalist and externalist perspectives it is no virtue of the agent that she ignores or is ignorant of defeaters in her environment. That environmental luck is a serious worry and that certain contexts of inquiry are properly describable as inductive contexts, are nearly synonymous.

Simple evidential luck does not violate the safety principle; it is the luck of being situated in a way that others might not be to have supporting evidence for a true belief. Ernest Sosa uses the simple paradigm example of coming to hold the true belief that there is a crow in the yard, but only because one happened to glance out the window at that particular moment it flew by. By contrast, environmental luck does violate the safety principle. It is the luck that one's belief *is true,* given a set of modal or other epistemic circumstances that are *inhospitable* to the reliability of the utilized doxastic strategy (mode of belief-uptake). What is importantly different between intervening (Gettier) and environmental luck cases is that in the former it is no matter of ability or competence or achievement that a true belief is acquired, whereas in environmental luck cases the agent's beliefs are the product of the exercise of a cognitive ability that *in more cooperative epistemic circumstances* might provide more positive epistemic status to their beliefs. The concepts of luck and risk help us analyze how agents achieve or fall short of more valuable epistemic states or standings—rationality, personal justification, knowledge, understanding, etc. But they may not apply in quite the same way.[68]

As an important methodological aside, recent work by Pritchard translates anti-luck epistemological concerns into anti-*risk* concerns. Pritchard's approach is able to explain when epistemic defeaters are genuine, either by "exposing the subject to significant levels of epistemic risk," or by "highlighting how the subject's safe cognitive success does not stand in the appropriate explanatory relationship to her manifestation of relevant cognitive ability."[69] Our study going forward, since it will be concerned to assess the limits of reasonable religious disagreement and with the strength and proper scope of de jure and de facto challenges to religious claims, invites asking when these conditions for genuine defeaters are met in the domain of religious claims. Chapter 2 more specifically will apply anti-risk epistemology by trying to show how the ascending degrees of inductive risk in an agent's doxastic strategy contribute to a philosophical account of how to distinguish between benign luck and the malign modal luck.[70]

CONCLUSION: EMERGING
PHILOSOPHICAL QUESTIONS

To review, theologians and philosophers of religion have begun to recognize how problems of luck affect theological accounts, and how they serve as tools for comparison and criticism. Some theologians themselves have taken up a call to articulate "luck-free" soteriologies and (as Kant called them) systems of eternity. But we should be worried when theologians pronounce their accounts luck-free, when they only push the appeal to luck from one form of it to another. Take Craig's response to the soteriological problem of evil: "What I suggested was that, if we are concerned that it would be unloving on God's part to condemn someone for rejecting His grace who would under other circumstances have accepted it, then we can hold that God in His mercy would not create such persons, but would only create individuals who would have rejected His grace under any circumstances." Arguably, this intended theological fix only hardens the moralized dichotomy between religious insiders and outsiders, giving theological sanction for viewing all actual non-Christians as damned, and quite culpably so, because they "must" be rejectors of God not just in this world, but "under any circumstances."[71]

I agree with Richard McDonough's critique of the way that fundamentalisms "inevitably must substitute human judgment for God's judgment."[72] But our own approach to problems of luck, which is philosophical, will not focus on theological debates or theological fixes aimed above all to maintain prior allegiances. We have introduced these debates only as examples to show that there are real instances of each described kind of religious luck that our taxonomy recognizes. Our approach will instead focus on this very tendency in many but not all religious believers to give asymmetric explanations of the value of religious insiders and outsiders. We want to ask what this tendency might reflect, psychologically, and what implications it might have for religious epistemology as well.

To emphasize this, we have made asymmetrical religious trait attributions, and exclusivist responses to religious multiplicity, the primary foci of this study. Both of these foci are open not only to philosophical examination, but also to social scientific study, for instance, through self-reports about attitudes, or perhaps through performance on assignable tasks. Neither, then, of the two foci of our study is reducible simply to a theological position, and it would be misguided to think that our concerns with problems of religious luck would be wholly resolved by a theological move from salvific or doctrinal exclusivism, to inclusivism. Chapter 4 will indeed directly examine two versions of salvific exclusivism, religion-specific and mutualist versions, and present a dilemma that challenges the rational coherence of each. But while we have already found problems of religious luck and theological doctrines of exclusivism to be overlapping concerns, they are far from identical. The ways that people ascribe moral traits to themselves and others, and their responses to religious multiplicity reflect attitudes toward otherness, and not simply what they take to be orthodox theology.[73] So the several problems of religious luck we have introduced draw our attention to questions about the multiplicity of different conceptions of faith that people operate with, and the effects of these different models on their understanding of religious difference.

Going forward then, our approach through problems of luck should be expansive, since these problems are not simply problems for theology or religious apologetics. They draw our attention to neglected assumptions about the relationship *between* reason and faith with which people with different models of conceptions of faith operate. They suggest new insights into the limits of reasonable disagreement, and into motivations and consequences of religious fundamentalism. These connections with psychology of religion, and what implications they may have for religious epistemology, are therefore also emerging questions that we will want to explore in later chapters.

While most writers who draw explicitly on the concept of religious luck have focused on moral concerns, we have shown through our taxonomy that categories of epistemic luck may be quite relevant to religious epistemics as well. Epistemic luck is ubiquitous in our lives, and has some salience in our true as well as false beliefs. This is why not all kinds of epistemic luck are malign. It is the kind of luck salient in a context of inquiry that most affects the positive epistemic standing of a belief. There are many aspects of being in a position to know which may be characterized as lucky, but where the luck is of a benign sort. So we need to better understand how theologians and philosophers parse in a principled (i.e., non–ad hoc or viciously circular) way between contexts in which self-attribution of epistemic luck is unobjectionably benign, and contexts where a "simply benign" attribution mis-describes the situation and constitutes a kind of self-privileging through ignoring one's broader epistemic context. Clearly, if the agent is in an inductive context then for positive epistemic status to accrue to her belief, her doxastic strategy needs to conform to inductive norms.[74] But what we are in need of are clearer ground rules for how philosophers and theologians can argue for one case-description—as benign or malign—over the other.

After the digression of the previous section onto problems of luck related to testimonial uptake and transfer, we are in a better position to respond to this question and to summarize other emerging questions for the later chapters of this study. Our Tess case helped us to understand when and how evidential luck is compounded by malign environmental luck, but we purposely said little about how pertinent environmental luck may be to epistemology of testimony. Rather than try to draw any over-broad conclusion, we held that while the Tess case is indeed quite closely analogous to the Barney case, the further question of whether the Tess case is closely analogous to cases of testimonial uptake and transfer in religious testimonial traditions, remains for us an open question, though we will later propose criteria for it. I will have considerably more to say about these issues, but I mean to invite critical responses that the Tess case only goes so far. It is enough for the present chapter if we showed that a philosophy of luck can help articulate the fair ground rules for that debate, one that has not yet been a focus of either secular or religious epistemology. So far we have merely tried to show why the differences between benign and malign epistemic luck, and the implications that different descriptions have for religious epistemics are concerns that theologians and philosophers of religion would do well to take as a focus for debate. Our main point, restricted to the development of a taxonomy of kinds of religious luck, was not to provide a definitive answer to this question, but more simply to clarify how that debate may proceed. In doing so we discussed the compounding benign with malign epistemic luck, and connected the compounding thesis with the need to avoid simplistic "all-evidential" or "all-veritic" answers to our question of what kind of luck affects the uptake and transfer of testimonially based religious beliefs.

The distinction between benign and malign epistemic luck, and more specifically between simple evidential and malign environmental veritic luck, clearly carries critical epistemological import.[75] Clarity on these matters seems essential for properly assessing the epistemic significance not just of religious disagreement, but of disagreement among controversial views more generally. So our approach through problems of luck raises what are arguably new and important questions for applied epistemology. Our approach is philosophical: the application of philosophy of luck/risk. But some of the questions that emerge for our initial discussion of models of faith most susceptible to problems of religious luck are questions that invite fruitful interactions among theologians, philosophers, psychologists, and religious studies scholars. If so, it is a virtue that we have to leave open certain questions.

We said that luck-invoking theological explanations or trait-ascriptions can feature in challenges to the well-foundedness of an agent's belief. But we have not approached the questions of how strong or weak arguments from contingency of belief are as motivations to an etiological challenge, and for what domains these challenges have the most force, and why. To develop answers to these questions we need to give closer attention to the proper scope and target of etiological challenges premised on the historical or cultural contingency of belief. In the next chapter, the New Problem will be constructed to more directly address some of these issues.

NOTES

1. For recent work on philosophy of luck/risk, see especially Ian Church and Robert J. Hartman (eds.) *The Routledge Handbook of the Philosophy and Psychology of Luck* (2019, forthcoming) and Duncan Pritchard and John Lee Whittington (eds.), *Philosophy of Luck* (2015).

2. Douglas 2000, 560–561. See Douglas's Preface and the authors' Introduction, in Elliot and Richards (eds.) *Exploring Inductive Risk* (2017) for fine overviews of the usefulness of the concept of inductive risk. Compare Biddle and Kukla's taxonomy of risk, in the same volume, and Biddle 2016. Inductive risk is understood as part of epistemic risk by Biddle, allowing for needed recognition of epistemic risks that are not well described as inductive risks. My book does not reduce the epistemic to the inductive, or philosophy of luck/risk to this especial focus. So it is quite consistent with Biddle and Kukla's view. But inductive risk is used here not to restrict, but mainly to broaden discussions of risky doxastic strategies. For the literature on managing inductive risk, as *applied* epistemology, includes the moral/social consequences that can follow from risky beliefs and actions, and therefore the need to recognize and manage these risks.

3. It is possible to take the etiological symmetry of religions of revelation, together with the generated contrariety (divergent teachings) as grounds for a stronger de facto challenge. From a large number of the generated beliefs necessarily being wrong (as shown by the contradictions among them), one concludes it more likely that all are wrong, then that some of them are, yet one might be true uniquely. I discuss this stance further in chapter 4, but a strong articulation of it is Philip Kitcher's 2013 Terry Lectures, published (2015) as *Life after Faith*. One might find strong analogies here with David Hume's treatment of miracles, though I find Hume himself to hang a bit ambiguously between making just a claim-focused de jure challenge and making a challenge to the very *existence* of miracles. By restricting myself to a well-qualified de jure challenge I am trying to avoid such ambiguity, as well as indicate my permissivist but responsibilist stance on the ethics of belief. Also, though many religious skeptics might insist the luck-based problems I articulate could be taken much further, in this study my comments about avoiding reductive naturalism stand. The presence of a plausible naturalistic explanation does not in itself *disprove* the claims of supernaturalism.

4. As we will later see, this question of sufficiency often plays into the rationale not just for de jure but for de facto challenges. Whether CSR provides "a complete or sufficiently complete causal account of how belief in God came about without reference to the existence of God" is one question. But related to it in de facto challenges is the thesis that if we have a sufficient naturalistic explanation in this sense, "then God does not exist." See Leech and Visala (2012, 167–8) for a formal reconstruction of criticism of this "argument against theism." Again, we are not pursuing this, but only a far more qualified de jure challenge to the exclusivist response to religious multiplicity. I think Thomas A. Lewis (2015, 50) is right to insist that the discipline of religious studies should steer clear of the metaphysics by taking the "What is really going on here?" questions as making normative claims. Indeed, explanation itself,

even where purely empirical is always partial explanation or selective, meaning that it is situated by particular questions and related *interests in explanation.*

5. Sessions 1994, 2. We will not pursue Sessions's *theological* project in his excellent book, *The Concept of Faith.* His project is a pluralism not just of extant conceptions but of idealized *models* of faith, of which he develops and compares six. But more interesting for us, he is also interested in analyzing extant *conceptions* of faith, and he offers interesting details on the proper use and limits of analogy between conceptions and between conceptions and his six models. Bradley Rettler (2018) also presents a clear contemporary discussion of the different dimensions upon which extant conceptions of faith differ and how this supports pluralism about the meaning of the concept.

6. I will employ "models" just as shorthand for Sessions's "conceptions" extant in actual faith-traditions. Still, our study takes note of Sessions's distinction between models and conceptions. His method also is a boon for our own project, as Sessions, far more than most philosophers of religion, consistently distinguishes descriptive or psychological questions from normative ones. For example, he quite carefully explains the difference between "conviction" and "certitude" as terms descriptive of one's psychological state, from "certainty" as normative in the epistemic sense of drawing upon norms of evidence and inference. Since I will later make more extensive use of Sessions's book, I also want to say that I think our account is neutral to, if not indeed supportive of, Sessions's primary thesis concerning the *unity* of the concept of faith. Sessions's key problem is whether and how far there is unity in the concept of faith, beyond its manifest multiplicity in extant faith-traditions. He argues that the concept of faith is analogical, not univocal, and that there is no categorical concept of faith (5).

7. Zagzebski, 397–398; 402.

8. Katzoff cites Paul, "Even before they had been born or had done anything good or bad, (so that God's purpose of election might continue not by works but by his call) she was told, "The elder shall serve the younger." As it is written, "I have loved Jacob, but I have hated Esau." Paul's account of election "may be likened to divine command theory in morals, according to which what is morally right or wrong is determined by God's will . . . [and] subject to no constraints, guided by no independent criteria." Katzoff, 102.

9. Katzoff, 9 Jewish and Christian accounts, Katzoff thinks, hold much the same view of *religious value*: "The lack of agreement between what a person deserves and how he is treated by God is fundamental to both accounts." But at least in terms of *attributing* religious virtue to the individual, Rabbi Judah's account Katzoff presents as less problematic, since unlike Paul, the virtues can coherently adhere to the character of the individual.

10. See for instance Imran Aijaz and John Bishop (2004). A more sweeping de jure challenge than either mine or Aijaz and Bishop's is Dawes and Jong's (2012): "A critic does not need to argue that what Christians believe is false. She could mount a direct attack on the Christian's claim to warrant, by offering a more plausible account of the causal mechanism giving rise to belief, one that is either indifferent with regard to the truth and falsity of the beliefs it produces or more likely to produce false beliefs than

true ones" (Abstract). I agree also with Bishop who argues "against the proposal that faith's similarities to interpersonal trust merit its being considered reasonable or virtuous. There is an important analogy between faith and trust that is crucial to understanding the content of faith. But the disanalogies between the two sever the attempt to justify faith along the same lines as trust" (Bishop 2014; compare Jennifer Lackey 2018 and 2014). I think this is correct even apart from what Fraser and others call testimonial pessimism. See Erik Baldwin and Michael Thune (2016) for a complementary account of the epistemological limits of experience-based exclusive religious belief.

11. Mill, 10–11.

12. Actually, the de jure interpretation would be the best for Mill, who acknowledged the value of people's "experiments of living," but in tune with the Enlightenment, was critical of claims of special revelation.

13. *Stanford Encyclopedia of Philosophy*, "Moral Luck," by Dana Nelkin, http://plato.stanford.edu/entries/moral-luck/. Bernard Williams's "Moral Luck" (1981) was also an influential early paper.

14. Nagel 1979. Page reference is to the reprint of chapter 3 in Statman 1993, 59.

15. See Rescher 2001. Other accounts of luck are possible, and indeed invited by the project of this book. Joe Milburn's *generics* (or *failure to exemplify a generic fact*) account of luck, is another emerging option (2015a, dissertation). Milburn (2015b) interestingly also holds that anti-luck virtue epistemologies, which have both ability and safety conditions, are able to support knowledge through divine revelation. However, this seems doubtful if luck is understood through generics. The naturalism which the generics account of luck is held to be consistent with arguably undercuts the externalist religious epistemology he appeals to in order to save knowledge by authoritative religious testimony. For generic pertinent facts would be recognized through empirical observation and inductive reason, while the purported truth of a special revelation would always be a supposedly "one-off reliable event": an event accepted *as* reliable only in the face of the generic facts, strong analogies between agents acquiring testimonial religious beliefs at different epistemic locations.

16. Pritchard (2015). J. Adam Carter (2017b) similarly points out, "There are many advantages to thinking about luck in terms of counterfactual robustness rather than control, and these advantages recommend a modal account of luck." Ian Church (2013) explores several specific ways to model degrees of luck in modal terms.

17. Nelkin (2013) "Moral Luck." Note that lack of control makes more sense in ethics than epistemology. Also, in philosophical ethics, adopting the lack-of-control account of luck should not mean that one must deny compatibilism or embrace the purported confusions that Frankfurt cases aim to root out.

18. Hartman 2017, 118. Excuse conditions may exist *doxastic* responsibility as well as moral culpability, as we will explore later.

19. Hales and Johnson hold that there is no fact to be discovered about whether someone is objectively lucky or objectively through the application of the probability, modal, *or* control theory of luck. On this basis they claim that "luck is a cognitive illusion and assignments of luck are merely a way to subjectively interpret our experiences; our encounters with the world do not include the detection of a genuine property of luck" (2014, 526). The authors hold that philosophers should take seriously the possibility that "there is no such thing as luck, and that worrying

about luck in epistemology, ethics, political philosophy and other areas has been a red herring" (506). But I think this view results from their not considering the risk or luck-related family of concepts as *diagnostic* of multiple types of norms that philosophers, theologians, and others are appropriately interested in. They arguably conflate folk attributions which might be explained as error with the theoretical interests that include risk, contingency, modality, etc. I grant experimental philosophy its studies of luck/risk attributions, but maintain that philosophers often illuminate the nature of the problems they study when they base these in terms of problems of luck/risk. Attribution studies in psychology should inform philosophy, but what they tell us falls far short of ground for concluding that judgments of luck are either wholly objective or subjective. See also Ballantyne (2014) for criticism of the ability of the concept of luck to aid the project of the analysis of knowledge.

20. D. Myers (2003, 247).

21. Kant, "The End of all Things," in *Perpetual Peace and other Essays,* 94.

22. John Calvin, *The Institutes of the Christian Religion,* III.21.7.

23. They cite *Ephesians* 1:11, that humans have been "predestined according to the purpose of him who works all things according to the counsel of his will," and are not at all bothered by the combination of divine-side predeterminism and human-side good or bad luck, including religious luck that comes through in *Proverbs* 16: 33: "The lot is cast into the lap, but its every decision is from the LORD."

24. Zagzebski (1994, 402).

25. Thus criterial luck might also be called aleatory luck, its seriousness as a philosophical and theological problem underlined by the close connection between aleatory and veritic, where veritic luck, as luck coming "betwixt the agent and the world," is considered a defeater to the epistemic status of any beliefs affected by it. "Randomness in the world and lack of certainty in a judgment have different sources. Randomness is a property of events in the world independent of the judge and uncertainty a property of a mental state of the judge. . . . Randomness refers to a principled and fixed limit on the accuracy of [in this case, human] prediction, whereas uncertainty can be reduced with more knowledge or expertise." S.A. Slomann, "Taxonomizing Induction" in A. Feeney and E. Heit (eds.) (2007), 330.

26. Just as actions and omissions are held by moral theorists to be asymmetrically related to the praise and blame of moral agents, differences between "actual" and "counterfactual" luckiness may affect how we understand both resultant and criterial religious luck. In a treatment of resultant moral luck that may have application to religious luck, Carolina Sartorio (2012, 74) writes, "There are, again, two opposed varieties of resultant luck: actual luck and counterfactual luck. And, although omissions are more subject to *counterfactual* luck than actions, they are less subject to *actual* luck than actions." Sartorio cites *three* potential sources of resultant luck for a given agent and an outcome: "First, agents may not fully control whether certain outcomes *occur.* Second, in cases where those outcomes do in fact occur, agents may still not fully control whether their behavior *results in* those outcomes. And, finally, in cases where their behavior does in fact result in those outcomes, agents may still not fully control the *way* in which they do" (85).

27. See especially Ted Sider (2002), who argues that "what I am calling the proportionality of justice prohibits *very* unequal treatment of persons who are *very*

similar in relevant respects. Whatever one thinks generally about the nature of justice, its proportionality should be acknowledged" (59). The problem is severe enough that Sider thinks it makes binary eternal Heaven/Hell contradictory to the justice of God. "There can be no such place as Hell, under its usual conception as part of a binary afterlife, for there is no criterion for judgment that God could employ. The continuity of morally significant factors is flatly in contradiction with God's justice (or at least God's non-arbitrariness) and a binary afterlife" (68).

28. US Catholic Church, *The Catechism of the Catholic Church*, section 847. 2nd ed. (New York: Doubleday Religion, 2003).

29. Calvinists and Molinists like Craig tend to support what Kvanvig terms the *strong view of hell:* "This strong view of hell involves four distinct theses. First, it maintains that those in hell exist forever in that state (the *Existence Thesis*), and that at least some human persons will end up in hell (the *Anti-Universalism Thesis*). Once in hell, there is no possibility of escape (the *No Escape Thesis*), and the justification of and purpose for hell is to mete out punishment to those whose earthly lives and character deserve it (the *Retribution Thesis*)." Jonathan Kvanvig, "Jonathan Edwards on Hell." See also David Alexander and Daniel Johnson (eds.) *Calvinism and the Problem of Evil* (2016).

30. Is a Molinist or Middle-knowledge soteriology logically compatible with the exclusivity of salvation through Christ? Craig, a Molinist, and David Hart, an evangelical critic of both escapism and Molinism, debate this. It would seem that Molinism requires giving up salvific exclusivism, since actual commitment to Christianity seems to be easily replaceable by a counter-factual conditional about what persons would have done if situated differently. This seems to imply *anonymous participation* in the one saving religion, potentially virtuous religious aliens, and salvific inclusivism rather than exclusivism. See also Robert J. Hartman (2014), and Robin Parry and Chris Partridge (eds.) (2003) *Universal Salvation? The Current Debate*.

31. Craig (1995, 120). This appears to save the expectation that the saved are only actual converts, or the baptized, not anonymous or post-mortem converts. Gordon Knight, in "Molinism and Hell" (2010) writes, "While the doctrine of hell is difficult to defend on any view of divine providence, Molinists are especially vulnerable to the charge that their construal of God, if it is not a universalist one, forces upon us a conception of deity as manipulative and unloving towards creatures. . . . The insistence on libertarian free will by itself does not remove the clear aura of cold manipulation from their eschatology. The God of the Molinists is indeed one who has great providential control over creation. But far from allowing an escape from the problem of hell, this providential control only makes the problem more intense." See also the exchange between Maitzen (2006) and Marsh (2008).

32. I thank my research assistant Katelyn Dobbins for these points, as she brought to my attention the connections between Craig's middle-knowledge view and his view on the condemnation of homosexuals. Re-describing them theologically as people who would reject God even had God not made them who they are, effectively just villainizes them, Dobbins argued in her term paper. The inference seems to be that God indeed made a large percentage of persons with naturally homosexual orientations, but he *must have* made them only out of such character types as God's

middle-knowledge reveals would reject God, "transworld." If it still seems odd that such folk are somehow culpable for their character, the apologist for this orthodoxy can just be selectively skeptical on that question, which functions rhetorically to say that we must leave the details to God.

33. Jensen, Chock, Mallard, and Matheson (2017) relatedly write, "While such an accommodation of biases might be the most effective route to harmony, it is surely not the rational course of action. When biases survive reflection, the subject's conscientious judgment is informed by prejudices that are both unfair and unfounded." Any account that recommends this will be both epistemically and morally inadequate: epistemically, because the hearer would maintain rather than try to discover and root out the error; and morally, because this strategy makes it easy to inflict an epistemic injustice on a person or community.

34. From my perspective, Hunt appeals to what we will term *environmental veritic luck*, while Craig's response only shifts this back to bad *constitutive luck* at reprobation (since it can only be God who so constituted people this way before they were born) and bad *criterial luck* (since few would likely assent to be born at all under such conditions as Craig describes, but are so committed by God).

35. We have been using the intuitively plausible but limited "lack of control" account of luck. But problems of luck are not all on the side of religiously determinist views. Steven Cowan in "Molinism, Meticulous Providence, and Luck" (2009) constructs a dilemma for theodicies on which God grants free will and relies on "middle-knowledge," or counterfactuals of freedom. Cowan distinguishes between two ways that God could use middle-knowledge to construct a world that would fit his divine plan, and tries to show that one of these ways is inconsistent with the meticulous providence Molinists hold God to exert over human history, while on the other way the Molinist must attribute to divine luck the truth of the belief that one possible creation of free agents like ourselves realizes the divine plan. Note that Open Theism understands God's relation to the world as one of limited rather than complete knowledge, and God's sovereignty as general in contrast to meticulous. For debate over Craig and the Molinist defense of Christian soteriological exclusivism, see Meyers 2003, and Perszyk, (ed.), 2011.

36. Sessions, 170. Lutherans and Wesleyans also have a teaching of predestination, but not in the double, Calvinist sense that they see as debilitating. They tend to see that as non-biblical speculation on the Calvinists' part, and as ascribing to God contradictory wills: for if, as is biblical, God wills the salvation of all and Jesus died for the whole world, God cannot simultaneously have *willed*, that is, decreed or reprobated, that some individual souls not be saved.

37. Blaise Pascal for example writes, "There is nothing which more shocks our reason than to say that the sin of the first man has rendered guilty those who, being so removed from this source, seem incapable of participation in it. This transmission does not only seem to us impossible, it seems also very unjust. For what is more contrary to the rules of our miserable justice than to damn eternally an infant incapable of will, for a sin wherein he seems to have so little a share that it was committed six thousand years before he was in existence" (*Pensees*)?

38. This Augustinian interpretation in turn shaped attitudes and teachings that humans do not deserve heavenly reward, but that God offers grace as unmerited gift

that is wholly to his own praise and glory. Indicative of intra-religious debate, Miller (2016) is highly critical of the Augustinian interpretation which influenced later Christianity greatly. Augustine he thinks "reinterprets the received tradition coming from 1 Timothy 2:4 that God wills to save all people [compare Titus 2:24: "For the grace of God has appeared, bringing salvation to all men"]. . . . Augustine maintains that God's will to save all people means either that those who are saved are those God wills to save or that God wills to save some from every class of human beings. God's justice is also altered. For Augustine, God does not will the salvation of all people and justly elect those whom God knows will respond favorably to God's grace; rather, by the sin of Adam and Eve, the whole human race has become a mass of perdition or a damned mass corrupted in its root. By the standards of justice, God does not need to save anyone, but God in mercy chooses to destine some for eternal life, the rest God justly let's go to eternal damnation. In his grounding God's election in God's sovereignty, Augustine limits the love of God" (141). Augustine's hostility to philosophy was not a strong as Tertullian's, perhaps, but his comments suggest using Greek and Roman philosophy in an ad hoc way, eliminating its independent normative force and instead treating it as theology's handmaiden, able to support but not to challenge faith-based dogmas.

39. Even in Catholic tradition, Aquinas's understanding of faith as "an act of the intellect assenting to the truth at the command of the will" strongly suggests that intellect is passive, and its role is to accept the *gift* of grace. The passivity aggravates constitutive luck concerns, because if one is not rightly equipped to receive or follow the "command of the will" then for reasons outside their control they will lose out on truth, and also on salvation.

40. K. Shaw (2017), "Faith as Extended Knowledge."

41. "If there were a perfectly loving God, He would see to it that each person capable of a personal relationship with Him reasonably believes that He exists, unless a person culpably lacks such belief. But there are capable, inculpable nonbelievers. Therefore, there is no perfectly loving God." This is the syllogistic description of Schellenberg's that turns to a strategy akin to skeptical treatment of the problem of evil, such that if the problem is substantial enough, then the God of the "Three O's" cannot exist. See Howard-Snyder and Moser (2002, 4); also Maitzen 2006.

42. Robert McKim begins his book *Religious Ambiguity and Religious Diversity* (2015) by noting, "The religious ambiguity of the world has many aspects, one of which is the hiddenness of God." Various soteriologies may subscribe to the value of mystery and fideistic assent, criticizing as faithlessness the attitude of "doubting Thomases" along the way. But the exclusivist claim that God demands a religion-specific cognitive component under conditions of ambiguity of total evidence is especially threatening to the rationality and morality of God as so conceived.

43. J.S. Mill *On Liberty,* chapter 3.

44. By way of comparison, some religions and models of faith more so than others embody teachings and models of faith that explicitly recognize the plurality of individual temperament, and its accommodation in the hereafter insofar as it supports virtue. The Hindu *four margas* is the classic example of recognition and accommodation of personal temperament, stages in life, etc. The Buddhist *Suttanipāta* (translated

by Bhikkhu Bodhi) contains a story how the Buddha once spent the months of an annual rain retreat: "The Blessed One explained meditation subjects suitable for the 84,000 different kinds of temperament in this way: . . . To those of a discursive temperament, he taught such meditation subjects as mindfulness of breathing and [symbolism in mandalas]. To those of a faith temperament, he taught such meditation subjects as recollection of the Buddha. And to those of an intellectual temperament he taught such meditation subjects as the delineation of the four elements" http://www .wisdompubs.org/landing/loving-kindness.

45. In *A History of God,* Karen Armstrong (2017) [1994] develops a fourfold model of divinity, consisting of two crossed distinctions. The first is the distinction between *Transcendent* and *Immanent*. This is a question of divinity's standing relative to our lived natural and social world. The second is the distinction between *The Personal* and the *Ineffable*. This is a question about how we as humans relate to divinity. What James calls our "live options" arguably always situate themselves somewhere on this model. This is why we should take taxonomies of faith such as Armstrong's as a source of diversity or multiplicity in models of faith. And while many authors treat James's idea that the only candidates for belief are what a person takes to be "live options" as something idiosyncratic to individuals, James himself treated temperament more socially, as including "imitation and partisanship, the circumpressure of our caste and set" (*WTB* Sec. III). So Armstrong's taxonomy of conceptions of Godhead may be used to gauge *personal* temperament, but it more historically gauges broad *theological* shifts. Thus she writes that periods where a transcendent or an ineffable God is emphasized theologically, often gives way to psychological need-responding turn to the other side of these scales, a god who is immanent and personal. Theological adequacy, this "history of the idea of God" suggests, is dependent on people's actual psychological needs, which are not quite the same in every era. What is a live option for belief is not merely what tradition or past theology tries to dictate, but what spiritual needs people express in each age. People essentially want all four characteristics, but the tensions between these traits make that logically challenging. Dipolar theology might then be seen as the most explicit attempt to "have it all"—that is, to somehow embrace all of these contrasting positive characteristics in a *single* conception of God without inviting charges of conceptual incoherence.

46. Although cast in terms of doctrinal rather than soteriological exclusivism, the following introduction might be taken as background to the epistemological issues to which we are turning: "A plurality of religions raises and epistemological issue. It is the issue of how believers can be entitled to make claims for the objective truth of their religion and therefore the objective reality of the God of that religion, given the many religions of the world. The question might be posed thus: given that we know that there are numerous competing and incompatible religions, how can anyone be confident that his or her own religion is the true one since, no matter what reasons we might give for the truth of our own religion, practitioners of other religions can do exactly the same?" Paul Helm, *Reason and Faith.*

47. *Circumstantial* and *Evidential* religious luck are among further possible categories of epistemic luck, but I will not treat them extensively or offer definitions. Thomas

Nagel treated circumstantial luck as one of his three kinds of moral luck. A perfectly harmless German émigré to Argentina would have chosen to obey orders from Nazi superiors to commit atrocities if his family had not migrated from Germany while he was young. This kind of luck bears on subjunctive conditionals, and so is partially addressed in debates about God and middle-knowledge we have already treated, but circumstantial luck could certainly be individuated if one wants. "Circumstance," though, is ambiguous between moral and epistemic situations, and since the subjunctive conditionals I am from here out most interested in are epistemological in nature, we can most easily just proceed to discussing epistemic kinds of religious luck directly. Nagel 1979, 29. The example's pertinence to kinds of religious luck is discussed by Mark B. Anderson, 2011.

48. In the extensive literature on epistemic luck, Mylan Engel (1992; 2017) first distinguished evidential luck as "benign," or consistent with knowing, from veritic luck as malign, or knowledge-precluding. We can all understand an evidential luck that raises no particular concerns of malign effect. I rarely glance out my window, and had I not happened to glance out the window a moment ago, I would not have seen that there is a blackbird in the tree. But since I did glance, I came to know that there is a blackbird in the tree. The question is not whether there *is* benign epistemic luck—epistemic luck that is compatible with knowledge. Certainly there is. The question is rather whether information and access-related religious luck can properly be thought of as *like that*, or whether it instead displays the characteristic features of any of the forms of epistemic luck whose impact most epistemologists believe undermines positive epistemic status. Duncan Pritchard developed the contrast further in his 2005 book, *Epistemic Luck*, and presented a fuller taxonomy. Since this is a contrast that we will extensively pursue later as we extend the analogies with previous ethical and epistemological work on luck into philosophy of religion, I will treat evidential religious luck as something of a placeholder for luck in access to information or experiences that are prima facie benign.

49. Bondy and Pritchard 2017, 4. Susanna Rinard (2018a) supplies examples that might usefully fit what Bondy and Pritchard describe as propositional luck (see also 2018b). Her examples would seem to best fit for domains of our controversial views, in contrast to our everyday beliefs: "[I] argue that evidence can play a role in bringing about belief without being a motivating reason for belief, thereby leaving room for practical considerations to serve as motivating reasons. I present two ways in which this can happen. First, agents can use evidence as a mere means by which to believe, with practical considerations serving as motivating reasons for belief, just as we use tools (e.g., a brake pedal) as mere means by which to do something (e.g., slow down) which we are motivated to do for practical reasons. Second, evidence can make it possible for one to choose whether or not to believe—a choice one can then make for practical reasons." Abstract for Susanna Rinard, "Believing for Practical Reasons," 2018. In neither of Rinard's types of cases would the agent (aside from an unfortunate presumption of naïve realism on their part) be "in the market for knowledge"; this is another respect in which Rinard's cases seem to fit Bondy and Pritchard's description of being deeply affected by propositional luck.

50. Lisa Bortolotti and Matthew Broome (2009, 205) argue that "by appealing to a failure of ownership and authorship we can describe more accurately the

phenomenology of thought insertion, and distinguish it from that of non-delusional beliefs that have not been deliberated about, and of other delusions of passivity." The several forms of religious luck under discussion might be thought to give specificity to what has sometimes in the literature on epistemic luck been termed "reflective luck." Therefore I have not found it necessary to include *reflective religious luck* as a separate type in this taxonomy, although others might find more examples of it. But "reflective" luck is very broad and perhaps a worry only of radical global skepticism, or the naïve realism that motivates it as a response. See also Breyer, D. (2010 & 2013), and Pritchard (2005) for discussion of reflective luck. For Breyer and Greco (2008) cognitive integration is a condition on virtuous belief-forming methods for the reasons that integration underwrites a kind of first-personal belief ownership, which in turn underwrites all that subjective justification and doxastic responsibility share in common. But more important for us, Breyer and Greco hold that a putative ability is well-integrated not just if the agent *owns* the belief, but also *only if the (real or putative) process or ability is not subject to any defeaters to which the agent has access.* And I will argue in later chapters that counter-inductive methods of belief formation have defeaters to which the agent has access. Lots of defeaters.

51. This delineation of propositional luck may indicate a rethinking on Pritchard's part of his earlier (2005) treatment of how evidential and doxastic luck can come apart, or again, of how internalist and externalist concerns each affects the analysis of knowledge. Propositional luck probably needs to be carefully distinguished from another kind of benign luck besides evidential luck: what Pritchard terms *reflective luck.* My description of religious propositional luck may be considerably too loose to adequately capture Pritchard and Bondy's meaning. But as I am taking it, recognizing the category of propositional religious luck strongly supports Pritchard's (2003) criticism of Alvin Plantinga that in going radically externalist, the form of Christian apologetics associated with the basic belief apologetic appeals to the *wrong kind* of virtues (because it devalues the responsibilist or character virtues). But I hope to pursue more fully integrating propositional religious luck to my taxonomy and to anti-evidentialist apologetics in a later paper.

52. Theists and naturalists will understand this coming apart in different ways, but both are relevant to the assessment of the impact of propositional luck. At least some theists understand faith in such a way that the "real" cause is quite other than the apparent or proximate cause of true religious belief. While the apparent or proximate cause might be early childhood identity-building and education in a religious community setting, strong fideism leads to holding that the apparent cause, while the real cause of the beliefs of religious aliens, is not the real cause of belief, at least for those in the one true religion of God. That is instead a working *sensus divinitatis,* or at the religion-specific level, for Christians, the work of the Holy Spirit. They invoke, in other words, a final cause explanation. Now religious studies scholars employ methodological agnosticism, and so while acknowledging the adherent's supernatural, final cause explanation, they do pay attention to the radical asymmetry in the religious subject's theologically cast explanation. Within their attempt at description and naturalistic explanation, the religious studies scholar and the uncommitted philosopher of religion is entirely correct to compare it for similarities and difference to the explanations offered by adherents of other religions, to see the self-exemption (where

truth-guaranteeing final causes operate here and not elsewhere) as inductively illogical, yet widely spread. They are correct to see this separation of reasons and causes as part of the *uniqueness* and *superiority* claim which adherents of religions so often indulge in. Non-committed philosophers of religion will tend to see the proximate causes of social identity and early childhood exposure to a religion through family or local culture as the real reason, different from the adherent-alleged one.

So the situation we have that I want to suggest bears upon problems of propositional religious luck is that the supernaturalist and the naturalist *both* see reasons and causes as coming apart in the case of religious belief. The supernaturalist at least on highly fideistic models of faith prefers causes to reasons, and even says that epistemically well-founded belief is not real faith. The naturalist also points to the coming apart of reasons and causes, but in the form of mis-attributions of divine causes to defend religious uniqueness: Mis-attributions because the proximate cause of being raised in a different family or different culture explains divergence of nurtured religious belief much more symmetrically. These first-personal and third-personal attributions of epistemological irrelevance, and of a serious split between reasons and causes, I am suggesting, should both sometimes motivate taking the etiology of the agent's belief as subject to propositional luck.

53. A person's initial personal or prima facie justification for a target belief is, in an instance of bad epistemic luck, defeated (whether the defeater is recognized or not by the agent). It looks like the agent is headed for a personally justified yet false belief. But this anticipation of falsehood is then "reversed" by a second instance of epistemic luck, this time *good* epistemic luck, such that what the person comes to have is a true belief after all. Their personal justification remains as it was, but success in having a true belief comes in from the side, as it were. This is why it is said that in Gettier cases the truth of the agent's belief is not connected in the right way with her justification for that belief.

54. Griffiths, 152–153. Barth himself writes, "No religion *is* true . . . A religion can only *become* true. . . . The true religion, like the justified human being, is a creature of *grace*. . . . Revelation can adopt religion and mark it off as true religion. And it not only can. How do we come to assert that it can, if it has not already done so? There is a true religion: just as there are justified sinners. If we abide strictly by that analogy—and we are dealing not merely with an analogy, but in a comprehensive sense with the thing itself—we need have no hesitation in saying that the Christian religion is the true religion. . . . On the question of truth and error among the religions only one thing is decisive . . . *the name Jesus Christ.*" *Church Dogmatics Vol.1.*

55. If utilizing the type/kind distinction would lend further clarity, we have discussed multiple "kinds" of religious luck, in that "kind" is generally used to link an individual to a group. "Type," when distinguished from kind, is used to differentiate one grouping from another, by way of some important distinguishing characteristic(s). The root meaning of type is "impression." If we take our interest in epistemic luck to be focused in part on normative differences between benign and malign effect—that is, the standing of what we claim to know or justifiedly/rationally believe—then benign and malign we should recognize as two *types* of epistemic luck, and we can fit the appropriate kinds under one type or the other. Thus, I treat veritic luck (two kinds)

as being of the malign type, while recognizing that there are also kinds of epistemic luck (like simple, uncompounded evidential luck) that are of benign type. This allows both that there could be disagreement about what is malign epistemic luck or not, and that type distinctions might be drawn beyond the standard one concerned with normative effect on epistemic standing. It also allows that I may simply have not identified all of the kinds of religious luck. But we have endeavored to pattern our treatment on the existing literature on luck.

56. On this distinction see especially King (2008) and McKim (2012; 2015).

57. Griffiths notes that many theists and non-theists today find salvific exclusivism morally repelling: "You might think, for example, that, since people's religion is usually given to them by causes beyond their control (parents, teachers, local culture) it is unfair that their eternal destiny should depend upon it. Or you might think it is so obvious that nothing of deep importance of anyone can really be beyond their control that when you come across a view (like exclusivism) that claims just this, and does so in very stark terms, the fact that it makes such a claim is enough to make you reject it" (2001, 151). Using Barth as his paradigm, Griffiths goes on to say why he confirms exclusivism in the face of these moral objections.

58. Pritchard 2010, 47. For his recent turn from anti-luck to anti-risk epistemology, see Pritchard (2017).

59. My reasons for preferring "epistemics" are well-articulated by Dominic Marbaniang (2010): "The term 'epistemics' was coined by Alvin I. Goldman to contrast it with traditional epistemology that didn't take modern psychological studies in cognition into consideration. For Goldman, on the social arena, epistemics concerns 'itself with the interpersonal and institutional processes that affect the creation, transmission, and reception of information, misinformation, and partial information.' As such, it would be appropriate to use the term 'epistemics of religious fundamentalism' to refer to that branch of philosophical enquiry that deals with active beliefs that fundamentalists hold to be justified and true, and that subjectively and/or intra-socially (within a particular community) appear to justify fundamentalist behaviors. By 'active beliefs' is meant those beliefs that readily occur to the mind in the given situation where fundamentalism is obvious" (Marbaniang 2010, quoting Goldman 1978, 509).

60. As Rachel Fraser points out, "Recent epistemological history has inclined towards 'testimonial optimism,' keen to stress the division of epistemic labour and the ubiquity of our dependence upon the words of others" (2018, 204). Several authors have explored testimonial pessimism, which takes a more dour view of testimonial transmission in domains like morals. See also Howell 2014, and Mogensen 2017b. In developing her perlocutionary account of pessimism, Fraser presents a dilemma: "Moral testimony will not typically give rise to testimonially based belief. Agents without the resources to grasp the proposition they are told will not end up believing it. Agents with the resources to grasp the proposition they are told might end up believing it, but they will not, in general, believe it in the right sort of way to count as having testimonially based belief" (214).

61. The objectivity of defining her epistemic environment as fake news "county," can certainly be challenged. There is nothing wrong with isolating on her local

environment as salient for safety or sensitivity failure, but what defines the threshold for salience, like how the belief-forming method of process should be described, are aspects of the *problem of generality*, a major problem for both internalist and externalist epistemologies.

62. Baker-Hitch (2018, 189) uses a parity approach to argue that contingency arguments like Mill's will "result in excessive skepticism concerning a range of ordinary testimony cases." But Mill already mentioned political ideologies in his argument, and we have already conceded that the epistemic location problems affect domains of controversial views. The question is between nurtured and non-nurtured views, and between controversial views and other, perhaps more truth-apt domains. I will develop the difference between robust and rhetorical broad parity arguments later in this chapter, as the broad parity "gambit" is commonplace in Christian apologetics, and many are satisfied that controversial domains are minimally truth apt. It is the apologist who want to set them apart as truth apt in a way that miracles claims, for example that Jesus walked on water or was birthed by a virgin, are to be understood literally, either as true or as false claims about historical events.

63. As we will later extend Pritchard's "turn to risk" (see his 2017 and epistemic dependence papers), I argue that high risk derives from epistemic situations inhospitable to the epistemic strategy one is employing. Riskiness marks epistemic luck as veritic and malign. Note that the sensitivity principle imposes a modal constraint on true belief: if the proposition believed were false, one would not believe it. Sensitivity requires that one would not believe P by the same method were P false. The safety principle imposes a somewhat different modal constraint: if the agent forms a belief, not easily could it have been false. Both will be important going further, but it is not claimed that they map directly onto the two kinds of veritic luck. For other recent work on the turn to epistemic risk, see Carter (2017), Freedman (2015), and Riggs (2008).

64. Inquiry into aporetic or ambiguous problems and into *unknown* truths is what the Greeks meant by the *zetetikos: inquirers*, in contrast to knowledge-claiming dogmatists, sometimes including certain "settled" or rationalistic philosophers settled anti-rationalistic skeptics. *Global* or cross-domain skepticism is often motivated by anti-rationalism. Parity of belief-kinds is combined with a concession to the skeptic of the lack of capacity to know even so-called hinge propositions. But *domain-specific* skepticism is not usually this concessionary, and will often assume some minimal common-sense and/or scientific realism. For a religious skeptic, for example, there are strong arguments that show that there is more disparity than parity in the reliability of claims across domains, for instance scientific theory and theology. Domain-specific skepticism is more likely to be associated with evidence, and with comparative risk-related issues of the safety and sensitivity, the reliability and responsibility, of the inquirer in their zetetic methods, their methods of inquiry.

65. It may not even be the case that one needs to know that the ratio of true to false publications one would acquire by Tess's method is very low, just that there is a good chance she would get a false belief if she could about as easily have been directed to a different box. This is what defeats the "objective" or "epistemizing" justification of the agent even though, as I am supposing, she is subjectively justified.

66. See the exchange between Sandy Goldberg and Charlie Pelling.

67. Barney's "knowing" is produced by automaticity. But if reflection and inference was actually called for by the agent's comprehensive context of inquiry, propositional knowledge cannot be attributed without equivocating over the meaning of "knows," equivocating between the desired reflective knowing and mere externalist knowing on the basis of unreflective automaticity. I might agree that if I put my dog's food dish in among many visually, etc., identical but fake bowls, yet he manages to run straight for the genuine article and does not even appear to notice the others, I should not deny that in an animal sense, Fido *knew* that was his bowl. But if so this is because he does not have what is distinctive about "reflective" agency and reflective knowledge, the wherewithal to consider one's doxastic strategy and how well or poorly it operates in one's epistemic environment. His good luck will not count against his brute knowing as it would against reflective knowing.

68. Risk is especially salient in environmental luck cases because of the inductive reasoning that these cases require. Risk and responsibility are a common pair. But Gettier cases seem not to involve inductive risk as directly. Also, luck but not risk is salient in the denial of understanding to the agent (at least where understanding is taken as irreducible to knowledge-that).

69. Pritchard 2016b, 1.

70. "Our judgements about knowledge are . . . sensitive to the modal closeness of error as opposed to its probabilistic closeness" (Pritchard 2016, 554). Modal accounts characterize possible worlds in the standard way in terms of a similarity ordering. See also Bondy and Pritchard (2017).

71. Craig 195, 124.

72. See Richard McDonough (2013) for a critique of fundamentalist commitment to divine command as "conceptually incoherent," insofar as its proponents "inevitably must substitute human judgment for God's judgment." I take it that most Christian theologians take the following syllogism as consistent with Christian orthodoxy: 1. An act of forgiving can never be predicted (Hannah Arendt, 240); 2. God acts freely in an act of forgiving; 3. So, an act of forgiving by God can never be predicted. This seems right, but isn't this conclusion quite inconsistent with a language of necessary conditions, as "*blank* alone" surely is? The absolute sovereignty of God itself conflicts with God's judgment being cast in the language of a necessary condition—faith alone, or confession to the creed of religion x.

73. This is highlighted also by the distance between what is considered theologically correct belief and what is actually held by people as part of popular religiosity, a gap that cognitive science of religion scholars have begun to study empirically. These differences might in fact operate in both directions, such that popular religiosity could display inclusivist responses to religious multiplicity in traditions where exclusivism is orthodox (thereby to a degree mitigating concerns about soteriological luck), *or* instead exclusivist responses where inclusivism is orthodox (thereby exacerbating luck-related concerns).

74. The conception of positive epistemic status I employ here is that of well-founded belief, or belief that meets a "grounding" expectation. It is possible that an externalist apologetic would counter my "clearly" claim with a stark reliability about

which the agent need have no internal access. An agent needs no good epistemic reasons for belief, because belief is unstable if based on reasons and inferences at all. My short response is that this "basic belief apologetic" just invites another form of malign epistemic luck, propositional luck.

75. Bondy and Pritchard (2017) have recently expanded Pritchard's taxonomy of forms of epistemic luck, arguing that "propositional epistemic luck" is a malign form not previously delineated in the literature. If so, the distinction between evidential, or perhaps reflective luck and propositional luck also carries critical epistemological import. "(PEL) S's belief B is propositionally epistemically lucky iff S has a good reason R (and therefore, propositional justification) for B, but it is only a matter of luck that she does. . . . All cases of propositional epistemic luck are cases where a subject has a belief which is propositionally but not doxastically justified (though, as we will shortly see, not all cases of beliefs which enjoy propositional but not doxastic justification will involve propositional epistemic luck). There are two ways in which a belief that is propositionally justified can fail to be doxastically justified: it can be held on the basis of a bad reason, or it can be held on the basis of a good reason but in a bad way."

I cannot think of religious cases of the second sort, but indoctrination-cases where one believes on the basis of what is taught, but there is, or the agent *later* finds that there is good evidence to support what she believed on other, perhaps authoritarian basis, may easily have religious examples. This potentially saps much strength from the claim that testimonial authority assumption can result in positive epistemic justification if the agent studies and learns more about theology and theological problems subsequent to forming religion-specific beliefs.

Chapter 2

The New Problem of Religious Luck

QUALIFYING AND REFOCUSING ETIOLOGICAL CHALLENGES BASED ON CONTINGENCY

As we earlier saw with our example of J.S. Mill, contingency arguments allege a kind of accidental quality to most people's culturally nurtured beliefs. Our obvious psychographic differences—differences in such things as attitudes, values, and most importantly for this study, what John Rawls terms *comprehensive conceptions of the good*—are strongly conditioned by our historic, geographic, and demographic location. Religious identity and whatever faith-based beliefs one has are a prime example of this familial or cultural inheritance, and the apparent contingency of such nurtured beliefs. Although certainly not the only example, the proximate causes of one's religious identity and the formation of attendant beliefs are, for most people, a matter of their epistemic location, which in turn appears to be an accident of birth.

Michel de Montaigne gave a version of a "contingency" or epistemic location argument when he wrote,

> We receive our religion in our own way and by our own hands, and no differently from the way other religions are received. We happen to find ourselves in the country where it has been practiced; or we value its antiquity or the people who have supported it; or we fear the threats it attaches to wrongdoers, or we follow its promises. . . . By the same means another country, other witnesses, similar promises and threats, could in the same way imprint in us a contrary belief.[1]

Arguments like Montaigne's and Mill's have strengths and weaknesses that are rarely carefully noted. They can be wildly over-ambitious if (mis) interpreted to have the implication of reducing to epistemic irrelevance the evidence for all beliefs that are even tinged by cultural contingency (Muscat 2015). Nathan Ballantyne (2015) is correct to find that in arguments from contingency both ancient and modern, "pointing is typically all we get—worked-out arguments based on variability are uncommon."[2] Although religious beliefs are usually the ones singled out, epistemic location has a conditioning or shaping effect over *all* of what in the epistemology of disagreement is termed our "nurtured beliefs." George Sher (2001) re-ignited philosophical interest in nurtured belief; Sher asks us to study "the implications of the fact that even our most deeply held moral beliefs have been profoundly affected by our upbringing and experience—that if any of us had had a sufficiently different upbringing and set of experiences, he almost certainly would now have a very different set of moral beliefs and very different habits of moral judgment."

As Sher indicates, etiological challenges and the contingency anxiety they arouse in those who take them seriously may attach to a far broader group than just religious beliefs.[3] They affect the epistemic assessment of culturally nurtured beliefs more generally. Several philosophers have given thoughtful treatment to contingency arguments in recent papers.[4] Among them there is much agreement that to improve the epistemology of controversial views, philosophers need to focus more carefully on the a) right target, b) proper scope, and c) epistemological force of arguments of the sort that Montaigne and Mill share.[5] We will follow J. Adam Carter (2017) and others who use the term *controversial views* to refer to the broader class of nurtured belief/opinions which include our moral, political, and philosophical views.[6] But each of these domains has unique characteristics such that philosophers cannot be treated indifferently.[7] Retaining our central focus on religious beliefs, one main etiological challenge starts from what are essentially thought experiments about how different our beliefs in the religious domain might easily be had we been raised in a different geographic or demographic location. The challenge is that if raised elsewhere demographically or by family, you would likely accept different such beliefs than you actually do. Is this true? Empirical data is clearly relevant. I think the specific question that needs answering here is, "What percentage of adult religious adherents are adherents of the religion in which they were raised as children?"

It would be good to see experimental philosophers fill in the gaps if sociological surveys do not adequately engage the empirical questions like this one, which epistemic location arguments lean upon.[8] But sociologists of religion are quite interested in the study of "religious mobility," and while I cannot claim to have exhausted the literature, from studies in the America's it appears that there is solid survey data on this question: the relevant percentage stands right around 90 or 91%.[9] This figure if correct surely does provide formally strong empirical support for the generalization behind John Hick's argument, similar to Mill's and Montaigne's, that in "a great majority of cases" religious people (presuming adults) practice that particular religion in which they were raised, or had "instilled" in them from an early age.

More than the obvious fact of inheriting aspects of collective identity from family, or from the culture or subculture in which they are raised, this strongly suggests that whatever affiliation-changes people may make later in life, they tend strongly to initially reach out to a religious option most readily available to them in their epistemic location. These known facts are reflected in the *thesis of descriptive fideism* developed in chapter 3. They are sufficient for motivating the seriousness of contingency or epistemic location arguments, even if, as we have seen, the normative force of etiological challenges is debated in the literature.

Etiological challenges to controversial views are concerned with the how routinely our views in these domains bear marks of contingency and of what John K. Davis (2009) terms trait-dependence. Davis writes that trait-dependent belief is widely acknowledged in domains where informal logic, interpretation, weighing factors or norms, and the exercise of judgment are normal aspects of epistemic assessment. In the acquisition of trait-dependent beliefs, "the subject reasons competently from justifying considerations to a belief, but would not do so if he or she lacked some trait that appears to be epistemically irrelevant, even if the subject and the situation were the same in all other respects." The agent "would not take those considerations to justify that belief if she had a different socioeconomic background, religious affiliation, temperament, political ideology, or the like, even if she were otherwise in the same epistemic circumstances"[10]

The epistemic location problem is clearly involved in the psychographic differences Davis discusses as trait-dependent. I will not in this book be able to develop a full epistemology of disagreement for controversial views. In the recent literature on disagreement, the focus questions seem to be whether disagreement should undermine one's confidence in some target belief or proposition. While I will remain neutral on some of these issues, I do not think there is a one-size-fits-all answer either to this question or to an over-broad question about how people should rationally respond to recognized peer disagreement. Our approach holds that the normative upshot of the prevalence of trait-dependent beliefs in the domains of controversial views is not that they are never well-founded. Although many nurtured beliefs may be biased, we cannot assume that all are without begging the interesting philosophical questions.[11] It is better to say (as seems to be the intent of both Montaigne and Mill) that what normative upshot philosophers should draw crucially depends upon the varying degree of blind spot bias that particular agents exhibit with respect to beliefs in particular domains. Blind spot bias might be thought to be exhibited in various ways, through over-estimation of the epistemic status of their views, through rhetorical and unsupported asymmetries of explanation, and more defensively through rhetorical peer denial. It is the dogmatic ways in which nurtured beliefs are sometimes held that motivates a serious de jure challenge.

So our inductive risk account starts out in agreement with Rawlsian *reasonable pluralism,* and with Davis's permissivist view that recognized trait-dependent overdetermination of a belief in the domain of controversial views does not undermine the basing relationship in any sweeping sense: it undermines that relationship only if and when that trait-dependence manifests or mirrors known personal or social biases. We will return to develop specific, scalar markers of this in part II. But when it does *not* undermine the basing relationship the agent reasons competently, and the influence of personal traits need only be regarded as one of the many sources of the faultless cognitive diversity that John Rawls explained as grounds for *reasonable pluralism.* Davis makes the connection between trait-dependence and Rawlsian reasonable pluralism explicit by quoting the deservedly famous "burdens of judgment" section of *Political Liberalism*: "To some extent (how great we cannot tell) the way we assess evidence and weigh moral and political values is shaped by our total experience, our whole course of life up to now; and our total experiences must always differ" (25).

The epistemic location problem is one of the most unavoidable of these sources of contrariety, being basic to the human condition, and closely related to the evidential ambiguity that affects so many views we hold on morals, politics, philosophy, and religion. The epistemic location problem might suggest grounds for challenging especially our culturally nurtured beliefs, and these range far beyond the domain of religious ideas. But these epistemic worries that contingency arguments raise do not necessarily fall evenly across *cases,* let alone *domains.* This is partly what philosophy of luck and our inductive risk approach to the limits of reasonable disagreement can help us to see. They need not fall evenly across the four mentioned *controversial domains.* Indeed part of what motivates the etiological challenge I am about to lay out is that the sharply asymmetric value ascriptions associated with religious exclusivism are much more prominent in some models of religious faith and responses to religious multiplicity than in others. It is the philosophy of luck that brings the implications of asymmetric trait-ascriptions into focus, and that will help us identify the more and less morally/epistemically plausible models. I will argue that focusing on asymmetric religious value ascriptions and the specific conditions that make them morally, epistemologically, or theologically doubtful helps to illuminate the *limits* of reasonable religious disagreement.

Since we need to think carefully about epistemic location if we are to explicate the force of the epistemology-related religious luck problems, the New Problem tries to present a qualified and refocused set of concerns. It carefully delimits the scope of its de jure challenge. In general terms, a de jure challenge implicates dereliction of epistemic duty, intellectual viciousness, or some other sense of epistemic unacceptability to some target class of religious belief, narrow or broad (Plantinga 1995). By engaging facts of religious multiplicity and understanding an epistemological anti-luck condition in terms of the degrees of inductive risk entailed by a mode of belief-uptake, we can state the specific challenge of the New Problem as a challenge to the reasonableness of religious exclusivist a) conceptions of faith and b) responses to religious multiplicity.

Let us clarify some terms before going further. *Inductive risk is the study of the chance or possibility of getting it wrong in an inductive context.*[12] Debate in the second half of the twentieth century over the role of values in scientific research introduced the concept of inductive risk. Philosophers of science like Carl Hempel reasoned that because no evidence can establish an explanatory hypothesis with certainty, "acceptance . . . carries with it the 'inductive risk' that the hypothesis turns out to be false."[13] Based on this admirably broad definition, the conversation about risk-management with respect to scientific research and the applications of technical knowledge expanded in later decades. Government or corporate science policy-makers dialogue over risk-assessment together with stakeholders: all those potentially impacted positively or negatively by the decisions made. The concept of inductive risk, if portable beyond philosophy of science and epistemology, might serve equally well as common ground for discussions between philosophers, theologians, and researchers in cognitive science of religion. There are a number of concepts in the risk-related family of concepts—risk, probability, chance, luck, fortune, fate or destiny, and so on. Risk is an especially useful diagnostic concept in epistemology because it is connected with what is calculable, in contrast to concepts like destiny or fate.

Counter-inductive thinking entails the highest degrees of inductive risk. The definition of counter-inductive thinking is independent of any special concern with a special domain of inquiry. *Counter-induction is defined in dictionaries as a strategy that whether self-consciously or not reverses the normal logic of induction.* One example would be ignoring the normativity of a strong pattern of how things are within our past and present experience, while making a prediction about the future. For instance I predict something will happen that is quite counter-point to what the evidence and inductive reasoning would suggest. Another example, closer to our concern, is a strategy of taking a mode of belief-uptake that we ourselves assert or are committed to holding is unsafe/unreliable for the production of true beliefs in *other people*, as a truth-conducive mode of belief-uptake in *our own case*. For our purposes counter-inductive thinking primarily describes a prima facie logical failing: a failure to see reason to apply to oneself our ingroup a judgment that one readily and even eagerly applies to others (and their epistemic situations); or a failure to supply sufficiently independent and non-circular epistemic grounds for one's self-exemption from an inductive norm.

We are now in position to lay out the New Problem formally. It will consist of three theses, and a fourth which follows from the first three. The first two theses are about *formal* symmetry, symmetry in the belief-forming cognitive process. The first thesis is:

Familial-Cultural Displacement Symmetry

(DS) For the great majority of religious adherents, had s/he been raised in a family or culture with a different predominant religious identification than that in which s/he was actually raised, but with the same natural capacities and intellectual temperament, s/he very likely would come to identify herself with that religion, with roughly the same degree of personal conviction.

Next we propose a belief-forming cognitive process-type salient in the formation of religious beliefs of widely divergent content. The process-type should be wide, since our purpose is to challenge as unsafe not the etiology of *all* religious beliefs, but the etiology of beliefs associated with a fideistic uptake of a testimonial tradition. Max Baker-Hytch (2014) points out that what a modal reliability (or safety-based) version of the contingency argument should do to serve its purpose is *not* to pick out a process-type whose specification involves particular religious texts or particular testimonial chains. Rather, "selecting a wider process type, whose specification includes no such particulars . . . achieve[s] the desired result: locating a process type a significant proportion of whose outputs are mutually inconsistent, thus whose overall truth-ratio cannot, even given the truth of one or other consistent subset of the process's outputs, be high enough to satisfy a process type reliability condition."[14] In line with this useful point, our second symmetry thesis is:

Etiological Symmetry

(ES) The epistemologically-relevant level of generality at which to characterize the belief-forming cognitive process by which persons in a great majority of cases, and across epistemic locations, acquire their religion, denomination, or sect-specific beliefs is a level of *testimonial authority-assumption*.

Testimonial authority assumption is our proposed "wider process type, whose specification includes no such particulars." We can all recognize that accepting the unique authority of a purported revelation is a common way to acquire a religious identity, and often in testimonial traditions such acceptance by the individual is tantamount to what they are taught from an early age that faith consists in. So now we follow up these two (difficult to deny) claims about symmetrical processes of testimony uptake with a thesis about exclusivist *asymmetric* ascriptions of truth and falsity to the beliefs acquired through this mode of belief-uptake. (EA) makes a qualified contingency argument *specific to religious exclusivists*:

Exclusivist Asymmetries

(EA) Religious believers of exclusivist orientation in the actual world whose original mode of belief acquisition is aptly described by (DS) and (ES) would likely, if raised in a different epistemic location with a different but still exclusivist dominant testimonial tradition, a) adopt as uniquely true and salvific beliefs that in the actual world they hold to be erroneous; and b) ascribe falsity and error to beliefs that in the actual world they hold to be true.

Finally, (CIT) draws out the key implication that prior concession to all three of (DS), (ES), and (EA) logically commits one to:

Counter-inductive Thinking

(CIT) Religious believers in the actual world whose mode of belief acquisition and maintenance is aptly described by (DS), (ES), and (EA) ascribe to a mode of belief acquisition and maintenance that should by their own lights be acknowledged as *counter-inductive* thinking.

The intention of this argument is to demonstrate how the mind-set of religious exclusivism is enabled only through counter-inductive thinking. The exclusivist ascribes falsehood to the theological systems of religious aliens, but truth to their own, through what any non-committed party would judge to be a common mode of belief-uptake: testimonial authority assumption. (CIT) shows this to be an unmotivated self-exemption from the normal logic of induction, where if a form of belief-uptake is judged unreliable for others to use, it is very probably unreliable for ourselves. Religious exclusivists are among those who are most likely to deny that religious aliens are peers, to dismiss the epistemic significance of religious disagreement, and to maintain themselves as fully rational in what Griffiths refers to as "non-accommodationist" attitudes toward religious aliens. But (CIT) strongly implies that peerhood is not easy to dismiss; it indeed suggests that dismissing it proceeds the same way—by a self-serving self-exemption from inductive norms (i.e., by counter-inductive thinking). Denial of the epistemic significance of religious disagreement is shown vain if the fact of persistent disagreement directly affects the assessment of whether the luckiness of people's epistemic situations implicates benign evidential, or instead malign environmental luck.

In order to deny acknowledging (CIT) exclusivists must deny one or more of (DS), (ES), or (EA), but this is not easy to do. The primary challenge that follows from being logically constrained to accept (CIT) is that the well-foundedness of the exclusivist's belief will then be shown negatively impacted by environmental veritic luck not just in the counter-factual but also in *the actual world*. Your beliefs in both the counterfactual *and* the actual world are acquired on an unsafe basis, under conditions of very high inductive risk, which in turn should be recognized as a strong de jure challenge to their epistemic standing. How can one respect the morality and rationality of a mode of belief-uptake that generates sharply *asymmetric* moral, epistemic, and theological trait ascriptions directed by *some* of its users against *other* of its users? The de jure challenge stemming from the New Problem of religious luck is that that the mode of belief-uptake characterizable as testimonial authority assumption is from an externalist viewpoint *unsafe*.

Are they also from a responsibilist viewpoint *intellectual vicious*? That is a somewhat different question, and would involve us more deeply in discussion not just of the safety but of the sensitivity of belief. The epistemic location problem, and the way we have articulated its force in the New Problem, plausibly shows that the contingency of so many of our nurtured, or testimony-dependent beliefs, involves a question about the basing relationship. I believe this is correct, but sensitivity is often criticized as a strong demand and I am not assuming that it is a condition of knowing.[15] Still, it seems to track some relevant aspects of reasonableness, and to be pertinent to an epistemology for controversial views.[16] For a culturally nurtured belief to be insensitive, we do not have to imagine radical deception scenarios.[17] We only have to make some quite modally close changes, such as growing up in a politically or religiously conservative family instead of a liberal one, growing up in our same society but in a different religious tradition, growing up in a different society that has a different majority religious tradition, and so on. Whatever we can say about the truth-aptness of beliefs in domains of controversial view, and about trusting putative moral or religious experts, it is clear that beliefs in these domains are exceptionally insensitive.[18] But their insensitivity and their causally overdetermined etiology are almost indistinguishable.

THE EXCEPTIONALIST DILEMMA

"Genuine tragedies in the world are not conflicts between right and wrong. They are conflicts between two rights."

—Georg Wilhelm Friedrich Hegel

The question just asked leads me to a complementary description of the New Problem in terms of a dilemma for religious exclusivists: *The Exceptionalist*

Dilemma. The exclusivist, it holds, is caught between embracing two responses to the New Problem, neither of which proves philosophically adequate. The first horn says that the exclusivist cannot without great cost just concede that the formal mode of belief-uptake for adherents of the home religion is of the same general type as that of religious others. For one who grabs the first horn and makes a "same process response" will still want to maintain that the faith-based believing of adherents of the home religion results in *true* belief. But given that they themselves hold that it this general process-type results in untruth and error in a vast majority of cases, they certainly cannot say that the process is *safe*, as epistemologists use that term. The cost of grabbing this first horn is being saddled with recognition that one's mode of belief-uptake is unsafe. The claim seems to be that the symmetry of proximate causes of belief just does not matter so long as truth is claimed. What was an inductive pattern of causal conditions quite saliently applied to religious aliens in judging their falsehood does not apply at home. The same proximate causes at work in those other cases produce true belief *in their own case.*

Note that lack of safety is entailed by an inference being counter-inductive, since (in more internalist terms) a counter-inductively derived conclusion is locatable at the *Weak* pole on the standard scale of inductive arguments, running from strong inductive arguments where the premises make the conclusion *probable* or highly likely, to weak inductive arguments where the premises fail to make the conclusion probable. So we should think of weak inductive inferences as being unsafe *by definition.* Inductive weakness and inductively risky belief immediately re-raises problems of religious luck: If the religious insider's beliefs, like all the religious aliens who got theology wrong, are grounded on counter-inductive thinking, then doesn't it follow that the religious insider's beliefs are, if true, only *luckily* true from the epistemic point of view? It is lucky that in some way—for whatever reasons—the inductive finger points only outward and does *not* point back at you. But the moral, theological, scientific, and philosophic disciplines have a right and obligation to press the counter-inductive conclusion further, asking *why* not.

The safety or reliability of a belief-forming process is a condition on knowing and related epistemic standings, and we should conclude that we lack personal doxastic responsibility if we believe on the basis of a mode of belief-uptake that we allow is unsafe.[19] Grabbing the first horn then comes back on the initial asymmetrical positing of truth: the truth status exclusivist confers on their own specific theological system is now counter-inductive to the falsity they claim for all other theological systems.

It is likely a more appealing option for exclusivists to make a "unique process response," thus denying the charge of counter-inductive thinking that comes with affirming that their beliefs are generated by the same general process of adherents of other testimonial traditions. But the second horn of our dilemma is that all attempts to justify the uniqueness of the mode of belief-uptake ascribed to adherents of the home religion either will be empty or will implicitly rely on self-favoring ascriptions of good religious luck.

To effectively grab the second horn, the uniqueness asserted must genuinely be of *process type*, not just of content. One cannot just appeal to content by saying the process type is a "one off," for instance, by claiming the input to it is the one true revelation of God, or the process must be reliable because it outputs the one true creed. By strength of analogical inference, the seriousness of the charge of engaging in counter-inductive self-exemption is not avoided by such form/content conflating responses, but actually re-enforced. To avoid vicious circularity, a response that grabs the second horn of our dilemma needs to argue for the uniqueness of process-type in an adequately formal sense. The challenge I put forth is that no such unique process response can be given to the Exceptionalist Dilemma that is not empty and cannot be shown to lean once again on a self-serving religious luck ascription.

There are different responses that might be tried out, and numerous counter-analogies or disanalogies that might be raised to try to dislodge our challenge. So rather than claiming that the New Problem or the Exceptionalist Dilemma is strictly inescapable I present them primarily as a useful focus for a new discussion between philosophers of luck, theologians, and proponents of CSR. But if *neither* "same process" nor "unique process" responses to the dilemma prove satisfactory, then the adherents of our different religious faith-traditions should concede that the de jure objection reveals the intellectual poverty of exclusivist conceptions of faith and responses to religious multiplicity.

EXPLANATORY ASYMMETRIES AND CRITICAL REASONING DISPOSITIONS

Attributional asymmetries shed a good deal of light on explanation, and what makes for a well-founded causal explanation. In the social as in the natural science asymmetry, understood basically as "the arrow of causation," plays a central role in many debates about explanation.[20] So before returning to discuss the New Problem or even religion specifically, let's look at asymmetry in the sense of the arrow of causation. Daniele Molinini introduces the importance of asymmetry for scientific reasoning this way: "Explanatory asymmetries appear when we have pairs of deductively valid arguments which rely on the same law(s) but which differ radically in explanatory potential." The classical example of such a pair is that of the flagpole and the shadow. Let Figures A and B, below, represent these arguments.

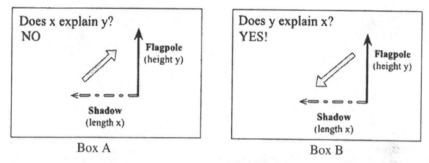

Figure 2.1   A and B. Figures 2.1 and 2.2 reprinted compliments of Daniele Molinini.

Figure B's argument represents a reasonable causal explanation of why the shadow has that particular length, but Figure A's argument does not:

> The problem with this second derivation, in the context of explanation, is that it seems nonsense to say that the length of the shadow explains why the flagpole has that particular height. . . . In the tower and the shadow example we intuitively recognize that there is a direction which gets the explanation right. . . . The height of the flagpole *causes* the length of the shadow, while the converse is not true.[21]

Besides comparing how asymmetry is understood in empirical and in mathematical cases, Molinini draws a more general lesson that we should pay attention to when genuine causal explanations are hypothesized in any domain, or when competing explanations are weighed:

> There are pragmatic constraints which operate in scientific explanation. These pragmatic constraints are specific abilities to reason (for instance, the ability to reason analogically, or the ability to reason causally) which are used in non-scientific explanations as well. . . . Our ability to reason causally acts as a pragmatic constraint in the case of the flagpole and the shadow, thus permitting us to discriminate between the two putative explanations.[22]

That there are constraints on a well-founded explanation both inside and outside the empirical sciences is a point worth highlighting. Abilities to reason inductively and conceptual resources combine in the judgment that B but not A is a good explanation. All cases of "getting it right" in a putative causal explanation involve constraints and criteria. Molinini indeed gives examples from multiple fields to show "how explanatory asymmetries shed light on explanation" in scientific and non-scientific domains alike. The light this sheds is that the constraints on acceptable explanations are *critical thinking dispositions* that help us to assess one explanation as better than another. To do so we must acknowledge the force of inductive norms, compensate for our

Chapter 2

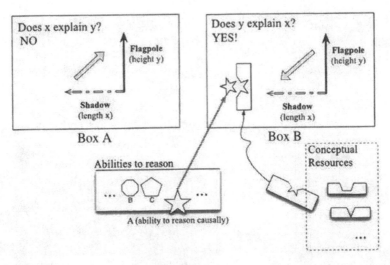

Figure 2.2   A and B. Figures 2.1 and 2.2 reprinted complements of Daniele Molinini.

own cognitive and motivational biases, and avoid relevant fallacies. Beyond this, the abilities needed in the scientific context are especially abilities to employ cause-effect, generalization, and analogical reasoning. But these same abilities are widely used in all domains, for in all domains we need to be able to distinguish strong from weak causal claims, strong from weak analogies, or generalizations. For us, these sometimes quite general and at other times very specific abilities for assessing inductive strength are simply the tools a person has in his or her inductive risk toolkit.

From a psychological perspective, Keith Stanovich, Richard West, and Maggie Toplak take Myside bias to occur "when people evaluate evidence, generate evidence, and test hypotheses in a manner biased toward their own prior opinions and attitudes."[23] Avoiding myside bias or other known biases has little to do with intelligence, but far more with habituation to higher-order critical reasoning skills and dispositions. The cultivation of general intellectual virtues that help attenuate cognitive biases and inappropriate heuristic responses to problems calling for reasoning leads Stanovich and his colleagues to study how well or poorly people are able to engage their *fluid rationality.*[24] When lacking in fluid rationality or working memory, thinking tends to be dominated by what Stanovich terms "crystalized inhibitors," or just plain "miserly" processing. These inhibitors as Stanovich describes them include egocentric processing, over-reliance on one's own introspective powers, and assuming the superiority of intuition. Effective problem-solving seems inextricably connected with the agent's fluid rationality, which in turn involves utilization of skills of inductive reason. How an individual performs on an assigned task involves skills with inductive reason that give power and portability to fluid rationality.

But why is this relevant to the asymmetric attribution of religious truth or value? Why should it matter to religious practitioners, and to philosophical theologians? How is the centrality of inductive norms for sound inferences involving cause and effect, generalization, and analogy/disanalogy supposed to place suspicion on any putative explanation that a theology offers for religious difference? How is it supposed to "reveal" all, most, or many such theologically cast asymmetric trait-ascriptions as the products of crystalized inhibitors, and inductive illogic?

Our argument is not brought forth on the basis that every favoring of prior opinions and attitudes deviates from the judgment of an ideal reasoner. As a pragmatist account it is one that can respect background beliefs and the important senses in which we are children of time and can only start from where we are, and that we "live forward" and therefore face all kinds of pragmatic constraints. But as a pragmatist account it is also one that preserves and supports the functions of criticism, and the ample resources that inquires have available to them. Religious thinking at the level of practice and theology are both shot through with cause-and-effect talk, with the drawing of generalizations about events and populations, and the application of such generalizations to particular actions, persons, or groups; they are also shot through with analogies and disanalogies between events and populations. These are the specific focus of our inductive risk account in terms of what it criticizes and in how it takes studies of moral and cognitive to apply to philosophical concerns with assessment and guidance. So to turn the previous questions around, we should start from a clear acknowledgment that there are well-established inductive norms and skills that fuel success with problems of inquiry involving inductive risk. But then how are we to understand the positing of final in contrast to efficient or proximate cause explanations? Are there experts on extra-scientific cause and effect?[25] If so, on what skills and dispositions does this expertise depend to distinguish good from bad explanations about religiously relevant traits, if *not* skills articulated in terms of inductive reason? If our best cognitive assessments in all other walks of life indicate and utilize these skills, then what exactly would lead a religious believer to hold that processing religious experiences and religious testimony should follow a *different* logic entirely?

Our interests are primarily epistemological rather than metaphysical. The proximate causes of religious belief appear symmetrical with beliefs in other domains of controversial views, in that epistemic location and nurturing importantly help explain differences in belief. But in a theologically cast final cause explanation all those formally symmetrical proximate causes—everyday cause and effect—are typically left in place, while the asymmetry in God's action, as a supernatural event, is conceived as quite independent of them. Were a religious disagreement neutrally describable as the exchange of contrary putatively causal explanations without observable causal effects, what should the real inference to the best explanation be? How could this radical asymmetry among unfalsifiable final cause explanations between one religion and the next *not* have implications for broader debates over realism or fictionalism about religious language? In what ways could a neutral observer, under such conditions, even confirm that final cause explanations are genuine explanations in contrast to misrepresentation of products of religious imagination?

I mention these questions really only in order to set them aside. Such questions best pertain to de facto challenges, and are therefore outside the purview of our de jure focus. The New Problem targets the reasonableness of religious exclusivist responses to religious multiplicity, not realism about religious language, so I will occasionally connect the inductive risk account to motivation for so-called "debunking" theses, but our study takes no stance on them. Chapter 6 will involve us in cognitive science of religion, and there we will examine more closely different view about the relationship between (weaker) de jure and (stronger) de facto challenges, but again without taking any strong stance on the matter. What we can ask is, why should the domain matter this much? Why should we think that resistance to miserly processing, overconfidence, myside bias, and inductive illogic are in principle *less* pertinent understanding religious ideas and theologically cast explanations than they are to beliefs and explanation with non-religious content?

At the start of this book we posed the question of what is going on when persons, theologies, or purported revelations ascribe various kinds of religiously relevant traits to insiders and outsiders of a faith-tradition in sharply asymmetric fashion. This is a *diagnostic question*, and in these terms the New Problem offers what one leading college critical thinking textbook terms *diagnostic arguments*:

> These are arguments in which we reason *by* explaining certain data we encounter, and when explanation becomes a tool in our reasoning, it provides a huge increase both in the vocabulary we may exploit in talking about reasons and in the apparatus we may employ in analysis.[26]

Moral, epistemic, and also religious luck are diagnostic concepts—concepts that play an important role in psychological, philosophical, and theological answers to diagnostic questions. The concept of religious luck grants us significant insights into the epistemological significance of religious disagreement. Pervasive disagreement and epistemic risk make the epistemic context an *inductive* context for agents: contexts in which a person cannot assess his or her own reliability apart from considering how reliable others would likely be using a formally similar method, and how reliable they themselves would likely be still using their same method but under a range of modally varied circumstances. So a philosophy of luck should necessarily be concerned with inductive risk. To say that a religious ascription appears to lean on luck or that a particular way of thinking aggravates problems of lucky belief or luckily true belief, is almost synonymous with saying that the group or agent makes the ascription in a way that violates default norms of symmetry and induction. Our argument in this chapter shows that the degree of inductive risk implicit in an epistemic strategy is a formal and sometimes readily assessable issue. It also suggests that the high degree of inductive risk in contexts in which testimony-based claims to religious knowledge are typically made is a fully sufficient criterion for determining it to be a context of malign environmental, rather than benign evidential, luck.

Finally, degrees of incurred inductive risk may not only be a sound criterion for taking the etiology of a belief to be affected by malign epistemic luck; they may also prove a useful means of measuring where a particular theology falls on the scale between religious rationalism and religious fideism.[27] Rationalists claim that to be entitled to a religious belief, there should be no more risk involved in it than in other more everyday beliefs. The denial of this claim holds that at least for religions-specific beliefs, it is necessary to believe by faith. Further, the fideist may go on to valorize supra or even counter-evidential "belief," on the grounds that a commitment matched only to the degree of rational confidence in one's evidence provides at best a conditional and hence unstable faith. So our approach suggests that these same concerns with inductive risk and safety-principle violation also supply a way to distinguish moderate and strong (sometimes called radical or counter-evidential) fideism on the basis of recognizable formal markers—something that might be quite useful in religious studies and CSR.

By circumscribing the de jure challenge of the New Problem rather narrowly, it should be clear that I am not using this or any of the other problems of religious luck as a blunt instrument to delegitimize religious faith *en toto*. But family resemblances among historical faith-traditions, as we have noted, are important to take notice of. Moreover, that the Abrahamic religions have often given quarter to religious exclusivism is, in good part, a function of shared characteristics that feature in religions of special revelation. Religion-as-revelation seems both to generate variety and at the same time to aggravate problems of religious luck in ways that will bear further attention in part II of this book. But to reiterate, the New Problem as presented here targets only the reasonableness of strongly counter-inductive models of faith, and of the exclusivist response to religious diversity.

A key approach we have taken to the issue of religious rationality is to re-cast safety and sensitivity concerns as indications of high *inductive risk* entailed by the cognitive strategies people rely upon in acquiring or maintaining their belief.[28] The concept of inductive risk is one we will continue to develop throughout the book, but one debate that seems to bear upon it is debate over whether rationally maintaining one's belief in the face of genuine peer disagreement requires one to offer "independent" reasons. Independence requires that, when you assess whether to revise your belief in P upon discovering that someone disagrees with you, you should not rely on the reasoning that led you to your initial credence in P. Baldwin and Thune (2008) for example discuss religious multiplicity as a defeater for religious exclusivism, and attempt to rule out "defeater-defeaters" that are not *independent* of the initial basis of the belief whose defeat is at issue.

David Christiansen writes that an independence requirement "essentially gives us a way—to use Mill's terms—of taking precautions against our own fallibility." This seems especially important when theological claims are asserted in the face of polarized contrariety. Again I do not think the epistemology of disagreement literature has paid enough attention to the significance of *polarized* contrariety, and how part of what explains it is fideistic denial of any independence requirement on the true believer. Christiansen adds that J.S. Mill's position on free speech and diversity in the marketplace of ideas "is straightforwardly epistemic: Mill would have us treat the opinions and arguments of those who disagree with us as an epistemic resource." The need for such constraints "stems from the realization that we often err by overlooking, or failing to attend carefully to, arguments opposing what we're inclined to believe. And engaging carefully and honestly with those who disagree is the natural precaution against this sort of fallibility." Christiansen further notes that his own version of an independence requirement "flows from the realization that our fallibility runs a bit deeper than Mill suggests: we also often err in coming to settled, all-things-considered judgments, *even after the most careful reflection and conscientious engagement with our opponents.*"[29]

While an independence principle is seen, by those who acknowledge it, as applying to the reasoned defense of *all* of our controversial views, the special problem in regard to religious disagreement specifically is the tactic of responding to epistemological objections with theological, hence metaphysical, answers. So as a stab at a principle of explanatory constraint that takes account of our special concerns with asymmetric trait-attributions, consider EGO, or "Epistemically-Grounded Only" Principle:

(EGO) Reasonable religious disagreement recognizes that trait-ascriptions applied asymmetrically to religious insiders and outsiders—that is, ascriptions of asymmetrical religious status or value explanations—require independent epistemic justification, and not just purely theological, or home-scriptural justification.

Independence is in the first instance an attempt to determine common principles of reasoned dialogue. I am sensitive to critics who hold that strict independence may be an impossible ideal for disagreement with respect to domains of controversial views. Accordingly, I will not treat adherence to an independence principle as a strict requirement of reasonableness.[30] The force that it has is a matter of degree, not all-or-nothing, and for us this means that radical denials of Independence are direct indicators of high inductive risk, and only through this, of agent unreasonableness. (EGO) still supports Baldwin and Thune's (2008) argument for the inadequacy of the reformed theological uses of "internal" and "external rationality," and of the circularity of their ways of discounting defeaters.[31] Against these philosophers' recognition of epistemological limits of experience-based exclusive religious belief, are negative apologetic works such as Jeroen de Ridder's aptly titled article, "Religious Exclusivism Unlimited." de Ridder (2011) uses the notion of external rationality to claim that

> an exclusivist can rationally hold religious beliefs in the basic way without having anything by way of a reason or argument to defeat the defeater of religious pluralism. The exclusivist would simply have to find herself with a firm conviction that her beliefs really are right, in spite of counter-testimony from seemingly trustworthy sources.[32]

Once an exclusivist has "defeated the defeater of pluralism" by a simple reiteration of the same basic or non-inferential cognitive process she claims originally produced the beliefs, her "structure now includes a belief that adherents of other religions are epistemically less fortunate than she is; this belief being inferred from her reproduced properly basic first-order religious beliefs" (455).

This "iterative" response, would clearly fail an independence principle like (EGO). The Reformed view is re-iterative, but Jerome Gellman's much more subjectivist-internalist response, or others that appeal to a subjective method would clearly fail it as well.[33] The asymmetry between religious aliens "epistemically less fortunate" than adherents of the home religion is diagnosed, in our inductive risk account, as a simple iteration of the author's prior appeal to *constitutive* religious luck for the unique truth of his own religion-specific beliefs. It is epistemically circular to attempt to justify one's framework through reference to that very framework.

How vicious or virtuous should we take this circularity to be? It is not as if we are not permitted a worldview. (EGO)'s standard of reasonableness I think is not asking too much in a world where few but the most isolated tribes do not have regular exposure to religious diversity and religious unbelief. Tess, in the basic Tess Case of chapter 1, was not highly blameworthy that she gained so little perspective on news sources. Even if we cannot say she only manifested a virtuous agency and credit for her true belief if she had confirmed or challenged it by looking beyond the Blue newsstand publications, her belief that its stories are the actual history of Land of Lakes County is not well-founded. Tess could have and should have done better since she had other boxes available to her to supply some perspective independent of what her uncle and the Blue newsstand publication told her. She knew there was deep disagreement between their contents, as this was announced in bold letters on the back of the paper: "Remember, trust only the news from this box! All of the other boxes contain fake news." But since the possibility and even the desirability of meeting an independence principle are said to be debatable matters, we can leave (EGO) up for debate. I conclude that in the first instance, the radical rejection of any independence principle, and what will be more closely argued to be the associated logical circularity of exclusivist responses to religious multiplicity, are among numerous indicators of the high-risk doxastic strategies prescribed in strongly fideistic conceptions of religious faith.

AN OBJECTION AND REPLY

Consider this objection: The claim crucial to the New Problem, that as a doxastic strategy home religion testimonial uptake is *unsafe*, unfairly totalizes over religions. It is easy for the exclusivist, whether on epistemologically internalist or externalist assumptions, to deny this. More particularly they can deny (ES), the Etiological Symmetry thesis, which seems to say that *testimonial authority assumption* is all one needs to know about the causal etiology of belief to determine both its ubiquity across religions and its epistemic viciousness. But the analysis is too course-grained. For these same reasons it is therefore easy to grab the second horn of the Exceptionalist Dilemma: to maintain that the uniqueness of my religion's testimonial tradition qualifies its transmission as a "different process" than that used by adherents of other faith-traditions. The safety of testimonial chains needs to be assessed singly, not in the totalizing way posited by the dilemma. Looked at that way, it can be safe even as I, as an exclusivist, hold that testimonial authority assumption indeed results in false belief for adherents of alien religions.

In response, let me first remind the objector of the requirements of grabbing the second horn: "To effectively grab the second horn the uniqueness asserted must genuinely be of *process type*, not just of content. One cannot reasonably just appeal to content by saying the process type is a 'one off,' for instance, by claiming that the experiential or testimonial input to it is self-authenticating, or that the process *must* be reliable because it outputs the content of the one true creed." As this passage hints, religious exclusivism has champions who defend it through an internalist apologetic, and others who use an externalist apologetic. If the conditions I place on a "different process" response are correct, the question is whether either apologetic strategy can escape circularity well enough to establish reasonable debate-independence for its supporting reasons.

Starting with internalism, the appeal to unique phenomenology, as de Ridder (2014) points out, is an appeal to internal evidences, evidences such as what it *feels like* to read the Bible and feel its inspiration, or to participate in a ritual or other communal practice. These factors are vitally important to one's religious identity. Indeed, that every religion comes with unique concepts and experiences is an important aspect of my permissivist ethics of belief. Religious narratives place readers where they can feel what it is like to have certain sorts of experience, but they appear not to situate them well for making truth claims, let alone exclusivist ones, on their basis. The question at hand is not whether the inner evidences count as personal or subjective justification—they do—but whether the exclusivist can infer epistemological differences from phenomenological ones.

Appeals to a first-personal perspective and phenomenology seem ill-equipped to break the default symmetry among people as epistemic peers on a certain matter. They can be used to deny peerhood, but only, I think, in a rhetorical way, by the insulating moves of saying the evidence-sharing condition on peerhood is never met across traditions, and that religious disagreements therefore are not peer disagreements. Adherents of alien religious traditions can easily mirror a self-guaranteeing claim that "I feel it so strongly, it can't be false." The next move, again shared by all, is to "logically" infer the falsity of any view contrary to one's own orthodoxy. The claim of the self-guaranteeing authority of the home scripture or experience is something religious studies scholars associate with strongly fideistic models of faith, but these claims have never settled any actual disagreement. At their worst, exclusivists about the truth and worth of purported special revelations generate their own "enemies in the mirror." Let us use the resources of a philosophy of risk and luck to erase, as I have tried to do, the phenomena of self-constructed enemies in the mirror. Doing so it seems to me is genuine religiosity—at least, it requires no anti-realism about religious language.

Those who appeal instead to externalist epistemology in order to defend an attitude of religious exclusivism, such as Alvin Plantinga, may also often appeal to unique phenomenology. But they would have us accept that we can deny etiological and peer symmetries by starting from the other end, from the posited truth of their religious worldview and from the religious knowledge they purport to have. Unfortunately, jumping ship on the epistemic level and the requirement of independent reasons, by telling a metaphysical/theological story about the *causes* of one's experience that set it apart as especially veritic, has never resolved religious disagreement either.

Despite the twists in Plantinga's account of a divine design plan, I hold the basic belief apologetic to be no less fideistic and circular than a phenomenal conservative apologetic strategy. Both make religious knowledge very easy, but falter over why views contrary to their own do not also count as properly basic, warranted, and safe. All that either apologetic strategy ultimately does is to say that warrant (externalism) or undefeated evidence (internalism) only follows the true, and that beliefs running contrary to the Christian's are not true. Here again epistemological questions are given metaphysical answers. On Plantinga's externalist apologetic strategy, a reliable etiology (safety or warrant) is assured for general theistic and also for Christian teachings infused irresistibly by the work of the Holy Spirit. But ask him about the logical possibility on which the Holy Spirit and God do *not* exist and we find Plantinga forced to concede that neither his religion-specific nor his theistic beliefs would in that case be *warranted*, either. Their warrant depends upon supposition of their truth: no truth, no warrant. This explains why the potential mirroring of contrary views that also assert properly basic beliefs in the Great Pumpkin–believers cases, for instance, became such a serious problem for Plantinga.

One might think (ES) paints religious belief acquisition with a broad brushstroke, and that when you look in finer detail, the similarity and formal symmetry of the grounds of belief are very different. It is true that (ES) is framed broadly, but this is a reasonable level of generality at which to describe a good deal of belief-uptake, and the location-switching thought experiment works to confirm that something very like this is the causal etiology of the religious beliefs of most people who grew up in a testimonial faith-tradition.

This is of course a claim only about observable proximate causes. That the perspective on causal etiology in (ES) attends only to proximate causes is a methodological limitation, but it does not beg the question by presupposing that all religions are epistemically on a par. The reader should not confuse the charitable defeasible presumption of peerhood when faced with disagreement, with question-begging. I am not committed to the metaphysical claim that no religious perspective or experience is especially veritic. Similarly, there is nothing in (ES)'s identification of a common proximate cause (home religion testimonial authority assumption) in the acquisition of religious belief that is blind to the claims that some persons use a safer method than others, and that whatever tradition they acquire their belief from, some persons work harder than others to *improve* their epistemic positions. The New Problem encourages attempts to make good on symmetry-breaking reasons, just in order to understand them more clearly and to analyze their formal structure. Default symmetry, a weaker notion than parity or peerhood, is a defeasible posit, but one that allows us to focus directly upon particular attempts to *break* symmetry, and on the inductive risk explicitly or implicitly accepted in these attempts.

So contrary to the objection, I think that the inductive risk approach pre-supposes qualitative or epistemic differences, and *invites* looking for "finer detail." It looks for this especially in symmetry-breaking reasoning, and in the various models of faith that lead adherents to their response to religious multiplicity. But "finer detail" should not be reduced to an opportunity to sub-stitute a sacred narrative in place of a call for epistemic situation-improving reasons. If this closer look reveals that the purportedly unique process mirrors know group biases and inductive fallacies, then far from its uniqueness being established, this would further support (ES) being a good description of it. So this goes case by case. If the reasons offered in attempts to grab the second horn are reasonably independent of the disagreement, then symmetry-break-ing may be on inductively strong grounds. But if these reasons turn out to be circular or to lean explicitly or tacitly on asymmetric attribution of religious luck, then it starts to look like there is far less genuine uniqueness in claims to religious uniqueness than exclusivists would like us to think.

CONCLUSION

Chapter 2 argued that the concept of religious luck grants us significant insights into the moral, theological, and epistemological adequacy of dif-ferent models of religious faith and the responses to religious multiplicity that they motivate. The concept of religious luck has to earn its keep by the value of the diagnostic questions it raises, but it is well able to do so. This is in part because it draws needed attention to variations among belief policies or doxastic methods, "theological methods," as some religious studies call them, prescribed by different actual traditions of religious faith. This diversity among conceptions or models of faith allows keener insight into attempts of theologians to produce "luck-free" soteriologies, and into attempts by philosophers and religious studies scholars to study the logic and illogic of radically asymmetric religious trait ascriptions.

The study of symmetry-breaking attributions, especially through a phi-losophy of luck or risk, provides theologians, ethicists, epistemologists, and cognitive science of religion new insights into the causes of religious disagree-ment and the limits of reasonable religious disagreement. The New Problem of religious luck presented reason to think that denial of epistemic symmetry, and the assertion of asymmetric value in God's eye between adherents of the home religion and all others, will always on close examination be seen to self-attribute one or another type of religious luck. Our discussion of the New Problem also began a process of translating the rather vague concepts of moral, epistemic, and religious luck into terms of *risk* that are more scalable and open not just to thought experiments, but to close psychological study. This translation will be developed through part II.

The presence of pervasive disagreement and epistemic risk make one's epistemic context *inductive*. So our argument in this chapter shows that a philosophy of luck applied to religious epistemics must necessarily be concerned with inductive risk, and that the degree of inductive risk in an epistemic strategy is a formal matter, and potentially measurable. Our study further suggests that the high degree of inductive risk in contexts in which testimony-based claims to religious knowledge are typically made is a fully sufficient criterion for determining it to be a context of malign environmental, rather than benign evidential, luck. Testimonial authority assumption is on this standard a strategy of high inductive risk, even if one holds themselves to have attained truth through it. For it is counter-inductive that one's own testimonial authority assumption should succeed in delivering the epistemic goods, while it is conceded that all symmetrical authority assumptions on the part of persons in a different testimonial faith-traditions would fail rather than succeed.

Finally, part I has given initial reason to think that degrees of incurred inductive risk is a sound criterion for taking the etiology of a belief to be affected by malign epistemic luck. If so, this suggests new means for measuring where a particular model or conception of faith falls on the scale between religious rationalism and religious fideism.[34] Over-strong rationalism (religious *or* skeptical) and over-strong fideism both function to undermine the possibility of reasonable religious disagreement, as well as to obscure a theory of its moral and intellectual limits. Religious rationalism in the form of natural theology provides arguments for God's existence that do not depend upon scriptural sources.[35] Religious fideists by contrast hold that faith is necessary because a person whose assent to theistic beliefs is matched only to the degree of rational confidence in one's their evidence has only an unstable faith. So our approach suggests that these same concerns with inductive risk and safety-principle violation also supply a way to distinguish moderate and strong (sometimes called radical or counter-evidential) fideism on the basis of recognizable formal markers. These markers are the implications and applications of the theoretical issues regarding luck/risk introduced here in part I. In part II we will develop their more specific connections with comparative study of religious fundamentalisms (chapters 3 and 4), with religious exclusivism (chapter 5), and with cognitive science of religion (chapter 6).

NOTES

1. Montaigne, *Apology for Raimond Sebond* [1580], 6.

2. It is hard to say, for instance, just what the conclusion of Mill's argument about the "London Churchman" in *On Liberty* is. Ballantyne (2015) starts from this same "pervasive and disconcerting worry about intellectual life: our controversial beliefs regarding morals, politics, religion, and philosophy depend on facts about our personal history." Bogardus (2013) very plausibly suggests that the alleged wrong—and the basic reason for contingency anxiety—is a violation of safety. "For Mill, there are nearby possibilities in which one forms religious beliefs via the same method she actually used, and yet in which she would believe something which is, by her own lights, false." But it also seems to involve not-insignificant insensitivity. See also Nathan Ballantyne (2013) and Baker-Hitch (2014).

3. The truth-aptness of philosophical judgments has been challenged in similar ways. See Amia Srinivasan (2015) for a treatment of "genealogical skepticism" about philosophical judgments. Srinivasan's account overlaps mine where she provides a discussion of different arguments for genealogical skepticism and in response to it; more especially, in her noting that "epistemologists differ over the extent to which luck plays a role in the acquisition of knowledge. All epistemologists will agree that luck has some role to play. . . . Where epistemologists disagree is on just how much knowledge we can acquire through good luck" (347). The Tess case argued that this is a matter of the kinds of luck in play, and not merely the domain.

4. See Mogensen 2017a; Ballantyne 2013; Vavova 2014; DiPaoli and Simpson 2016. Sometimes these same contingency arguments are called arguments from evidentially irrelevant causes of belief, or debunking arguments, because they threaten to explain the etiology of these beliefs in a way that has nothing to do with their likelihood of being truth. Vavova 2018 also argues that evidence of irrelevant belief influence is sometimes, but not always, undermining. It is surprising how little this quite plausible thesis has been systematically explored, but epistemologists of disagreement have enamored of universalist answers.

5. See Axtell 2019 where I develop etiological challenges to well-founded belief as directly related to a belief's being highly overdetermined by trait-dependent factors. Although I will not explore them here, my understanding of these issues has benefited from papers (see Bibliography) by Baker-Hitch, Ballantyne, Bogardus, DiPaoli, Mawson, Mogensen, Simpson, and others. Religious mobility sometimes occurs for practical reasons of marriage, and another big reason why young adults aged 16–30 are far and away the most mobile or identity-shifting age-group, is suggested in multiple studies to be parental divorce. The data on religious mobility show some trends, but that people are mobile in both directions between religious and secular identities is a basic fact. The overall rise of religious mobility, or what are called "total mobility" levels, compared with decades ago, suggests to me a national trend toward greater reflection, and personal responsibility and active, autonomous pursuit of options in a marketplace of ideas. This trend toward increased religious mobility

would clearly suit Mill, a strong proponent of "experiments of living," and James. It suits this book as well, supporting the openness not only to choice but also to criticism of every historical conception of faith, every doxastic method, and every degenerative research program in any domain.

6. According to J. Adam Carter (2017), recognition of peer disagreement implies that "we are rationally obligated to withhold judgment about a large portion of our beliefs in controversial subject areas, such as philosophy, religion, morality and politics." He recognizes that a thorough-going agnostic suspension or the kind recommended by some epistemologists is open to objectionable consequences of "spinelessness," and impracticability—un-livability. So he distances his version of controversial view agnosticism from these worries, qualifying it such that it allows for "suspecting that" but not "believing that." In a nutshell I would draw the lines differently, and would not accept a non-permissivist view. In defense of permissivism, see Kelly (2014), Kopec and Titelbaum (2016), Booth and Peels (2014), and Schoenfield (2014).

7. Philip Quinn identifies a crucial shared assumption between evidentialists and the others like phenomenal conservatives: "One should demand no more, and no less, by way of justification for beliefs in one area of inquiry than one does in another. Equally stringent standards of rationality should apply in all cognitive domains" (1991, 317). The first group thinks religious belief fails these standards, and the latter thinks it meets them. But by setting aside this faulty shared assumption of religious evidentialism in favor of pragmatism, we can make a similar reply to epistemic parity arguments like those of Plantinga. The project of a broader epistemology for our controversial views is indeed one that I am interested in, but will require another book. But Quinn finds the argument unsound: "It may be that there is no way to prove that the skeptic is mistaken, and so perhaps the only escape from skepticism is by means of a leap of faith. But even if this is so, it does not follow that all leaps of faith are, so to speak, equal in size. Some leaps of faith may be, as it were, bigger than others" (340; compare Penelhum 1983).

8. A PEW study (2009) put the number of adult respondents "who have changed from one major religious tradition to another" at 9%, a figure that closely corroborates earlier surveys I have seen that asked this question. This group includes "converts from a variety of different backgrounds, including converts to Catholicism and converts from or to religions other than Catholicism or Protestantism." Somewhat contrary to the contingency argument assumption, the study finds that "Americans change religious affiliation early and often. In total, about half of American adults have changed religious affiliation at least once during their lives. Most people who change their religion leave their childhood faith before age 24, and many of those who change religion do so more than once." But at the same time, the authors of the study also say, "The group that has grown the most in recent years due to religious change is the unaffiliated population."

9. Studies of religious mobility certainly undermine the simplistic nurturist claim that culture is destiny. For recent studies of religious mobility, see also T. Smith (2005). The PEW study published in 2009 used a re-contact survey years after the original religious Landscape 2007 survey, found only 56% of respondents were in the same Christian denomination as that in which they were raised. "The 2007 survey

found that more than one-in-four American adults (28%) have changed their religious affiliation from that in which they were raised." Thus the 56% would increase very substantially to just above 90%, and corroborate the 1988 figure, if remaining in the same "affiliation" were taken as remaining Christian, etc. These are strong numbers, but I suggest we ask more directly what the empirical presuppositions of properly qualified contingency-of-belief arguments are, and whether there are extant studies that bear upon it. If not, what would an empirical investigation on this matter look like—what specific questions would it need to ask? How would these questions differ between the domains of controversial views?

10. Davis (2009, 23). See Axtell (2019) for development. Davis defines "trait" broadly to include "not only personal traits such as gender or features of one's personality, but also such properties as socioeconomic background, rigorous training, exposure to certain individuals or groups, subscribing to a certain ideology or religion, or having a certain personal history."

11. Davis does not think it is correct to say that traits consist of holding particular beliefs, though the trait may involve holding some beliefs. (24) A bias in cognition "is a tendency towards a certain kind of distortion in one's process of reasoning and belief formation." But in trait-dependence cases as Davis wants to understand them, ex hypothesi "there are no such distortions—just the dependence relation. . . . Trait-dependence is not a cognitive distortion unless trait-dependence defeats the basing relationship—and that is the question before us; we cannot assume an answer to it" (24).

12. See especially Bishop 2007a and b on how moderate fideism can constrain doxastic ventures. Note that my account does not depend on testimonial knowledge being inductive or inferential; it is neutral with respect to debates between reductionists and anti-reductionists. But if testimonial uptake is inferential, then this still further substantiates logical connections between belief-acquisition through testimonial authority assumption and high inductive risk.

13. Hempel 1965, 92. See Douglas 2000 for discussion.

14. Baker-Hytch, 190.

15. This, despite the fact that the belief of the victim of a malin genie that he has a physical body is as insensitive also. My entitlement to hold fast to my metaphysical beliefs in a physical universe, other minds, etc., where all sources of empirical evidence support my causal story does not extend an entitlement to hold steadfast in the case of more controversial views. My thought here, which relates to epistemic parity arguments, is roughly that sensitivity tracks reasonableness when the closest error-possibilities are modally close, but it does not track reasonableness when the closest error-possibilities are distant. Thanks to Patrick Bondy for helping me articulate this suggestion.

16. Kevin Wallbridge (2018) argues that while inductive knowledge may not be strongly sensitive, it is weakly sensitive. The point is supportive of the importance of the insensitivity of counter-inductive thinking to epistemic rationality or reasonableness, even though I do not take sensitivity as a general necessary condition on knowing.

17. Insensitive belief that is not based upon shared facts but rather on private intuitions or other subjective factors cannot claim the same reasonableness as the belief that I am not radically deceived. My entitlement for the latter does not imply entitlement to the former, potentially much more temperamental choice.

18. James Fritz (2018) writes, "Many writers have recently argued that there is something distinctively problematic about sustaining moral beliefs on the basis of others' moral views. Call this claim pessimism about moral deference. Pessimism about moral deference, if true, seems to provide an attractive way to argue for a bold conclusion about moral disagreement: moral disagreement generally does not require belief revision. Call this claim steadfastness about moral disagreement." Fritz then goes on to argue that there no easy or compelling root from pessimism about moral deference to steadfastness about moral disagreement.

19. Relatedly, Rik Peels (2016) argues that responsible belief "is compatible with its being a matter of luck that we hold that belief." The present analysis, however, shows that it very much matters what kind of luck is salient, and whether an appeal to religious luck for holding the beliefs one does is morally as well as epistemologically concerning. This does not mean that I disagree with Peels; indeed I very much agree that if we want to act responsibly, we should believe responsibly, and that doxastic responsibility has diachronic and not merely synchronic aspects. Peels develops the interconnections between ethics and epistemology through the problem of doxastic involuntarism, which I agree with him gives in many of its forms a distorted view of belief. Peels goes on to give a detailed account of how we can still believe responsibly "if we are excused for our belief by force, ignorance, or luck." My term constitutive epistemic luck seems to be broken down further by Peels into mechanism and aretaic luck.

20. For a thorough introduction to this important topic, see Molinini, Pataut, and Sereni (2016).

21. Molinini 2012.

22. Tables 1 and 2 reprinted complements of Daniele Molinini.

23. Stanovich, West, and Toplak 2013, 259. See also the authors' 2008 study. Their many studies show that the magnitude of the myside bias shows very little relation to intelligence (or to whatever IQ tests, tests). Studies demonstrate quite substantial individual differences on tasks normed to commit or avoid myside bias; these demonstrated differences, cognitive science has sufficiently established, are due largely to differences in critical reasoning skills and dispositions.

24. Fluid rationality describes a range of available critical reasoning dispositions, together with ability for sustained de-coupling of their default, heuristic thinking. When utilized by the agent, he or she exhibits resistance to misery informational processing and my-side bias.

25. Carter (2017) usefully develops conditions of the "centrality" and "symmetry" of disagreement in a domain as a criterion for challenges to the well-foundedness of belief in domains of controversial views. In our terms, when these conditions are met, the discourse is likely only minimally truth-apt, and extrinsically adequate theories need to take account of this fact that propositions can only be "quasi-asserted."

26. Wright, *Critical Thinking*, 2013, 206.

27. According to David Hume, "All those opinions and notions of things, to which we have been accustomed from our infancy, take deep root, that 'tis impossible for us, by all powers of reason and experience, to eradicate them" (A Treatise of Human Nature). D.J. Hanson tries to show that Hume is the first English utilizer of fideism, and that his "fideism" was a solution which he found to extricate himself from his skepticism (5). Bayle was "the chief Pyrrhonist influence on Hume," and led Hume to be a fideist in both his philosophy of religion and his metaphysics. Penelhum puts Bayle along with Catholics Montaigne and Erasmus, in the skeptical rather than the evangelical fideism camp. Penelhum defines prescriptive fideism as "the insistence that faith needs no justification from reason, but is the judge of reason and its pretensions" (quoted by Hanson, 10). Richard Popkin suggests that if a person accepts "metaphysical doctrines of cause, personal identity, substance, or external objects (common sense beliefs), or even religious doctrines of miracles, immortality, or the existence of God on non-rational basis, we should judge him a fideist rather than a skeptic. For he then accepts non-rationally what he rejected on a rational basis" (quoted by Hanson, 5). But Bayle like Erasmus encourages his readers to turn away from doctrinal disputes altogether. This separates him from Pascal and Kierkegaard as evangelical fideists, where most of the other Protestants appear. So Penelhum puts Bayle along with Catholics Montaigne and Erasmus in a skeptical rather than evangelical fideism camp.

28. Safety and sensitivity are both externalist conditions, so that to the extent that it is more plausible to take them as failing than as being met in an exclusivist belief, they rebut the kind of claim de Ridder and Plantinga make, that defeaters are defeated by a reiterative application of how strongly one "feels" one's belief to be true. That is an appeal to phenomenal consciousness. J. J. Ichikawa and M. Steup (2014) point out that sensitivity, like safety, is "an externalist condition on knowledge in the 'access' sense. It is also externalist in the 'state' sense, since the truth of the relevant counterfactuals will depend on features outside the subject."

29. Christiansen (2014). Kelly discusses another passage by Christiansen (in Christiansen and Lackey eds. 2013, 37): "The motivation behind the principle is obvious: it's intended to prevent blatantly question-begging dismissals of the evidence provided by the disagreement of the others. It attempts to capture what would be wrong with a P-believer saying, for example, 'Well, so and so disagrees with me about p. But since P is true, she's wrong about p. So, however reliable she may generally be, I needn't take her disagreement about p as any reason at all to change my belief.' There is clearly something worrisome about this sort of response to the disagreement of others. Used as a general tactic, it would seem to allow a non-expert to dismiss even the disagreement of large numbers of those he took to be experts in the field." While Christiansen treats acceptance or rejection of an independence principle as a crucial divide between conciliationism and non-conciliationism, Kelly suggests certain qualifications to this equivalence, and to Christiansen's proper formulation of the principle itself.

30. The combination of (DS) and (ES) poses a defeater for the radically asymmetrical trait-attributions and explanations of religious status that are part and parcel of attitudes of religious exclusivism, and (EGO) places the reasonable constraint that

one cannot just appeal to the notion that "everyone has an equal right to an opinion," or that "my religious phenomenology or my religious authority is unique," is the end of the story and sufficient rational grounds to dismiss the epistemic significance of geographic—psychographic epistemic location problem.

31. I here focus on Plantinga's claim of external rationality, but Baldwin and Thune nicely articulate related objections to reformed epistemologists' use of internal rationality. An iterative response to a potential defeater, a response of simply saying that a defeater is itself defeated by reapplication of the "If properly produced, then warranted" claim, is viciously circular because it just privileges itself to the truth of the antecedent of this conditional, even though that was precisely what the potential defeater challenged. "Plantinga's external account of warrant includes the stipulation that a belief must be internally rational if it is to be warranted. And he tells us that "internal rationality includes, in the first place, forming or holding the appropriate beliefs in response to experience." The appeal to experience cannot be watered down so much that anything firmly believed is internally rational. That just confuses psychology and epistemology; "it is hard to see how a belief could come to be indefeasible in this way" (446–447).

32. De Ridder 455. Plantinga appeals to what he calls "impulsional evidence," something that might be present in cases of necessary truths but which he applies far more generally. Todd Long (2010) argues that Plantinga assumes (1) one's impulsion to believe (i.e., the experience of the impulse alone) causes the proposition to seem true to one; thus, (2) "impulsional evidence" is evidence for the proposition believed. He continues, "But, the inference from (1) to (2) is doubtful. Note first that feeling impelled to believe a proposition is not always epistemic. A proposition such as "everything will turn out all right" may be so attractive to a person in a desperate situation—because it is reassuring—that the person feels impelled to believe it. But its being reassuring does not itself provide any epistemic reason to believe the proposition. An epistemic reason to believe a proposition just is an indication that the proposition is true. The desperate-situation example shows that one may feel impelled to believe a proposition even if one has no epistemic reason to believe it. So, if one does have an epistemic reason to believe a proposition, that reason is something other than the impulsion to believe. The upshot is that an impulsion to believe is not itself evidence. Second, reflection suggests that Plantinga has backward the explanatory relation between seeing the truth and feeling impelled to believe. One doesn't see the truth of a proposition because (in part) one feels impelled to believe it, but rather one feels impelled to believe the proposition because one sees its truth" (11).

33. Gellman's "contented" religious exclusivist also clearly fails an independence principle like (EGO). Gellman (2008, 381) concedes, "My defence of a rational exclusivism, therefore, cannot rationally be invoked as a protective strategy by just any want-to-be exclusivist." Gellman's thesis is that "religious beliefs may go rationally unreflective for the religious believer in the face of other religions. A believer may rationally invoke her unreflective religious belief to defeat opposing religious claims, without having to consider the question any further" (375). But then the notion of rationality which Gellman employs for showing when exclusivist responses to religious multiplicity are not a protective strategy, is a psychological notion: whether for

the individual, her religious beliefs "squeak in the face of religious diversity." But then this subjective method cannot answer the question, which was, "Is the contented exclusivist derelict in any epistemic obligations?" It can only change the topic, and if that is not a merely evasive maneuver it is a kind of teleological suspension of the epistemological.

34. On religious rationalism compared with fideism, and the relationship of natural theology to particular faith ventures, see Bishop 2007 a and b.

35. Natural theology presents proofs for the existence of God, and aims to provide reasoned support for monotheism, through non-revealed sources. For a CSR perspective on the "enduring appeal" of natural theological arguments, see de Cruz (2014). Blanshard (1974, Chapter vii), a skeptical rationalist, writes, "The rationalist in philosophy need not, so far as I can see, deny revelation in religion. But he will say with the best will in the world, he cannot accept a revelation that contravenes his reason, because such a revelation he could make no sense of. . . . Once reason is in abeyance, the best of us are not safe against confusing our preconceptions with leadings from on high." But that is a high mark since all religions shock and contest our everyday reason to some extent. So I take "contravenes" and reason "in abeyance" in the strong sense of a kind of teleological suspension of moral, epistemic, or logical norms.

Part II

APPLICATIONS AND IMPLICATIONS OF INDUCTIVE RISK

Our eyes see nothing backward. A hundred times a day we mock our neighbors, and detest in others certain defects which are much more apparent in us; yea, and marvel at them with heedlessness and audacity. . . . *Oh, importunate presumption!*

—Michel de Montaigne[1]

NOTE

1. Montaigne, "Of the Art of Discussion," *Montaigne's Essays, Book III.* Renascence Editions.

Chapter 3

Enemy in the Mirror

The Need for Comparative Fundamentalism

In part II of this book our focus largely shifts from the unwieldy but diagnostically useful concept of religious luck to that of moral and intellectual risk. Of course, risky doxastic strategies, or what in the literature are often called belief-forming functions, may be a rather special concern; they do not illuminate all aspects of religious orientation. But people's penchant for inductively risky inference inside the religious domain indicates for psychologists and religious studies scholars a useful means of measuring the *degree of fideistic commitment* characteristic of a particular religious grouping. This can be determined along a scale from minimally to strongly fideistic. Risk-based measures allow for a more direct focus on the degree of fideistic orientation. They also enable psychologists to study the ways in which strong fideism correlate with an agent making judgments that "mirror" known personal and social biases.

The questions I will suggest to expand fundamentalist orientation scales and give them broader comparative grip are questions about the connections between strong fideism and risk tolerance. From our theoretical background in part I, we might reasonably hope to formulate not only new research *questions*, but also new *scales* and *measures* that help cognitive and social psychologists measure the degree of fideistic orientation displayed by religious subjects, or inherent in the particular conceptions of faith (theological methods) they adhere to. So one central thesis of part II is that the concept of inductive risk I propose helpfully operationalizes radically asymmetric trait-ascriptions. My thesis is that the inductive riskiness of religious doxastic methods that individuals use, or that are prescribed by different models of faith, helpfully *operationalizes* the broader social scientific, philosophical, moral, and theological interest that people may have with problems of religious luck. Accordingly, we will speak less about luck in part II, and more about specific markers of high inductive risk and their complex relationship to the study of human biases.

In this chapter and chapter 4, my special focus is on the need for compara-tive fundamentalism (hereafter CF), and on how a better inductive risk "toolkit" can empower its development.[1] I explain why an empirically informed study of inductively risky patterns of inference on the part of agents allows for a signifi-cant expansion of the scales used by psychologists to study religious orientation, and most especially fundamentalist orientation. We will take time to carefully describe the thesis of *psychological (or descriptive) fideism,* the distinction between psychological and *religious fideism,* and the different ways that this distinction is important for social scientists, philosophers, and theologians.[2] Psychological fideism is an explanatory thesis, and one that can be tested and continually revised. Chapter 6 develops certain aspects of it by asking about connections between our own focus on *counter-inductive thinking,* and research in CSR focused on the appeal of *minimally counterintuitive religious ideas.* If our application of the inductive risk account in part II help to connect the study of fundamentalist orientation and with more general work in CSR, then one result should be that philosophers, psychologists, and theologians should all find overlapping interests in the violation of inductive norms, just as I hope, after part I, that they all find interesting connections to their own field in what we first described as problems of religious luck.

Understanding and predicting religious radicalization is important to what-ever resources we have for responding to it. Whitehouse and McQuinn (2013) bring additional theory to help analyze religious radicalization in the form of DMR theory, or *divergent modes of religiosity.* It highlights that the more severe or risky are the requirements for entry into a group identity, the greater the liking or emotional connection with group members.[3] But beyond predic-tion and control, what about risk and doxastic *responsibility* with respect to such attitudes? How will we develop our inductive risk account of the limits of reasonable religious disagreement? That is a normative and philosophical question. Developing this normative or philosophical side of the inductive risk account is the second central thesis of part II.

In developing this side of the inductive risk account concerned with guid-ance, we must endeavor to keep the psychology and the censure/critique of strong fideism (or for that matter, fundamentalist orientation), properly sepa-rated. Psychological fideism deserves to be studied, but morally risky belief that exhibits markers of bias-mirroring, I argue, deserves censure. So morally risky belief (and however explained theologically) deserves censure. This is to say that my de jure argument against theological defenses of the reasonableness of an exclusivist response to religious contrariety, as it will be developed further in part II and especially in the arguments of chapter 5, is a *philosophical* the-sis. It is based on moral, logical, and epistemological concerns, even though it draws heavily upon psychological studies. Remembering this we can boost the strength of our de jure argument by making it more "proper." Chapter 6, while it focuses on CSR and is mostly concerned with the first side of the project, also clarifies my critique of religious exclusivism and attendant apologetic strategies by examining more directly the relationship between de jure and de facto objections. The result of development and application of the inductive risk account's normative side should ideally be this. The reader agrees with me that reasonability and doxastic responsibility are closely tied, and that while there are many reasons to be permissive of faith ventures, the exclusivist response to religious multiplicity does not deserve to be given a free pass as reasonable; the reader agrees that what Griffiths describes as "polemical apologetics" among exclusivist religions or sects is not reasonable disagreement.[4]

FROM PHILOSOPHY OF LUCK TO AN INDUCTIVE RISK TOOLKIT

Enlightenment *philosophes* who contributed to the rebirth of toleration were generally concerned not with all forms of religiosity, but with what they called "religious enthusiasm," which they took to be manifested cross-denominationally. This is as much to say that comparative philosophy must strive to understand fundamentalism's varied forms through more careful attention *both* to particulars about distinct sects *and* to formally common features within and between whole families of religion. Fundamentalist orientation is not only—I daresay not *nearly*—so much a matter of *what* is believed, as about *how* religious beliefs and moral rules are taken up and maintained; these recurring patterns are best studied comparatively.[5]

There have been a number of fundamentalism scales put to use in psychology, and our project of explaining the value of measures connected with moral and epistemic risk will try to build off of these. Until recently few such scales aimed to be comparative enough to work even with populations across the Abrahamic religions. Fortunately, there are now scales aimed at illuminating the "multi-dimensionality" of fundamentalist religiosity, scales which provide better comparison across religious affiliations.[6] Jose Liht, Sarah Savage, and their research team, for example, approach comparison within Abrahamic religions by identifying seven areas symptomatic of the tension between traditional religiosity and modernity. Like Altemeyer and Hunsberger (2004), Liht, Savage, and their colleagues take a sensible approach to establishing scales that support cross-cultural or comparative study of fundamentalism. Consulting with experts from the three Abrahamic faiths in order to ensure the face and construct validity of the scale, these researchers went on to design multiple items (questions, half pro-trait, half anti-trait) for each of these seven areas:

1. Protection of revealed traditions versus rational criticism
2. Heteronomy versus autonomy and relativism
3. Traditionalism versus progressive religious change

4. Sacralization versus secularization of the public arena
5. Secular culture perceived as a threat versus secular culture embraced
6. Pluralism versus religious centrism
7. Millennial-Messianic imminence versus prophetic skepticism.

What the authors term their Multi-Dimensional Fundamentalism Inventory (MDFI) addresses *attitudes* and *group dynamics*, and not just beliefs. But while it appears to be a substantial improvement over older scales, from the approach we are taking, few of the items engage very directly with character-istic patterns of inference and their inherent riskiness. Only #1 and #6 begin to get at how people reason when they *ascribe* traits and *explain* differences between religious insiders and outsiders. If psychologists take my sugges-tion to be well-motivated and feasible, then one important result would be to establish more direct connections between current research programs in psychology of religion and philosophy.

We will return to these concerns about how philosophy or luck/risk might enable more accurate and useful scales of fideistic orientation later in this chapter and the next. But as a more general methodological point, there are likely to be different understandings of problems of religious luck, and differ-ent views on their philosophical and theological implications. My expressed purpose is to improve our ability to understand and respond to fundamen-talist religiosity, but this may well differ from the use that others want to make of problems of religious luck, either philosophically or theologically. The safety-based concerns for faith-based belief can cut a number of ways: against knowledge, truth, rationality, or moral responsibility. Our normative concern in this book is primarily with the limits of reasonable disagreement, and so with this narrowed purpose in mind we should avoid getting side-tracked onto other issues about epistemic status that might lead us astray.[7] I do not want to say a lot about its implications beyond its contributions to CF, since as noted earlier I have no strong thesis to promote in respect to the debate between theists, atheists, and principled agnostics over the truth of theism. Similarly we do not want to go astray by confusing our de jure challenge targeting salvific exclusivism with a different kind of challenge, a de facto challenge.

Salvific exclusivism is one of the attitudes characteristic of fundamental-ists of different faith-traditions. Faultless disagreement does not occur under conditions of self-deception, and so the inductive risk account says that we should not take it as occurring under conditions of counter-inductive thinking. Ways of acquiring or maintaining a belief dependent upon apparent violations of inductive norms are far from faultless, and the beliefs of agents who rely on such methods are especially exposed to serious etiological challenge.

Returning to our main topic, the first question that this chapter should propose in connection with CF is, "Can counter-inductive thinkers come to recognize their mirror images?" The "enemy in the mirror" is a metaphor which researchers of comparative fundamentalism and religious radicalization have sometimes used to describe a concern of special interest.[8] On the view to be developed, the enemy in the mirror is a direct consequent of counter-inductive thinking when applied to a multiplicity of narrative testimonial traditions. This *Enemy in the Mirror Phenomenon* (EMP) will be a technical term for our study, as this will aid our attempt to explain in the next section how religious contrariety arises on the basis of etiological symmetries. The final section brings the discussion back around to our de jure challenge to religious exclusivist response to religious multiplicity. There I distinguish two forms of exclusivism that we find defended in the literature, *particularist exclusivism* and *mutualist exclusivism,* and I present a dilemma that aims to expose the serious inconsistencies of each.

Persons of fundamentalist orientation tend to identify certain fundamentals of the faith and elevate these to absolutes. Of course, I have not claimed that fideism is rendered extreme *only* by engendering exclusivist attitudes about religious truth or salvation. It can also be rendered extreme in other ways, for example by placing faith into conflict with reason; by conflating subjective or psychological certitude with objective justification or warrant; by engaging in purely "negative" apologetics, by distaining philosophy and science, or using them only in an ad hoc manner; by asserting that nonbelievers should live under the yoke of divine command, Sharia law, or an institutionalized religious authority—a theocratic state. Like "religion," "fundamentalism" is a *family-relations concept,* a concept with multiple aspects such that manifesting different combinations of these aspects may be sufficient to fall under the description. Religious fundamentalism identifies ways of reasoning that go beyond conservativism and orthodoxy.

Religious fundamentalism has forms that arguably can be active in all religions. Yet the common characteristics of fundamentalism, including especially exclusivist attitudes about religious truth and salvation are features of some religions, and some models of faith, more so than others.[9] The need for scales that measure a propensity among religious subjects for inductively risky doxastic strategies is our main concern, but of course in the broader context of CF, I am only arguing that the markers of inductive risk be recognized as one marker of religious extremism among others.[10] The thesis of descriptive fideism (hereafter psychological fideism, in short) fideism is a thesis about how affective elements impact how people understand faith and the particular commitments faith binds one to.[11] It does not presuppose that people are always self-aware, as writers like James and Kierkegaard most clearly are, about the influence of emotion or affect and related extra-evidential factors over what religious or theological statements they accept as true. Getting clear about the thesis of psychological fideism is important, because it can be the basis for predictions of characteristic ways of thinking. I argue that inductive risk gives definition to the thesis of *descriptive fideism* as a working hypothesis in the science of religions.

In "Faith and the Right to Believe," William James defines faith tendencies, for the purposes of an empiricist approach that might aid development of a science of religion, as "extremely active psychological forces, constantly outstripping evidence." Let's call this James's *psychological fideism*; it is his claim that the psychological dynamics of religious faith, as studied through its "characters" and "varieties," integrally involve the will or the passional nature of human agents. This descriptive fideism is best illustrated in what James termed the "faith-ladder" and its progressive rungs or steps:

1. There is nothing absurd in a certain view of the world being true, nothing self-contradictory;
2. It *might* have been true under certain conditions;
3. It *may* be true, even now;
4. It is *fit* to be true;
5. It *ought* to be true;
6. It *must* be true;
7. It *shall* be true, at any rate true for *me*.

Famous for a "subjective method" he shared with Kierkegaard's, James's ethics of belief is often criticized for its radical level of permission to believe that which fulfills certain needs for meaning and value in life, even when undermined by evidence. While I am a permissivist, I think that James presented a too one-sided an account of the "courage" and "caution" principles with regard to faith-based "doxastic ventures." But my main point here is that James is quite correct, *descriptively*, that epistemic risk is undeniable in religious assent, whatever doxastic attitudes we ascribe to it. The "faith ladder," as James terms it, crosses the philosopher's division between "Is" and "Ought" claims, and from an analytical perspective is "no logical chain of inferences." But the agent's perspective is often far from an analytical perspective, and psychological fideism needs to be carefully distinguished in a science of religion from religious fideism.[12] One cannot properly address the question of one's "right" to believe (or the limits to that right), without accepting something like the faith-ladder's psychological descriptions of how the believer—especially the believer of fundamentalist orientation—typically reasons.[13] Psychological fideism should therefore also be distinguished from any religious apologetic strategy, and from any thesis bearing directly on the ethics of belief. A skeptic could accept it as well as a theist, though these two radically disagree about what a person *should* believe. It was quite evident to James that faith tendencies are value-charged schemes of thought;

religious cognition not only reveals leaps from *ought-to-be* to *is*, and from *might be true* to *is true,* systematic theology often wears such leaps on its sleeve. So how ironic it must have seemed to James that that almost in inverse proportion to the strength of a person's fideistic orientation, they tend to try to "sink the fact" of the evidential underdetermination of what James aptly termed their religious "overbeliefs." For how could James, a forger of the fields of empirical psychology and of East/West comparative philosophy of religion, not acknowledge how religious characters habitually "live upon the faith-ladder"?

One reason for favoring the concept of inductive risk in our approach to religious epistemics is that, since this concept is a well-recognized concern in science policy decision making, any ability to carry it over to philosophy of religion opens up some methodological parallels between theological and scientific reasoning. Being a proponent of the Dialogue Model of the relationship between science and religion, this is something I would like to encourage. The risk of getting it wrong, we all recognize, is potentially a moral as well as epistemological risk. Risk-management is as much an issue for the limits of reasonable religious faith ventures as it is for decision making over practical affairs. For our study, the concept of "reasonableness" is not given to any pet theory of evidence; our use of the concept relates it to lack of blameworthiness, as responding to *both* epistemic and ethical norms. Any agent's doxastic method that is inductively risky from a non-religiously committed standpoint marks itself as a potential target for criticism, or what we will call *censure.* The more so as other persons are done an epistemic injustice by it, censure of the agent's doxastic responsibility may range over moral as well as epistemological concerns. Any of the markers of religious fundamentalism noted above can be considered from the perspective of risk that one person or group's faith venture may affect others in adverse ways.

Arguably, that fundamentalist faith ventures *risk others* in ways that more moderate religious faith ventures do not, is as clearly observable as that, in game theory, *defectors* risk *cooperators,* while cooperators do not similarly risk defectors. In *Tragedy of the Commons*, for example, the cooperators do not really risk others, because their choices aim for the best available outcome for *everyone.* But a defector by contrast makes choices that, in order to maximize personal (or group) gain, severely risks destruction of the goods of broader trust and cooperation. The non-cooperators are often studied in game theory as following strategies that impede the social evolution of cooperation. Why isn't the logic of fundamentalist religiosity analogous to this sort of asymmetry exhibited by defectors?[14] Why shouldn't the habits of inference descriptive of Barthian fideism be studied in light of game theory, where the concept of a "magic circle"—a shielded but never fully self-enclosed space where normal rules and expectations as suspended—is central to a good deal of theory?[15]

This suggests that responsible faith ventures are maintained only with awareness of and appropriate responsiveness to inductive risk. On the present account, the limits of responsible faith ventures are set not by any one type of adequacy that the religious agent recognizes—epistemic, moral, or theological—but by the agent's recognition of each of these functioning through checks-and-balances on the other two.[16] Permissible or virtuous faith ventures will thus be assured to be balanced between the courage of religious virtue and religious particularity, and the caution of independent or universal moral and intellectual virtue; they will be balanced between responsiveness not only to risk to one's own person, but to risks that my faith venture might pose to others, physically, socially, or psychologically.

Risk and responsibility are closely connected: the riskiness of one's method of forming one's religious beliefs is central not just to explanatory concerns in the psychology of religion, but also to normative concerns with the ethics of belief. For many kinds of harm, the exposure of others to it already constitutes the main de jure issue. An exposure to harm is already a harm in the placing on others an unconsenting risk. Permissivist accounts in the ethics of belief need to set the limits of reasonability: they need to have "teeth" in the sense that moderate fideism and recognition of a fideistic minimum in all of our faith ventures, is the best corrective to immoderate or radical fideism. When they fail to do so, it is not a form of permissivism as I understand it. It is an apologetic strategy that "rides shotgun" for religious absolutism by defending for the laity an unqualified steadfast response to peer disagreement: theological non-accommodationism.

There are positions in the epistemology of disagreement that are self-described as dogmatist, and religious proponents of this position are also proponents of religious particularism.[17] Dogmatism as a thesis is perhaps better described as mutualist impermissivism, than as permissivism. But we will examine it more closely in chapter 4.[18] People are not necessarily intellectually vicious for accepting nurtured beliefs and holding them without a great deal of reflection. But neither does such a permissivist account rationalize dogmatism or imply the reasonability, *tout court,* of holding to what we are taught. Permissionism should *sharpen* reasoned criticism rather than lead to its abandonment, and an inductive risk-focused account, as we will argue throughout this book, does much to show us how.[19]

Responsible agency implies that we have moral reasons to monitor, modify, and moderate how we think about disagreement with epistemic peers. In the broad domain of controversial views, bias-attributions may fly in both directions between proponents of competing systems of belief. Now ascribing error to another's view *can be* a mark of respecting shared norms of rational criticism. Even doing so by attributing a bias to someone with whom one disagrees might be made honestly, in the hope that pointing out a bias will stimulate reflection on the part of that agent, and greater future habituation to critical reasoning dispositions. And not all ascription of error, or even of bias, is grounds for further ascription of culpability or blame. But the kind of metaphysical truth-declaration and peer denial we find on display in exchanges between aggressive atheists and religious fundamentalists draws courage from the persuasive appeal to informal fallacies such as genetic fallacy, psychologizing the other, appeal to ignorance, ad hominem, bandwagon, strawman, appeal to fear, and so on.[20] Employment of informal fallacies is certainly not praiseworthy, but the great difficulty humans have, cognitively and motivationally, with recognizing their own biases and trying to redressing them makes doxastic responsibility an especially difficult yet vital topic. I agree with Paul Thagard's call for avoiding a longstanding conflation between "thinking" and argumentative "reasoning." Taking a more empirically informed approach, "[W]hen arguments fail to convince, we should rarely look for the explanation in terms of the traditional fallacies, but rather in terms of the multitude of error tendencies that psychological research has shown to operate in human thinking."[21] This is why a more general or domain-neutral review of personal and social biases is methodologically important to us. Evidence of bias supplies etiological information that may present a strong de jure challenge to a particular agent.

Paradoxically perhaps, vice-*charging* can be aimed either at encouraging needed doxastic responsibility in the person so charged or at insulating the vice-charger from criticisms of a similar sort directed at him by others. Peer denial in its most common form, as a dogmatic way to claim higher authority for one's beliefs or values while insulating them from criticism, is something we see throughout the broader domain of controversial views. Those loudest voices in our culture wars over science and religion attribute bias to each other. Often they are both right, but it is "bunk de-bunking" whenever the attribution of a bias functions like (or simply as) a circumstantial ad hominem argument. Ian Kidd suggests that to begin to approach the question of sound versus simply self-protective instances of vice-charging, we should distinguish two types. *Rhetorical complaints* contrast with *robust charges*, where only the latter qualify as legitimate modes of criticism:

A rhetorical vice charge involves an agent expressing a negative attitude, opinion, or evaluation of some other agent, whether expression is oral, literary, or bodily—a curt tweet, audible grown, eye-rolling, and so on. But, crucially, that agent could not elaborate or "unpack" the charge if asked to, for instance by explaining the reasoning that supports the negative judgment. Rhetorical charges involve reportage of one's negative judgments, but not the presentation of any reasons, evidence, or feelings in support of them, so they do not do any real critical work.[22]

Kidd's condition on a rhetorical vice charge would need to be strengthened to apply to the manner in which religious apologists could and sometimes do engage in rhetorical vice-charging. We will see examples of this later. But Kidd goes on to develop conditions of robust vice-charging. These require first a clear concept of epistemic responsibility, and so "should be sensitive to the etiology of vice and the ecological conditions of epistemic socialisation."[23] If evidence of irrelevant influence is sometimes evidence of error, rationality demands that the vice attributor not ignore it as a defeater to personal justification. Where contingency anxiety and attendant epistemic humility is appropriate yet lacking in the agent, we can hypothesize that unconscious motivations will be triggered to engage in confabulatory explanation.[24] For virtue theorists like Kidd, Vainio (2017, discussed below), and myself, de-biasing means encouraging the shared resources of the moral virtues of open-mindedness and reciprocity, and of intellectual virtues of epistemic humility and intellectual fair-mindedness.[25] We can disagree about what balance of reason and faith to recommend, and whether to weigh risk of error higher or lower than desire for truth. But without valuing and habituating ourselves to inductive norms, what a person advances as generalizations, analogies, and explanations that help us understand religious difference arguably has the character of a story, a *mythos,* not *logos.*

FUNDAMENTALIST ORIENTATION AND THE RISKS OF TELEOLOGICAL SUSPENSION

Religious fundamentalism is a term for tendencies that can be studied comparatively. So is religious fideism. Both concepts must be understood *descriptively* as befits academic religious studies, without the pejorative connotation put on them in popular writing and the culture wars more generally.[26] Connotations that condemn whatever is called fundamentalist religiosity do not encourage dialogue, and strawman characterizations always serve to enable equally over-simple "that's not us" reposts. While religious radicalization and violence are a focus of keen concern by academics, these are not synonymous with fundamentalism, which some see as just a way of being religious no more harmful than any other.[27] This however might be to overgeneralize in the opposite direction. At the height of theological hostility is often found an apocalyptic narrative of cosmic war, a narrative which invokes a moral dualism splitting earthly and supernatural beings into two basic camps of the good and the evil. Apocalypse and religious utopia/dystopia (since what is utopia for insiders is typically dystopia for outsiders) are among the most extreme uses of religious imagination, and often play a role in religious radicalization. Personal psychologists have looked at "the genesis of the need to divide the world into rigidly polarized, warring camps . . . at the heart of religious fanaticism."[28] As Mark Juergensmeyer, a sociologist noted for his work on religion and violence puts it, "the religious imagination . . . has always had the propensity to absolutize and to project images of cosmic war. It has also much to do with the social tensions of this moment of history that cry out for absolute solutions, and the sense of personal humiliation experienced by men who long to restore an integrity they perceive as lost."[29]

So my approach agrees with Malise Ruthven that "whether or not we like the term, fundamentalist or fundamentalist-like movements appear to be erupting in many parts of the world [and] the phenomena it encompasses deserve to be analysed" (6). Patterns of religious authority and leadership that characterize fundamentalism are, like "religion" itself, a matter of family relations. The concept of fundamentalism I deem to be quite legitimate, but is not well captured by a set a necessary conditions, since *different* combinations of features may be sufficient for describing one's orientation as fundamentalist. What is clear is that fundamentalism has many forms, and that in some subset of those forms it gives rise to epistemic injustice, political and psychological harm, but only in extreme cases to a specific act of religious violence.[30] There are numerous moral concerns that I believe make the comparative study of fundamentalism a pressing demand today. These moral concerns can briefly be broken down into three points.

Firstly, fundamentalism threatens to cut off dialogue and the search for points of commonality, because it sees only the side of different, contradictory beliefs, not the side of common proximate causes and formal symmetries in the culturally nurtured manner of belief-uptake. This neglect is indeed one of the clearest signs of unacknowledged similarity between fundamentalists of different sects. Trumping epistemological norms by "truth-first" strategies can lead to an over-easy rejection of peerhood, and therefore also of the epistemic significance of religious disagreement. "Metaphysics is first philosophy" is the simple, pre-modern way of expressing a strong fideism, and of insulating a religious worldview from rational scrutiny even by religious insiders. For the average religious adherent who knows the narrative but is not a theologian, the effect may be that moral and epistemic concerns are discounted. What is taken as true metaphysically is whatever is accepted through testimonial authority assumption, and the theological categories of the home religion.

In *On Religious Diversity*, Robert McKim writes, "Members of religious traditions generally think that their tradition is superior to the competition. So they are committed to there being criteria of evaluation in virtue of which this is so."[31] This does not mean that folk religiosity has the character of religious rationalism, or adheres to the evidentialist maxim that 'the wise proportion their belief to their evidence.' It rather means that an evidentialist *apologetic strategy* is often adopted, on which ample reason and evidence are said to be available to justify the home religion's theology, even though the actual basis of faith is maintained not to be inference from evidence but as something more direct, and for the agent irresistible.[32] But here of course the problems of circular reasoning and of the subjectivization of evidence sufficient to rationalize belief come to the fore. Chapter 2 briefly introduced (EGO), my version of an independence-from-theory demand on reasons given in support of asymmetric attribution of religious truth or value to group insiders and outsiders. (EGO) says that ascribing differences to people needs to be supported with *relevant difference reasoning*, and it adds several constraints on this reasoning.[33] Mainly it constrains us to appeal only to agent-level considerations to justify the ascription of an agent-level asymmetry: one ought to only appeal to epistemic considerations in justifying purported asymmetries of epistemic states and standings. Rationalists, whether religious rationalists who believe God's existence to be provable (a priori or a posteriori), or skeptical rationalists who set a high bar for rational belief and claim arguments for God's existence do not meet that bar, agree on one thing: these rationalists agree that the beliefs we hold should be reasons-responsive, and supportable by neutral or *independent* reason. Traditionally, fideistic orientation is by degrees suspicious of rationalism, and with it of natural theology and religion-specific evidentialism. Reason is to be allowed to support but not to challenge first assumptions: philosophy is the handmaid of theology who must always deliver a happy ending. The more threatening that reason and science are taken to be to one's faith, the more that the model of faith invites fundamentalist orientation, and with it a disregard of (EGO)'s norm of appealing to independent reasons to support one's beliefs.

A second well-motivated concern motivating the comparative study of fundamentalism is that it is a common denominator in cases of religious violence where there is what Kierkegaard describes as an agent's "teleological suspension of the ethical." A problem with acts of unconditional assent to an authority is the possibility of fanaticism, and fanaticism sometimes drives either taking divine commands as the final arbiter of moral justification, or appropriating religious authority in the name of violent means to one's own ends. For those of us reliant on human modes of inquiry, such appeal to God to support, or even to motivate, moral and epistemic divisions may be all that can be meant by "getting it wrong." The truths to which the believer assents are purportedly transcendent truths not open verification, or it seems to falsification. But this is a psychological fact: a decision on the part of the believer to accept certain tenets of faith as absolutes. Too often these contents, however, are identified as things culturally particular rather than culturally universal. As I ate lunch today, I read of a case where a recently radicalized Islamist yelling "God is great" stabbed a woman to death at a train stop in Marseilles, ran away, came back, and stabbed a second woman who had gone to her aid, and when soon thereafter confronted by police, charged at them as was shot. How is it that a just and great god authorizes or demands violence against countrymen and civilians? How is it that the surety of one's metaphysical beliefs as a guide to action supersedes not just basic moral intuitions, but as it appears at least in cases of religious hate crimes such as this, *any* genuinely universal moral principles? If we do not want to be politically naïve, we should not discount how complex and varied the causes of radicalization are, and the extent to which religion may not be a primary driver, but sometimes only a pawn, of conflict between ethnic groups or political ideologies.[34] The politics of identity may involve numerous factors, and religious differences may be just one of these. But fundamentalism tends to breed ideologies that neglect private/public distinctions, and that are increasingly both religious *and* political in nature.[35] The proximate causes of religious radicalization often involve highly selective interpretations and applications of a testimonial tradition's religious virtues and teachings. The idea that if you had *enough* faith you would do God's will without experiencing the moral dissonance between ones actions and universal moral principles like the Golden Rule, etc., is surely an idea of radical fideism: however counter-intuitive it is that a just God would demand the indifferent slaughter of innocents, if you had *enough* faith you would act on the (perceived) will of God and not demand independently good moral reasons.[36] In this sense radical fideism is still closely associated with the "enthusiasm" or "fanaticism" that Enlightenment *philosophes* identified as driving back-and-forth persecution between Catholics and Protestants.

We see teleological suspension of the ethical in the biblical narrative in which Abraham responds to a perceived command to sacrifice his beloved son Isaac, quite the opposite of what any loving parent would want. The particularism of divine commands and their potential conflict with universal morality is seen in this same Biblical narrative since God, in treating Isaac merely as a tool in a test of Abraham's faith, seems to act contrary not only to what one would think a just god would do, but also to the universal principle to treat others always as an end in themselves and never merely as a means. Kierkegaard in his deep reflection on this Biblical passage in *Fear and Trembling* does not mention this latter point, but he does describe a teleological suspension as a subordination of the "universal" to the "particular." In *Fear and Trembling* Kierkegaard writes, "The ethical as such is the universal, and as the universal it applies to everyone." So in suspending the ethical, Abraham "acts by virtue of the absurd, for it is precisely absurd that he as the particular is higher than the universal. . . . By his act he overstepped the ethical entirely and possessed a higher *telos* outside of it, in relation to which he suspended the former."[37]

While teleological suspension of the ethical, in which the individual "becomes higher than the universal," has garnered a great deal of critical attention, what seems to have gone unnoticed in philosophy of religion is that this same fideistic suspension can attach to the logical and epistemological as well. Religious virtues can as easily come undone from universal logical and epistemological norms just as they can from universal ethical norms. Each such divergence of religious virtue from independently recognizable moral or intellectual virtue holds its own danger with respect to facilitating religious extremism. Emil Brunner, an early post-liberal theologian like Barth, claims that "God takes over all responsibility for our action."[38] So later we will take time to elaborate this threefold typology and identify psychological markers of these parallel concerns: teleological suspension of the ethics, the logical, and the epistemological. But briefly here, *teleological suspension of the logical* is an apt description of religious uniqueness maintained through counter-inductive thinking. *Teleological suspension of the epistemological* is an apt description of purely negative religious apologetics, and of at least some forms of an externalist or "basic belief" apologetic. In many normal cases, the falsehood of a belief is consistent with its having been rationally held by an agent: rationality is independent of truth, yet a good indication of what may responsibly be held *to be* true. But every instance where, if truth were to go missing, *so would* the agent's warrant and rationality in assenting that belief, can plausibly be seen as an instance of teleological suspension of the epistemological. For here external warrant and internal rationality were never allowed their natural independence. They are never treated as indirect indicators of truth; rather, the faith-based *assumption* of truth or divine authority is employed as a *guarantor* of the warrant and rationality enjoyed by the true believer.

My third point about moral concerns that make the comparative study of fundamentalism a pressing demand today is that fundamentalism threatens to make religious toleration an "impossible virtue." The difficulty with tolerance as Bernard Williams wrote, is that it seems to be a *necessary* and yet on certain assumptions an *impossible* virtue:

> It is necessary where different groups have conflicting beliefs—moral, political, or religious—and realize that there is no alternative to their living together, that is to say, no alternative except armed conflict, which will not resolve their disagreements and will impose continuous suffering. These are the circumstances in which toleration is necessary. Yet in those same circumstances it may well seem impossible.[39]

To be sure, there can be good moral and pragmatic reasons for tolerating others even when we feel sure that their beliefs are erroneous or their ways of life are immoral. This may even be so in a situation where you are part of a religious majority that could impose paternalistic laws. Also, "intolerance" is difficult to characterize, and it surely is not the case that fundamentalists are all personally intolerant. We need to be careful here of course since the characterization of certain groups as intolerant is sometimes a result of one-sidedness in one's descriptions. But religious exclusivism and absolutism are two (among the multiple) marks of fundamentalist orientation, and those who argue that religious toleration is impossible are almost exclusively self-described exclusivists. There are clear *logical* connections between exclusivism and the "non-accommodation" of non-believers, at least soteriologically, in the doctrine of salvation if not also in the social sphere.

We can leave it open just how "accommodating" the reasonable accommodation of non-believers should be. Part of the problem with this recognition may be that on assumption of religious absolutism and the one true sect or religion, the very idea of theological if not also moral and political compromise can appear counter to God's plan. If you know the will of God, your duty is to see it enforced as you claim God intends it.[40] But there is always an intellectual viciousness and an epistemic injustice done by the exclusivist in denying religious others as peers, and in not accommodating *their* virtue and reasonableness some reasonable way.

> But they do me wrong. They do me . . . a great wrong in this, that they make the same words which accuse my infirmity, represent me for an ungrateful person . . . [and] from a natural imperfection, make out a deficit of conscience.
>
> —Montaigne[41]

CONCLUSION

In part I we saw that how far a theology, theodicy, or apologetic response to unbelievers to or religious multiplicity "leans of luck" is a largely descriptive and readily assessable matter once one understands what "leaning on luck" means. It helps greatly to have a working taxonomy of the different *types* of religious luck ascriptions people make, and examples of debatable problems associated with each type. We said that part II would work to apply part I's theory to religiosity in the wild by translating questions discussed among theologians and philosophers as problems of religious luck into more empirically approachable questions of degrees of epistemic risk, including especially the risk of getting it wrong in an inductive context of inquiry.

So starting from what may most easily be tested for by psychologists, a test subject displaying dispositions toward counter-inductive thinking in the religious domain functions in my account as a key marker both of high doxastic risk toleration and of the strength of that individual's fideistic orientation. This together with other measures on a scale of strength of fideistic orientation becomes, in turn, a revealing new marker of fundamentalist orientation. So these proposals are aimed at giving the scholarly study of fundamentalism more tools and greater comparative validity. This chapter has accordingly argued that new scales related to ingroup–outgroup attitudes but focused on measuring propensities for inductively risky patterns of inference are what would provide interesting new and testable hypotheses in regard to fundamentalist orientation in particular. Scales for fideistic orientation and fundamentalist orientation can be hypothesized to correlate to a high degree. A third possible scale, a scale for propensities to think counter-inductively, helps to tie these other two together; it potentially brings needed clarity to the scholarly study of religious fundamentalism and related areas such as the psychology of religious radicalization and religious violence.

The inductive risk account holds that exhibiting comparatively risky doxastic methods indicates strongly fideistic orientation. But our discussion of bias studies in this chapter was quite general; we insisted only a) that personal and social biases affect many beliefs in domains of controversial views, and b) that the domain of religious ideas is no exception to this general fact. But the "mirroring" of known biases, as the next chapter will further elaborate, is important psychologically and philosophically. So the introduction to research on biases in this chapter is mainly background for the further development of our inductive risk account. Although these proposals may be quite sketchy and this point, we will continue to sharpen them in the next chapter, and especially in chapter 6, which develops a number of more specific research questions, questions that might also serve to more closely connect comparative fundamentalism (CF) and cognitive science of religions (CSR).[42]

NOTES

1. "It's important to understand that opinions are often influenced by what we value. This mixing of beliefs and values sometimes makes it difficult or confusing to assess their truth. But a good critical thinker's toolkit provides the tools for tackling this seemingly tricky task" (Foresman, Fosl, and Watson, 2017).

2. As a methodological aside, despite our concern with narrative testimony we will not need to engage debates in the epistemology of disagreement, or even the epistemology of testimony very directly in this chapter, but will rather try to remain neutral. We do not, for instance, need to decide between the two normative theories,

the "concessionist" and the "steadfast," in the epistemology (see Christiansen and Lackey 2013). And while our central argument that the religious luck ascriptions that people make illuminate epistemological issues that are really concerns about inductive risk might be rendered stronger if testimonial transmission is inductive, nothing in our approach presupposes or necessitates that we take an inductive or reductionist position in the epistemology of testimony. Again we can perhaps serve the interest of connecting philosophy of luck to CF and CSR if we remain largely neutral on these "in-house" philosophical debates.

3. Supporting this theory of modes of ritual group formation, the authors cite studies showing that "traumatic ritual ordeals increase cohesion and tolerance within groups, but they also seem to intensify feelings of hostility and intolerance towards outgroups" (Whitehouse and McQuinn 2013, 600). Introducing DMR theory they write, "The theory distinguishes a doctrinal mode characterized by routinized ritual, diffuse cohesion, hierarchical structure, and rapid dissemination to large populations from an imagistic mode characterized by rare and dramatic ritual ordeals and intense cohesion within small cults" (598). It has usually been used to explain the formation and spread of religious traditions, but the authors argue for its value in explaining association with armed groups, both religious and nonreligious, engaged in civil conflicts.

4. By contrast, Leo D. Lefebure in *Revelation, the Religions, and Violence* argues that dialogue and nonviolence are tightly interdependent: "The struggle to overcome violence and form a healthy global community is one of the strongest reasons for interreligious dialogue. Indeed, the series of international movements of nonviolent resistance are among the most important fruits of interreligious exchange. . . . To proclaim the revelation of God in Jesus Christ today calls for Christians to critically appropriate our own tradition in dialogue with other religious voices" (2000, 23).

5. Robert C. Neville (2018, 147) holds the need for comparison even in a theological project: "All serious theology should take place in and arise out of a solid grounding in the comparison of religious ideas. This is my hypothesis. Too many people believe that theology should be the reflection of religious ideas from the standpoint of a religious tradition by itself, exclusively in its own terms. For instance, many Christian theologians, influenced by Karl Barth, think that theology is a reading of the Christian word of God on its own terms without any serious mention of Jewish, Buddhist, Daoist, or Muslim theology. Sometimes this kind of theology is called "confessional" because it takes its rise from some theological starting point to which it confesses allegiance and then derives what follows from that. While confessional theology can be helpful for the fulsome expression of the implications of the theological starting point, it runs the grave danger of abandoning theology for intellectual sociology."

6. Liht et al. (2011).

7. If we are to parallel Hume to a considerable extent, our focus should be on *rational credibility*—in our case not of testimony to miracles as interventions in the natural order, but of testimonial traditions and transmissions to radically asymmetrical attributions of religious value to insiders and outsiders of the home religion.

8. Roxanne Euben's (1999) *Enemy in the Mirror* focuses on Islamic fundamentalism but through an approach to political theory that is inherently comparative. She

does not mean by this that movements presupposing nonrational, transcendent truths can be held to the bar of Enlightenment reason. Rather, Euben argues, conceptions of reason vary as do conceptions of faith, and a sound understanding of fundamentalism must test the scope of Western rationalist categories. For an advanced study of the dynamics of religious and ideological radicalization, see Alimi, Demetriou and Bosi, 2015.

9. Jakobus Vorster points out that "the three religions of the Book, namely Christianity, Islam and Judaism have, in spite of deep-rooted differences in theology and ethics," have a remarkable similarity in being "prone" to fundamentalist orientation through a propositional or literalist view of the contents of their scriptures, or an infallibilist view of the *vehicle* of revelation. Psychological needs condition these particularist assumptions: "Scripturalism meets the need for certainty and authority for many people and gives them confidence in their pursuits. The appeal of these fundamentalisms is great because of the use of proof-texts that are easy to understand and to follow. Nationalism and patriotism combined with self-centric ideals create dangerous forces where violence for the sake of furthering a holy agenda becomes a romantic and even sacral strategy of change" Vorster (2008), 49.

10. Un-safe belief raises concerns about the cognitive and moral *risks* of our various faith ventures. This is true to varying degrees with doxastic commitments we take on in all controversial fields. Allen Buchanan (2013) draws attention to "credibility prejudicing" as a major aspect of the moral and prudential risks of our social epistemic dependency. Where the New Problem of religious luck is unique is partly in focusing on the most extreme and serious of risky belief in this particular field, which is why I initially described my purpose in articulating it as a contribution of comparative religious fundamentalism.

11. While most philosophy of religion textbook glossaries define fideism only in its religious and not also its psychological sense, David Shatz (2002, 559) laudably takes the more careful approach: "Fideism: (1) The view that religious belief *is* based on faith and not reason. (2) The view that religious belief *should be* based on faith and not reason" (italics original). The unequivocal "not" here likely skews Shatz's definition to fit only *strong* fideism, rather than the full range; yet I applaud his clear recognition of the need to make the psychological/religious distinction.

12. As J.C. Wernham correctly points out, "The ladder is not advocacy but description. . . . If one compares James' will-to-believe doctrine and the ladder, one finds differences between them and similarities too. The will-to-believe doctrine is advocacy" (1987, 113). This may also indicate that as his thinking matured James became clearer about the need to distinguish the two senses of the term in order to avoid an overt Is-Ought fallacy.

13. For more on descriptive fideism see also Louis Pojman (1986), Chapter 9, and John Bishop (2007a and b).

14. Of course, this is only half the story because groups are typically cooperative internally even as they are competitive between groups. In evolutionary theory, *social selection* involves groups of cooperators outcompeting other groups. According to Darwin in *The Descent of Man* (1871, Vol. I: 182, 179), "There can be no doubt that a tribe including many members who [. . .] are always ready to give aid to each other

and to sacrifice themselves for the common good, would be victorious over other tribes; and this would be natural selection." So the "defector" analogy perhaps fits a relationship of competing groups, but *within* groups cooperation is high. Certainly religious groups are internally cooperative. But "primeval man," Darwin argues, "regarded actions as good or bad solely as they obviously affected the welfare of the tribe, not of the species" and corresponding vices, if practiced on other tries, typically "are not regarded as crimes."

15. The strong interest in the *magic circle* among some game theorists draws upon Durkheim's distinction between the sacred and profane. Especially as one understands Barthian fideism as an Independence model (more akin of Wittgenstein's language games) the strong reading of the circle metaphor as a circle enclosing and separating a faith community from the rest of the world, fits. Much fundamentalism is isolationist, with a narrative of being the city on a hill. This shared interests in entry of the circle and negotiation of its borders I suggest makes discussions of digital games relevant. See Stenros (2014) for a fine introduction. "The *magic circle of play* is the social contract that is created through implicit or explicit social negotiation and meta-communication in the act of playing. This social contract can become societal as other social frameworks (law, economics) can recognize it. . . . The participants are supposed to treat the encounter within the borders of the social contract as disconnected from the external world and they are not supposed to bring external motivations. . . . As a contractual barrier is established, the events within the border are loaded with special significance."

16. While I admire his many valid criticisms of Feldman's assumptions, the normative upshot for J. Adam Carter (2017), his controversial view agnosticism, is still a form of impermissivism. For exemplary work in support of a permissivist ethics of belief, see Haack (1997), Audi (2011), Kelly (2014), Kopec and Titelbaum (2016), and Booth and Peels (2014), Schoenfield (2014), and Simpson (2017). Permissivists hold that "the gap between the ways in which we are meant to normatively assess belief and action may not be as wide as has been thought." According to Booth and Peels, the Permissivist Thesis holds that "responsible belief is permissible rather than obliged belief. On the Unique Thesis (UT), our evidence is always such that there is a unique doxastic attitude that we are obliged to have given that evidence, whereas the Permissibility Thesis (PT) denies this." Although a fuller account of the ethics of belief and what James called religious "overbeliefs" is outside the purview of this book, my own work in this area has aimed to provide a virtue-theoretic account of permissivism, an account I term *doxastic responsibilism* (Axtell 2006, 2011a, 2011b, 2013, 2018, 2019).

17. Examples of philosophers taking these positions are McCain (2008) for phenomenological conservativism, and Fantl (2018) and Tucker (2010) for dogmatism.

18. Mutualism as a moral and epistemological thesis about mutual recognition of reasonableness seems to fall under permissivism. But when it is mutualist exclusivism, it is akin to a claim of holding purely negative rights, rights that one cares only about their own, but allows to others also not on principle of desert, but only pragmatically, to *secure* their own. Dogmatism and phenomenological foundationalism are two examples of the mutualist exclusivism that is self-titled as dogmatism

or as phenomenological foundationalism. Both seem to be in bad faith in regard to people's mutual recognition as each other as reasonable; for they grant the point only in order to justify the reasonableness of each person in denying any positive epistemic status to beliefs contrary to their own. Mutual steadfastness is a term we can use for the claim that higher order evidence, including evidence of peer disagreement, need not be taken as being epistemically significant. The agent is fully reasonable in maintaining their preexisting degree of confidence toward the first-order propositions that the disagreement is about. This claim may be permissivist if qualified to that it *need not* have such an impact. Few defenders of steadfastness claim we *should never* allow higher-order evidence to change first-order views antecedently held. But strong religious fideism and the broader position simply called "dogmatism" seem to me to come close to embracing this absurdity. I would remind the reader of Jean Jacques Rousseau's famous claim, "Those who would separate civil from theological intolerance are, to my mind, mistaken. The two are inseparable." In development of this, William James spoke of the spirit of inner toleration that empiricism promotes, and that he hoped a science of religion together with philosophy of religion could promote: "No one of us ought to issue vetoes to the other, nor should we bandy words of abuse. We ought, on the contrary, delicately and profoundly to respect one another's mental freedom: then only shall we bring about the intellectual republic; then only shall we have that spirit of inner tolerance without which all our outer tolerance is soulless, and which is empiricism's glory; then only shall we live and let live, in speculative as well as in practical things."

19. The appeal to supernatural or final causes as trumping any and all philosophical and scientific standards of epistemic risk does not provide an avenue for bypassing inductive normativity as based on shared, observable proximate causes. It always carries the rider, "in the home religion but not others," which is itself an asymmetry that demands neutral criteria if not to be seen as but an article of faith. This is a retreat from reason and accountability for faith-based commitments. Such theologically cast, religion-specific appeals to final causes as discounting shared, neutral evidence, are inevitably claims that 'the pattern stops here'; but doing so marks it as an authority-based claim or a fideistic article of faith. This objectively, that is, in the shared natural and social world we inhabit, increases the alethic and epistemic (and potentially also, moral) riskiness of the faith ventures based on such assumptions. One can say that "metaphysics is first philosophy," but from the interest of neutrality where truth claims need to be justified and not simply assumed, this as I argue is descriptively an instance of *testimonial authority assumption,* a clear marker of religious fideism.

20. Employment of such informal fallacies points us to the rhetorical dimensions of the "culture wars" over science and religion, and typically to voices defending the least defensible positions on each side of the debate. When I refer to our "culture wars" over science and religion, this should *not* be taken to suggest that I support a Conflict or "warfare" model. Indeed I defend a Dialogue model and try to develop its advantages in Axtell (2013).

21. Thagard (2011), 164. Ken Manktelow (2012) explains how centrally important in experimental psychology is the distinction between reasoning and thinking. It makes possible the testing of agents against logical norms—the *Normative-Descriptive Gap*—and the better recognition of heuristic strategies and ecological on the

part of agents rather than ideal rationality. The "new paradigm" as Manktelow and other psychologists describe it aims to integrate the study of reasoning and decision making. It recognizes lots of traffic between the traditional precincts of theoretical and practical reason. My complaint about a lot of what goes under epistemology of disagreement fails to make these crucial distinctions. The objection I would make is that whether they hail from skeptical or religious evidentialism, the broader approach that they take is extensionally inadequate. Evidentialists like Richard Feldman I think do so by reducing human thinking to an argument model. Christian evidentialists like Richard Swinburne and phenomenal foundationalists like Kevin McCain (2018) do so by reducing norms of good evidential reasoning to simple conservation of the agent's phenomenological seemings. As Paul Sands rightly points out, "One might say that evidentialism sacrifices faith on the altar of probabilism, while fideism substitutes self-assertion for adjudication when challenged by religious pluralism" (147). Note that the objections I present (2011) to Feldman and Conee's explicitly *epistemic* evidentialism are meant to be complemented by my direct response (Axtell 2018) to the over-weaning *moral* evidentialism of Scott Aikin and Rob Talisse (2018). Both parties I think mis-apply the *Rational Uniqueness Thesis* to the epistemology of controversial views, but I can only hope to write a book on these issues in the near future.

22. Kidd (2016), 183.

23. Kidd notes the ubiquity of "vice-charging" in social contexts outside of religion, acknowledging that it can often be intended to promote responsibility. Kidd's distinction is valid in many contexts, but may be less clear where religious value attributions reflect religious teachings and alternative theological methods. Part of the asymmetry between religious luck attributions is that while the in-group's good luck is usually attributed to God's will, the religious outsider's bad religious luck is typically attended with vice-charging. Still, there are definite differences in the extent to which adherents of alternative models of faith are committed to interfaith dialogue, and to positive as contrasted with merely negative apologetics.

24. The concept of confabulation should be related back to our discussion of *contingency anxiety* in chapter 1. Contingency anxiety could be taken as descriptive of what agents self-report, but when one adopts a normative conception of rationality and applies it to experimental design, we are using a normative account of rationality. What *should* induce some contingency anxiety, as we discussed with the epistemic location thought experiments, is ignoring formal symmetries of belief acquisition and maintenance with epistemic peers. Arguably, the failure of rationality in the agent who identifies religious truth with content such that etiological challenges are like water off a duck's back, is a failure to abide by inductive norms that operate in other domains of our social world.

25. For new work in virtue-theoretic approaches in philosophy of religion, see Callahan and O'Connor (2014). One strong overlap between Vainio and myself is a strong emphasis on virtue theory as championing diachronic, in contrast to only synchronic justification of beliefs (Vainio 2010, 142–143; Axtell 2011). Of course this is consistent with naturalism's focus on the reliable etiology of belief, which in turn makes inductive norms salient for all forms of a posteriori knowledge. Vainio finds that "in religion people rarely if ever use synchronic justification for their beliefs. The synchronic view of religious beliefs is like a static snapshot, whereas the diachronic

view takes beliefs as a sort of narrative that develops over time. . . . The belief system does not rest on a single basis but it is a complex mixture of experiences, truth claims, witnesses, and other data" (143). I take this to correctly hold that beliefs core to one's religious identity needs to be supported holistically, not atomistically or as a matter of "synchronic fit." That is a view I have also defended.

26. Vainio makes this point clearly, as did Thomas D. Carroll (2008) in another careful, historically informed discussion. As Vainio comments, "to Carroll the problems regarding the concepts of fideism are due to its common pejorative use, the lack of historical precision . . . and the complex philosophical background of the concept itself" (3). Vainio seems to note, but I would emphasize, that those for whom the term is used in a pejorative way are not just those with a skeptical bent, but often those to whom one in historical perspective one might suppose to fit its objective description. This is pure Alvin Plantinga, who seems to me rhetorically to define "fideism" by its most *anti*-rationality extreme, in order to easily dismiss the description of reformed theology as a form of fideism.

27. Ninian Smart (1995). "Interfaith movements can engage fundamentalism in a more positive fashion. 'Fundamentalism' functions as a heuristic device teasing into relief typological 'family resemblances' that unite religious protest movements across the globe. Militant Zionism, political Islam, Hindu nationalism, and sectarian Buddhism all share 'generic characteristics' that invite comparative treatment. Using 'fundamentalism' as a cross-cultural analytical category, this approach views fundamentalism not as an aberration but as one religious phenomenon among others." http://www.crosscurrents.org/Huff.htm.

28. James W. Jones (2013, 391–392). "Religions almost always idealize and sanctify some ideas, beliefs, institutions, books, codes of conduct, or various leaders. . . . So denoting something as sacred appears to have significant emotional and behavioral consequences even when that something is the jihad, ending abortion, turning the United States into a biblical theocracy, restoring the boundaries of biblical Israel, purifying the Hindu homeland, or converting the Tamils to Buddhism."

29. Juergensmeyer (2003, 242). That religious studies scholars and theologians themselves may refer to an active role of religious imagination in the fostering and transmission of religious ideas does not assume that personality traits are sufficient for understanding why people adopt or do not adopt religious orientations. No single factor could explain something as complex as religious orientation or religious radicalization, but individual factors can still play an important role. Social-psychological analyses may be necessary to understand things like ritual identity, religious violence, and so on, even though not sufficient. Religious imagination from any scholarly approach needs to be recognized as playing a role in the home religion if it is seen as playing a role in alien religions. But too often talk of imagination, like talk of historical critical methods of scriptural interpretation, is rejected outright by those of fundamentalism orientation because inconsistent with the literalism and inerrantism of their view.

30. See Fricker (2007) *Epistemic Injustice: Power and the Ethics of Knowing.* On the psychological and epistemic motivations for religious violence, see also Marbaniang 2008.

31. McKim (2012), 152.

32. As one theologian aptly put it, I do not believe in miracles because I have proved them, but I forever try to prove them because I believe them.

33. One might think here of Mill's Method of Difference as an inductive norm.

34. Quassim Cassam's approach to "the epistemology of terrorism and counter-terrorism" (2018, forthcoming) focuses not on prediction but on "making the turn to violence *intelligible* in specific cases . . . without any expectation of general laws or the ability to *predict* violence. It works backwards from effects to causes and, instead of positing generic psychological mechanisms to explain why some people carry out acts of terrorism, emphasizes the extent to which pathways to terrorism tend to be highly individual, idiosyncratic and contingent." The holy of counterterrorism he says has been "prediction, and governments and intelligence agencies are attracted by the idea that radicalisation predicts political violence. [On this view] . . . the key to explaining the turn to political violence is to understand 'the radicalisation process.'"

By contrast, as a self-described *epistemic particularist* Cassam thinks that there is no *general* answer to the question of what leads persons to turn to political violence. While I worry that epistemic particularism shares the content-focused "can't compare across traditions" thesis with post-liberal theologians, and against CSR, Cassam makes a useful distinction that may bring us closer: "In its most extreme form epistemic particularism would deny the existence of *any* interesting generalisations about the turn to political violence. In its more moderate form epistemic particularism allows that there may be such generalisations but insists that they are of limited value when it comes to understanding the actions of a specific individuals."

35. Rawlsian "reasonable pluralism" I see as based negatively upon the burdens of judgment, and positively on agents' holistic reasons for adopting a religious identity, whether in a testimonial faith-tradition or something less traditional but still potentially a "comprehensive doctrine" covering all recognizable values within a systematically articulated system or worldview. It is important to note that the argument for Rawlsian reasonable comprehensive conceptions is explicitly political, and that the burdens of judgment are epistemic. Now Rawls and Rorty both do connect the dialogical principles or criteria of reciprocity that supports behind pluralism to a demand for "privatization" of religious belief in the sense of it being just to keep religious belief out of the public sphere. But that is a different argument and one that should not rely on such broad generalizations. The personal and the private are not the same, and personal or experiential aspects of spirituality do not subjectivize the object of faith, or contrast it with collective life. Both authors should be seen as adhering to what Rorty calls the "Jeffersonian Compromise," though they both perhaps exaggerate how directly relevant their describing religion as, in a liberal democracy, a personal search for perfection, answers that question of religion and politics. Much debate about democracy and moral paternalism, the establishment clause, and other questions would have to come between. So my presentation of the inductive risk account, and my use of the Rawlsian notion of "reasonable pluralism" is largely neutral to that whole debate about the place of religion in the public sphere.

36. Partly what is meant by "radical" fideism is an absolutistic bent, whether it be more cognitive (demand for creedal assent) or practical (demand that everyone live under Sharia law).

37. Kierkegaard continues, "For I should very much like to know how one would bring Abraham's act into relation with the universal, and whether it is possible to

discover any connection whatever between what Abraham did and the universal . . .
except the fact that he transgressed it."

38. Brunner 1937, 155. See Blanshard's (Chapter vii) discussion of Brunner and
Barth's central role in the post-liberal turn.

39. Bernard Williams, "Tolerance: An Impossible Virtue?" Many fundamentalists
traditionally viewed politics as anathema and were isolationist, but may have displayed benevolent attitudes when circumstances forced their interaction with broader
society.

40. It appears that "friendly" atheism and theism (see Greco 2008) may be
described as a de facto position independent of a de jure one. For instance, say that I
hold that evidence and argument best supports theism (or atheism), but not that others, given the trait-dependence of both of our views, are necessarily unreasonable or
outside their intellectual rights to hold a contrary view. One of the best things about
contraries is that they can both be wrong! I see no reason why a narrow-target de jure
objection like our own against exclusivism cannot be combined with a de facto objection to theism that finds no justification for censuring theism, or deism, or pantheism,
etc., more generally. Indeed, such a combination may be how Rawlsian reasonable
pluralism is best motivated, since Rawls' view is permissivist, yet has the "teeth" to
censure the unreasonability of the those who eschew their burdens of judgment the
putting the culturally particular above the universal: those "discontents" of Rawlsian
reasonable pluralism.

41. Montaigne, *Essays* book 1.9, ebooks@Adelaide.

42. I do not find comparative philosophers of religion to be drawing as readily as
they might from the empirical studies of CSR. From the other direction, "religious
orientation" as studied by psychologists proceeds without the focus on symmetry or
asymmetry of trait-ascriptions that philosophy of luck/risk brings to bear. But the new
research questions that I hope will serve to more closely connect these two fields of
study are ones we have already laid the basis for: they are questions informed by close
study of how religious groups make and justify asymmetrical ascriptions of religious
truth or value to group insiders and outsiders. They connect with problems of religious luck, and still more directly with modes of belief acquisition and maintenance
that are cognitively unsafe (because inductively risky), or morally dubious (because
of the attitudes toward religious outsiders they engender, and the irresponsibility of
risking others *besides oneself* through one's doxastic faith ventures).

Chapter 4

"We Are All of the Common Herd"

Montaigne and the Psychology of our "Importunate Presumptions"

PSYCHOLOGISTS AND PHILOSOPHERS
ON OUR BIAS BLIND SPOT

Let me begin this chapter by bringing back to attention the epigraph to part II, Montaigne's quote:

> Our eyes see nothing backward. A hundred times a day we mock our neighbors, and detest in others certain defects which are much more apparent in us; yea, and marvel at them with heedlessness and audacity . . . Oh, importunate presumption!

Montaigne's recognition of our many "importunate presumptions" captures quite well a central claim in contemporary psychology, that our species suffers from our common *bias blind spot*. The judgments we make in ignorance of our own biases Montaigne calls our importunate presumptions, and he suggests a host of practical factors that make these presumptions appealing to us. Montaigne associates many of our errors with one or another kind of presumption, often about our similarity or differences from others, or from God. Our obvious psychographic diversity and the polemical dynamics involved in our "culture wars" are compounded on the agential side by the invisibility of our biases to ourselves. "We are all huddled and concentrated in ourselves, and our vision is reduced to the length of our nose. We are all unconsciously in this error, an error of great consequence and harm."[1] So many of our presumptions are ego, ethnic, or anthropocentric. Some indiv- may do much better at the reflective task of recognizing and/or compensating for their biases, but none of us are above them. Montaigne emphasizes their costs as well as their causes, a cost that is both moral and cognitive. Morally, he finds it a sad irony that "our religion is made to extirpate vices; it covers them, fosters them, incites them." Cognitively, there is a matching irony: "For it comes to pass that nothing is more firmly believed than things *least* well-known." Here again, while these points focus on extremes, and reflect times of intra-Christian warfare in which Montaigne lived, I find them quite relevant today.

This chapter is concerned with connections between the comparative study of fundamentalism and the psychological study of biases and heuristics. In what ways might biases and heuristics play a special role in aiding our understanding of, and response to, fundamentalist orientation? The first section looks at efforts to provide useful scales for fundamentalist orientation; it also introduces research on a number of personal and social biases that plausibly affect *all* of our beliefs in domains of controversial views, religious views included. This is background for the second section. The comparative study of fundamentalisms, religious radicalization, and religion and violence all recognize *formal similarities* among groups of religious believers. The proximate causes of belief are all that we can study, and in these there may be significant etiological symmetries. Yet those groups themselves, especially to the extent that they are exclusivist, are tunnel-visioned on claims of doctrinal uniqueness: on *content differences* of a theological sort. Todd Tremlin makes a point similar to this when he writes,

> [W]hen we cut beneath the variegation in religious representations found around the world, we find a basic set of cognitive building blocks that simultaneously constrains possible variation and betrays an underlying unity to the diversity that does exist. . . . It is attention to this shared psychology, and to the conceptual unity beneath cultural diversity, that revivifies the "comparative" study of religion.[2]

The second section turns our attention to this intriguing tension between form and content, or between etiological symmetry and doctrinal uniqueness. It asks how we get from etiological symmetry with respect to the proximate causes of belief, to not just religious "diversity," but to religious "contrariety" and to even to contrariety of a polarized and polemical sort. Under what conditions can etiological symmetry be predicted to give rise to religious contrariety? There I present a kind of "genealogy" of religious absolutism and exclusivism—importunate presumptions in the religious domain—broken down into steps where the role of biases can hopefully be more easily recognized.

As a brief aside before moving to the first topic, allow me to reflect on the fortunes of comparative philosophy of religion. Tremlin mentions "revivifying" this field, and this strikes me as the right goal particularly with respect to comparative fundamentalism (hereafter CF). This field seems to have gotten off to a strong start, but then languished in recent decades, even as a lot of good work has been done in CSR. There are multiple reasons for this. One reason why interest in CF has not been strong is that it has followed a path similar to that of comparative philosophy and comparative methods in religious studies more generally. When I was a graduate student, comparative philosophy and comparative religious studies enjoyed a higher profile than they do today. Today, Hickian or neo-Kantian "essences" of religion are for many scholars out; for the most part, so is the "correctness" of the religious pluralist's attempt to stress theological similarities rather than differences, ecumenism, and common ground rather than different ground. Radical "particularity" and the uniqueness of each tradition is back in. Under these conditions studies of similarities across religions or families of religion are largely uninteresting and possibly irresponsible projects conducted by individuals who do not really know what it is like to practice a particular faith-tradition and to make it the basis of one's worldview.[3]

Reported dissatisfaction with Kantian essences, with Hick's Realin-itself beyond human categories of thought, and with Tillich's broad notion of religion as ultimate concern, is arguably only part of the reason for recent relative neglect of comparative methods. The larger reason is the post-modern and post-liberal "turns" in theology beginning around in the 1970s. The two latter movements, post-modernism and post-liberalism seem in many ways counter-point to one another. They make strange bedfellows, as many have noted, since while they both champion particularity, post-modernist epistemology tends toward relativism and social constructionism, while post-liberalism as I understand it is the rejection of liberal theology in favor of religious absolutism and biblical literalism.[4] But however different post-modern and post-liberal trends in theology may be, they do overlap at points, and on the view I will present, one of those overlaps is that they both tend to detract from the recognition that there are features of religion that can be compared across traditions, and made the basis of scientific study. Those who think we need, or have entered a "post-liberal" or "post-Enlightenment" era, are often also the same who discount far too quickly the possibility and value of comparisons, both in theological content and in the proximate causes of belief, across families of the world's religions.[5] In philosophical terms of the twentieth century, the "myth of the given" morphs into its mirror image, the "myth of the framework," simplistic foundationalism into radical anti-foundationalism and relativism. But of course cognitive relativism does not sit well with religious absolutism, and celebration of cultural particularity of the sort that post-modern theology supports for post-liberals like Griffiths (1991; 1994) becomes grounds for rejecting the value of ecumenism and even of inter-religious dialogue. Proselytizing may be part of one's evangelical religious identity, but "dialogue" in the sense of opening one's own nurtured beliefs to criticism by religious aliens is described as pointless. For religious belief systems are taken as closed or sacrosanct in a way that makes *inter*cultural critique normatively impotent, and compromise unthinkable. So "particularity," "uniqueness," and especially "intratextuality" have become buzzwords of post-liberals, whether simply conservative or influenced by post-modernism. Why not instead say neither post-modern nor post-liberal, but simply *retribalized*?[6] We should worry with Jeffrey Stout and the editors of the *Comparative Religious Ethics* collection (2016), that "tradition" can be employed rhetorically or in triumphalist ways that shut down understanding rather than as a term that engages recognition either of similarities *or* specific differences: "Of course, attention to particularism can move from a salutary and humbling recognition of the contingencies and contestability of one's own location to a form of ideological identity politics that turns into a presumptive insistence that *this*, simply by being *this*, cannot also be *that*."[7]

Neglect of etiological symmetry comes not just from fundamentalists. But the study of fundamentalist orientation is one area where etiological symmetry and asymmetry in trait-ascriptions are both highly relevant. Against the combination of neglect of etiological symmetry and over-estimation of content-uniqueness, I suggest we start over with Montaigne's recognition that "Each man bears the entire form of the human condition," and that "We are all of the common herd."[8] These are two claims that are being confirmed to us in study after study in psychology and evolutionary theory. Humans appear hardwired to be part of a group, and we rely on our ingroup for many of our ideas. Mark van Vugt, who has studied group biases extensively, writes, "Human belongingness needs are embedded within a marked ingroup/outgroup psychology. Many studies show that our social identities are boosted through inducing competition, either real or symbolic, between groups."[9]

Turning to the psychological understanding of fundamentalist orientation, Hood, Hill, and Williamson (2005) organize their fundamentalism scale around six attitudes that fundamentalists characteristically maintain toward their sacred text. Fundamentalist adherents to traditions of revelation "are forced to defend a particular text elevated to distinctiveness as *the* sacred text containing *the* revelation from *the* Supreme Being":

> From the outside, there are many sacred texts, allowing us to speak of various "fundamentalisms." But to do so is to be keenly aware that one has moved into a study of the *structure and process* of fundamentalist belief and away from a study of the *content* of fundamentalist belief, which . . . is best viewed as orthodoxy [and] orthodoxy is by definition tradition–specific.[10]

A recent article in *Scientific American Mind* highlighted a range of de-biasing strategies and theoretical approaches to religious radicalization that the authors believe may help us break what they term "the cycle of co-radicalization." People sometimes have different core values. In the healthy cultural salad bowl or melting pot this is fine, but "when groups start becoming isolated from conventional society, this innate propensity to 'swarm and norm' can form a springboard for cliques, cults and other kinds of extremists."[11] Intra-communally these behavioral tendencies can become a platform for groupthink conformity, and for not carefully questioning consensus opinion. Inter-communally, or between groups, they can become a springboard for group polarization. In certain group settings, people report experiencing "identity fusion," where boundaries between individual and group identities break down and we empathize with our peers to an extraordinary degree. But at the same time, our moral empathy often evaporates when it comes to out-groupers. "The mind-set of us versus them—the psychological Ground Zero for all discrimination and prejudice."[12]

This statement makes our Bias Blind Spot one of the deeper and more intractable problems, both morally and epistemologically. Let's discuss seeing others as more prone to bias than yourself, since this has been demonstrated with groups in addition to individuals. There is a substantial body of work in psychology, a good deal of it due to Emily Pronin and her collaborators, which evidences "a broad pervasive tendency for people to see the existence and operation of bias much more than others that in themselves."[13] This is the exact insight, it seems to me, that Montaigne expresses in his point about our importunate presumptions and the difficulty of recognizing them as such!

Our bias blind spot and our tendency to engage in doubtful, sharply asymmetrical characterological trait-ascriptions are intimately connected. Both can be a reflection of what psychologists working on human conflict and conflict resolution refer to as naïve realism. One manifestation or marker of our bias–blind spot is self-versus-others asymmetries; another is attributions involving ingroup–outgroup traits. In Pronin, Gilovich, and Ross's terms,

> Important asymmetries between self-perception and social perception arise from the simple fact that other people's actions, judgments, and priorities sometimes differ from one's own. This leads people not only to make more dispositional inferences about others than about themselves . . . but also to see others as more susceptible to a host of cognitive and motivational biases."[14]

Our social biases make self-privileging strategies of explanation appealing to us; charging others with bias can be a self-exculpating strategy. Bias-charging is sometimes well-motivated and sometimes not, but it is almost always attended with an implicit assumption of asymmetrical insight on the part of the attributor. In "You Don't Know me, but I Know You: The Illusion of Asymmetric Insight," Pronin, Kruger, Savitsky, and Ross analyze studies that test the hypothesis that people often exhibit "an asymmetry in assessing their own interpersonal and intrapersonal knowledge relative to that of their peers."[15] We see it when our peers make self-serving attributions on tasks like explaining one's own and others' test performance. We judge them as biased. But we are more likely to judge our own similarly self-serving attributions to be free of bias. It is not just doctors who report that other doctors but not themselves are susceptible to perks from the vendors of the pharmaceuticals they prescribe. In addition to seeing others as biased when they are, but largely exempting ourselves, we can also go so far as to infer that others are biased when such an attribution is *merely* self-serving, and not based in fact. We can even impute motivational or cognitive bias (impugning motives, or doubting the sincerity or competence of others) *just because* they differ from us in what they believe; such evidentially unmotivated bias-charging is itself a marker of this extreme form of bias.

Psychologists recognize multiple specific social biases, and different contexts in which they are commonly displayed. Specific concerns with symmetry and asymmetry in explanations were crucial to the design of many of the cited psychological experiments, and to the hypotheses they test. Pronin and Ross in particular have also suggested broader application of their findings by describing more of the psychology of "naïve realism" that biased trait-attributions often presupposes: "Although this blind spot regarding one's own biases may serve familiar self-enhancement motives, it is also a product of the phenomenological stance of naive realism."[16] These psychologists therefore raise theoretical and practical questions directly relevant to our own project, questions about "the relevance of these phenomena to naïve realism and to conflict, misunderstanding, and dispute resolution."[17]

Now if, as seems plausible, religious thinking sometimes plies upon social biases and heuristics, this should not lead to positing biases that are completely unique to the religious domain. Comparative philosophers and CSR scholars seem to agree on this. Even if there could be some bias that is unique to inferences from statements with religious or metaphysical content, it would be a strange assumption to think that the biases affecting religious ideas are somehow domain-specific. Rather, although manifesting in religious ideas, they are more likely to be the effects of biases like *Ingroup–Outgroup Bias* that psychologists have identified through more general studies of biases and heuristics. The point is that an array of cognitive, perceptual and motivational biases affect human judgment and decision making, and what would be miraculous is if this were not the case only in one particular domain, or for adherents of one religion or sect. Our biases affect our social interactions in all domains, and all that we need to presume at this point is that religion is no principled exception to this rule.

Cristina Cleveland points out that when social biases like *Ingroup–Outgroup Bias* do take hold—in whatever sphere of life—"the tendency to cling to rigid and oversimplified categories of other groups quickly leads us to exaggerate differences between *us* and *them*." She also adds,

> We want to be perceived as different from *them* so we exaggerate our differences with the other group. . . . In fact, we often distinguish ourselves from other groups even when there's no logical reason to do so. . . . This natural inclination to obsess over the characteristics that distinguish our group from other groups is exacerbated by the fact that we spend the majority of our time with fellow group members who confirm our beliefs, culture, and way of life. . . . Exaggerating differences also gives way to wider differences in viewpoints. This is called *perspective divergence*—[or] *the gold standard effect*—and is one of the main causes of divisions between groups . . . lead[ing] us to believe that not only are we different from them, but we are also better than them.[18]

False consensus effect, according to Tricia Yurak, "demonstrates a kind of bias to which people fall prey in their typical thinking, thus often referred to as a cognitive bias. Unfortunately we fall prey to a number of such biases. This is problematic when we consider how often in our daily lives we make judgments about others."[19] False consensus effect occurs when people believe or estimate that others are more similar to them than is actually the case.

Pluralistic ignorance refers to cases of actual similarity being interpreted as dissimilarity:

> Unlike the other biases which seem to be self-serving, pluralistic ignorance emphasizes the individual's distinctiveness and even alienation from others. . . . Several studies have shown that people underestimate the proportion who also behave in a socially desirable way—an indication of false uniqueness. For example, persons who regularly engage in physical activity tend to underestimate the actual proportion of other people who exercise. For undesirable attributes and behaviors (such as smoking cigarettes), people overestimate the proportion of peers who behave the same way they do. . . . This bias is thought to be the result of a self-enhancement or self-protective motivation: By underestimating the number of other people who behave desirably, the person can feel distinctively positive. On the other hand, perceiving one's undesirable behaviors or attributes as more common than they actually are can create a feeling of safety in numbers, and help to justify irresponsible practices.[20]

False consensus effect and pluralistic ignorance arguably have especially strong connection with counter-inductive thinking. They are essentially egocentric biases. By contrast, *Ingroup–Outgroup Bias* and *False Uniqueness Bias* regard us/them relations. Russell Spears writes, "One of the key objectives of research in intergroup relations has been to explain evidence of ingroup bias in its various forms, as a necessary step to reduce and resolve intergroup discrimination." Social identity theory is one of the leading available theories, aiming to explain why, for more symbolic reasons than simple self-interest or self-protection, people discriminate in favor of their group. According to Spears, "The explanation proposed for this [is] that such discrimination provides the group with distinctiveness that can enhance the identity and self-esteem of ingroup members. . . . More recently social identity theory has been extended by emotion theory to explain the more malicious forms of prejudice and discrimination towards outgroups and the different forms this may take."[21]

Bias may be detected even where superiority is not assumed, as people naturally enough use their own culture as the touchstone for making comparisons. Correlations between ingroupers and outgroupers are not always negative for ethnocentric thinkers. But often when they *are* negative, they elicit a false uniqueness bias. False uniqueness permits an individual or group to self-attribute exceptional traits or behaviors. "This perception may support general feelings of self-worth, but it also might contribute to overconfidence and lead to negative impressions of peers."

Another, sometimes related effect is *confabulation*. William Hirstein writes, "Confabulation involves absence of doubt about something one should doubt: one's memory, one's ability to move one's arm, one's ability to see, etc. It is a sort of pathological certainty about ill-grounded thoughts and evidences." More than simple rationalization, "Confabulators don't know that they don't know what they claim." Hirstein gives these conditions: "Jan confabulates if and only if:

1. Jan claims that *p* (e.g., Jan claims that her left arm is fine).
2. Jan believes that *p*.
3. Jan's thought that *p* is ill-grounded.
4. Jan does not know that her thought is ill-grounded.
5. Jan should know that her thought is ill-grounded.
6. Jan is confident that *p*."[22]

Confabulation is arguably of special philosophic concern when it manifests in connection with the holding of controversial views for which there are strong etiological challenges. Confabulation is counter-point to contingency anxiety, though they could be seen as two different ways to deal with cognitive or moral dissonance. If we fill in that claiming or believing "that p" in the above is a claim or belief *about a trait asymmetry between Jan and another person or persons*, then we can see that asymmetry and confabulation are often found combined. Often we confabulate to actually hide a bias from ourselves. Rationalizing an asymmetric ascription or explanation on weak rational grounds *incites* psychological contingency anxiety or another form of cognitive dissonance, which may in turn leads to confabulatory explanations. Because the operation of bias typically eludes conscious awareness, introspection is a poor tool for its discovery. Favoring intuitional methods invites myside bias, where people evaluate evidence, generate evidence, and test hypotheses in ways biased toward their own prior opinions and attitudes. Critical thinkers need a solid understanding of general human biases and heuristics, and of their potential effects on our cognitive and moral judgment. For purposes of our study we should delve beyond bias blind spot, with its interpersonal and group asymmetries, and describe a number of more specific social biases that affect the ways that people acquire and maintain beliefs across various domains. I do not make direct connections to religion in this section, but simply ask the reader to keep in mind how these biases *could be* instanced where persons, narratives, or theologies ascribe traits differentially to religious insiders and outsiders. More specific connections between bias studies and religious apologetic strategies can be approached later.

We could pursue this line of reasoning, but the more general psychological tendencies to resist epistemic norms, and hence to incur inductive risk, are simply *directional thinking*. Michael Philips gives many examples to show how widespread directional thinking is, and cites studies showing that humans are not very good at recognizing it in ourselves.[23] Seeing directional thinking and its effects as centrally important, he argues that philosophers often ignore it and that psychologists have not gone far enough in constructing markers and tests. It is not easy, but directional thinking can be tested for:

> Since few of us realize that our thinking is directional when we are doing it, experimenters can't rely on what we tell them to identify directional thinking and discover how widespread it is. Instead, they test it by asking experimental subjects to evaluate a theory (a study, or a packet of information) that is unwelcome news to some of them and either welcome or neutral news to the others. If the group to whom the results are unwelcome reject or criticize them significantly more often than the group to whom they are welcome, experimenters infer that they are not evaluating what they have read or heard on the basis of the evidence alone (however much they may think they are). That is, they infer that what the subject wants to believe plays an important role in determining what they *do* believe. If the experimenters can run these experiments with enough variation of belief types, circumstances, and subjects, they can determine the extent to which and the conditions under which we believe what we want to believe.[24]

If Philips is correct that both philosophy and the experimental literature on directional thinking remains underdeveloped, more attention on trait-attribution symmetry and asymmetry could help: "If it is to have important practical implications, the experimental literature needs to be much more fine-tuned than this. It needs to tell us how to recognize directional thinking in ourselves and others. It also needs to tell us what the so-called reality constraints are for different people under different circumstances and to what degree they constrain us."[25] Relatedly, classical *Attribution Theory* tends to treat explanations as a purely cognitive activity, and the worry with this is that there is no accounting for the social functions of explanation. Without such attention, psychologists may fail to identify psychological factors besides raw information that influence the explanations people construct. Specifying these factors, however, is arguably key to predicting such important phenomena as actor–observer asymmetries, and self-serving biases.[26] Our suggested measures for counter-inductive thinking, while they are far from precise, are intended as a contribution to the study of directional thinking.

Researchers have done quite a bit of work on asymmetries in children's induction projections, and on category-based induction more generally. These studies begin to illuminate the conditions under which disparities between ingroups and outgroups, and asymmetries of trait-ascription arise.[27] In attribution studies there is research on actor–observer differences in people's behavioral explanations, and we have reviewed some of this "ingroup–outgroup attribution research." But Knobe and Malle (2002) argue convincingly that attribution theory has sometimes been burdened by efforts to reduce a multiplicity of different effects to a single, unifying one. They sketch a very different framework for understanding folk explanations of behavior, a framework on which different processes are more readily acknowledged, and allowed to involve different effects. Amenable to our own concern to develop better scales for fundamentalist orientation, the authors suggest, "This new framework gives a central role to the distinctions among various types of explanations. How do actors and observers choose which events to explain? How do they choose whether to give reason explanations or causal history explanations? When do they choose to offer beliefs and when desires? And how do they choose whether or not to linguistically mark belief reasons?"[28]

This brings us back around to the attribution of luck, whether religious luck or some other kind. Explanations in terms of good or bad luck we have seen are often highly asymmetrical and applied in a manner favoring the ingroup. They may for these reasons be akin to what psychologists in more clinical psychiatric settings call *confabulatory explanations*. If so, our approach through problems of religious luck and the inductive risk that asymmetric ascriptions of religious value entail, provides resources. It arguably provides the right kind of theory to suggest fruitful hypotheses, and to improve psychological markers and measures of confabulation. That agents "mask" their explanations and value-ascriptions in distinctly theological terms is to be expected, and does not mean that ascriptions of religious value/luck are not prime examples of this more general phenomena.

We need significantly more studies of laypeople's perceptions of luck, including religious luck. What Hales and Johnson (2014) investigate experimentally about attributions of moral luck is potentially of still stronger validity and import with regard to attributions of religious luck: practices of asymmetric trait-ascription that appeal to luck in a "masked" way. The authors hypothesized that "the luck attributions of naïve participants are shot through with various cognitive biases, including the cognitive bias of framing," where framing is understood as a change in the wording of a problem. Participants in their studies read and answered questions about the luckiness of events in various short narratives of "vignettes." For these investigators, the deep worry is that

> the existence of pervasive bias raises the possibility that there is no such thing as luck. It may be that attributions of luck are a form of *post hoc* storytelling, or even mythmaking; that they are merely a narrative device used to frame stories of success or failure. . . . [L]uck is a cognitive illusion, and assignments of luck are merely a way to subjectively interpret our experience.[29]

So what implications might studies of bias have for intra and inter-religious relations? In summary thus far, we have reviewed important individual and group biases, but they are biases that can affect us in all domains of controversial views. If I cannot show that exclusivist attitudes toward religious multiplicity *manifest* known specific social biases we have reviewed, I can argue that they often *mirror* them, and that when they do, this fact is a marker of high inductive risk. But before going on to explain how etiological symmetry can give rise, when it plies on bias, to polarized contrariety, I want to acknowledge that there are a good number of religious philosophers who are today encouraging more critical thinking about religious disagreement, and even taking deliberate steps to incorporate bias studies into their religious epistemics. To introduce someone whose work we will discuss at some length in later chapters, Olli-Pekka Vainio carefully examines causes of disagreement in two books, *Beyond Fideism: Negotiable Religious Identities* (2010), and *Disagreeing Virtuously: Religious Conflict in Interdisciplinary Perspective* (2017). Vainio closely relates these issues to the need to understand religious fideism: "While the social theories of this postliberal theological wave are predominantly communitarian, their philosophical theories of religion have been claimed to be 'fideistic.' What does this concept mean?"[30]

Looking ahead, we will develop an answer to this question in chapters 5 and 6 that incorporates Vainio's (2010) work clarifying different types of fideism, and his emphasis on the need to recognize variety in the ways that faith and reason are understood to be related in the "belief-policies" or "theological methods" recommended in different faith-traditions. While I will make some specific criticisms of *Disagreeing Virtuously,* I broadly agree with his virtue-theoretic approach to philosophy of religion as common ground between theologians and philosophers, and with his attempt to use psychological studies to make theologians and laypersons aware that "if we were more conscious about the way our minds work, we could be more effective in resolving our disputes" (80).

HOW ETIOLOGICAL SYMMETRY BEGETS RELIGIOUS CONTRARIETY IN TESTIMONIAL TRADITIONS

Our approach to "scaling" the brick wall of religious fundamentalism directs us to identify some unique ways in which fundamentalists think, rather than what specific beliefs they hold. This more formal rather than belief-based approach I think coheres with the approach of researchers in the field of comparative fundamentalism. James Peacock and Tim Pettyjohn for example argue that narrative is an especially useful analytical window into fundamentalist religious traditions. "The analysis of narratives leads us to look at representation instead of looking for essence. Our materials are stories told by fundamentalists about themselves, not abstract categories such as 'belief' or 'faith' (although these certainly find their way into the narratives)."[31] Starting with this excellent methodological suggestion, we can next describe four "steps" that illustrate a common way that etiological symmetry begets polarized and polemical religious contrariety.

Step One: Narrative Content Confounds Our Source Monitoring

Source monitoring is a very important concern both for comparative fundamentalism and CSR. Naïve realism, as psychologists like Pronin and Ross use the concept, seems to be exhibited in agents in cases of the kind that philosophers such as Lisa Bortolotti and Matthew Broome (2009) refer to as *failures of belief ownership and authorship.*[32] Robert McCauley, a leading figure in CSR, notes that under certain circumstances we can all be prone to failures in distinguishing *inner* from *outer* sources of phenomenal experience. He studies source monitoring primarily through focus on popular religiosity and on people who report experiences of hearing voices. How, and how reliably or unreliably, do agents attribute their phenomenal experience to an outer versus an inner source? In pathological cases such as schizophrenia the agent disowns or is unusually confused about the status of sources that are in fact internal. "Self-disownership" (or "disowning") of the sources of one's experience of course does not always manifest a pathology, but is also ever-present in religious belief, and is similarly a phenomenon open to psychological study.

What interests us here is that source monitoring studies open out onto more epistemological issues concerning the reception of *testimony*. The concern with source monitoring can easily be extended to include psychological studies of how competently people recognize differences between simple and narrative testimony, or again, between *assertive* and *narrative* testimonial transmissions.[33] Even apart from a specific interest in religious narrative, it is clear that basing beliefs upon narrative testimony is a complex matter that goes far beyond a simple matter of trust of the author or authors.[34] The difficulty of interpreting a narrative and its characters as being intended as history, as moral allegory, or as some mixture of each, is compounded as the recipients of the testimony become separated in time from the authors and their original intended audience.[35]

Rachel Fraser (2017) has codified some of these points by detailing how and why our reliability in source monitoring is particularly challenged when we deal with *narrative* testimony. If we are interested in whether narrative testimony is a good source of beliefs about what the world is like, we should, Fraser argues, find empirical studies on *narrative credulity* quite concerning.[36] Test subjects in these studies quite often fail to reliably monitor the differences between historical fact-assertion and storytelling. Charged with the task of interpreting short, written vignettes, a substantial portion of test subjects are highly unreliable at such tasks even when the written vignettes include markers of their narrative intent.

We are less reliable in processing narrative, in contrast to simple testimony, since narrative testimony is often ambiguous as to what elements are factual, and what elements are products of imagination. To interpret it, we need a context that allows us to make educated assumptions about author intent. This is generally not an issue either with simple testimony, on the one hand, or with fiction on the other. Fiction is narrative, but contrasts with other forms of narrative like biography and autobiography, which while they always "sharpen" and "level" certain aspects of their subject matter deemed important or non-important, also purport to *inform* us about how things are in the historical world.

Narrative testimony is attended with a unique and rich phenomenology, Fraser argues, one that, especially in recognition of the somatic and modal elements of the reception of narratives, places one in a good position to understand *what it feels like* to have certain experiences.[37] You can have knowledge *of the story* without thinking yourself well situated to have a settled view about whether the personages and events within it are historically accurate, or what the authorial intent was. One can know the story without knowing or claiming to know what specific audience it was originally a story for, or what the author's intent was with respect to that audience.

Fraser argues that differences between narrative and simple testimony show up at the epistemic as well as the phenomenological level. Arguably, the claims of post-liberals and post-modernists that religious texts can only rightly be understood "intratextually" need to be understood with these *provisos*.[38] Narrative testimony behaves in *epistemologically* distinct ways, and there is a crucial trade-off. Narrative testimony comes with a distinct phenomenology, a sense of being enveloped in the story world. We associate no such phenomenology with simple testimony. So the relationship between them is hydraulic: Simple testimony is phenomenologically poorer but epistemically richer, while narrative testimony is phenomenologically richer but epistemically poorer.[39] Fraser's strongest thesis is that (religious) narrative testimony places one in a good position to understand what it is like to have certain sorts of (religious) experiences, but in a *poor* position to make factual claims or to gain knowledge of empirical/historical facts.

Unfortunately, the unique features of narrative testimony often go unacknowledged in epistemology –even in the recent resurgence of research on epistemology of testimony! Similarly, the role of imagination in religious understanding is understudied, and despite some efforts to rehabilitate it, is routinely ignored by most theologians and religious philosophers.[40] Both the unique features of narrative testimony and the special problems people have processing it are generally ignored in discussions of testimonial transmission, trust, and the proper limits of trust. Beyond the claim that these special problems with narrative testimony are often conveniently ignored, I agree with Fraser that extent models in the epistemology of testimony are rather ill-suited to capturing the unique features of narrative testimonial exchange:

> Epistemologists interested in testimony have, for the most part, explored the epistemic dimensions of very simple, one sentence assertions ('simple testimony'). But our testimonial lives are richer than this picture suggests: much of what we tell each other comes packaged as narrative. This matters: the phenomenology typical of reading or hearing narrative is very different to the phenomenology typical of simple testimony –when we read or hear narrative, we often feel immersed or enveloped in the story-world, or feel like the events being described are happening to us in ways rarely associated with simple testimony.[41]

We can argue about whether there are religious experts and about what constitutes evidence in the domain, but it is almost unanimously affirmed that unusual testimonial claims, such as claims of psychic power or supernatural occurrence, demand especially strong evidence. We monitor sources of claims as well as claims themselves, and authority or expertise sometimes leads us to accept a claim because an authority figure conveys it. In other areas, there may be no recognized expertise, only self-appointed experts.[42] When we confuse narrative and simple testimony we don't give the source of the testimony its proper scrutiny. Critical thinking texts teach that responsible reception of testimony involves evaluation both of *claims* and of *sources of claims*. But narrative form appears to distort our credibility judgments about content, and a narrative presented to people as canonized scripture may do the same by distorting one's credibility concerning a particular source of testimony.[43] This is not the place to discuss it, but if this is correct it may have direct implications for discussions of trust and our epistemic dependence on one another.

Step Two: An Adopted Revelation Becomes the Ground for a Self-Awarded 'Prize'

It is directly relevant to the connections that I want to establish between strong fideistic theological methods and polarized contrariety that Karl Barth writes at the very outset of *Church Dogmatics*, "The basic problem with which Scripture faces us in respect of revelation is that the revelation attested in it refuses to be understood as any sort of revelation alongside which there are or may be others. It insists absolutely on being understood in its uniqueness." This might well be an example of self-disownership of a belief (something discussed in Step One) since it is the text itself that "refuses" any alternative non-absolutistic understanding. We also earlier (in chapter 1) used Barth's evangelical account of the testimonial authority of Christian scriptures as an example of a theological method that makes leans for support the intervening type of veritic religious luck. We analyzed the formal structure of Barth's soteriology, where God intervenes to make the Christian revelation the lone true means of salvation, and found it highly analogous to if not a clear instance of, a standard Gettier case. The uniqueness of Christianity for Barth as for other strong conformist fideists is manifested by God's *intervention* to make human religion the vehicle of genuine revelation and salvation, an intervention lucky or unlucky for the individual, depending on how one is situated.

What should strike us as logically odd in Barth's account is how easily the exclusivist narrative could change. With no more or surer epistemological signposts for humans, God could have "meta-chosen" a different religion, for Barth pulls back from and even explicitly denies any inherent epistemic superiority in the one chosen.[44] The uniqueness demand that Barth makes so primary is also inextricable from his way of dealing with religious difference.[45] *Church Dogmatics* is a long book, but Barth very quickly dispenses with any concern about religious multiplicity. He is not completely flippant about it since he does place himself briefly in conversation with Gotthold Lessing, the Enlightenment-era thinker who's Parable of the Rings in his play *Nathan the Wise* "forbade evangelical theology to award itself the prize in comparison with other theologies." Barth does not engage with any of the reasons that Lessing's tale of the three rings provides for being skeptical of the exclusivist claim that one's own ring or faith-tradition is the only one with the truly authoritative "roots."

A sacred narrative is a source of testimonial belief, but that testimony is itself a contingent fact, and so cannot prove historical facts from a position independent of faith. Lessing argued both through his play and in his philosophical and theological writings that no historical truth can be demonstrated, and if no historical truth can be demonstrated, then nothing can be demonstrated by *means* of "historical proofs." The soundness of this *modus ponens* argument, would undermine the appeal to scripture as a "proof-text," where this means that it somehow overcomes or bridges the difference between the strength of faith-based conviction, and objective or evidence-driven reasoning.[46]

What our descriptive fideism recognizes as the *fideistic minimum*[47] to any model of religious faith is just my more formal way of describing the "ugly, broad ditch" that Lessing found that he, or any honest inquirer, must acknowledge. It is closely associated with what prevents Lessing from the prize-awarding decision he wishes he could make. For he recognizes the intellectual poverty of it, and how it perpetuates conflict over authoritative "roots" or special revelation.[48] If historical evidence underdetermines faith-based assent, then as Lessing saw, faith-based assent also underdetermines claims about history. Yet while Barth notes Lessing's point he does so only to immediately reject this *epistemological* objection on the *phenomenological* ground that true religion is "self-proclaiming." Prize awarded, it is already time to move on: "For this reason we will dispense with any comparison or evaluation that would separate or synthesize various theologies. Instead, let this simple pointer suffice: the theology to be introduced here is *evangelical* theology."

We see here why Barth believed he need not worry that the testimonial authority assumption he makes may be mirrored by adherents of *other* testimonial traditions or purported revelations. He explicitly asserts at one point that phenomenological differences *cannot* decide on matters of truth, yet (as I read him) seems to miss the point that what he means by the gospel being "self-proclaiming" can only be something phenomenological —something along the lines of what it *feels like* to experience reading the gospels, or to have been a witness to events in a biblical narrative. This suggests that no text "refuses" or "insists" on being treated differently than another, but that these are judgments made only consequent to a personal experience of being emotionally moved by reading the text.

Related self-contradictions appear in Barth's *Church Dogmatics* where some pages further on he writes that evangelical theology is a *modest* and non-boastful theology even though it is "fundamentally and totally different from that of other theologies." This latter claim must mean that Christianity is unique in God's eyes, by his making it and it alone his vehicle for salvation. The claim is *not* that it is fundamentally and totally different on phenomenological, historical, philosophical, etc., grounds, since Barth rejects that. But superiority in the special status God confers on Christianity is clearly presupposed. This superiority lies wholly in Christianity's all-or-nothing truth, but this truth is, from the epistemological perspective, an evidentially underdetermined assumption that can be and is made by adherents of other faith-traditions as well. So the grounds of the superiority are epistemically circular.

The circularity of debates over authoritative roots was of course what Lessing's parable was about. Lessing's key contrast is between "roots" and "fruits," that is, between the circular debate over the divine authority of a special revelation and a more enlightened acknowledgment of spiritual fruits to be found in many forms of religiosity, and expressed through mutual respect and toleration. True religiosity bears moral fruit, and this is what the ring was originally supposed to function to do for its wearer: bring love for and all others. Pragmatic fruits are not, in Lessing's parable, something different than Barth's or Lindbeck's "prize." But for Barth and Lindbeck, it is different: what is prized is prized because authoritative. The uniquely authoritative roots of their special revelation are what constitutes it as a prize, and as *to be* prized by the Christian.[49] Justification by faith alone takes on a radical, arguably new interpretation when taken as Christian commitment to authoritative testimonial roots *rather than* anything substantiated by pragmatic fruits.

George Lindbeck, like Barth a noted proponent of exclusivism, writes, "What, then, of other religions? *There can be any number of claimants . . . but the prize winner stands alone.* The notion of a truly comprehensive outlet defines a class of, at most, a single member."[50] So none of Lessing's *reasons* for censuring a theology from awarding itself "the prize" seem to be engaged by these post-liberals. After quickly dismissing the significance of disagreement, Barth thereafter treats contrary theological systems as false, and their followers as epistemically vicious. The logical circularity of his fideism could not be more evident than when Barth goes on to assert that the true believer's knowledge of God is all of "the God who reveals himself *in* the Gospel" (emphasis original). Barth even describes a person's assent to the unique truth and authority of Christian revelation as encompassing them in "the magic circle."[51]

Step Three: *"Have Their Ditch and Cross it, Too,"* or, Testimonial Authority Assumption Comes to be Identified with a Propositional View of Revelation

Barthian theology's truck with religious luck-leaning asymmetrical ascriptions of religious truth and value was explored earlier (in chapter 1) when we

considered its strong formal similarity to a Gettier case. But to push further
the common formal features of religious fundamentalisms, it can be compared with the Avishai Margalit's *propositional* view of revelation, and with
Paul Griffiths's defense of the "absolute claims" of religion. In "The Ring,"
Margalit provides a formal argument for this exclusivist conclusion: "A religion based on constitutive, redemptive, and revealed truths cannot ascribe
value to a religion that contradicts these truths. Thus, each religion sees itself
as the only true religion and ascribes no value to the others."[52]

The first premise of the argument for this conclusion, and what is needed
to get it off the ground, is that "Revelation is propositional." A propositional
view of revelation is presupposed in soteriological and doctrinal exclusivism.
Essentially this is the view that God said it, and that what constitutes faith is
that one believes it. "A proposition is generally an indicative sentence that
makes a statement that can be either true or false. . . .When the revelation is
transmitted in book form (the Koran, for example), the transmission itself is
propositional." The propositional view asserts that revelation is God's Word,
and the agent's role is to assent to it *as* truth. 'God said it, and God said
believe it,' or 'God said it, so I believe it,' is what religious faith and virtue
are basically said to be.

We can easily see how narrative content is reduced to what Fraser called
"simple" testimony, such that events in narrative are also either "true" or
"false," simpliciter. But Margalit then adds, "However, I see the concept
of propositional revelation as including commandments as well, such as
'Remember the Sabbath day to keep it holy.'"[53] This adds a second reduction,
in this case from value-charged imperatives to human reception as simple
fact-asserting about piety or divine command. But the second reduction is not
more logically suspect than the first, where narrative "becomes" fact by an act
on the part of an interpreter.

Narratives are retained, shared, reinterpreted, and sometimes modified.
Narrative and ritual are closely linked in most religions, but how the narrative
dimension of religion relates to its doctrinal dimension varies widely by the
view of scripture that one assumes. The propositional view fails to recognize
differences between simple and narrative testimony; it treats the canoniza-
tion of scripture quite ahistorically. Creedalism and the propositional view
go hand-in-hand. Arguably, if the meaning of narrative cannot be reduced to
a group of assertive empirical statements, then by conflating these kinds of
meaning the propositional view both over- and understates its religious meaning. If so, this easily leads to an impoverished view of faith. This is the sense
in which many theologians themselves have noted that fundamentalism based
on biblical literalism/inerrantism is something rather new rather than being
the longstanding orthodoxy it claims to be. Religious language as treated on
the propositional view not only cannot distinguish narrative meaning and

historical truth, but also does not allow enough distinction between empirical and metaphorical uses of language, or between univocal, equivocal, and analogical predication.

An agent's affectively conditioned appropriation of scripture is not logically associated with their meeting a basing requirement for propositional faith. The conflation is evident in various places, including perhaps most especially, for inheritors of a testimonial tradition, in a disregard for differences between narrative and fact-assertive content.[54] Faith *in* a promise, or *in* one's relationship with the divine gets reduced to faith *that* the teachings, and even narratives, are inerrantly *true*. On the propositional view of revelation, revelation is historical and not existential or dialectical. As one author puts it, "Revelation according to this theory is originally given to a few privileged recipients, to whom the word of God comes directly. Prophets receive the word of God as an interior gift. . . . Revelation, having been received by the prophets and apostles, is then handed down in scriptures and tradition, which constitute the written and oral vehicles of the word of God."[55] This relates to the absolutistic ways that religious assertions will be treated on the propositional view. Griffiths writes,

> Religious claims to truth are typically absolute claims: claims that explain everything; claims about the universal rightness and applicability of a certain set of values together with the ways of life that embody and perpetuate that; and claims whose referent possesses maximal greatness. These tendencies to absoluteness, although they have certainly been typical Christian doctrines, are not typical only of them; they are characteristic also of the most interesting claims made by the religious virtuosi of non-Christian traditions.[56]

Griffiths makes at least two logical mistakes here: failing to distinguish universal from absolute claims, and attributing absolutism to "religions" rather than to fundamentalists within various religions. Because he takes his own model of faith as normative for everyone, he also fails to acknowledge that many believers even in his own tradition find no need to absolutize as he does.[57] It is true to say that theologies almost without exception make *universal* claims: claims valid not just for themselves but for all people.[58] Paul Knitter responds to Griffiths on this point by distinguishing universal and absolutistic claims:

> To give up what we are calling *absolute* claims to truth would not mean abandoning both the particular and the universal claims to truth that are inherent in both religious experience and in the teachings of most religions. . . . Particular and universal claims are not at all denied when religions are asked to pull in the range of their absolute claims. Each religion continues to announce that what it contains is really true and important for all people. But in abandoning their

absolute claims, each religion would also be open to the possibility (if not probability) that other religious figures or events may also bear truths—very different perhaps—that are also really and universally important.[59]

To be clear, the social phenomena of our construction of "enemies in the mirror" is explicable in philosophic and social psychological terms as prize-awarding, together with the counter-inductive thinking necessary to rationalize one's fideistic assent. In its most formal sense, counter-inductive thinking is something much more specific than weak inductive reasoning. It is not just weak analogy, weak causal inference, or faulty generalization, to refer to the three forms of inductive reasoning. We must follow inductive norms when we draw a generalization about a population or apply such a generalization to predict something about individuals within a population. We follow inductive norms anytime we draw disanalogies and analogies between two things, and also when we draw a causal implication from things observed to be either positively or negatively correlated. Counter-inductive inference is the logically illicit move of reasoning *oppositely* to what induction suggests. This puts our definition of counter-induction in sync with dictionaries, which define it as a pattern of inference *reversing* the normal logic of induction, a strategy of taking the way things are within our past and present experience not as a *guide*, but as positively *counter-point* to how we should take them to be outside our past and present experience. For our purposes it is more simply a logical failing to apply to one's self (or to one's own epistemic situation) an explanation that one applies to others (and others' epistemic situations).

Step Four: Biased-Closure Inferences Rationalize Peer Denial and Pave the Way for "Easy" Knowledge

We have discussed inductive reason a great deal but deductive reasoning can also be co-opted by adherents of strongly fideistic models of faith. It is said by some that "fundamentalism proceeds rationally from its own first assumptions." I think this gravely overlooks violation of inductive norms, but there is something to it on the deductive side when people accept a deceptively simple "closure principle" as a way to close out the significance of any claims inconsistent with one's own. The "logic of exclusivism" according to Gavin D'Costa is that "there are certain claims to truth and those other claims that do not conform to these initial claims, explicitly or implicitly, are false."[60]

Christian philosopher Dick-Martin Grube (2015; 2005) understands what we have called biased-closure inferences in terms of the doubtful assumption of a bivalent truth-focused account of religious beliefs. Bivalence "implies a particular way of dealing with that which is genuinely different: It implies that, if position A is true and position B differs from A, B *must* be false. [Yet] . . . B's falsity is not affirmed after careful scrutiny by default, viz., simply by virtue of the fact that A is held to be true. Under bivalent parameters, there is no other choice than to consider B to be false. Since only A *or* B can be true but not both, B must be false if A is true. I summarize this point by suggesting that bivalence implies an *equation between difference and falsity.*"[61] Rejecting bivalence as a sound basis for religious epistemics, Grube argues that we cannot "overstep the limits of what is humanly possible to know in order to maintain positive religion."[62]

Following these suggestions, let us call *biased-closure inferences* (BCI) the kinds of "natural" but very self-serving inferences people often make from their own belief being true, to any belief contrary to it being false. In biased-closure inferences, the third option with regard to contraries, that they could *both* be wrong, is neglected, and so is the evidence that the disagreement provides that may support inferring that neither the thesis nor its contrary is strictly true. As psychologically driven inferences, biased-closure inferences reduce contrariety to simple contradiction, and the central theological or religious claims of the home religion as true or false, simpliciter.[63]

Epistemologists often focus on a closure principle being necessary to "save knowledge," but rarely do they give study as to how closure reasoning easily lends itself to a host of *easy knowledge problems*. Closure inferences are biased when they are valid but not sound. If I start with a false belief then closure reasoning will close off truth, simply because truth will be contrasted with the false belief which is held as true. Even if I start with a justified belief, an uncritical application of a closure principle invites the agent too easily to conclude that no belief incompatible with her own can enjoy positive epistemic status. By this reduction one is enjoining to "go binary" and infer contradiction from what may very well only be contrariety of a lesser sort.[64]

The "contented religious exclusivists," whose rationality Jerome Gellman defends, is a believer who, as a result of biased-closure inferences, does not care to investigate religious disagreement or to consider adjudicating any causes of disagreement besides what their accepted testimonial authority says about idolaters and unbelievers. Gellman's thesis about contented exclusivism is not just that "religious beliefs may stay rationally unreflective," but also that "a person's religious beliefs acquired as described earlier, can legitimately, and without impugning full rationality, serve for assessing other religions or religious claims outside one's own religious circle."[65] One sees the world *very clearly and satisfactorily* through rose-colored glasses, and if other persons wear other shades and see the world differently, it is of no concern to me as a contented exclusivist. Necessarily then, this contented fellow is unconcerned about etiological symmetry problems, or about any alleged bias-mirroring in their own perspective. It is enough to know that these etiological challenges are *challenges*, to know that, whatever their basis, they are false and so can and should be ignored. As Hood, Hill, and Williamson write,

> It is when openness is lacking that fundamentalism more easily takes hold. Attitudes of fallibilism that should be accorded to our answers to ultimate questions are supplanted by attitudes of absolutism, and the sanction for those attitudes is exported to a source outside the agent: the inerrancy of Pope, of the home religion's elders, or of special revelation. A special revelation is provided to God's chosen but still understood as normative for every person because true of the world absolutely.[66]

According to these authors, for fundamentalists their sacred text guides its own interpretation, being perceived as true and complete in itself. Thus intratextuality rules—the brick wall of fideism. "The issue for fundamentalists is more correctly one of inerrancy, not one of literality. . . . Furthermore, inerrancy is crucial, since finding an error within the text can only be claimed on the basis of criteria outside the text." Lack of openness is also at issue with failure to recognize etiological symmetries and similarities among believers in different faith communities. Different attitudes toward comparative study are on display in Silverstein and Stroumsa (eds., 2015), *The Oxford Handbook of the Abrahamic Religions*. Stroumsa wonders why modern scholarly study has shown "a remarkable lack of interest in thinking and studying the three religions together, in comparative fashion" (56). He suggests that resistance to the idea of a family relationship, of a *suggeneia*, between Judaism, Christianity, and Islam" reflects the "zero-sum-game polemics" to which the Abrahamic religions have often been given (69). But reflecting post-liberal theology, Remi Brague associates "Abrahamic family" talk, and the "three rings" discussion, primarily with a debunking "three imposters" thesis. Thus he criticizes the whole language of families of religion along with a drive for comparative study he thinks "masks real differences underneath a surface harmony" (104). But other contributors including Weltecke and Ruthven supply historical evidence which limits the kind of brute appeal to tradition that Brague and Margalit make to support their doctrinal and/or salvific exclusivism.

CONCLUSION

Bias is clearly *part* of the reason for cognitive diversity, but a good deal of diversity is arguably generated without the need to appeal to overt bias on the part of some or all agents as explanatory of differences in belief. What has drawn our critical attention in this chapter is the puzzlement that symmetric or essentially similar doxastic strategies should give rise not just to cognitive diversity, but to what we can call *polarized or polemical* contrariety, contrariety of a kind where each view adamantly rejects all others. This is certainly possible in other fields besides that of religious ideas, but is most apparent in that domain where political and theological intolerance have so often been conjoined. It is indeed a surprising outcome, and a concerning one, if and when the very similarities shared by members of a *family* of religions generate and maintain exclusivist attitudes about religious truth and salvation. Such, indeed, I believe to be the case with the sons of Abraham: *It is not nearly so much their different sacred narratives or their doctrinal-level differences, but what they have formally in common, that makes them fight.* As we will continue to develop, bias studies take on a much stronger salience in explanations of religious contrariety under such conditions of bias-mirroring effects.

Inductive risk and related concerns about the doxastic riskiness of a strategy of belief formation or maintenance, is a largely descriptive and scalar concern. These scales could be used to test and revise what we described as the hypothesis of psychological fideism. But the concept of high inductive risk also lends itself to *normative* applications. The connections between strong fideism and counter-inductive thinking do not just have explanatory implications of interest to psychologists, but also normative implications for the well-foundedness of belief, in terms of both the reliability and the reasonableness of a religious belief premised upon an act of testimonial authority assumption. But rather than argue for any overgeneralized thesis about how highly risky doxastic methods impact the epistemic status of religious, we tried to invite a broad-based discussion of these matters. We insisted only that luck aggravation and high inductive risk provide are concepts that help us to determine different *kinds* of normative adequacy, theological, moral, and epistemic. A highlighted point was that a person's specific inherited or adopted model of faith is as open to critique and to rethinking as is any other aspect of religious identity. Indeed, it would behoove us all to take better notice of the various models of faith we operate with, since conceptions of faith we have shown differ significantly in how far they aggravate problems of religious luck, and these differences bear quite directly upon their theological, moral, or epistemic appraisal. Criticism of a particular model of faith may involve more than one kind of adequacy, especially as concepts of moral and epistemic risk are intertwined.[67]

The "four steps" were intended to be descriptive and explanatory, but they also invite a more direct critique. The next chapter begins by defending reasonable disagreement in domains of controversial views, but also returns us to the de jure side of the inductive risk account, and to direct concern with the *limits* of reasonable disagreement. There I argue more directly that exclusivist responses to religious multiplicity, and associated self-serving peer denial and vice-charging, lie beyond the pale of reasonable disagreement.

NOTES

1. Montaigne (D. Frame, ed.), 116.
2. Tremlin 2010, 146.
3. Compare Dostoyevsky's related insights: "So long as man remains free he strives for nothing so incessantly and so painfully as to find someone to worship. But man seeks to worship what is established beyond dispute, so that all men would agree at once to worship it.... This is the chief misery of every man individually and of all humanity from the beginning of time. For the sake of common worship they've slain each other with the sword. They have set up gods and challenged one another, 'Put away your gods and come and worship ours, or we will kill you and your gods!' And so it will be to the end of the world; even when gods disappear from the earth, people will fall down before idols just the same." From "The Failure of Christianity."
4. Other key contrasts are that post-modernists tend to be explicitly non-foundationalist, while post-liberal theology is foundationalist about revelation. Post-modernists are radically constructionist and anti-realist, while post-liberalists arguably evince naïve realism in their reading of scripture.
5. We will focus on self-described post-liberals like Paul Griffiths, since this fits best with our special concern with critical examination of religious exclusivism and contemporary forms of fundamentalism. Griffiths and Blanshard's historical descriptions of the post-liberal turn are interestingly very similar, although they assess it from very different perspectives, the one championing it and the other highly critical of it. Both see post-liberalism as claiming that faith is not aided by philosophy or natural theology; it is "a descent of grace. Don't try to defend Christianity; take the offensive against rationalism as a stupid misunderstanding and irrelevance" (Blanshard, Chapter vii, "The Revolt against Reason in Theology"). The relationship between post-liberalism and post-modernism is difficult, since post-modernism had many more varieties, some of which do, and others do not, militate against propositional conceptions of faith. For an excellent introduction to post-modern theology, see Pamela Sue Anderson (2010).
6. Their particularism provides only a *notional response* to etiological challenges of the sort elaborated through the thought experiment of chapter 2. By 'notional' responses I mean to suggest responses more grounded in religious imagination than in anything sustainable by appeal to facts, evidence, or logical reasoning. The *absolutizing* of the particular is different from theism or deism in the sense of belief in a universal creator from natural facts or reason. This point is suggested by Hume: "We often find, amongst barbarous nations, and even sometimes amongst civilized, that, when every strain of flattery has been exhausted towards arbitrary princes, when every human quality has been applauded to the utmost; their servile courtiers represent them, at last, as real divinities, and point them out to the people as objects of

adoration. How much more natural, therefore, is it, that a limited deity, who at first is supposed only the immediate author of the particular goods and ills in life, should in the end be represented as sovereign maker and modifier of the universe? Even where this notion of a supreme deity is already established; though it ought naturally to lessen every other worship, and abase every object of reverence, yet if a nation has entertained the opinion of a subordinate tutelar divinity, saint, or angel; their addresses to that being gradually rise upon them, and encroach on the adoration due to their supreme deity" (Hume 2009, 151–52).

7. Mathewes, Puffer, and Storslee 2016, "Introduction to Volume III," 8. The editors see the field expanding even though they say it would be hard to find another area of study whose "several component pieces are more fundamentally contested than CRE" (3). They point out that a one-sided focus on 'sameness' and un-self-critical appeals to neutrality or objectivity have been subject to much opprobrium, but at the same time that making all understanding 'internal' to a tradition stunts its growth.

8. Montaigne (Frame, 611; 429). Between psychology's meliorism and the biblical 'bent wood' of humanity, afflicted with error, there seems to be only consistency. The problem is just resolved in very different ways. The psychologist finds us a herd animal, and our nature human, all too human; theology finds us equally flawed, but giving a primordial moral/spiritual reason for it, and prescribing moral and spiritual nourishment the cure for a universal sickness of soul.

9. Mark van Vugt, "Averting the Tragedy of the Commons," 171.

10. Hood, Hill, and Williamson, *The Psychology of Religious Fundamentalism,* 191–192.

11. K. Dutton and D. Abrams, "What Researchers Say about Defeating Terrorism," March 2016.

12. Or as Dick Simon puts it, when we allow our "themification process" to carry us along without correction, "we lose much of our capacity to reason, and to empathize.... We label others as THEM rather than doing the hard work of trying to garner a more nuanced understanding of complex situations. We categorize others as THEM to protect us from ambiguity. We stereotype others as THEM to rationalize our own behavior." Dick Simon, "The Most Dangerous Four-Letter Word." Accessed from http://www.huffingtonpost.com/dick-simon/the-most-dangerous-fourle_b_455555 1.html.

13. Pronin 2007, 37. Ballantyne calls this the *bias bias:* "-a bias that sways judgment and reasoning *about bias.* One of the several cognitive mechanisms that it has been found to manifest the bias blind spot is "evidential asymmetry between judgments of self and others" (150). There is a form of irrationality (associated with confabulation) that consists in thinking one believes on one basis, when in fact he or she believes on another. There is also a form of irrationality (associated with directional thinking) that consists in confusing subjective factors with objective ones. These problems arguably affect religious belief more so than other of our controversial views, since the "basis" of belief is often a claimed supernatural event. We rarely can *know* on the basis of self-deceived evidence, and we rarely know when we *are* self-deceived.

14. Pronin, Gilovich, and Ross (2004, 781). "[W]e feel that our own judgments reflect the true nature of things, and thus assume that, to the extent that others perceive

events or objects of judgment (including "us" and "them") differently, those others reveal in impact of various perceptual, cognitive, or motivational biases" (Pronin et al. 2001, 640). If we are objective, people who disagree with us must be uninformed, or irrational. See other works by Lee Ross for a fuller general account of naïve realism and its ill-effects on human judgment. I would relate this assumption to what Keith Stanovich terms a "crystalized inhibitor," and contrasts with the critical reasoning dispositions of "fluid rationality."

15. Pronin, Kruger, Savitsky, and Ross (2001), 639.

16. Pronin, Gilovich, and Ross (2004), 781.

17. Pronin, Lin, and Ross (2002), 369.

18. Cleveland, *Disunity in Christ*, 68–70.

19. Tricia J. Yurak 2007, 344.

20. Roughly put, pluralistic ignorance is the case when a group of interacting agents all experience a discrepancy between their private opinions and the perceived opinions of the others." Yurak, 344.

21. Russell Spears, "In-group-Outgroup Bias," 484.

22. William Hirstein (2005) *Brain Fiction: Self-Deception and the Riddle of Confabulation*, 209 and 187. Compare Lisa Bortolotti: "When people confabulate they ignore some of the psychological processes responsible for the formation of their attitudes or the making of their choices, and produce an ill-grounded causal claim when asked for an explanation" (2018, 235). Confabulation theorists like Hirstein concede that studies in this area treat themselves to some strong assumptions about rationality. But this potentially fits cases of sharply asymmetric religious luck attributions exchanged between adherents of different religions. Further evidence that it does fit might be that confabulation involves failure to meet the norms of both internalist and externalist epistemologies. Internally the confabulator's failure is unaware of the implausibility of her claim, or holds it in such a way that she does not downgrade confidence even in the face of evidence of the unreliability of her doxastic strategy. In the religious case this might be the failure to be aware that her reasoning is fideistic and that those she attributes either vice or bad religious luck to can utilize very similar reasons for their own incompatible religious views. Externally the confabulator's failure might be insensitivity to the etiological symmetry between her own belief and those of other religious believers, often even as she attributes falsehood to what similar processes produce in other agents.

23. Michael Philips, *The Undercover Philosopher*, 90. "One reason it's hard to say when directional thinking occurs is that it's difficult to come up with a model or theory of how directional thinking happens. That is because directional thinking seems to involve a kind of self-deception, and self-deception is difficult to model. . . . How exactly do we pull this off? What are the processes by which we recognize evidence as relevant so that we may hide from ourselves? . . . The fact that we don't have a successful theoretical model for self-deception seriously hobbled scientific study of directional thinking" (93).

24. Philips, 89–90.

25. Philips, 91.

26. Bertram Malle, "Attributions as Behavior Explanations: Towards a New Theory," (unpublished manuscript, University of Oregon, 2003. Copyright by Bertram F. Malle). The actor–observer asymmetry is made relevant by evident due to belief reasons being more dominant over desire reasons among actors than among observers, and due to belief reasons being favored over desire reasons whenever an explainer tries to present the agent in a rational light.

27. While there are a variety of interpretive theories, the studies show among other things that causality and similarity can each form the basis for drawing a generalization. Bob Rehder, "Property Generalization as Causal Reasoning," 2008, 84. In the same volume, see also Douglas Medin and Sandra Waxman, "Interpreting Asymmetries of Projection in Children's Inductive Reasoning."

28. Malle and Knobe, 22. See also Michel and Newen (2010), and Christina Borgoni (2015).

29. Hales and Johnson, 60 and 75. But I here risk using Hales and Johnson out of context by turning the attention to the participants rather than the adequacy of theories, since the authors argue that the three main philosophical theories of luck cannot adequately accommodate their empirical results. So to stop here with luck attributions in 'folk' morality, etc., is a bit unfair to authors who argue that experimental results just as well make hay with philosophical theories of luck. My basing the value of the concept of religious luck on its diagnostic value is my main response to their skepticism about philosophical theories. These theories can allow us to articulate the implications of these empirical findings, and to frame new testable hypotheses.

30. Vainio (2010), 2.

31. Peacock and Pettyjohn 1995, 115. For a well-informed recent discussion, see Christina M. Gschwandtner 2016. For essays on faith and narrative, see Yandel 2001. Munivar (2017) connects narrative identity with still broader functions of *literature*: "Some literary scholars have begun to see literature as adaptive, and thus they think that a proper understanding of this art must be carried out in biocultural context. This is not to say that natural selection somehow adapted humans to literature, but rather that the skills that give rise to literature, when so exercised by literary art, then prove advantageous" (415).

32. If this is correct, then strong connections between *failure or belief ownership and authorship* and appeals to constitutive (moral) religious luck, and to both propositional and veritic luck, become obvious. We could give religious examples of each of these types of appeal. Bortolotti and Broom argue that "by appealing to a failure of ownership and authorship we can describe more accurately the phenomenology of thought insertion, and distinguish it from that of non-delusional beliefs that have not been deliberated about, and of other delusions of passivity." Breyer and Greco (2008), in their account of the epistemological importance of cognitive integration and the ownership of belief, hold that a belief is well-integrated in the way that brings ability and epistemic credit to the agent, not only if the subject *owns* the belief, but also *only if the (real or putative) process or ability is not subject to any defeaters to which the agent has access.* But contrary to these authors, I argue that counter-inductive methods of belief-formation have defeaters of which the agent has access. Disowning grounds for the truth or justification of belief of one's belief, against inductive pattern,

is *itself* a most serious violation of the second condition of the absence of accessible defeaters.

33. The genuine distinction between narrative and simple testimony is supported in CSR by the differences between *modal* (visualized or sensory-engaging) and *amodal* (propositional) forms of representation and processing. Modal processing is exploited by narrative to engulf the hearer in the narrative setting and make her feel what is like to have certain experiences.

34. For a well-motivated attempt to balance the intentional, world-making stance on narrative with research in the cognitive sciences, see David Herman 2013.

35. "[Claims] are statements that indicate a position has been taken. ... One of the first judgments a good critical thinker must make, then, is to determine in just what way a statement is presented. ...There are countless things one can do with words and other forms of expression" (Foresome, Fosl, and Watson (2017), *The Critical Thinking Toolkit*, 8).

36. Studies of this include instances where test subjects receive hints about (but fail to pick up on) non-literal/factual authorial intent, and others where there are no such hints but some passages read by test subjects have what most people would consider fantastical elements of some sort. Studies of this sort can be seen as focusing on another major concern of monitoring, not this time our ability to reliably monitor inner and outer sources of ideas of experiences, but of our ability to reliably monitor differences between *narrative and assertive* testimonial transmissions.

37. The stories about persons and events to whom we trace our heritage *are us,* in an important sense. Narratives, especially communal ones and ones of an epic nature, are deeply connected with people's sense of identity. Nietzsche talks about "the happiness of knowing oneself not to be wholly arbitrary and accidental, but rather growing out of a past as its heir, flower and fruit and so to be exculpated, even justified, in one's existence." The problem is when this antiquarian sense of reverence for a people's history no longer preserves life but mummifies it; when it constrains people to a very limited field of vision and when the new, or newfound facts inconsistent with it, are treated with hostility. Then it is properly countered by a critical sense of history that Nietzsche says drags it to the bar, interrogates it, and condemns what is worth condemning. Nietzsche *One the Advantage and Disadvantage of History for Life,* 21. Some of the recent best work on the distinctive features of narrative testimony is being done by in ways informed by enactivist theory. We are not just narrative but *enactive* selves: The bodily and emotional components of our awareness, and the "background to consciousness" blends with culture and contributes to diversification in ways that enactivists have studied. More attention to embodied religious practices follows from giving proper due to the role of the body in cognition (see Axtell 2018b).

38. The point was recognized in ancient Greek thought. In a quote attributed to Hypatia of Alexandria, "Fables should be taught as fables, myths as myths, and miracles as poetic fancies. To teach superstitions as truths is a most terrible thing. The child mind accepts and believes them, and only through great pain and perhaps tragedy can he be in after years relieved of them." Hypatia's point is at base a criticism of a common mistake in source monitoring –of not telling the difference between strictly historical and imaginative narratives. Even religious studies scholars struggle with the

classification of some narratives as mythical, others as religious, where the difference may only be that the mythical designation refers to dead religions—one's for which there are no present defenders who may be offended by that characterization of their sacred narrative. They are not well differentiated by content.

39. If this is correct then narrative testimony is *not* well suited to placing the agent in position to have well-justified testimonially based beliefs, beyond one's about the structure, plot, or themes of the narrative itself.

40. Roger Pouivet (2002) is an exception. He tries to rehabilitate healthy respect for the role of the religious imagination, tying this to classical tradition (Aquinas) as well as to contemporary narrative theology.

41. Rachel Fraser, "The Pragmatics and Epistemology of Testimony." Podcast of her at the Moral Sciences Club (Cambridge), May 16, 2017. Accessed from https://sms.csx.cam.ac.uk/media/2481645.

42. Montaigne points this out when he writes, "It comes to pass that nothing is so firmly believed as that which we know least; nor are there any persons so sure of themselves as those who tell us fables... to which I would join, if I dared, a host of persons, interpreters and verifiers-in-ordinary of the designs of God." *Essays,* Bk. I, 32.

43. Hume and James both correctly argue that first-personal experience may rationally ground someone's belief in something that it would not rationally ground for someone else who only heard testimony of the experience second-hand.

44. This is also why Kierkegaard also finds Lessing compelling, and the gap between subjective conviction and objective knowledge impossible to bridge. Purported truths of revelation are not plausibly synthetic a priori.

45. Arguably, with no less and perhaps substantially more plausible grounds in the traits of a good and loving God, God could have used his freedom to allow *more* that more than one prophet, revelation, or religion is a vehicle of genuinely salvific revelation. In so doing, this unbounded God would also be addressing the problems of epistemic location, selective access, and evidential ambiguity from the human perspective, since decision under conditions of underdetermination by evidence impacts both theism versus non-theism, and one particular testimonial tradition over others.

46. A more accurate term than proof-texting here may be *Eisegesis,* which can refer to a whole text rather than a selective passage being taken out of context. Eisegesis refers to interpreting a text in a way that imports one's own presuppositions, agendas, or biases *into* and/or *onto* that text. This term also makes for a strong connection between fideistic uptake and the previously discussed issue of conflating narrative and simple testimony. I would relate this to how, in the field of biblical exegesis, it is sometimes said that *'eisegesis* is poor *exegesis,'* and in post-liberalism it is arguably present in the notion that all genuine understanding comes from studying a text "intra-textually."

47. Carroll (2008, 18), notes, "If 'fideism' were defined loosely as the idea that the truth about religious matters cannot be established by natural reason alone, then the vast majority of religious thought—among the many religions in the world—would be fideistic." This is close to what I mean by a fideistic minimum. Descriptively, few come to their beliefs by objective reasoning.

48. Lessing, 55. Lessing writes, "That, then, is the ugly, broad ditch which I cannot get across, however often and however earnestly I have tried to make the leap." Asserting the "fact" that the source of religious truth is revelation, or that, as special revelation is inerrant, can gloss over this gap to make it less noticeable, but it never can never truly bridge it.

49. The bees, working collectively, spiral up above the fruits. But the interpretation of faith that apologists for religious exclusivism leads them to dig for roots, and has the potential at least to go spiraling down into an alethic stalemate between exclusivist communities. For Lessing's parable, good relations between the 'three sons of Abraham' are judged to be an indication of the veracity of the ring(s): its blessing upon its wearer is in good part that it is able to bring harmony and flourishing. We might interpret their prize *as* the ring(s). Lessing's tale is of a ring of many colors and bright stones, a ring inherited by the son from his father, going back many generations. It was a *prized* ring, this "ring of inestimable worth [whose] real value lay it its ability to make its wearer beloved of God and humankind." So the ring(s) take the shape of the prize, and Barth and Lindbeck are certainly talking about the same thing in so far as the "prize' involves a person's trust in veridicality of their personal and group experiences, and the sincerity of their own testimonial tradition's elders/founders.

50. Italics added. Lindbeck continues, "Thus of all the religions and professedly non-religious *Weltanschauungen* which aspires embrace without being embraced, only one, if that, can be ultimately successful" ("The Gospel's Uniqueness," 430). But in Lessing's tale, this is exactly the claim that leads the three proverbial 'sons of Abraham' to fall into quarreling. For the ring had come down to a father with three sons, whom he loved equally, so before dying he went to a smythe, and upon his deathbed called each son in alone, and gave him a ring as his own final blessing. But barely had the father been put into the ground before the sons took notice that they each had a ring indiscernibly different to all who looked on them without wearing them, and took to quarrel over who had the true one of the father. A wise judge had to intervene into this sibling rivalry to challenge the sons by saying that if this ill-will were the practical result of wearing a ring from the father, likely the true ring was lost, or had now lost its powers and its value: for outward practical and social fruits had originally been a big part of its blessing, and that which is most evident to a neutral judge.

51. Many theists embrace the religion-specific exclusivist 'leap of faith,' understood as courageous and heroic, or as humble and pious; but others have denied its necessity, and still others have acknowledged it but been embarrassed by it, since moral objections follow the epistemic ones. Gary Habermas (1991) points out that "Lessing's 'ugly ditch' and Kant's 'mighty chasm,' which we do not jump, have become an 'abyss' [in Barth's words] into which we take a leap by exercising faith in Christ." Barth's distinction between [Habermas, Gary R., "An Appraisal of the Leap of Faith" (1991). Faculty Publications and Presentations. Paper 398. http://digitalcommons.liberty.edu/lts_fac_pubs/398].

52. Margalit, 1996, 150.

53. Margalit, 150.

54. Unless there is the clearest consensus about authorial intent and the relation of narrative to historical fact, narrative testimony should very plausibly be treated by philosophers of religion as only minimally truth-apt. This supports theologians who argue that faith and belief should be distinguished, and that fundamentalist inerrantism and literalism is both too strong and too weak as an understanding of religious faith.

55. A propositional view of revelation is presupposed in salvific and doctrinal (sometimes called alethic) exclusivism, a view on which revelation is God's Word, and the agent's role is to assent to it *as* truth. 'God said it, and God said believe it,' is pretty much all one needs to know. Faith in a promise, or faith in one's God gets reduced to faith *that* the teachings and the narrative are inerrantly *true*. On the propositional view of revelation, revelation is historical and not existential. As one author puts it, "Revelation according to this theory is originally given to a few privileged recipients, to whom the word of God comes directly. Prophets receive the word of God as an interior gift. ... Revelation, having been received by the prophets and apostles, is then handed down in scriptures and tradition, which constitute the written and oral vehicles of the word of God." Dulles, "The Problem of Revelation," 78. On non-propositional views, by contrast, "the term 'Christian revelation' is not itself exclusive or intolerant. A Christian can acknowledge the existence of 'Mosaic revelation' or even 'Islamic revelation.' There is no impossibility of God revealing himself at different times in different ways, as Hebrews 1.1 asserts that he has in fact done. The alleged superiority of God's revelation in Christ is not an automatic consequence that follows from belief in Christianity as a particular revelation." If the exclusivist attitude takes hold, it is usually more through an all-or-nothing Christological doctrine than from the concept of revelation.

56. Griffiths, Apology for Apologetics, 2.

57. Barth's language suggests that Christian faith is virtuous while that of religious aliens is vicious. He and Alvin Plantinga thus serve as examples of *particularist exclusivism,* which we will later contrast with the *mutuality exclusivism* of Gellman, Griffiths, and Margalit.

58. Several authors have done extensive work on debates over the implications of religious diversity for religious epistemics. These include Paul Knitter, David Basinger, James Kraft, and Michael Thune, though I will only treat Knitter here (see Bibliography).

59. Knitter (2002, 233).

60. D'Costa 1996, 225. Note that Plantinga and D'Costa both hold that Knitter's "inclusivism" collapses into exclusivism. My own taxonomy is simplified rather than expanded from the standard one that includes pluralism as a separate position from inclusivism. My treating inclusivism as the denial of exclusivism has the advantage of saying that the complete dichotomy resolves Plantinga and D'Costa's claim. But in practice way that in inclusivism the religious alien's potential "fulfillment" of the goals of their religion through the goals of the home religion (for instance, through Christ's sacrifice) makes inclusivism look like warmed up exclusivism. Given the way we have defined the dichotomy, this is not how we are using the term. My proposal is that the luck-free theology project, and the "three kinds of adequacy" rule, enables distinguishing the cases where inclusivism seems to collapse into

exclusivism. Theology of religions could be an example of this, but so could other comparative theological research projects such as Neville's pragmatic theology.

61. Grube (2015), 421. For fuller development, see also Grube and van Herck (eds.) 2018. Grube argues that this is one of the ways (another is sociological or other (including post-modernist 'reductionisms') *of depriving the concept of truth of its normative function*. He points out Joseph Margolis (1991) as arguing against bivalence as a general logical principle taken as holding indiscriminately across domains of inquiry. Margolis argues that there are many domains where applying a bivalence principle is misguided.

62. Grube describes a "critique of bivalence" and the "standard model" prioritizing truth over epistemics as "a springboard" for developing his constructive alternative. Grube's form of (what I call) mutualist religious epistemics is *also* consistent with holding that some doxastic ventures are responsible while others are not, and with moral and intellectual norms leading to recasting theological/soteriological accounts. Grube does not comment on salvific exclusivism or soteriological evil, but does indicate that there are good *theological* reasons for respecting other religions" (419). Grube calls for "criteria to distinguish between" responsible and irresponsible faith ventures, and of course this book considers not 'nurtured,' but counter-inductive aetiology and asymmetric 'privileging' (or simply, luck-leaning), along with risk to others, as prime criteria.

63. John Locke's *A Letter Concerning Toleration* contains a related critical reflection on what we are calling biased-closure inferences among the religious enthusiasts of different testimonial faith-traditions: "But if one of these churches hath this power of treating the other ill, I ask which of them it is to whom that power belongs, and by what right? It will be answered, undoubtedly, that it is the Orthodox Church which has the right of authority over the erroneous or heretical. This is, in great and specious words, to say just nothing at all. For every church is orthodox to itself; to others, erroneous or heretical. For whatsoever any church believes, it believes to be true and the contrary unto those things it pronounce; to be error. So that the controversy between these churches about the truth of their doctrines and the purity of their worship is on both sides equal; nor is there any judge, either at Constantinople or elsewhere upon earth, by whose sentence it can be determined" (124).

64. Aikin and Talisse (2013) explain what I am calling easy knowledge problems in simpler terms in their textbook *Why We Argue (and How we Should)*. They relate the *Simple Truth* and *No Reasonable Opposition* theses. The first says that disagreement over Big Questions "always admit simple, obvious, and viable, and easily—stated answers. [It] encourages us to hold that a given truth is so simple and so obvious that only the ignorant, wicked, devious, or benighted could possibly deny it." They see the second thesis as a corollary of the first: "According to the *No Reasonable Opposition* thesis, argument and debate with those with whom one disagrees is a pointless and futile endeavor. If in fact the answer to a given Big Question is a Simple Truth, then there is no opponent of that answer who is not also woefully ignorant, misinformed, misguided, wicked, or worse" (61).

65. Gellman, 403. Kelly (2008) connects what I am calling biased-closure inferences to belief polarization, and to Kripke's account of it. "It is characteristic of the

Kripkean dogmatist to treat apparent counterevidence in a dismissive manner. Indeed, a Kripkean dogmatist need not even attend to the specific content of such evidence: as soon as he knows that a given piece of evidence tells against one of his beliefs, he knows all that he needs to know in order to employ his general policy; he thus pays it no further heed" (8). Kelly discusses the *principle of the commutivity of evidence,* but goes on to give an alternative account of belief polarization. But the issue is that whatever I believe *first,* can then be used to dismiss as not relevant to learning, anything that contradicts what I learn first. It is certainly pertinent to an epistemology for controversial views that the justification for our nurtured beliefs seems rarely to abide by the evidentialist principle of the *commutivity of evidence.* Rather, earlier-acquired evidence generally settles belief in such a way that reinforcements on a pattern of confirmation and myside bias seem to be the norm for humans, and the individual making a break due to an assessment that total evidence does not support the initial enculturated belief, is rare.

66. Hood, Hill, and Williamson, 2005, 194. "[For some Christians, for example] trusting that Jesus' words are not intentionally deceitful and that the Gospel accounts are historically accurate is an act of faith. . . . [I]t is only when the sacred text emerges and is understood as sufficient in itself, and as the ultimate criterion of truth, that fundamentalism emerges—not as a religion, but as a way or process of being religious within a given faith tradition." If any part of the sacred text is allowed to be shown in error by such means, the entire text loses authority, as many scholars both in sympathy with and in opposition to fundamentalism have noted" (192). Brand Blanshard voices the classical dilemma for inerrancy: "It is sometimes argued that the human author must either be a passive agent (which raises all the problems of inerrancy as well as being psychologically implausible and plainly inapplicable to many of the biblical writers) or be employing his own creative capacities to the full (leaving no room for the alleged activity of God). ... Either revelation is totally immune from rational criticism, or it is subject to such criticism. If the former, it is wholly discontinuous with our ordinary standards of what is reasonable and right; if the latter, it can have no independent authority" (quoted and discussed in B. Mitchell 1973, 144).

67. My arguments may not have convinced all my readers that the strength of religious fideism is an important orientation to develop psychological scales for, or that strong fideistic orientation tracks formal features of highly counter-inductive thinking. But I take the book thus far to have provided ample reason for concluding that belief-acquisition, revision, or maintenance that plies on highly counter-inductive thinking may be challenged as epistemically vicious *wherever* it may be found.

Chapter 5

Scaling the 'Brick Wall'

Measuring and Censuring Strongly Fideistic Religious Orientation

THE MANY SOURCES OF RELIGIOUS DIVERSITY

Before we discussed the epistemic location problem in part I, we located concerns about the historic, geographic, and demographic contingency of people's nurtured controversial views within a much broader set of recognized sources of cognitive diversity. The epistemic location problem is one of the most unavoidable of these sources of contrariety, being basic to the human condition. But on the present view there are multiple sources of cognitive diversity that any balanced approach to the limits of reasonable disagreement should recognize. This is why we brought up the close relationship between beliefs that are underdetermined by evidence, and beliefs or doxastic strategies that are overdetermined by what John K. Davis terms trait-dependent factors. This chapter will develop those connections, and will largely conclude the side of the inductive risk account that challenges religious exclusivism with a de jure objection. Here we also discuss more generally what force, what censure, a proper de jure objection can have for those against whom it is made.

The first section looks at trait-dependence together with evidential ambiguity, since the ambiguity of total evidence, experienced especially in domains of morals, politics, philosophy, and religion, heightens the ensuing need to render holistic or all-things-considered assessments of claims made these domains. We will examine especially different *attitudes* toward evidential ambiguity, and what psychologists and religious fundamentalists say about it. This is background for the ensuing sections of this chapter. The second section continues our study of fundamentalist orientation by distinguishing psychological (or descriptive) from religious (or prescriptive) fideism. This in turn allows us to better recognize not only that the multiplicity of models of faith that religious adherents adhere to, but also that the relationship between forms of fideism is *scalar*: there is a spectrum of views running from rationalism to fideism, and at the fideistic end of this spectrum are important differences between moderate and strong forms of religious fideism. I further explain why developing tests and markers for a high degree of fideistic orientation is important to all those who study religion.

We have already talked a good deal about salvific exclusivism, and about exclusivist responses to religious multiplicity. But we have not yet made one crucial distinction reflected in the literature: the distinction between religion-specific and mutualist exclusivism. The mutualist does not talk just about the right of adherents of one specific religion to assert exclusivism, but the adherents of any and all "home" religions. So in the remaining sections of this chapter I return to the de jure challenge, arguing that some previously unrecognized problems for the reasonableness of exclusivist responses to religious multiplicity are brought to light when we make this distinction between these two basic ways to understand the claim that exclusivists are making. I then try to put particularist and mutualist defenses of exclusivist responses to religious multiplicity on the horns of a dilemma. Paying special attention to apologetics for exclusivism that run along mutualist lines, I argue that despite the popularity it presently enjoys among post-liberal theologians, a close examination reveals that the very conceptual coherence of mutualist exclusivism is in serious doubt.

Ollie-Pekka Vainio's work, as mentioned earlier, is exemplary of Christian philosophy that is empirically informed by social and cognitive psychology. In *Beyond Fideism: Negotiable Religious Identities* (2010), the author affirms the value of religious identities, together with "a framework of negotiability" and a sharp critique of what he calls the current wave of post-liberalism. Vainio's analysis of religious fideism and its various kinds adds to Terence Penelhum's earlier distinction between skeptical and conformist religious fideism. Vainio identifies conformism mainly with *non-reflective fideism,* where an individual accepts a religious identity and associated beliefs under influence of their surrounding family or culture, and without much care for epistemically good reasons, or for etiological challenges.

Vainio goes on to say that "Non-reflective conformist fideism . . . is not very interesting (while being without doubt of the most common belief-forming methods in the world)."[1] Here, however, I will take issue. Vainio seems to be setting normative standards for what is better seen as a descriptive distinction between skeptical fideism (where adherents hold that there is no religious *knowledge,* though there may be responsible belief) and conformist fideism (which simply assumes the authority of the "home" religious culture).[2] Conformist fideism as a category used by psychologists does not impugn the adherent's virtue or categorize them as non-reflective. But contented religious exclusivism, by the very description given by its defenders (Gellman; Margalit;

D'Costa) places itself in Vainio's "non-reflective fideism" category. For Gellman describes this agent's complete "unconcern" for what religious aliens have to say about the validity of their own religious way of life. Of course, one wants to encourage virtues of doxastic responsibility, and at least in every other area of life this would seem to require careful reflection about disagreement.[3] But the doxastic methods (or "policies" as Vainio puts it) that are most common among us are far from being of little interest to theorists who study religion. Indeed, CF and CSR likely should be *most* concerned with those modes of belief-acquisition and maintenance that are most common; conformist fideism and its default, relatively unreflective style are of high, not low, interest. So while it is commonplace for theologians to admonish the mere rule-followers, or those who merely say the words but do not mean them as they should, that admonishment of conformist fideism indicates a theological value in favor of holding belief in a more passionate embrace.

These considerations show us that Vainio's reflective/unreflective fideism distinction is prescriptive rather than descriptive. For instance he writes, "In philosophy, fideism usually means a mode of thought or teaching according to which reason is more-or-less irrelevant to (religious) belief, or even that faith is strengthened, not undermined, if one judges that reason is unable to give it support."[4] The mode of thought or teaching here is understood as something *prescribed* by a model of faith. We will discuss prescriptive fideism at points going forward, but while it may be of theological interest in psychology of religion, descriptive fideism is the proper focus for psychology and religious studies scholars. It seems to be a fault of Vainio's book that the author does not better mark these distinctions. Descriptive fideism does not provide an account of what faith properly is, but rather of how people acquire and hold their religious beliefs through passionate attachment. It recognizes that their inferences are not bound by evidence and argument. But it recognizes a range of supra and counter-evidential models of faith, and does not define fideism by the extreme of counter-evidential belief.

The models of faith (theological methods) most like one another in fideistic orientation are those most likely to take a propositional view of their scriptures. They are those, indeed, which cycle through some or all of the 'steps' discussed in chapter 3, that foment fundamentalism. What from the standpoint of logical norms is an 'inductive fail' is from the strong fideist's perspective the grounds of difference that allow denial of the epistemic significance of disagreement. McKim points out that "Advocates of large-scale systems of beliefs that include discrediting mechanisms are not in a position to appreciate the appeal to systems of belief they think to be discredited. They are not likely to be able to give them a fair or sympathetic hearing."[5]

McKim's point seems confirmed by Gellman's definition of the contented exclusivist as one for whom "the home religion will teach that it is true and that other religions are false to the extent that they clash with the home religion. One's home religion will include as a matter of course, a ready explanation for the failures of other religions to recognize the truth."[6] But if adherents of each home religion can do this to every one of the others, then given 100 home religions, 99% would be judged false by all others, all of the time, and nobody has any reason to ever take a close look at anybody else's discrediting or vice-charging reasons. How does this not implicate what we earlier termed rhetorical vice-charging? That implication is only strengthened given that the right to ascribe such negative traits to outsiders and to take an exclusivist attitude is, for Gellman, clearly independent of any connection with truth. This is why the New Problem's thought experiment of our switching places with a religious other, is a step forward to seeing the force of inductive norms. It might be better, though, to reverse the order, asking if under these conditions the exclusivist could plausibly deny that they would be likely to also come to believe that the faith the individual *in fact* holds as the uniquely true and salvific one, is false and non-salvific.[7] For if the experiment leads to conceding that they would in other circumstances have come to hold religious beliefs that *are by their own lights erroneous* and to reject beliefs *by their own lights uniquely true*, disagreement may begin to be taken as more significant. Its reasonableness is arguably shown up. No longer can disagreement be treated as a 'bare fact' easily explained by relevant metaphysical, epistemological, or moral differences between home and alien religions or sects. The exclusivist's discrediting mechanisms of denying epistemic peerhood with unbelievers, and of explaining this denial by asymmetrical metaphysical, epistemological, or moral trait-ascriptions, becomes harder to motivate.[8] The thought experiment bears directly on whether the bias charges that are supposed to confirm the errors of the religious alien's ways are better seen as "robust" or merely "rhetorical." The discrediting mechanisms of exclusivist apologetics are much better developed than in other domains, and they very often involve strategies of vice or bias-charging. The religious alien's failure to see the truth of the home religion calls for explanation, and how would that be accomplished without charging unbelievers with ill-motivation or bias? So for Gellman, "[M]y contented exclusivist may rationally believe that all religions other than the home religion are works of the devil, and that the devil tricks others into believing them."[9] Here I would simply question what the author means by "rationally believe"?

Some philosophers who study fundamentalism note how ambiguity is unreasonably devalued in fundamentalist and exclusivist religiosity. Imran Aijaz (2014; 2013) critiques this devaluation and the attendant denial of inculpable non-belief in traditional Islam, arguing that these attitudes are philosophically unsound. As Jamie Holmes also points out, fearful or highly negative/dogmatic responses to moral or cognitive ambiguity by fundamentalists do not reflect a balanced view. The feeling of ambiguity, including evidential ambiguity for theistic belief, is not *inherently* negative. Holmes understands the feeling of ambiguity as an "emotional amplifier," but this feeling "is not always unpleasant" and can spawn creativity. Psychologically, "we're programmed to get rid of ambiguity, and yet if we engage with it we can make better decisions, we can be more creative, and we can even be a little more empathetic." Holmes' research highlights the many ways embracing ambiguity improves people's ability to problem-solve and think critically.

> A lot of times it [ambiguity] is threatening, just because of the content of what we happen to be facing: whether I'm going to be fired, or a physical threat, or the uncertainty of a medical diagnosis. But there's also great research that shows that if we're uncertain about whether someone's romantically interested in us, or if we're uncertain about whether something good or really good might happen to us, then those experiences are even more pleasurable than they usually are.[10]

Holmes's psychological perspective on the benefits of ambiguity, whether experienced as pleasant or not, supports more philosophical discussion on religious ambiguity and the difference between exclusivist and inclusivist responses to religious multiplicity. McKim (2012) provides a complementary philosophical perspective, distinguishing between contexts of *simple, rich,* and *extremely rich* evidential ambiguity. He then argues that even the question of the existence of God exhibits rich ambiguity, the main defining features of which are:

> that there is an abundance of relevant evidence; that this evidence is diverse in its character, multifaceted, and complicated; that it contains discrete pockets of evidence that are particularly congenial to the advocates of particular interpretations of the evidence; that one group regards as evidence phenomena that are not so regarded by other groups; and that it is extremely difficult to tell whether there is more evidence for one side or the other.[11]

This sounds very much like the epistemic situation that William James describes before going on in his famous "The Will to Believe" lecture to reject "the veto . . . which the strict positivist pronounces upon our faith," and to affirm a person's intellectual right to self-aware religious doxastic ventures that suit their affective character:

> For such a half-wild half-saved universe our nature is adapted. The deepest thing in our nature is this dumb region of the heart in which we dwell alone with our willingnesses and our unwillingnesses, our faiths and our fears. As through the cracks and crannies of caverns those waters exude from the earth's bosom which then form the fountain-heads of springs, so in these crepuscular depths of personality the sources of all our outer deeds and decisions take their rise. Here is our deepest organ of communication with the nature of things.[12]

Many writers focus on one source of contrariety in domains of controversial views. William James and J.S. Mill focus on character types and "crepuscular depths of personality," hinting at the recognition of the partly somatic "background" to conscious experience, and the foreground/background distinction that John Dewey would later develop. Kidd (2013) follows James in focusing heavily on individual temperament as a key source of reasonable disagreement,[13] while Hick and McKim focus much more on the religiously ambiguous nature of evidence for deciding between what James would call "the religious hypothesis" and the "naturalistic hypothesis." I am here focused more on social identity and doxastic risk-taking, but also want to show the complementarity of the various sources of psychographic diversity. For our study the main point is that the sources of diversity, especially but not exclusively found in our controversial views, are *many*. They include symbolic aspects of cultural identity, religious ambiguity, confirmation holism, and what John Rawls calls the "burdens of judgment."[14] Pragmatic reasons for belief, when they are recognized, are another source of cognitive diversity.[15] We should keep in mind that the different forms of inductive reasoning –generalization, cause-effect reasoning and analogy/disanalogy– are not always kept distinct in our reasoning, and especially not in inference to the best explanation. The holistic nature of evidence for worldviews and ideologies is correctly recognized as a source of diversity, as is the balance a person must choose between intellectual courage and caution, believing truly versus not believing falsehoods.[16] What we should aim at in the next section's account of descriptive fideism is a more balanced view of these sources of religious multiplicity, and of the trait-dependent factors that overdetermine belief when belief or another propositional attitude is logically underdetermined by agent-neutral evidence and argument.

To summarize this section, models of faith (theological methods) that are like one another in strongly fideistic orientation are ones most likely to take a propositional view of their scriptures and to run adherents through the other 'steps' that foment fundamentalism, or the enemy in the mirror effect (EME) more precisely. These morally and intellectually paradoxical forms of faith establish responses to multiplicity that devalue dialogue across traditions, apart from evangelizing where that is part of the group's perceived mission. All truth being contained within the home religion, there is nothing really to learn from "dialogue" with non-believers, and perhaps even a positive moral danger in associating with them in any relationship other than an evangelizing one.

DESCRIPTIVE AND PRESCRIPTIVE FIDEISM: A CRUCIAL DISTINCTION

Fideism has been the subject of a good deal of interest in both theology and philosophy of religion. I want to start by saying that it is clearly one of numerous philosophical concepts that it is crucial to recognize has distinct descriptive and prescriptive senses.[17] To clarify this with other examples, think of the concepts of ethical relativism, or again, of ethical egoism. The former is a metaethical theory, while the latter is a normative ethical theory. But in both cases, the thesis the concept identifies is a normative one about how people *should* understand ethical claims (relativism) or about what motives moral agents should act from (egoism). But there is in the attendant argument for these positions, an appeal to psychology, and to how ethical statements *actually* function, or the motives for which people *actually* act (psychological egoism). Textbooks and online encyclopedias of philosophy routinely note the centrality of the descriptive/prescriptive (or psychological/normative) distinction when engaging either of these debates, and I take it that philosophy which fails to do so is never able to articulate a clear question for debate. To follow the egoism example further, confusion in philosophy itself between *is's* and *oughts,* between claims about how people do act and how they normatively should act, etc., makes it easy to wind up in a pseudo-debate. This can also reductively make the 'how we ought to' question follow simply from the 'how we in fact do make judgments' question, when there is really quite a large gap between these two questions.

The same is true in regard to philosophical and theological debate surrounding reason and religious faith: without distinguishing psychological observations or claims about human nature from how different models of faith prescribe thinking about reason and faith, it is easy to talk past one another. But once the distinction is made, the relationship *between* "allowing" a descriptive claim and "endorsing" a normative one can be better approached.[18] The Clifford–James debate over the ethics of belief might be an example of this. I have heard it said that Clifford could have come closer to James had he taken a wider view of "evidence" and of "sufficiency" of evidence, accepting pragmatic reasons along with strictly epistemic ones. And reciprocally, James could have come closer to Clifford had he taken a wider view of "faith ventures," accepting that they may take something other than the status of beliefs. Both proposals make a good deal of sense, but for both men their shared assumption of volitionism actually served to harden their positions, leading each into the kind of conflation in question. For Clifford a person *ought* not to accept faith-based believing, because in fact such beliefs are evidentially underdetermined. For James one's passional nature *ought to* decide for or against the religious hypothesis, because given the fact of underdetermination, it *must* be the deciding factor.

Psychological fideism is a unitary thesis, and one that makes a testable claim. Prescriptive fideism stands for any instance of multiple models of how the faithful *should* think, especially about the relationship between reason and faith. Those psychologists who try to confirm or disconfirm the hypothesis of descriptive fideism will need to recognize numerous proximate causes of religious multiplicity, including epistemic and psychographic location, a religiously ambiguous world, individual temperament and aesthetics, etc.[19] In *Varieties of Religious Experience,* William James insists that "among the buildings-out of religion which the mind spontaneously indulges in, the aesthetic motive must never be forgotten." This is a description of one of several factors causally involved with the 'building-out' of particular religious identities.

The plurality of models available by which to understand the relationship between reason and religious faith is not well acknowledged in our debates, which is part of the problem. The major religiosity and spirituality scales utilized in religious studies and psychology do not aim to sort between different types and degrees of fideistic orientation. I do not believe great progress can be made in this debate until we recognize the diversity of conceptions of faith, even within Christian tradition itself. A specific model of faith is often the unquestioned first assumption that guides a religious grouping's way of attributing religious value or disvalue to group insiders and outsiders. This does not mean that the model one adopts as authoritative is simply dictated by one's religion. Each major world religion allows for interpretation and for a range of different models of faith, models that may have *different types of objects* and that may express different ways in which an adherent is *related to those objects.*[20]

It seems descriptively true that what is taught at an early age to be religious faith's demands will for most people tend to become for them a first assumption, and something inviolable. But it also seems correct that many of these faith models are more problematic than others from logical, epistemic, and moral points of view. So we must insist that models of faith are not 'above the battle,' but are for reasonable and responsible agents subject to normative criticism of at least the three kinds we have identified. Models of faith should be the first rather than the last thing that a doxastically responsible agent assesses for adequacy. The plurality of these models, and how they are expressed in patterns of thinking along a spectrum from weak to strong fideism, should be an explicit concern for CF, and as we will argue more specifically in chapter 6, for CSR as well.[21]

Our study in chapters 1 and 2 focused critical attention on how particular models of faith can aggravate luck-related worries, and this also suggests a need to recognize a plurality of models of faith operant in religious communities. This descriptive pluralism about theological methods complicates religious epistemics. Let me outline for the reader several reasons why comparative fundamentalism should focus upon differences among *models of faith* rather than *denominational* differences. Firstly, the debate among adherents of different religions is largely a matter of theology and apologetics, and when they are, they fail to readily engage philosophy and the human sciences. Secondly, the differences between Catholic, Orthodox, and

Protestant branches of Christianity, or related main branches of Judaism or Islam, suggest that "orthodoxy" is and has always been a more fluid concept than fundamentalists allow, since, as Voltaire put it, each religious viewpoint is orthodox unto itself.

Thirdly, conceptions of theological adequacy are subject to broad intellectual movements such as progressivism and liberalism, which sought to render faith acceptable to reason and to modern sensibilities even if this leads to theological revisions. These movements often hold even across religions, while at the same time, almost all major world religions show a range of conservative to revisionary positions. Fourthly, even within sects, as seen vividly in Protestant traditions but well-evidenced elsewhere as well, there is no single agreed model of faith –no single view that uncontroversially designates what faith is and means. Therefore, to emphasize differences between religions or between denominations would be to focus only on the content claims of different religions but to miss seeing models of faith as what so often drives substantive differences among doctrines and attitudes.

When the proximate causes of religious beliefs or avowals are roughly symmetrical, fideistic orientation is strong, and purported prophets or special revelations are numerous, we have an environment for religious epistemics that is rife for the generation of exclusivist ideologies. Similarly generated, each becomes a 'sibling rival' of all others. Inductively speaking, the greater degree of conflicting beliefs that spawn from a formally similar pattern of belief-acquisition, the weaker its grounds. Think of this as the inverse of the famous *diversity of evidence principle* which is ubiquitous in the different forms of induction, accruing to generalization, causal, and analogical reasoning. This combination of inductively weak grounds and contrariety in the output of a belief makes disagreement in such cases *quite* epistemically significant. But among theologians and not just apologists, instead of recognition of this we too often get merely a notional acknowledgment of etiological symmetry.[22]

If a person is relying on testimonial transfer, or even appeal to facts to support their beliefs, there are very basic inductive norms that reasonability demands conformity with. These norms prescribe that we: acknowledge that people may be mistaken about what they believe to be fact; be cautious in characterizing a statement as making a factual claim if it is equivocal between 'is' and 'ought'; be cautious with claiming factuality or historicity for things not widely agreed upon; use facts that have been verified by reliable sources, and where there is no consensus among experts, consult multiple and diverse sources; and consider whether sources of claims are neutral or given to directional thinking.

Then there are inductive risk norms: Where beliefs are a ground for decisions and actions, we must agree that reasonableness demands that we recognize the risks, to others as well as oneself, of holding beliefs unsafely. Responsibility demands that we spend extra time to verify facts where the risk of getting it wrong could result in harm to others; and that we abide by the diversity principle by looking for the sources of cognitive and moral diversity, and by considering the empirical, conceptual, and axiological (valuative) issues in any particular disagreement from diverse points of view.

Now, to say that a mode of thinking is counter-inductive is also to characterize it as counter-evidential: this would seem to follow by definition. The implicit but clear claim is just as Wittgenstein put it: "The pattern stops here." How counter-inductive one's claim is depends entirely, it would seem, on how strong the violated pattern was, and what reasons one has claiming a violation of the pattern. How strong the pattern was is determined scientifically, when it can be determined at all, by employing the diversity of evidence principle. Phenomenal seemings are controversial grounds for assuming other-worldly, or even this-worldly truth. But if it does not matter to someone how counter-evidential the ground of their belief is, either because they think faith requires subjective certainty and expulsion of all doubt, or because they shut down critical reflection by conflating subjective certitude with objective *grounds* for a truth claim, then the 'shoe' of *radical fideism* clearly fits. Our theory suggests that persons who easily dismiss etiological challenges through responses that violated inductive norms will scale at the high end of the spectrum of orientations running from moderately to strongly fideistic. Those who deny or rationalize-away the epistemic force of inductive norms, and the moral concerns with risking others in our practical reasoning, similarly exemplify the radical fideistic view that faith 'needs no justification from reason.'[23]

Counter-inductive religious thinking is on our account an indicator of a strong as contrasted with a moderately fideistic theological method. The reader familiar with philosophy of religion might therefore assume that I intend to employ the distinction between "supra-evidential" and "counter-evidential" fideism, since this is perhaps the most common way that philosophers of religion have tried to mark kinds or degrees of fideistic orientation. However, I hold that the supra/counter-evidential distinction is helpful neither to philosophy nor psychology of religion. The idea behind that distinction is that some *beliefs* are consistent with total evidence yet go beyond it (moderate fideism), while other beliefs 'fly in the face' of total evidence (strong fideism). While such a distinction may aim to get at what encourages those who John Locke and other Enlightenment thinkers described as religious enthusiasts, it does a poor job of it. The related distinction between "reflective" and "unreflective" fideism that Vainio employs I think has some of the same flaws, since it does not distinguish critical self-reflection from a use of reason in the service of apologetics, where one's pre-existing beliefs are never genuinely questioned, but only defended. The post hoc and ad hoc use of reason when so enlisted to defend unquestioned first principles is often an indication of more rather than less extreme fideism.[24] When it comes to tribalistic particularism, the defense of the worldview may be purely negative, a "basic belief" imbued by God, not by culture; or it may an evidentialist apologetic, taking on the trappings of science, as in new speciation-denying 'scientific creationism.'[25]

This book's concern with counter-inductive thinking has a clear association with counter-evidential fideism, and the old distinction between "supra" and "counter" evidential fideism seems to recognize the importance of there being degrees of fideism. So why shouldn't we accept it? The supra/counter contrast is a blunt tool; the concept of "counter-evidential" imports a belief-focused account inconsistent with the methods of the sciences. What the total evidence is for something like God's existence is of course disputed, and matters get still murkier with respect to claims derived from purported special revelations. Social scientists should not be tied to classifying agents and their beliefs in this way, a way that makes them judge the synchronic level of evidence supporting a belief, in order to recognize the agent's theological method as either moderately (supra-evidential) or strongly (counter-evidential) fideistic.

These points are worth elaborating because they explain why I take an inductive risk-based approach to classifying forms of fideism as far more helpful to philosophers and psychologists both. The main reason why the approach to identifying and measuring strongly fideistic orientation is in need of rehabilitation is that the supra/counter distinction leaves the researcher with unwanted "Who decides?" questions. Who decides the level of total evidence for a religious belief, in order to know whether it is supra or counter-evidential? The 'strong fideism equals counter-evidential' approach seems to assume a belief rather than agent-based approach. It neglects *how* the agent makes inferences, focusing instead on degree of epistemic justification.[26] By contrast, we have proceeded from a twin focus, the first focus being asymmetrical religious trait attributions as a primary psychological concern, and the second being problems of religious luck as reflected in moral, epistemological, and theological perspectives on this primary data of asymmetrical religious trait attributions. These two grounds led us to interest in a broader study of fideistic orientation, one that, by focusing on epistemically risky methods of belief-acquisition, directly addresses *how* the agent makes inferences.

But few persons who are descriptively (i.e., from a third-person perspective) fideistic in their conception of faith describe *themselves* as holding beliefs counter-evidentially. Tertullian, Kierkegaard, and paradox-embracing Buddhists and Sufis get classified as counter-evidential and hence as extreme fideists, mostly just for honestly admitting mysteries of faith, and the limits of reason and knowledge in religious metaphysics.[27] Pascal opined that "Man is more inconceivable without this mystery than this mystery is inconceivable to man." The problem is not in recognizing paradoxes in faith-based belief, but in *failing* to recognize them, an act of trying to deny the intellect and to simultaneously claim it for oneself. Propositionalism can withstand paradox no more than support reasonably disagreeing peers. While there probably has been no historical instance of a conception of faith that eschews reason *completely*, there are clearly instances that engender a Conflict model of the relationship between religion and on the one hand, and science on the other. Yet in fact how much more extreme are those who exhibit self-delusion about total evidence? Affectively driven evaluations of total evidence thrive on conflation between the *de dicto* and *de re* standing of evidence, that is, roughly, between subjective conviction and objective certitude.

Relatedly, we should reject definitions of *normative* fideism that identify it with claiming a right or mandate to believe counter-evidentially, or *against* reason. This creates a straw man characterization of fideism, and ironically has been a rhetorical tool *both* for aggressive atheists like Dawkins, and for religious exclusivists like Plantinga. The former are happy to straw-man all religious believers as advocating acceptance on insufficient evidence. And this same overly narrow definition, where all fideism is characterized by the extreme, is also a rhetorical device that serves Plantinga by allowing him to maintain that his "basic belief" apologetic for Christian exclusivism is *not* a form of fideism. Yet on our own inductive risk-based account, this apologetic clearly has all the marks.

As a side-note on the just-mentioned similarity between fundamentalists and aggressive atheists as usually being proponents of a conflict model of the relationship between science and religion, let me mention that Richard Dawkins takes religious orientations generally, and not religious extremism, as responsible for acts of atrocity. On the topic of martyrdom he writes, "The take-home message is that we should blame religion itself, not religious extremism."[28] I strongly disagree: Even violent forms of radical Islam are not simply religious phenomena as Dawkins here assumes. As Karen Armstrong puts it, Dawkins is "not correct to assume that fundamentalist belief even represents or is typical of either Christianity or religion as a whole."[29] The dynamics of radicalization may have as much to do with political autonomy and hegemony in an era of globalization, and with maintenance of a politics of identity, as they do with religious doctrine or religious ethics.

Now although fideistic orientation is a degree concept best measured on a spectrum, this does not mean it varies *only* in degree, as the supra versus counter-evidential distinction might suggest. Many more factors might be involved. For example, some models of faith acknowledge mysteries, puzzles, or paradoxes of faith. Others do more than acknowledge them. They try to resolve them in systematic theology by showing why they need not be challenges to the reasonableness of faith. Or they embrace the mystery of a reality transcending our natural and social being, taking our relationship to it to be found in fleeting direct experience of ultimate reality and not through "secondary" systematic theology. Some even revel in paradox and make it a direct focus of reflection; Kierkegaard seems to do this does almost as much as does practice-oriented Buddhism. Mystery and the call of faith determine that religious insight into the nature of the universe comes through primary experience and sometimes rigorous ritual or meditative practice. Philosophers and natural theologians generally want to render faith acceptable to reason, but acknowledging limits to rational understanding can be *honest*. The strong fideist who acknowledges mysteries of faith may maintain a basic religious realism, and still respond to them as did Kierkegaard: "If I am capable of grasping God objectively, I do not believe, but precisely because I cannot do this I must believe." Or as James did, they may respond by bidding that we not take as "necessities of universal reason," what are "at bottom, accidents more or less of personal vision which had far better be avowed as such."

Kierkegaard insisted that faith "has in every moment the infinite dialectic of uncertainty present with it." His understanding of faith was of "an objective uncertainty, held fast through appropriation with the most passionate inwardness."[30] Let us identify this as a tenet of at least this self-aware type of *prescriptive* fideism, that faith requires acceptance of the condition of objective uncertainty. Risk-acknowledging intellectual honesty is the logically necessary prelude to *taking responsibility* for doxastic risk, and for seeing how peerhood is not plausibly denied in any domain where efforts to acquire justified beliefs are especially challenged by evidential ambiguity or underdetermination. This is the case with respect to most of our nurtured beliefs, but peer denial is rarely as dogmatic as in those that deny objective risk on the basis of a metaphysical truth claim, while at the same time prescribing faith as supra- or counter-evidential belief. Prescriptive fideism –still more explicitly defended by William James through a permissive ethic of belief that validates faith ventures comporting with one's individual spiritual and intellectual temperament– becomes incoherent apart from Jamesian–Kierkegaardian acknowledgment and acceptance of epistemic risk. Hence James insists that the world is religiously ambiguous, and that under conditions like this, the individual is the rightful "chooser of the risk" that his or her doxastic strategy entails, notwithstanding qualification by harms that one's faith-based commitments may visit upon others who do not share them.

Risk and venture are nearly synonymous because our human curiosity and desire for knowledge exceeds our human competence. But risk-taking and personal identity overlap as well –a point well-recognized in personal and social psychology.[31] Psychological studies show that shared risk-taking promotes social bonding. So Kierkegaard insists, "To venture causes anxiety, but not to venture is to lose one's self. . . .The most common form of despair is not being who you are."[32] This again is simple *honesty* on the part of a fideistic thinker to accept the riskiness of their faith venture. But moderately fideistic claims like this one and radically fideistic claims are often expressed by the same author. The most radically fideistic (and morally and philosophically objectionable) comment that I see in Kierkegaard's writing is not any of these acknowledgments. Rather it is, "For without risk there is no faith, and the greater the risk, the greater the faith."[33] Does taking a good idea to its furthest extreme always, or even regularly, result in a better one? The greater the risk the better the faith is a fitting motto for the Flat Earth Society perhaps, but it is not a doxastic method that supports reasonable faith ventures. It is the opposite of a moderately permissive account that allows place for doxastic responsibility, since it lends credence to religious virtues conceived as free-floating from intellectual virtues. But this latter view should itself be theologically inadequate, should it not? At any rate, how much one believes something does not make it true, and such a doxastic policy would clearly be under the bar of reasonability.

No disagreement will be a reasonable one where one or more parties to it cops a 'risk-maximizing' attitude. In this direction truth becomes subjectivity, with neither objective uncertainty nor the constraints of facts, moral principles, or the beliefs of our fellows allowed purchase. Believing that *p* on the basis of "the most passionate inwardness" resolves evidential ambiguity, but assumes inordinate epistemic risk, and ignores doxastic responsibility. The issue again is more about self-awareness of risk, and of assumption of responsibility in the second-personal claims and demands we make upon each other. Elsewhere I have argued against the internalist–evidentialist ethic of belief, partly on the grounds that it cannot preserve the reasonable disagreement that Rawlsian *reasonable pluralism* would establish.[34] But that Kierkegaard and much of Protestant Christian apologetics in Europe and the Americas move so counter-point to the claims and demands made by evidentialists like William Clifford, clearly indicates why epistemic and moral risk-related measures should be foremost among the marks of radically fideistic models of faith.

These claims might draw support from Robert M. Adams's careful treatment of Kierkegaard. Kierkegaard famously describes faith as "holding fast the objective uncertainty so as to remain out upon the deep." Adams finds it interesting that Kierkegaard's prescriptive fideism held that "it is precisely a misunderstanding to seek an objective assurance," and that "it is impossible in the case of historical problems to reach an objective decision so certain that no doubt could disturb it."[35] He describes Kierkegaard's "decision of faith" as "a decision to disregard the possibility of error [. . . a decision] not to be unaware of it, or fail to consider it, or lack anxiety about it." Adams's corrective to Kierkegaard's radical fideism is that "faith ought not to be thought of as unconditional devotion to a belief." This sets up "an impossible ideal." Perhaps this is what invites teleological suspension of the ethical. Adams says it "would set the religious interest at enmity with all other interests, or at least with the best of them."[36]

Adams's last point makes an especially strong reply to Kierkegaard and, by extension, to religious virtue divorced from concern with moral and intellectual. His point is well supported empirically because the technique of exposing people to a 'taken-to-the-limit' version of a good idea, and having them learn and articulate what went wrong in that movement to the nth degree, is one of the notable techniques of *debiasing* that Dalton and Abrams think encouragingly about as sometimes able to break the cycle of co-radicalization.[37] Most people, when exposed to this thought experiment, tend to moderate their views and thereafter exhibit more sensitivity to difference. In essence they are starting to reason inductively rather than think counter-inductively. If taking the idea to an extreme did not work or was not well motivated in my view in all these other cases, how can I say it will work and be well motivated in my own case? Apparently people can see through the idea that the nth degree is always better than a moderate degree; they tend to avoid rather than seek such a fast track to truth-as-subjectivity. The concept of religious truth is a very *thin* concept, but one that is thickened in different ways in scriptures and theologies. Still, propositional belief on the basis of non-propositional evidence such as temperament, wishfulness, practical interest, etc., challenges the positive epistemic status of those beliefs. The more passionate the motivation to believe, the less the "truth" claim resembles anything we can connect with evidence, and with formal modes of reasoning, the more we are concerned with inductive reasoning, the less credence will we place in statements of passionate commitment to contrary religious propositions.

Let us summarize the stated reasons for wanting to rehabilitate discussion of fideism so that it can be employed with more scientific and philosophical acumen. Firstly, fideism is one of numerous philosophical concepts that, it is crucial to recognize, has distinct descriptive and prescriptive senses.[38] The two senses of fideism are important for scholars to keep distinct, because fideism tends to confuse the psychology or phenomenology of belief with epistemology. The result of such confusion is a muddling of descriptive and normative categories.[39] Secondly, the old way of marking differences in degrees of fideistic orientation by contrasting 'supra'- and 'counter'-evidential belief has outgrown its usefulness. It needs to be replaced with more sophisticated models, which philosophers of luck and risk can help design. This old way was belief based, and given to a propositional model of religious commitments. It focused on a relation between a proposition with religious content and the overall or all-things-considered level of evidence for that proposition. But what makes Kierkegaard's 'best faith equals highest risk' formula so symptomatic of strong fideism is not *what* was believed, but *how* one's religious belief is to be formed, and how risk-inviting one's doxastic method is while acquiring and maintaining beliefs. The "how formed" question refers us not to a belief-content, but to an agent and a context of inquiry.

Our study of descriptive (psychological) and prescriptive (religious) fideism suggests turning back to *formal* features of doxastic methods (i.e., of how people process), features that may be straightforwardly tested for in studies utilizing scales of religious orientation. So the chapter thus far has mainly been about with what, to serve the research interests of theologians, philosophers, and cognitive scientists, should *replace* the supra/counter-evidential fideism distinction. How can we better distinguish the relevant types of fideistic inference that people actually employ? How can we better understand the philosophic and social scientific interest in each type? If our focus on inductive risk is worth anything, it should allow us to rebuild the spectrum of religious orientation from the ground up. The psychological effects that the thesis of descriptive fideism predicts are scalable: There are measurable degrees of fideistic orientation, which are opened to empirical investigation when we take note especially of patterns of inference that violate inductive norms.

BRIDGE BUILDING, OR BURNING? A CRITIQUE OF THE BELIEF MODEL

William Lad Sessions's *The Concept of Faith* develops and compares six distinct but often overlapping models: Personal Relationship, Devotion, Attitude, Confidence, Hope, and Belief.[40] In this section I want to more directly critique the naïve realism of the belief model of faith, and the practical consequences of a theist accepting this particular model. We will not be able to comment on each of the models directly, but we earlier cited psychological work supporting the claim that our blind spot regarding one's own biases is exacerbated by an agent's phenomenological stance of naive realism. I want to put a focus on the belief model and provide reasons to think that it is rationally challenged in ways that other models need not be.

As Sessions characterizes the belief model, "faith is propositional belief. . . . Belief is not 'believe in' but 'believe that,' belief that such and such is the case, or belief that a certain proposition is true." But also on this model,

> Faith's belief lacks adequate evidence. . . . S's faith that p is not at all a matter
> of proportioning one's belief or degree of conviction to the evidence, and any

conception of belief that essentially ties belief or level of conviction to evidence must forge a different conception of faith. . . . Unlike rational conviction or knowledge, faith's believing involves going beyond, perhaps far beyond, the evidence – it requires an evidential risk or 'leap.'[41]

Here I hope the reader will agree that the truth claim and the fideism or anti-rationalism about grounds that we see expressed, are deeply in tension with one another.[42] Firstly, there is a mismatch between the description of faith as belief, and the belief model's denial of the need for or desirability of epistemic reasons or arguments as grounds for assent.[43] Secondly, there is deep ambiguity in the belief model of faith between what are supposed to be the voluntary aspects of faith, and what are supposed to be the irresistible effects of grace, or the involuntary status of faith-based belief more generally.[44]

Relatedly, we earlier endeavored to explain why the belief model invites cognitive dissonance.[45] It combines the propositional attitude of belief (as essential to a state of faith) with anti-rationalism about grounds. This is considerably different than saying either that what we take to be evidence is broad or that revelation or religious authority is a kind of evidence. It is asserting normatively that belief based on evidence does not meet the bar of what genuine faith *is*. So for our purposes the belief model nicely articulates much of the strong end of any scale running from religious rationalism to religious fideism. Connections with naïve realism appear strongest where the belief model allows that agent to 'disown' his or her own agency in coming to have theistic, and even religion-specific, beliefs. Disownership allows for discounting the moral and epistemic risks of their faith-based belief. Faith-based and God-caused will be happily conflated if this alleviates cognitive dissonance.

Sessions's "model-theoretic" methodology also allows him to describe each different model of faith by what cognitive stances its adherents deem *inconsistent* with faith. So we learn much more about the belief model when he writes that for it, "[f]aith's opposites are nonbelief, disbelief, evidential belief, and tepid belief. Each opposes the central conditions of faith according to the belief model, but in different ways."[46] This side of the belief model reinforces moral ownership of faith qua personal sincerity and response to perceived divine command. Sessions's project does not involve attempt at philosophical justification of any one of his models of faith over others. While he does describe some actual conceptions of faith as embodying the belief model, Sessions does not point to any single denomination let alone religion that takes it as orthodoxy. The main point for us to take away from Sessions's work is, "Evidential risk is therefore ineradicable for the belief model."[47] In this model more so than others, we have a clear prescription for taking up and maintaining belief through a high-risk, perhaps even explicitly counter-probabilistic, doxastic method.[48]

While I share much the same criticisms of the belief model which Philip Kitcher (2011) articulates, I am happy to concede several points to the knight of faith who might champion it. First, let me agree with Sessions's claim that "proportioning conviction (and belief) to evidence need not be the only way of being rational in one's doxastic economy, for there may well be nonevidential considerations bearing on rational believing."[49] Second, I heed Sessions's caution that "one must be careful not to overdramatize such evidential inadequacy. In particular one must not equate belief lacking adequate evidence with irrational belief, much less with irresponsible fanaticism. . . . [I]nadequately evidenced belief is not always [but is sometimes] irrational belief." Third, I confirm Sessions's pragmatism on which "truth is not the only interest of reason in believing." And fourth, I confirm his claim that "actions, emotions, and attitudes may all be rationally justified, and not always, or even often, is this justification a matter of evidence." Still, as Sessions in turn concedes, "The force of evidence-rationality derives from the obvious interest of reason in truth and hence in believing true rather than false propositions; since evidence is what bears on the truth of propositions believed, reason takes note of evidence."[50]

The pronounced tendency among heart-felt believers to confuse their subjective conviction with objective certitude is part of Sessions's argument that claims of unique-access-to-truth are difficult to maintain, whatever model of faith one espouses. There is a form of irrationality (associated with directional thinking) that consists in confusing subjective factors with objective ones. But ironically enough, as Sessions notes, the drive to affirm the conceptual uniqueness of one's own faith-tradition is not itself unique to any one sect, any one religion, or even any one family of religions.

But let us return to a key point: "Evidential risk is therefore ineradicable for the belief model, and it prevents faith from pretending it is knowledge." This is Sessions's fuller claim about this model. Let me note a big concern, because the "prevents" is here intended by Sessions as a *logical* and *epistemological* implication. But this seems odd since the belief model is explicitly anti-rationalistic in its understanding of grounds. So if a suspension of the logical and epistemological are already made by the agent, what force is this 'implication' supposed to have for him or her? Why should adherents of the model comply in not contending that they possess religion-specific knowledge even in the face of strong religious contrariety?

The problem I am pointing out is this: Sessions clearly identifies a logical implication of the belief model as *skeptical fideism,* but the idea that a person can believe, perhaps believe truly, while fulfilling religious virtue *yet still not know* – this idea does not register for most people. *Of course* the true believer knows any true proposition he or she believes! The Thomistic, Calvinist, and Lutheran conceptions of faith that Sessions identifies as sharing in the belief model are not in general *skeptical fideisms* that deny positive knowledge. To consistently fit Sessions's abstract belief "model," champions of actual extant "conceptions" of faith attracted by the belief model would need to acknowledge that all faith-based belief falls short of knowledge (perhaps because of safety and epistemic credit concerns discussed earlier). Proper intellectual humility and religious virtue would take this form of separating belief in the religious domain, from knowledge.

Indeed there have been times when fideism and skepticism were more closely aligned, as Sessions's model prescribes. But do we find this implication accepted today? Hardly. In fact what we more often find is the *opposite* claim or assumption: that whatever appeal to epistemic luck might be implicit in their theologies, when it comes to religion x, the adherent's epistemic luck 'must' be benign luck, because it *must be* that the true believer in *that* faith-tradition knows what he or she (truly) believes. To put it another way, to accept personal responsibility in the faith venture would mean to accept that while "non-evidential firm belief is central to faith on this model . . . the belief is a matter of conviction, not certainty" (68). But aside from the odd Kierkegaardian or Jamesian, strong fideists are the least likely to assent to this difference. Or to reverse that, those least likely to assent to this difference are the strong fideists. Ignoring the resulting circularity, they often make the *tu quoque* argument, under the veil of "broad parity," that secular faith and even belief in other minds, or a material universe, is always in the same situation.

To his credit, Sessions does appear to recognize that extant conceptions of faith sometimes run roughshod over his clear logical distinction between psychological conviction and objective certitude. This is a key reason why he points out barriers to claims of religious exceptionalism. So what I surmise from this odd situation is that in general, the more strongly fideistic and risk-inviting is the conception of faith which one is studying, the more likely one will find endorsement of just this conjunction of a truth claim and an extra-epistemic basis.[51] For it is a clear case of what we earlier described as teleological suspension of the logical and of the epistemological.

Let us return to my mention of broad parity arguments. How are they entangled with naïve realism in the belief model? Pritchard describes parity arguments:

> This is the idea that when we consistently apply the epistemic standards in play as regards ordinary belief, we find that religious belief is no worse off. . . . Assuming this claim is correct, it is dialectically significant because, radical skepticism aside, there isn't thought to be a standing challenge to the epistemic

standing of perceptual belief. Hence, given that skepticism about the rationality of religious belief is meant to be specific to religious belief (i.e., and not a trivial consequence of radical scepticism more generally), then it follows that there is not a serious epistemic challenge to religious belief.[52]

Parity arguments show that claims about symmetry and asymmetry can play a large role not only in philosophy of religion but in a broader epistemology of controversial views more generally. But the best religious candidate for a permissive parity argument to basic beliefs like other minds or a material world would be a quite generic theism or deism. The less plausible both the broad parity and the basic belief defenses become, the more specific and diverse the specific beliefs defended on these bases are.[53] We can debate the merits of broad parity, but let us coin the term *rhetorical parity-claiming* as the apologetic complement to rhetorical vice-charging. There *are* instances of rhetorical parity-claiming, though this charge may need to be made on a case-by-case basis. But *tu quoque* arguments are a general example of rhetorical parity arguments, and even if broad parity arguments are not abused in this way, I think they are based on weak analogy and should be rejected on that basis.[54] Consider also that epistemic peerhood is standardly understood in the literature in terms of cognitive and evidential parity between individuals *vis-à-vis* some target question. So it stands to reason that the more closely concerns about cross-domain parity are conceptually connected with concerns about *peer* parity that heighten the epistemic significance of disagreement, the *less* philosophic sense can it make for a person to hope to use broad parity across domains to his or her advantage, while at the same time tossing such epistemic symmetries to the side in order to claim religion-specific knowledge for oneself alone.

One thing we tried to be clear about in chapter 4's four-step genealogy of religious contrariety arising out of etiological symmetry in testimonial faith-traditions, was the epistemological importance of the "ugly, broad ditch": a problem that Lessing, Kierkegaard, Barth, and many others have each individually struggled with. James's talk of the faith-ladder as no ordinary 'chain of inferences' from evidence, and Kierkegaard's talk of the disconnect between passionate appropriation and objective certainty, are related expressions of the 'ditch.' James says this about our self-serving failure to acknowledge the 'mood of faith' in so many of our controversial views, and the doxastic responsibility that comes with a doxastic faith venture. Acknowledging the broad ditch and the moral-epistemological challenge that it presents is itself an accomplishment, not only because so few do, but also because all sides to the debate should recognize that it is bad faith that does not recognize itself *as* faith. Lessing reports that the ugly, broad ditch is something "I cannot get across, however often and however earnestly I have tried to make the leap." Kierkegaard also finds Lessing compelling, by which I mean he agrees with

Lessing that the gap between subjective conviction and objective knowledge is impossible to bridge in a way that is not a paradox to reason. Purported truths of revelation are not plausibly synthetic a priori, which they would have to be to avoid such paradox and get over the 'ditch' safely. Barth and Lindbeck by contrast have no problem taking that leap and holding the Christian uniquely successful in it. Unlike Lessing, Barth's response was classically that of the personal 'leap' of the crevice, the simple sort of *testimonial authority assumption* that leads him to self-attribute the religious "prize." This is truly the fideistic 'leap of faith.'

Scholars have discerned multiple senses of the "ditch," and perhaps we could delineate these. There is the underdetermination of supernatural beliefs by natural facts, and the underdetermination of the historicity of biblical miracles by agreed empirical facts. There is also the *over*determination of 'prescribed certainty,' and there is the elevation of one's acquaintance with a purported revelation into possession of a kind of a priori synthetic knowledge (since the first assumption is that God said it, and the conclusions are that the Bible must be inerrant and that it must recount literal truth about creation and early human history). The only way to avoid the force of inductive norms over causal explanations and generalizations about groups is to treat one's experience of a putative revelation as a priori synthetic apprehension. But the specific sense of the ugly, broad ditch that I want to highlight is the assumption of an objective metaphysical absolute on the basis of an epistemology that is based on a subjective method. We spoke of how, for Kierkegaard, the passionate appropriating of objectively uncertain propositions is a definition of faith.[55] But importantly for the subject of religious epistemics, Pojman points out that Kierkegaard's definition of faith "in turn is used to characterize the concept 'truth.' The passionate appropriating of objectively uncertain propositions is 'the highest truth attainable for an existing individual.'" Kierkegaard says that "only the truth that edifies is truth for you."[56]

Following Kierkegaard, James's early subjective method placed "It *shall* be true, at any rate true for *me*" at the top rung of his 'faith ladder.' Both strongly suggest an indexical or a subjectivist-relativist notion of truth. It no longer looks like the fideist is allowing "truth" its normative function.[57] For how are such truths, which are not *normative* over other persons, supposed to provide explanations that genuinely *apply* to others? The adherent still thinks he or she is asserting a cosmic truth, by which is understood one that has genuinely causal effect on every human and animals since the beginning of time. But in terms of epistemology, the fideist is using 'truth' or other terms like 'knows' in a non-philosophical sense and in a sense that no one else besides those of the ingroup would likely judge well-founded. The suspension of the logical and epistemological, it once again appears, is the only way that the chasm gets 'crossed' for adherents of the belief model.

Chasms are either uncrossable or their crossing requires a means and method. But here is the sad truth. The darkness of the proverbial blind faith leap in the dark is a self-imposed darkness. If one's goal is the self-assurance of truth or salvation, feeling the edge of the crevice with one's toe before leaping individually into the darkness one after another is much riskier than trying first to build a bridge. The bridge-building is a collective project, while the other seems to be pure existential risk. Now when some persons are recognized as having failed, it may be that the rest should come to expect that the chasm is just far too wide, not for one of them (brave soul) but for all. A person would have to far overvalue one's own ability to leap, as from one wall of the Grand Canyon, having already seen others of one's species fail at the task.

Bridge-building is the alternative means and method. There are indeed many ways to build a bridge, and each of them is connected with what Paul Knitter calls some kind of *religious mutualism*: an inclusive soteriology and response to religious multiplicity. "That religions mutually claim their superiority is the problem for theologies of religions, not a valid solution."[58] This means for us that bridges are not built in the dark of indifference to the experience and virtue of religious aliens, but in the light of ongoing dialogue over similarities and differences among faith-traditions, and through constant checks-and-balance between the three kinds of adequacy: theological, epistemic, and moral.

This first of Knitter's three bridges between faith traditions is the *philosophical-historical* bridge, which holds that salvation centers on God and not on any one particular faith or putative special revelation. God is a divine reality with many cultural expressions (Hickean pluralism). For example, the affirmation that God, for the Christian, is triune is at the same time affirmation, not denial, that Godhead is unified but experienced in substantially different ways.[59]

Second, there is the *mystical bridge*, in which one says with Rumi, the thirteenth-century Sufi seer and poet, "The lamps are different but the light is the same. It comes from beyond." In the story of the blind men and the elephant retold by Rumi but of South Asian origin, each of the men perceives the transcendent using human categories reflecting their own experience and applied method. Direct experience of the divine transcendent is what each sought, and how the mystical bridge is built. The construction of theological systems is at best secondary to religious experience and *praxis*.[60] But since they have all equally touched it, how each of the men describes it (its phenomenal forms) – as a tree, a snake, a rock, a rope, etc. – reflects a genuine *aspect* of godhead, not a merely human *perspective*. This is why Rumi says that, had our blind men been given sight, they would have each been shown as partly but substantially right, in contrast to all being shown wholly wrong. Like the philosophical-historical bridge, the mystical bridge is partly motivated by the gulf between human experience and concepts/language, on the one side, and transcendent or ultimate reality on the other. But it puts direct personal experience first, and agrees with those who think of theological systems as secondary constructions rather than as the life-blood of religion (Mill, James). Resistance to both of the first two bridges (it seems to me) comes especially from naïve realism, from creedalism, from group/institution oriented religion, and from what sociologists call priestly religion.

Thirdly there is the *ethical-practical* bridge, which Knitter describes as concerned especially with the fruits – the pragmatic, moral, and life-guiding consequences of holding any particular religious worldview. This was Lessing's moral in his parable of rings, since pragmatic and moral 'fruits' are confirmable in ways that authoritative 'roots' of one purported scripture over others, are not. This bridge is also supported by humanists and secularists. Enlightenment thought more generally tended to de-emphasize the importance of one or another special revelation in the religious life, abandoning creedalism as divisive and favoring a simpler (sometimes deistic or even humanist) *common faith*. James's descriptive fideism recognized that accepting or rejecting a metaphysical claim typically involves a blend of logical, empirical, and emotional considerations.[61] This psychological fideism is indirectly connected with James's permissivist ethics of belief, which holds that "By their fruits ye shall know them, not by their roots."[62] Theologians and philosophers who argue that we should promote 'friendly' theism, atheism, and agnosticism, such that while we disagree we make sure not to villainize others for not seeing things as we do, are also helping to construct and maintain the ethical-practical bridge.[63]

But the sad truth I alluded to is this: *Exclusivists are bridge burners, not bridge builders.* It is sad because, as Knitter argues, "All religious traditions, in various ways, recognize that the ultimate reality or truth which is the object of their quest or discoveries, is beyond the scope of complete human understanding"; and because, as Knitter also argues, all religions contain the *theological resources* to affirm some sort of inclusivist response to religious multiplicity.

Bridge burning occurs not by holding one's nurtured religious ideas to be true in some strong sense, and salvific, but only in the further and more specific endorsement of exclusivist attitudes and teachings. Proof-texts, scriptural inerrancy, biased-closure inferences, and easy religion-specific knowledge for the true-qua-home religion, are among the tropes of bridge-burners. We must look closer at the apologetic strategies that stoke these flames. We can only hope to convince more people of bridge-building resources within their own traditions: conceptual resources and dialectical commitments to inter-religious dialogue and reciprocity consistent with recognition of real and important theological differences among faith-traditions.

I do not think it is well appreciated how much the historical development of Abrahamic monotheisms out of a background of polytheism conditions the branding of religious others as idolaters and worshippers of a 'different god.' Does the divine plan plausibly prescribe a radically *agonistic* scenario of different faith communities battling it out for supremacy? Where it does prescribe this, it fits ill with the traits of a perfect being; on the other hand, such accusations are the quite predictable outcome of worship of a tribal god once that worship has grown absolutistic.[64] Absolutization of an essentially tribal god, as the means and method for crossing the chasm, has an unfortunate theological consequence: the consequence of suggesting an agonistic struggle between religious groups holding similarly derived but non-identical theologies, each now casting the worship of these others as idolatry.[65] This idolatry or false religion is something *their* god, the true god, detests and righteously punishes. Due in part to the problems of religious luck that afflict religious particularism, many consider this agonistic scenario pitting tribe against tribe to be a conception of providence unworthy of a genuinely benevolent and universally loving god. Really it is not a claim about systematic theology, but a vivid narrative of cosmic warfare until the end of time, now applied backward to religious epistemics. For how is it that a loving god would put us in such poor epistemic circumstance that the exclusivist *qua* true believer *needs* to mirror all manner of known biases in order to acquire saving knowledge? How is it that a philosophical ethics of belief is permissive, but God's judgment of us is not?[66]

Having just critiqued certain ideas that many or most religious exclusivists share in common, it is time to more carefully distinguish between different strategies for supporting one's exclusivist response to religious multiplicity. Particularist (or singly-virtuous) and mutualist (or plurally virtuous) defenses of religious exclusivism are distinct positions as one finds them in the literature, and making the distinction explicit will help us make sense of a marked ambiguity in the religious exclusivist's defining claim. You see, all forms of salvific exclusivism hold that one religion alone is the gateway to salvation; all forms hold that religious value in God's eye is held exclusively by just *one* religion. But when we look closer we find exclusivism's scholarly defenders are not all making the same claim. Is the exclusivist saying that the adherents of only one of the world's religions are rational and responsible in claiming uniqueness, and in 'awarding themselves the prize,' as Barth puts it? Or is the exclusivist saying 'I am rational and religiously virtuous in being an exclusivist of *my* home religion, and you are rational and religiously virtuous in being an exclusivist of *your* home religion'? *Any exclusivist must choose between these two claims.*

Griffiths terms the more traditional account "religion-specific exclusivism," and here we will term it *particularist exclusivism.*[67] Most philosophers of religion would take Karl Barth and other evangelicals to be committed to particularist exclusivism.[68] Particularist or religion-specific exclusivism is far and away the traditional sort, but in recent years it seems to have been largely supplanted, at least in journals of philosophical theology, by exclusivism along mutualist lines.

Let us now consider Griffiths's own influential redevelopment of exclusivism along mutualist lines. This we will term *mutualist exclusivism*. The mutualist element of this defense of exclusivist attitudes is the concession that religious aliens *to us* are symmetrically granted an intellectual right to analogous exclusivist belief about *their* home religion. The mutualist sanctions the same exclusivist attitude to all those who are religious aliens to him or herself.

While the two ways to develop exclusivism have not been very well-marked in the literature, the differences are quite apparent when we attend to the *language* that each employs. A particularist exclusivist, who says that only adherents of religion x are within their intellectual rights in making the exclusivist claim, will always use the *title* of that religion. In other words, who can rationally claim uniqueness and superiority is always a 'religion x-er,' where x does not change. This again is the case for Christians like Karl Barth, George Lindbeck, and very many more.[69] By contrast, the mutualist defense of exclusivism by such authors as Paul Griffiths, Jerome Gellman, and Avishai Margalit is developed without reference to a single, named religion, but instead using the *formal* terms of "home" and "alien." I call them *formal* terms because they act as placeholders. Each mutualist author of course is personally an adherent of one particular faith (Gellman and Margalit are both Jewish, while Griffiths is Christian). Yet the *thesis* of exclusivism as they develop it is a formal one, and brings indexicality with it, since Barth will be a religious alien to these latter two authors, and they will be religious aliens to Barth. Their mutualist arguments defend the rationality of the exclusivist attitude *generally, meaning for each against the others*. This is why I think its logical coherence bears very close scrutiny, for its implication seems to be an unlimited multiplication of enemies in the mirror.

The main initial point here is simply that mutualist epistemics cannot just be the empty claim of D'Costa, that I can use my earlier beliefs to judge false any claims that do not conform to them. Mutualist ethics/epistemology cannot just be saying, yes, you are both pious and reasonable, but you simply are not my epistemic peer because your religion is false. The mutualist claim *says* something. It commits the mutualist to the *rationality* of a person's exclusivist attitude, whatever home religion she hails from. While I do not agree with that claim, I do agree with mutualist ethics / epistemology. What mutualism commits a person to is crucial to the very conceptual coherence of mutualist exclusivism, so we will focus on it closely below.

THE CONCEPTUAL INCOHERENCE ARGUMENT

I now want to argue that an apologetic strategy to defend religious exclusivism along mutualist lines is deeply in tension with itself. Its very logical coherence can be called into question even apart from more specific concerns regarding its epistemological, moral, and theological adequacy. The mutualist exclusivist's core negative claim, that no religion based on constitutive, redemptive, and revealed truths can ascribe value to the religious lives of religious others (Margalit), is in danger of being recognized as what Aristotle termed "sophistic refutations: "What appear to be refutations but are really fallacies instead."[70]

First, let us get our definitions clarified. Griffiths defines in a formal and hence non-religion-specific way the exclusivist thesis he defends. "Exclusivism . . . makes belonging to the home religion essential for salvation," while inclusivism says that "belonging to the home religion is not necessary for salvation, that belonging to an alien religion may suffice."[71] While of course there are numerous soteriologies and many ways to combine theological ideas, Griffiths's manner of defining the relationship between salvific exclusivism and inclusivism quite formally seems quite practical and intuitive: inclusivism is essentially the denial of exclusivism.

Griffiths's position that I am calling mutualism defends not just Christian exclusivism, but "structurally similar forms of religion-specific exclusivism." Mutualist exclusivism we can therefore define as asserting the reasonableness of adherents of a plurality of faith-traditions in taking a salvific exclusivist response to religious multiplicity. We know what the exclusivists think about the falsity of the beliefs of religious aliens, and their status as persons unsaved. But what are the exclusivists saying about their *reasonableness*? The mutualist, as we have seen, defends it. Mutualism is intended to show proper awareness that judging another religion solely by the criteria and standards of one's own tradition is a highly problematic exercise. Mutualism must imply some positive moral and/or epistemological commitments, and we have seen those expressed in philosophical terms of the "rationality" of the agent. I will use the broader term "reasonable."

To add some specificity, let us understand mutualist ethics/epistemology as acceptance of (IGR), John Hick's much discussed Intellectual Golden Rule (IGR). This is "a rule of granting to others a premise which we rely on ourselves." The premise is that our own experiences and those of the religion-founders are veridical, and that our tradition's transmission and instruction through elders is sincere.[72] The denial of mutualism would be particularism, a view that denies this dialogical/epistemic rule. Shifting to acceptance of such a rule is perhaps the result of post-modern, or again 'Hickean' elements that post-liberal theology has tried to use to its advantage. But on closer inspection these admissions I will show are consistent only with the rejection of religious exclusivism, but not with its affirmation. Let us be still more specific about these elements that set mutualism apart from particularism. The difference between particularist and mutualist exclusivisms can be put in terms of Christopher Adamo's elaboration of Lessing through what John Hick termed the Intellectual Golden Rule (IGR):

> (IGR) If it is rational to trust my own experiences as veridical and my elders as sincere, provided I am open to defeating conditions, I must grant that it is rational for others to trust the veridicality of their experiences and the sincerity of their elders.[73]

(IGR) is very much in the spirit of Lessing's parable of the rings, though as we have seen that story is open to varying interpretations.[74] Those theists who allow (IGR) would seem to be granting that adherents of different revealed religions stand equally vulnerable in relation to Lessing's "ugly, broad ditch," and can be equally sincere in their religious identity. So mutualist ethics / epistemics and acceptance of (IGR) seem to me closely linked, and particularist ethics / epistemics with denial of (IGR).

With these definitions in place for salvific inclusivism as the denial of salvific exclusivism, and for particularist ethics / epistemology as the denial of mutualism (and more specifically of (IGR)), I now argue:

1. Mutualism implies the reasonableness of religious aliens in maintaining belief in their home faith-tradition even after exposure to ours.
2. The reasonableness of religious aliens in maintaining belief in their home faith-tradition even after exposure to ours implies the reasonableness of any one person's non-belief in any other person's home faith-tradition.
3. A just creator's final judgment of a person's religious value would not devalue transcendentally false but reasonable belief or non-belief in any one person's home faith-tradition.
4. If a just creator's final judgment of a person's religious value does not devalue trait x, then it allows for the value (actually or at least potentially) of trait x.
5. So by 1–4, a just creator's final judgment of a person's religious value allows for the religious value (actually or at least potentially) of religious aliens with the trait of reasonably maintaining belief in their home faith-tradition even after exposure to ours.
6. (5) is the thesis of salvific inclusivism, and the denial of salvific exclusivism.
7. Therefore, by 1–6, mutualist salvific exclusivism implies its own negation.
8. Therefore, by 1–7, mutualism is logically inconsistent with religious exclusivism.

The potential religious value of religious others is the thesis of salvific inclusivism, and at the same time the denial of salvific exclusivism. (1) and (2) seems to me straightforward applications of the mutualist thesis, and indeed they reflect the key difference between religious particularists and mutualists, that mutualist guidance does not ask you to convert to my religion, but instead says to stay within your own home religion, as where God intends you to be. (3) would seem to be the most debatable premise, but its denial seems to me to imply that God judges us not for sincere worship or moral virtue or intellectual reasonableness, or for anything but assent to what theological system is transcendentally true. The more that the human epistemic condition is religiously ambiguous, the more that this external success is far beyond anyone's control. So the denial of (3) strongly suggests a soteriology beset by problems of religious luck.

That we are each rational in thinking one another irrational I take to be deeply paradoxical, and I will assume that the mutualist exclusivist is not trying to defend *that* claim. But as I think the logical incoherence argument shows, they are defending something uncomfortably close to it. The mutualist but not the particularist allows that one has to embrace *plural* reasonableness to defend reasonableness of the exclusivist attitude at all. But then the content of the claim shared by other mutualists is not that they are 'really' reasonable, but that they are 'really' wrong, and in some sense that God (but no human?) understands, culpable for their wrongness. Mutualist exclusivism is non-traditional; it would not, for example, have been accepted by the authors of *The Fundamentals* (1910–1915). It was supposed to be how post-liberal theologians could effectively respond to the Enlightenment challenge, and also to nineteenth-century liberal theology and twentieth-century post-modernism.[75] And it was supposed to move post-liberal theology beyond them rather than simply denying them without some positive apologetic to plausibly explain how.[76] Our conclusion that mutualist ethics / epistemology is logically inconsistent with religious exclusivism would be significant, if the argument holds, because it would mean that this improvement simply does not hold water: a mutualist apologetic for exclusivism collapses back into the particularist doctrine it started out repudiating as small-minded and rationally unsustainable. The hope for a positive apologetic along mutualist lines collapses back into more purely negative religious apologetics.

DICEY ADVISING? DILEMMAS FOR THE TWO FORMS OF EXCLUSIVISM

The Conceptual Incoherence argument is pretty bare-boned, so adding another argument or two will help us to further elaborate problems of religious exclusivism, and to discuss other writers who defend versions of it. Avishai Margalit defines exclusivism, including his mutualist version, as the claim that an adherent of a revealed religion *cannot ascribe value* to a religion which contradicts the teachings of the home religion: There is no room for a different response to religious multiplicity, because on this view "false religious propositions are valueless" and the holders of them inherit this status as valueless. Thus, Margalit claims that his "one ring argument" demonstrates "that each religion denies the others intrinsic value."[77]

There are, as we have already seen, some major differences between two forms of religious exclusivism, particularist (or singly-virtuous) and mutualist (or plurally virtuous) exclusivism. Next I construct the following dilemma that challenges the conceptual coherence of the exclusivist response to religious multiplicity, whichever of these two basic forms it takes.

A Religious-value Focused Constructive Dilemma

This *Value-focused* version of the Dicey Advising Dilemma is in the form of a constructive dilemma. It takes the following valid form: (1) If A then C, and (2) if B then D; (3) But either A or B; (4) Therefore, either C or D.

1. If exclusivism is understood on Mutualist premises, then God's divine judgment *is sensitive* to the reasonableness of persons in maintaining multiple religious ways of life, and so God might well confer religious value on multiple religious ways of life.
2. If exclusivism is understood on Particularistic premises, then God's divine judgment *is not sensitive* to the reasonableness of persons in maintaining multiple religious ways of life, and so God's divine judgment makes personal salvation a matter of religious luck.
3. But God's divine judgment is either sensitive or not sensitive to the reasonableness of persons in maintaining multiple religious ways of life.
4. Therefore, either God might well confer religious value on multiple religious ways of life, or God's divine judgment makes personal salvation a matter of religious luck.

This Value-focused dilemma is intended to bring particularist and mutualist forms of exclusivism to task. If we accept the truth or plausibility of its premises, then we could conclude with a simple *modus tollens* argument:

1. If religious exclusivism is a reasonable response to religious multiplicity, then religious exclusivism's reasonableness must be adequately supported by either its Particularist or its Mutualist version.

2. Religious exclusivism's reasonableness is NOT adequately supported by either its Particularist or its Mutualist version.
3. Therefore, religious exclusivism is NOT a reasonable response to religious multiplicity.

A version of salvific exclusivism that expects conversion or baptism may be conceptually incoherent if combined with a strong view of grace as a gratuitous act on the part of God. For the latter view logically implies that there are no certain necessary conditions on God's judgment, and that humans are presumptuous and prideful to think so; but the former view takes conversion to a specific religion, religion x, as a humanly-known necessary condition on personal salvation.

While soteriologies are cast in theological terms, we have seen that some more than others are faced with problems of religious luck, and particularist doctrinal and salvific exclusivism have been highlighted as views deeply affected. Absolute sovereignty doctrines become conceptually incoherent the more that human judgment is substituted for God's judgment. Similarly to the above, I think it is clear that the cost of taking this particularist horn is simply appealing to phenomenal seemings plus religious luck, while being unable to say why people of other faith-traditions cannot do the same. Or again in other terms, to assume as Barth puts it, that the truth and uniqueness of religion x is self-authenticating, while being unable to put it in more objective terms than phenomenal seemings plus asymmetrical attribution of good religious luck to religion x-ers, and bad religious luck to all others. Green notes that "Barth is making no claim whatsoever for the superiority of Christianity on historical, philosophical, phenomenological, comparative –or any other non-theological—grounds."[78] But what exactly does this leave particularist exclusivists with? Apparently it leaves them with nothing but a negative apologetic and a wholly unpersuasive claim that only adherents of religion x are personally justified in making this sort of claim. Remember that religiously neutral scholars, in so far as they discern a phenomena of religious exclusivism, are going to express that phenomena in *generic* terms, with conservatives of religion x, and conservatives of religion being instances of that strong inductive generalization. As we earlier quoted McKim, "The *home* religion will teach that it is true and that other religions are false to the extent that they clash with the home religion. One's *home* religion will include as a matter of course, a ready explanation for the failures of other religions to recognize the truth."[79] If rationality is internalist, and we are just starting with how it feels to an individual, and not considering how it feels to others, then on what rational basis can I go on to claim that non-Christians are lacking on the internalist side of things, as Barth does in claiming they are vicious instead of virtuous?

Since I think that the manner in which particularist exclusivism leans on religious luck is insurmountable for it, I will be brief in commenting on those who would 'grab' the particularist horn of the dilemma or try to go 'between' the horns. But the problems for mutualist exclusivism may not be so clear, and these problems require our close attention.

Premise (1) summarizes this in a commonsense assertion that if God exists and is mutualist on the question of rationality and virtue across religious traditions, then he or she would not (and could not justly) disconnect this from divine judgment. On pain of issuing manifestly unjust judgments, God would confer at least some salvific value on persons living *different* religious ways of life. It would be a doubtful supreme deity, indeed, who says, 'You were conscientious and faithful in your inherited religion; but you got the wrong religion, period, and I do not want to argue about it.'

I will leave the support of the premises minimal. But we said that while we wanted to present a dilemma that puts these two basic ways of conceiving religious exclusivism on different horns, we also want to throw substantial critical focus on mutualism, since it has not received as much discussion in the literature, and its internal coherence might be doubted. So we move now to a more specific dilemma for mutualism.

An Advice-focused Dilemma for Mutualist Exclusivists

Knitter understands Griffiths's *Apology for Apologetics* as arguing that "if all religious people engage in such [exclusivist] apologetics, if in the dialogue they mark their differences and make their cases why one's own position excels over the others, everyone would find themselves more resolutely and happily on the road to truth."[80] This seems like a correct description of religious exclusivism defended along mutualist lines (though noting that our usage or the term "mutualist" differs substantially from Knitter's own).[81] But it should indicate that mutualist salvific exclusivism structurally resembles ethical egoism, and is subject to some to the same kinds of objection. Ethical egoism is a doubtful normative ethical theory in its principled as well as its unprincipled or merely opportunistic versions.[82] Principled egoism says that *everyone* should act egoistically. This is thought by its proponents to be an improvement over opportunistic egoism, which says to feign cooperation, and act egoistically when it is to your advantage. But principled ethical egoism provides *inconsistent* moral advice: it tells you that your actions are right when you are pursuing your self-interest, and that mine are right when I am pursuing my self-interest, but this predicts that these prescribed actions may clash, and it does not really say how such clashes are to be met. It just repeats that each should pursue his or her own interests in it. It seems that mutualist exclusivism is like that: it tells each person to be an exclusivist in his or her home religion, but this predicts clashes, and the theory provides no way to adjudicate those clashes, but just says to be exclusivist in attitude toward religious aliens, come what may in the present world, or in the hereafter. Principled ethical egoism at least has going for it that it promises us that egoistic actions by each will work to the collective good (Adam Smith's "invisible hand" argument). But what good is there in the prescription to stay in one's home religion if there truly is one saving faith but many contenders? This advice to stay put virtually guarantees damnation for the many, who now will never confess the true faith or coming to that saving knowledge, as the mutualist exclusivist must concede.

To drive home the cost of this concession (the cost of "going mutualist"), we can construct an advice-focused dilemma. In defending salvific or doctrinal exclusivism, the mutualist exclusivist must either:

Advise persons of a different religion than their own to go apostate in order to convert to their own religion (something that would violate rationality norms since they are affirmed to be already rational and justified in their own religion).

Or,

Advise persons of a different religion than their own to remain in the religion in which they grow up or otherwise find themselves (something that would respect their rationality but preclude their only chance at the religious goal of personal salvation).

This seems simple enough, but the rub comes when we consider that only the particularist can consistently take the first option. For the mutualist it would be dicey advising, because according to the mutualist, everyone is already rational and reasonable in holding the religion that they already do. Our dilemma does not, like the previous two, depend on any thesis around religious value. It depends only on considerations of what advice the exclusivist can consistently give.

To expand upon this, our dilemma gains force by recognition of a trade-off for the mutualist between two basic ways of framing advice: as epistemically fitting from an internalist or 'mixed' internalist / externalist point of view, or as what their own religious teachings would regard as theologically unsound. The trade-off is between giving religious outsiders what the advisor takes to be sound epistemic advice, and what you as a salvific exclusivist take to be sound theological advice. Let us define sound epistemic advice as advice that symmetrically applies virtues of responsible inquiry, and respects claims made on behalf of phenomenal feelings. That is how post-liberalism essentially describes itself. Sound theological advice will be understood as advice that aims at the salvation of the religious alien—something that in all the Abrahamic faiths, a just and loving God wants. The dilemma is that the exclusivist cannot supply both kinds of advice at the same time, since these two ways of advising the religious alien are complete opposites. Either way, the mutualist gives dicey advice. Should the advice a mutualist gives entail that the other commit the religious sin of apostasy? The particularist *qua* evangelist always says 'Yes, go apostasy' but the mutualist says 'No, you are rational to remain in your home religion's belief, since you are justified in them in a way that you are not if you go apostasy in order to convert to another.'

Besides driving a wedge between the more traditional and post-liberal defenses of an exclusivist response to religious multiplicity, our dilemma gains force if we affirm that the relationship between the two kinds of advice is *hydraulic*, or subject to a costly trade-off. For if the advice the mutualist exclusivist gives is from their own perspective sound epistemic advice, it is from their own perspective unsound theological advice: For why should one be guided to hold to their home religion, if it is not salvific but will result in their damnation? And if it is from their perspective sound theological advice, then it must also be from their perspective unsound epistemic advice. For why should one to give up the seemings of their home religion to embrace the seemings of another, when this would entail the religious vice of going apostasy, and the one faith-tradition is anyway conceded not to be epistemically discriminable as more objectively rational or well-grounded than the other?

Conservative theologies ask that we take difference seriously, and mutualism understood as endorsement of (IGR) does that. The question is whether exclusivism does that in any consistent way. If I acknowledge the sincerity, the piety, the morally strenuous mood that I experience in my religious identity and worldview, as following from having a 'home' religion to begin with, then what is alien to one is home to another. "Rationality" regards agential factors, like doxastic responsibility or personal justification, but is not truth-linked.

Since rationality is used almost synonymously with sincerity, it must be granted in some way to unbelievers on any form of mutualism. Religious inclusivism and pluralism are clearly consistent with mutual respect on the basis of perceived epistemic symmetries. But exclusivism is not, and that is what this discussion is about. There is a surface concession of epistemological similarity among faith-traditions when one appeals to the mutualist concepts of "home" and "alien," but this concession is insincere if it grants rational differences only to continue an attitude of indifference to that difference. For now the religious other is an epistemic peer and as such a resource one can learn from; it is unreasonable for me to ascribe rationality to someone disagreeing with me, and still not take my disagreement with them as significant to the well-foundedness of my belief.

Reasonability is a concept that seems to go with blamelessness. But an exclusivist is now supposed to charge the religious others with vices, unless the only difference between them is allowed to be sheer good epistemic luck of a religious kind. There cannot be undefeated defeaters to my home religion, so there must be to others'. But what are they? If these religious aliens are by hypothesis reasonable, quite possibly as reasonable as myself, with what vices should each charge the other?

Exclusivists like Griffiths and Gellman provide no clear account of rationality, but we can surmise that whatever "full rationality" means, on their view it does not rate highly with God. On closer inspection this position combining mutualist ethics / epistemics with exclusivism can succeed only upon a radical expansion of the gap between epistemic justification and truth. The foray into epistemology is supposed to serve to rebut challenges by non-believers to the reasonableness of religiously absolutist and exclusivist attitudes, but then it seems that what is given is quickly taken away as the true believers revert to their usual mode of metaphysics-as-first-philosophy: non-believers are fully culpable, and rightly damned, and this attitude, not that of mutual respect, rightly predominates within any particular religious person's life. Recognizing a gap, as mutualist epistemics does, between subjective justification and rationality, on the one hand, and objective truth (empirical or transempirical), is one thing. That is as it should be. But an exclusivism along mutualist lines seems to present the absurdity of a *complete bifurcation* between personal doxastic responsibility (rationality, right motivation, effort) and religious value (God's judgment). The mutualist exclusivist must charitably hold religious aliens as rational in adhering to their own discovered home religion, yet somehow still deny that they can hold value in God's eye. But how can this concession and this assertion cohere, given that personal justification and intellectual virtue are widely supposed to be what give us an intellectual right to think that our beliefs are true?

The big shift from apologists' giving religion-specific defenses of salvific exclusivism, to their giving a generalized defense along mutualist lines, should, for all the reasons discussed, have tempered the ability to grant religious others rationality, but deny them epistemic peerhood so as to claim truth all for oneself. But what mutualist exclusivism instead results in is essentially *mirrored disrespect.* We should say of those with such hatred of opposing or unorthodox theological views what J.S. Mill says of them in *On Liberty:* "the *odium theologicum,* in a sincere bigot, is one of the most unequivocal cases of moral feeling. . . . [S]o natural to mankind is intolerance in whatever they really care about that religious freedom has hardly anywhere been practically realized, except where religious indifference, which dislikes to have its peace disturbed by theological quarrels, has added weight to the scale."[83]

The mutualist must thus allow that there is real piety and spiritual commitment in alien religions, yet an exclusivist must somehow pair this with denying their epistemic peerhood. The theological adequacy problem is that the mutualist exclusivist, as a mutualist, must charitably hold religious others rational in adhering to their own discovered home religion (and even "fully rational" to use Gellman's odd phrase), yet somehow deny that they can hold value in God's eye. For salvific exclusivism, again, is this exact claim about religious value. But how can this be, given that personal justification and intellectual virtue are widely supposed to be what give us an intellectual right to think that our beliefs are true? If a deity only cared if you had true belief and not at all about your intellectual personal justification for your inherited beliefs, wouldn't that deity be basing divine judgment on what, from the human point of view, are the 'wrong kinds of reasons'?

Recognizing the gap, as mutualist epistemics does, between subjective justification and rationality, on the one hand, and objective truth (empirical or transempirical), is a big point in its favor. It works *against* confusing psychology (or phenomenology) and epistemology. But when one tries to run an argument for religious exclusivism along mutualist lines, this natural "gap" is expanded to unnatural proportion. It seems to present the absurdity of a complete *bifurcation* between religious value and personal doxastic responsibility, such that the former has nothing whatsoever to do with the latter. This would mean religious value really has nothing to do with a person's sincerity, rationality, effort, or even good moral motivations.

Insistence on this wide of a gap between truth-possession and agent rationality serves to rationalize peer denial that would otherwise be seen as baseless. The gap is related also to the fideistic circle, and to insulation of the truth-holding religion (but none other) from criticism. If you have the truth, what else do you need? No one else will be your peer, however reasonable or skilled they may be. So another way to pinpoint the logical inconsistencies in mutualist exclusivism is by a focus on the logic and psychology of peer denial. Gellman and Griffiths's mutualist exclusivist presumably holds that peer denial is fully rational. But if so, this is also logically odd, since peer denial needs to be based on something, and that is usually a kind of vice-charging. But how can a person both be fully rational, and at the same time be rightly charged with a vice or bias in the etiology of their belief? The mutualist exclusivist wants to defend the rationality of exclusivism whatever religion the home religion is, but at the same time to prescribe that each *individual* believer should deny all significance for one's own beliefs of this disagreement with rational others. But how can an intellectual right to peer denial track something *other than* normative concerns like those of rationality? What else would it track?

This suggests that the mutualist apologetic for exclusivism has a key flaw: A grossly expanded gap between metaphysical fact and human epistemic virtues. Gellman's claim that exclusivists are fully rational and deserving of respect asserts something about people's *normative* properties. These normative properties can be realized plurally, and quite independently of having true religious beliefs since for all exclusivists, one particular religion at most is true. But then as a condition of moral and theological adequacy it seems that God, as good and just, should value the normative stuff—responsibility, effort, virtue—and not the now purely metaphysical concern of assenting to just the one true set of beliefs. Indeed that latter, arguably, cannot *be* normative for us, since while we may all seek the truth, to possess it is by logical implication outside of the agents control *whatever* religious tradition they adhere to. If success in this is rendered radically independent from intellectual virtue and personal justification, then it is clearly outside of human control, and salvation will then in large part be a matter of luck from the perspective of even exemplars of intellectual virtue. Ditto for exemplars of religious virtue, so far as we take this from the point of view of someone in a faith-tradition which prescribes religious virtue. How can virtue and value be so opposed? How is it that God's judgment is said to follow a trait which people apparently have no control over – truth – but *not* one that they do – their rationality? If reasonableness does not go with what legitimates claims to truth and knowledge, what does it go with?

Another way to put this is that in particularist exclusivism, truth and justification are both rare, because these go together and are the basis for God's just condemnation of unbelievers; but on mutualist exclusivism truth is still rare, but justification or rationality broadly available. On both views outsiders to the one salvific religion still have to be morally culpable and complicit in their damnation. Just condemnation of heretics and unbelievers of the true opinion is, after all, exclusivism's basic claim. Yet a *desire* by persons of different faiths to be committed to the true opinion seems presupposed in mutualism's defense: otherwise their rationality would be impugned rather than supported. So if the mutualist is indeed defending religious aliens' a) motivation for truth and b) virtuous effort, then they go wanting for a reason how God could justly condemn unbelievers in the true religion. The rationality and virtue of the exclusivist becomes paradoxical in the extreme. Furthermore, the more this gap widens between good faith effort and veritic success, the more clearly are we again confronted with only a brute appeal to religious luck on the part of the one—or really the all—in *claiming* veritic success uniquely for themselves. The more parity there is on the side of ability, rationality, motivation, etc., the less independent grounds there are for the exclusivist claim that our own inherit religion is uniquely true and all others that conflict in any way with it, universally false. That the mutualist exclusivist says that *all* religious adherents should make that claim on the part of their home religions does not resolve this problem; it only increases it. I thus submit that there is no less circularity, and no more conceptual coherence in mutualist as compared with particularist exclusivism. Theologically, there is no more 'positive' apologetic strategy that 'going mutualist' can supply to advance beyond the purely negative apologetics associated with a particularist, or religion-specific exclusivist, view. If problems of religious luck are insurmountable for the one, they present no less an objection to the other.

To conclude this section, we have presented serious dilemmas for particularist and mutualist exclusivism, and we have argued that mutualist exclusivism even lacks conceptual coherence. Exclusivism is inconsistent with mutualist ethics / epistemics. Mutualist exclusivism has not escaped worries about implicit relativism and overt appeal to religious luck in the older particularist or singly-rational defense.[84] It has not built a better defense of the reasonableness of an exclusivist response to religious multiplicity.

OBJECTIONS AND REPLIES

As we did following the presentation of the *Exceptionalist Dilemma* in chapter 2, we can close with some objections and replies. The first objection, coming from an exclusivist perspective, asks 'Why target only the exclusivists? If the inductive risk account as you describe it is permissive of doxastic ventures (as you call them) in domains of controversial views, including religion, then how can it not be permissive of my exclusivist belief, which is, after all, just one more specific belief within my cohesive religious worldview? Also, most exclusivism comes from scriptural ground. How can it be doxastically irresponsible and epistemically vicious for me to believe *anything* biblical? Indeed, I would hold myself irresponsible and vicious if I *did not*.

The second objection is similar in challenging the scope of our de jure argument, though it comes not from an exclusivist but from a skeptical evidentialist or skeptical rationalist. It is not 'Why target only the exclusivists?' but 'Why *only* target the exclusivists? Why not extend your de jure objection to any belief about special revelation and religious testimonially authority, or indeed all theistic, or all supernatural belief? None of these beliefs are epistemically rational or well-founded. Doctrinal and exclusivist religious belief as you point out is encouraged by overtly anti-rationalist requirements on faith-based belief. But such irrationalism is true in some degree of all religious belief. So instead of limiting the de jure objection to a target as narrow as religious exclusivism, we should take disagreement in the whole domain of theology or religious discourse to be beyond the limits of reasonable disagreement. I more generally also contest what you call your pragmatist/

permissivist ethics of belief: There is no such interpersonal 'epistemic slack' as permissivists talk about or as your defense of Rawlsian reasonable pluralism requires.

Reply to Objection 1

Self-described post-liberals like Paul Griffiths bid philosophers to accept exclusivism as just one among other aspects of religious particularity. This reasoning may seem initially plausible. People are taught an attitude toward religious outsiders along with other substantial doctrines, and that some sects are more missionary or more evangelical in orientation than others is just one of the ways that sects differ. But on closer inspection this defense of the reasonableness of exclusivist responses to religious multiplicity falls apart, and I think even reiterates the strong grounds for criticism of exclusivist apologetics as a cornerstone of fundamentalist religiosity.

Firstly, scriptures teach that the faithful do not just perform rituals as a matter of course, but really take ownership of their faith. Scriptures admonish those who do not. But taking ownership of faith does not plausibly require the agent to *disown* his or her own doxastic responsibility; it must not be thought to require any of the three forms of teleological suspension: the logical, epistemological, or ethical. Where such a suspension is involved either in ascriptions of disvalue that one places on religious aliens or in dismissive attitudes one takes toward religious disagreement, what is really going on – or so our inductive risk account has argued – is that the agents are 'passing the buck' on their doxastic responsibility by outsourcing all risk and responsibility to a supernatural source. They are conveniently ignoring the etiological symmetries they share with religious others, on the false assumption that casting their moral and intellectual trait-ascriptions in theological, or final cause terms, makes the symmetry in proximate causes somehow no longer salient in the least. I think the inductive risk account is right in maintaining that where there is teleological suspension of the logical, epistemological, or ethical, there is a basic failure to accept doxastic responsibility for one's beliefs or actions. Appeal to tradition to settle the matter of belief reduces normative questions of what ought to be believed, or done, to some psychological or sociological facts.

Secondly, our inductive risk account of the limits of reasonable disagreement allows us to maintain that people are not necessarily intellectually vicious for accepting nurtured beliefs and holding them without a great deal of reflection. But neither does such a permissivist account as mine rationalize dogmatism or imply the reasonability, *tout court,* of holding to what we are taught. The exclusivist's objection treats religious beliefs as beyond criticism by any but persons in one's own faith-tradition. But the inductive risk account says that moral risk comes in degrees. High risk is not equal to moderate risk, and cannot claim the same immunity from censure. Inclusivism is not open to the same objections of bias-mirroring, or reliance upon counter-inductive thinking. Moreover, permissionism should *sharpen* reasoned criticism rather than lead to its abandonment.[85]

Thirdly, the objection does not deal with the problem of the practical consequences of exclusivism, in terms of epistemic injustices done to those persons whose moral and religious lives are judged by salvific exclusivists of other faiths as lacking religious value. Exclusivist attitudes and non-accommodationist theologies have profound effects on others.[86] The literature on testimonial injustice focuses on the injustice done to a speaker or group S by a hearer H when, due to a – in my terms, bias-mirroring—stereotype which H holds about S, H unjustly accords too little credibility to S's testimony.[87] Any of the markers of religious fundamentalism noted above can be considered from the perspective of moral risk that one person or group's faith venture may affect others in adverse ways. Griffiths claims that the ecumenical dialogue sponsored by the World Council of Churches or the Vatican "has no discernible benefits, many negative effects, and is based upon a radical misapprehension of the nature and significance of religious commitments."[88] All that is wanted by an exclusivist in the way of dialogue is what Griffiths terms "interreligious polemics." This seems to be as true of mutualist as of particularist exclusivism. If our thesis of bias-mirroring in fundamentalist religiosity is correct, such polemics do not plausibly contribute to the mutual discovery or recognition of truth. Indeed, victims of what Kennedy and Pronin (2012) term a *bias-perception conflict spiral* typically come to hold their disagreement situation as larger and more irreconcilable than do persons who do not necessarily impute bias to others.[89] Mutualist exclusivism just reflects desire for the *normalization* of such a spiral, or what we previously called not just polarized, but polemical religious contrariety. If they were reasonable they would acknowledge that the image in the mirror is their own.

The problem of the exclusivist ignoring practical consequences of their attitude towards unbelievers extends to the ills of bias-mirroring judgments of others. There is also the not-insignificant problem that on Griffith's mutualist approach, there is no way to criticize or rationally constrain exclusivist attitudes taken by adherents of religions other than one's own. This leaves Gellman and Griffiths with no resources at all to criticize praxis-oriented exclusivism that, as a prime example, aim at subjecting everyone—Jew, Christian and Muslim alike—to *sharia* law. So long as something is prescribed in their scriptures, they are being 'fully rational' by insisting that everyone should live under God's law as understood in those scriptures.

Griffiths points out that religious exclusivism is often motivated by conformity with scripture. It is undoubtedly true that this is one of the strongest motivations for it, and that a fundamentalist mind-set will throw out options that are judged not to fit with the scriptures of the home religion. Again this kind of 'disowns' responsibility for the way we treat others, but I will not return to that point. But differences between approaching questions of salvation by way of traits of a perfect being, on the one hand, versus by way of scriptural authority or appeal to a settled theological orthodoxy on the others, have very real-life consequences. This is why we have maintained that religious virtue does not plausibly stand independent of moral and intellectual virtue, nor the theological adequacy of a certain view from its moral and epistemic adequacy. It is why matters of potential injustice to others of one's response to religious multiplicity are not a concern that can responsibly be dealt with by appeal just to one's own scripture or tradition.

While I can only speculate about what my critics will say is theologically adequate, it looks to me that exclusivists are ignoring biblical resources and the fact that the Bible says things that can be and are interpreted in different ways. When used to support salvific exclusivism, a selective reading emphasizes some biblical passages while largely ignoring others.[90] This makes an essentially dead doctrine out of a living tradition that needs to constantly renew itself for each new generation, and knit together with what else we are learning about ourselves. According to theologians like Knitter, inclusivism is the best way to make sense of a very scriptural teaching: that the life of Jesus is a momentous event for all. Neither doctrinal nor salvific inclusivism presents a harm to *koinonia,* the Christian term for fellowship, and a concept which we may generalize as participative sharing in a common religious commitment and spiritual community.[91] Theological naturalism and supernaturalism can both support dialogical principles such as (IGR). But instead, "non-accommodationist" theology winds up excluding much of the middle ground between religious and humanist-naturalist ethics.[92]

Reply to Objection 2

This objection comes from a very different and more skeptical perspective, but shares with the previous one that neither objector sees a point in a targeted de jure objection such as we have constructed. I do not want to tie the inductive risk account too closely to my own pragmatism and neo-Jamesian ethics of belief. Depending on the ethics of belief one endorses, and its relationship with normative notions of rationality, reasonableness, etc., philosophers might derive more skeptical conclusions than I do from premises derived from considerations of luck/risk in part I of the book.

But acknowledgment of reasons for standing diversity was for John Rawls the largest stumbling-block to affirmation of "reasonable pluralism." The proper recognition of these many sources of cognitive diversity should make us expect diversity, and also respect it. I firstly hold that permissivism rather than impermissivism, and the affirmation rather than the denial of reasonable pluralism in the Rawlsian sense, is both advantageous and philosophically superior to impermissivism. I am happy to situate the normative side of my inductive risk account with a broadly permissivist ethics of belief. Disagreements in domains of controversial views are not necessarily unreasonable even if in the broader scheme one thinks that the domains of all or some controversial views are only minimally truth-apt, and that the debaters do not always make proper allowance for this. Trait-dependence is not necessarily bias: the kinds of overdetermination that we find manifested in beliefs in domains of controversial views are not especially troubling except under special circumstances.[93] Ill-founded beliefs are challenged from the side of philosophy by counter-inductive reasoning (violation of inductive norms) and rhetorical vice-charging. Ill-founded belief is challenged from the side of cognitive and social psychology by established markers of cognitive or moral dissonance, indoctrination anxiety, confabulatory explanation, or personal or social bias more generally. So while the dependence of nurtured beliefs on one's epistemic location is not *prima facie* evidence of bias, more specific things like the dependence of a belief on counter-inductive thinking, or the manifestation of those markers of bias that promote the *enemy in the mirror effect*, do strongly challenge the well-foundedness of an agent's belief. They do so far more than does the simple recognition of the cultural contingency of the agent having just that belief.

Others besides self-described pragmatists have argued that the *rational uniqueness thesis* is misapplied to the epistemology of controversial views. The defense of the universal applicability of the rational uniqueness thesis is the main dividing point between impermissivists and permissivists. Impermissivists, including evidentialists and principled agnostics, defend that principle, while permissivists deny its proper applicability to domains of controversial views. The defender of the rational uniqueness thesis claims that there is always one objectively right and epistemically rational way to weigh evidence bearing on a proposition of any kind, not many. For skeptical evidentialists, if it 'can't be determined,' that just means one's duty is to suspend judgment until it can. So the theist must stop believing and instead 'wait for the bell' of sufficient evidence, even if it is never likely to come. On these claims, however, I think Thomas Kelly (2014) argues cogently that the evidentialist conflates claims about intrapersonal and interpersonal epistemic 'slack.' Permissivism is a thesis only about the latter. Also, principled agnosticism concerning questions of moral, politics, and religion – the demand that people wait for a 'bell' that will likely never ring – has seemed to its many critics to prohibit actions where an act is forced.

In a sense the difference between low and high inductive risk is also reflected in disagreement about disagreement, or more particularly in the two sharply opposed "universalist" councils for how to respond to religious disagreement: conciliationist and steadfast councils. As a permissivist though, I reject universalist theories—those that claim there is one strong master principle that tells us how we ought to respond to disagreement. Both concessionist and steadfast guidance I take to be overgeneralized prescriptions about morally and intellectually responsible responses to genuine peer disagreement. So here I just note that my pragmatist ethics of belief, like John K. Davis's "divergentism," is more permissivist than either concessionism or principled agnosticism. Yet I will want to suggest that it may be more effectively able to challenge dogmatic thinkers' faulted attempts to epistemically privilege their own or their ingroup's nurtured beliefs, and to insulate certain of them from rational criticism.[94]

I have elsewhere argued that the norms that inform an ethic of belief are typically more diachronic than synchronic, and that guidance-giving takes place in the context of ecological rationality, not ideal agency where the *order* of acquired evidence should make no rational difference as all.[95] As the evidentialist thinks, censure *can* take the form of saying that the agent should reduce their confidence level in a proposition in response to undercutting etiological information. But *must* it? Many epistemologists of disagreement talk exclusively in these synchronic (and arguably voluntaristic) terms. The importance of the reliable etiology of belief for doxastic justification seems from my pragmatist or *inquiry-focused* epistemology to cast doubt on why doxastic responsibility and guidance-prescriptions should take a primarily or exclusively *synchronic* form. So while I appreciate J. Adam Carter's risk-focused account of controversial views, his principled agnosticism is still impermissivist.[96] If we, as Carter (2018) argues, should discern a more diverse set of doxastic attitudes than the Triad model (*believe, suspend belief, or disbelieve*) allows us to see, then we should also try to discern a more diverse set of permissible diachronic as well as only synchronic means of response to genuine peer disagreement.

For permissivists, moreover, guidance is not free to ignore the agent's ecological rationality in favor of such an atemporal ideal agent.[97] It is implausible that either on a moral evidentialist or epistemic evidentialist basis, guidance on doxastic responsibility given to agents should demand strict suspension of nurtured beliefs. The treatment both of epistemic assessment and of guidance-giving needs to be more contextual than this, and, granting reasonable credit to people for their background beliefs, different forms of normativity (epistemic assessment, personal justification or rationality, and guidance/censure) need to be much more carefully distinguished than they are in the stated objection.[98]

CONCLUSION

Religious exclusivism was given its most specific critique in this chapter. I critiqued its moral adequacy and presented commonsense reasons why theological adequacy should never be taken wholly independently, or in suspension of, moral and epistemic adequacy. Nothing could be riskier than that. The three kinds of adequacy were given more focused attention through our three formal arguments, and the comments I made about them. The Exceptionalist Dilemma of chapter 2 also targeted the reasonableness of religious exclusivism, but was focused around the costs and conceptual difficulties of making either a "same process" or a "unique process" response to the New Problem of religious luck. With its focus on attempts to break default symmetry among people in order to make the preferred response that one's own religious beliefs are caused in a different way than all purportedly false beliefs in the same domain are, that dilemma is clearly about epistemic adequacy. In this chapter, the Value-focused Dilemma hinges on basic differences between religion-specific and mutualist exclusivism, putting each on a different horn. The Advice-Focused Dilemma and Conceptual Incoherence argument each added to this; they allowed us to further flesh out problems specific to mutualist exclusivism, and to thereby to rebut the claim that it makes an exclusivist response to religious multiplicity any more reasonable than does standard religion-specific exclusivism.

My key claim about our inductive risk account is again not that it undermines knowledge claims, or is a general grounds for skepticism, but that it provides useful diagnostic and evaluative tools, including a way to measure degrees of fideism in particular agents or in the specific model of faith they employ. Our inductive risk toolkit helps us to address the sources of deep conflicts that often seem to make those debates intractable. If what we have contended is on the right track in terms of its methodology, the debates between religious exclusivists may not be as intractable as they seem. Disagreements characterized by mutual claims of uniqueness and superiority often reflect bias on all sides, and their reasonableness may be challenged by careful, empirically informed studies. Theological disagreements between exclusivists of different sects or religions are not exception to this, and indeed may be an example of what the social and cognitive science of religions are making good strides in explaining. We can explore this further in the final chapter.

NOTES

1. Vainio 2010, 59. Criticisms of unreflective conformism, whether religious or not, are common-place. For Bacon they fit as idols of the cave or of the Market-place. We are all susceptible to conformism in respect to our Controversial Views,

and so constant reminders are generally good. But these admonitions to avoid it are often also the stuff of unfair generalizations, like the New Testament criticisms of the Pharisees as rule-followers rather than as people of true faith. This not only over-generalizes, but implicitly puts in place a more cognitive or creedal conception of faith (that can be just as unreflective) in contrast to the practice-centered Jewish model. So the worry with over-simple denunciations of conformist fideisms, is that these are often just more self-serving us/them dichotomies used even intra-religiously to assure one of his or her own controversial views, and to accuse others of some failing on thin, 'psychologizing' evidence that assumes access to their motivations. normatively urging better motivations. In a religiously neutral way, President John F. Kennedy perhaps stated the general worry about cognitive idols of the cave and market-place best in a speech in which he stated, "The great enemy of truth is very often not the lie—deliberate, contrived and dishonest—but the myth—persistent, persuasive and unrealistic. Too often we hold fast to the clichés of our forebears. We subject all facts to a prefabricated set of interpretations. We enjoy the comfort of opinion without the discomfort of thought."

2. An example of skeptical fideism might be William James, who defends the right to personal doxastic risk while at the same time acknowledging the doubtful epistemic status of doxastic faith ventures. Montaigne is another example perhaps. One needs to allow the agent permissible doxa, but not religious knowledge to be a skeptical fideist.

3. Vaino holds non-reflective conformist fideism to be of little interest because "From the viewpoint of this study, it does not –although it definitely should!—really engage the question whether there exists adequate reasons for choosing a particular worldview over another more than the mere commonness of this worldview." (59) He thus puts both forms of conformism under his own broader classification, *pragmatic fideism* in contrast to the *communicative* fideism he argues for, which while still eschewing evidentialism, takes differences and reasons for belief seriously in ways that he thinks conformist fideism does not. He concedes, though that "there is a dose of pragmatism in all forms of fideism" (and I agree): "The ultimate test of truth is life itself, which makes the belief a part of public life and discussion" (64). Also, Vainio clearly allows that all these categories are gradational.

4. Vainio (2010), 2.

5. McKim, 152. Allen Buchanan (2004, 97) discusses a process of Credibility-Prejudicing via Isolation: "A person brought up in a racist society typically not only absorbs an interwoven set of false beliefs about the natural characteristics of blacks (or Jews, and so on), but also learns epistemic vices that make it hard for him to come to see the falsity of these beliefs. For example, when a child, who has been taught that blacks are intellectually inferior, encounters an obviously highly intelligent black person, he may be told that the latter "must have some white blood." Along with substantive false beliefs, the racist (like the anti-Semite and the sexist) learns strategies for overcoming cognitive dissonance and for retaining those false beliefs in the face of disconfirming evidence (11).

6. Gellman, 402.

7. See Muscat, 2015.

8. For notice that the need to hold beliefs by your own lights erroneous, or more especially to condemn as error and as especially a culpable error, is certainly *not* so of religious beliefs held in ways other than with the exclusivist attitude toward religious difference; neither is it true of the way we hold most of our moral, political, and philosophical commitments.

9. Gellman 2008, 382.

10. See Jesse Singal's 2015 review of Holmes for discussion.

11. McKim (2012), 143.

12. James, "The Will to Believe." There James affirms, "It is only by risking our persons from one hour to another that we live at all." See Axtell 2018 and 2019. James maintained that our "overbeliefs" or venturesome emotional and intellectual "visions are usually not only our most interesting but our most respectable contributions to the world in which we play our part" (*Pragmatism*, 10). With this I argue all permissivists (who are anyway the defenders of rational disagreement against religious dogmatists and strict empiricists) can readily agree. One can be virtuous in *responsibly-held* religious and philosophical faith ventures. Symbolic and analogical thinking, which James sees as affecting philosophical and religious overbeliefs, he associates with anti-rationalism.

13. "Understanding how temperaments regulate conviction, doubt, and other epistemic evaluations is essential to the project of critical inquiry, not least because it indicates that philosophical disagreements may reflect different 'ground-floor intuitions' . . . rather than necessarily indicating the obstinacy, dogmatism, or ignorance of one's interlocutors." Kidd (2013), 393.

14. The response of fundamentalists to religious diversity perhaps just stands out for the degree to which their conceptions of faith deny off these burdens, denying faultless non-belief in just the religious domain. It stands out also for the degree to the extent that there is an apologetic dimension in the historical religions which explains religious belief and unbelief in theological, and sometimes highly moralized language. And it stands out also for the degree to which religious apologists go unchallenged due to the authority they claim for themselves to define orthodoxy.

15. As children of time, we deserve respect not just for individual temperament, but for background beliefs and for many other effects of culture. Guidance that philosophers give must be consistent with psychological acknowledgment of pragmatism about reasons and of the ecological rationality of human agents. I would not presume to say that belief may never be permissibly responsive to non-epistemic reasons. We must not forget that we rightly reason holistically, and that as creatures of time as well as of place, we so inevitably 'live forward.' Looking backward, as Montaigne correctly says, is much more difficult for us, and this is where philosophy and the sciences help the most. We simply do not know, prior to careful reflection and honest dialogue with others, the 'real' causes for our beliefs. We need not agree with a broad skepticism that insists that 'ignorance of our ignorance is the death of knowledge,' in Whitehead's phrase. But again, what consequences to draw from the epistemic location problem are not clear-cut.

16. Gilbert Harman makes a related point when he contrasts the lack of "complete specification" in inductive reasoning, in contrast to our expectation for it in deductive

reasoning. He adds, "It is doubtful that anyone has ever fully specified an actual piece of inductive reasoning, since it is unlikely that anyone could specify the total relevant evidence in any actual case. The difficulty is not simply that there is so much relevant evidence, but also that one cannot be sure whether various things should or should not be included in the evidence. One cannot always be sure what has influenced one's conclusion" (1970, 844).

17. For further background on different kinds and senses of "fideism," see Quinn (2007), Amesbury (2005), Penelhum (1997), and Popkin (1960).

18. McKim relatedly argues that the availability of inclusivist responses to religious multiplicity "constitutes a difficulty for exclusivism insofar as they provide a way to give expression to much of what fuels exclusivism but that is free from its most serious difficulties" (2012, 68).

19. I treat "pluralism" as a position that needs support, but "multiplicity" and "diversity" as referring instead to a factual state of affairs.

20. What object of faith and how the agent is devoted to it are the main variables in light of which Sessions (1994) develops his taxonomy of six models of faith.

21. Debates over religion and science often seem almost intractable. Wittgenstein is right that scientists and theologians often talk past one another, making it difficult to see what the presumed disagreement is really about. But the reason for talking past one another is not to be that these groups are playing vastly incommensurable language games. It might also be that a person's very conception of what "faith" means, functions like the 'hard core' of a Lakatosian research program, being protected from refutation and revision, come what may. I do not believe great progress can be made in this debate until we recognize this diversity of conceptions of faith, even within Christian tradition itself, and address the merits—both philosophic and theological—of competing accounts of that relationship.

22. Penelhum defines fideism more in terms of an attitude toward the relationship of reason and faith: "the insistence that faith needs no justification from reason, but is the judge of reason and its pretensions" (Hanson 10). Penelhum's definition may capture the sense in which reformed tradition is fideistic, but the 'no' seems to be over-stated in that it does not capture any differences between moderate and radical fideism. I think that the relevant way to judge moderate versus radical as supra- versus counter-evidential is not quite right, but in regard to *how* counter-inductive it is, this still is helpful. If it *does not* matter to someone how counter-evidential, including how counter-inductive their asymmetrical attributions are, that does fit the radical, 'needs no justification from reason' notion.

23. This is Penelhum's definition. If one continues to hold that they know x, when the path to accepting or assenting to x was counter-inductive thinking, then an error theory arguably kicks in: It is better to interpret it as possibilist hope, wish, or some other propositional attitude than belief? This goes to the supra-evidential. H-S says you cannot have faith in what you hold improbably, but I really doubt that. Any football team, since they *all* have long odds, makes that clear. Faith can attach to 'better than the others' even when one has little insight of overall odds. Many, and perhaps most time that people engage in counter-inductive thinking, they are not aware that they are doing so. They are not thinking logically either about disagreement or about probabilities, or about modal environments. Emotion is one thing that clouds all of these.

24. An aggressive religious evidentialist apologetics appear on the surface as attempts to meeting independent standards of reason and evidence, but they can betray a more radical fideism in the descriptive sense especially when they treat one tradition's purported special revelation as objective evidence. The very fact of their confusion of subjective and passionate factors with being in a position to know, reveals the radical character of their fideism. Thus our basic scale running from rationalistic to fideistic is perhaps not best seen as opposite extremes, as we may have to bend the ends up into a circle to reveal how religious evidentialism – even about theism but especially about a particular religion, is an indication of self-deceived fideism. Rationalists in the primary sense will generally disdain holding the beliefs they think cannot be argued for by neutral or *independent* reason; fideists do not. For example, short earth creationists likely do not recognize themselves as fideistic, but are sure that their religious cosmogonic narrative is a question of historical facts. This is accounted for if, as I would hypothesize, those who responded to psychological measures as implicitly fideistic, will be some of the quickest to adopt explicit evidentialist stance in favor of the literal truth of their own sacred narratives. Relating the distinction between moderate and radical fideism to degree of violation of inductive norms (some of the evidence for which will be implicit measures rather than self-reporting) will be our preferred measure, and I will try to show why this is better-suited to reveal shared features of religious extremism.

25. The literature in dual-process theory uses the implicit-explicit distinction in another way, where implicit is basically automatic or Type 1, and explicit is slower but more self-conscious Type 2 processing. Partly what I am pointing out is the need for implicit as well as explicit (for example, self-reporting) measures of strongly fideistic orientation.

26. This in turn reflects ambiguity between whether we are treating fideism as a descriptive or a normative thesis, and also between subjective and objective perspectives on "total evidence." If this is correct then already it is not well suited to open up avenues for comparing models of faith and their relationship to religious extremism. Also, if it is the agent herself who decides whether her credence level is epistemically justified, supra-evidential, or counter-evidential, then the standard model will reward the self-deceived as being moderate, and punish with the 'counter' label those who simply concede that there are mysteries of faith that they accept but cannot provide "sufficient" evidence to rationalize.

27. As Pojman paraphrases Kierkegaard's argument, "If the objective uncertainty of the object [of religious faith] is not constantly recognized, the temptation is to 'confuse knowledge with faith,' transforming faith into pseudo-knowledge" (119).

28. Dawkins, *The God Delusion*, 306.

29. Karen Armstrong (2010), 304.

30. "In a human being there is always a desire . . . to have something really firm and fixed that can exclude the dialectical, but this is cowardliness and fraudulence toward the divine." Kierkegaard, *Concluding Unscientific Postscript to 'Philosophical Fragments'* I: 34–5.

31. For an interesting perspective on the social and psychological aspects of risk-taking, see Cynthia Lightfoot (1997): "Risks are actively sought for their capacity

to challenge, excite, and transform oneself and one's relationships with others. In this regard, risks are speculative, experimental, and oriented toward some uncertain and wished-for future" (2). There are two perspectives on risk that go far back in the history of ideas; one is of risk-taking-as-trouble, or as irresponsibility; the other is of risk-taking-as-opportunity. Conceived of as opportunity, "risk-taking is as bound to issues of experimentation, autonomy, and identity, development as it is to rebellion, trouble-making, and mischief" (17). On *cognitive* risk-taking and identity, see also Dan. P. McAdams (1997), Jennifer Welchman (2006) and my papers on William James.

32. Kierkegaard, *Fear and Trembling,*

33. Kierkegaard, *Philosophical Fragments,* 188. Pojman comments, "What is wrong with the argument is the inherent volitionalism. . . . By making faith, based on insufficient evidence, a virtuous act, it could be shown to follow—as Kierkegaard does—that it is clearly more virtuous to believe improbable propositions than probable ones . . . but I think it presents a consistent *reductio ad absurdum* of volitionalism. Kierkegaard's shrewdness lies in the fact that he saw these consequences, his weakness in the fact that he accepted them" (1984, 120). I am similarly critical of James' constant appeal to the need for an emotionally charged "strenuous mood" for faith (an idea that he takes from Kierkegaard) which presents the same dangers of inspiring zealotry. But Pojman notes that, though not well noted in the literature, the later Kierkegaard's 'attitude seems more favourable to the demands of reason' (129), and that he offers a more psychologically plausible view of faith. Much the same could be said for James, whose late views are far more qualified than his early, Kierkegaard-influenced subjective method. See Axtell 2018 for a critique of James' treatment of risk in faith ventures, but also 2013 for development of a fuller neo-Jamesian permissivism.

34. Elsewhere I argue against Richard Feldman that the combination of cognitive evidentialism and the *rational uniqueness thesis* (RUT) that they endorse functions to destabilize the "friendly" versions of both theism and atheism while empowering the "unfriendly" versions of each, instead. This is because of the positions it entails that undermine the philosophic support of reasonable disagreement. To do the opposite of this is what is philosophically and practically advantageous, but to be able to take this path requires rejecting internalist evidentialism or as a sound basis for a normative or prescriptive ethics of belief. The alternative I propose and develop more constructively in more recent papers is *zetetic* (inquiry-focused) virtue responsibilism. Virtue theory is the champion of the importance of diachronic norms, and the simple facts that we live forward but find ourselves already situated in the world are enough to explain why what norms should inform a sound ethics of belief are primarily diachronic. As children of time, we deserve respect not just for individual temperament, but for background beliefs and for much of the effects of culture. Perhaps this is why James said that for him, the most interesting and important thing about a person is their spiritual and philosophic 'overbeliefs.'

35. Adams (1998) says that "Kierkegaard, in the *Postscript,* is willing to admit a dispositional element at one point in the religious venture, but not in another. It is enough in most cases, he thinks, if one is *prepared* . . . but it is not enough that one

would hold to one's belief in the face of objective improbability. The belief must actually be improbable." (239).

36. Adams, 235, 241.

37. K. Dutton and D. Abrams, "What Researchers Say about Defeating Terrorism," March 2016.

38. For further background on different kinds and senses of "fideism," see Quinn (2007), Amesbury (2005), Penelhum (1997), and Popkin (1960).

39. Sands 2014, 147.

40. Pronin, Gilovich, and Ross 2004.

41. Sessions 50, 57. More formally, Sessions defines the influential belief model this way: S has faith that p only if S believes that p, S is (firmly) convinced that p, S has inadequate evidence for p, and S's belief that p is non-evidentially based (9).

42. This explains why one might expect a competent agent to respond to the tension by expressing some sort of cognitive dissonance, for example, feeling some genealogical or contingency anxiety. It is also why, if they do not respond in this way, one could suppose that the agent is self-deluded about the epistemic goods that she thinks her faith-based belief delivers to her. Her delusion, if it is such, could be confirmed by other measures, such as her recourse to confabulatory explanations and/ or rhetorical bias-charging and biased-closure inferences, in order to justify her belief and rebut all criticism.

43. This is why I earlier suggested that if there is a basing requirement on doxastic justification, the strong fideist fails it on account of their claim of religious knowledge being a claim dependent on propositional religious luck. What we have described as Kierkegaard's strong religious fideism, Louis Pojman analyzes in terms of a thesis of *prescriptive volitionalism:* "Kierkegaard accepted the prescriptive feature of volitionalism: it is good to tailor one's beliefs to one's deepest desires." Pojman qualifies this by saying that volitionalism is prescribed only for worldview-type beliefs. This sounds very much like early James and his subjective method. It is interesting, though rarely noted, that both men actually qualified their views substantially as they got older.

44. Proponents of the belief model of faith fall into the quandary that (a) faith is voluntary (bringing culpability into the picture), (b) belief is involuntary, and (c) belief is a necessary condition for faith. Relatedly, Hartman (2011) examines the coherence of the following claims: (1) one cannot have faith, (2) one has an obligation to have faith, and (3) ought implies can. For Kierkegaard, genuine faith, the faith that ventures, is a *choice*. Were it merely the working out of a prior divine decree: "subjectivity cannot be excluded, unless we want to have fatalism" (see Sands 65-66 for discussion of how Kierkegaard gets through this dilemma by viewing God's grace as *"indispensable but not irresistible, a necessary but not sufficient condition"* for faith).

45. There is a related literature on epistemic *akrasia* (weakness of will), understood as arising when one holds a belief even though one judges it to be irrational or unjustified. Scholars have debated whether this is even possible (Pojman's "volitionalism" charge against Kierkegaard and counter-probabilistic faith demands in the Bible) and whether and in what sense it might be reasonable or adaptive. I have chosen not to engage this literature, though I find it odd that the debate on epistemic

akrasia avoids the elephant in the room –the belief model of faith as Sessions understands as combining 'believing *that*,' and anti-rationalism about grounds. For here
norms of belief and of evidence appear to be deliberately violated or 'suspended.'

46. Sessions, 67. "Nonevidential firm belief is central to faith on this model, as
is shown by faith's opposites: Not believing, as well as believing contrarily, on evidence, or tepidly, all center on how (or whether) a person holds some proposition to
be true" (69).

47. Sessions, 65. In philosophical theology there is some interesting work utilizing
model theoretic approaches. See Jeanine Diller and Asa Kasher 2013. My differences
from Sessions might in a nutshell be that he thinks this strongly fideistic model can
rationally support belief but must deny knowledge, while I am not clear how in what
sense it supports "S believes that p," in contrast with the alternative of describing the
agent in such cases as holding some sub-doxastic attitude, or as having some truth-apt
conception of the propositional content, p. Not every believing *in* is something that
must be analyzed by epistemologists as a believing *that,* and the strong fideist seems
to commit this conflation in spades. Among theologians this conflation becomes
a motivation for *post hoc* evidentialist apologetic strategy, and self-ascription of
religion-specific "knowledge," in the face of religious contrariety and despite the
agent's belief being fundamentally supra or counter-evidential nature. Such claims
seem psychologically but not philosophically interesting to me. I explore this further
in chapter 6 with discussion of those who distinguish certain statements of religious
"credence" from belief. There are psychological markers of belief that so-called anti-
evidential belief seems to lack.

48. For Kierkegaard the life-crucial or existential types of commitments accentu-
ate the passional aspects of faith, marking differences between them and everyday
beliefs. The logic that Kierkegaard employs in regard to them, Pojman observes,
"seems to be counter-probabilistic: the less probability, the better!" (119). What is the
relevant difference between Kierkegaard's counter-probabilistic fideism, and Wittgenstein's religious adherent who says, "No. There it will break down. No induction.
Fear"?

49. Sessions 58, n.54. Here I would refer to my work on the centrality of diachronic concerns with responsible inquiry, in contrast to the merely synchronic notion
of evidential fit. I would also leave off speaking about "rationality" especially in its
bivalent 'rational or irrational' connotation, when we get to decision-making under
conditions of local underdetermination, and speak about reasonableness in a dialectical setting, instead.

50. Sessions, 59, 63.

51. This potentially comes back to haunt Sessions's commitment to be able to tell
when an act of propositional acceptance is indeed determinable as irrational (59).
He writes that "faith is indeed irrational in certain circumstances, in cases where the
evidence positively and conclusively counts against believing." But "conclusively"
is far too strong to be the norm of rational assent, and counter-inductive reasoning
is counter-evidential (and not just supra-evidential, *by definition*). So any belief-formation produced by a doxastic method rightly described as counter-inductive would

be 'irrational' – *epistemically* irrational – by his own definition, regardless of what pragmatic reason may say in its favor.

52. Pritchard (2017, 114).

53. So for example, skeptics like Michael Martin make the 'Great Pumpkin' objection of Plantinga's claim of properly basic religion-specific belief, while even other Christians like Linda Zagzebski charge Plantinga's basic belief apologetic with the violating a "Rational Recognition Principle: If a belief is rational, its rationality is recognizable, in principle, by rational persons in other cultures" (Zagzebski in Plantinga et al. 2002, 120).

54. See Quinn 1991, for what is one of the best papers of the use and potential abuse of broad parity arguments. Rhetorical status can be investigated case by case and we need not suppose all claims of parity across domains to be without merit.

55. This passionate appropriation conception of faith is how Kierkegaard himself appropriates the Lutheran conception of faith. Like Luther also, he affirms this appropriation of the Biblical narratives and Christian special revelation, but rejects, often in a fiery manner, natural theological attempts even to prove God's existence. Squaring Luther's passionate appropriation conception of faith his own denial of free will is considered by many to be theologically difficult, and part of the broader tension between grace and free will. How Kierkegaard deals with Luther's explicit rejections of free will, given Kierkegaard's Christian existentialist emphasis on our freedom in and responsibility for our choices, is also philosophically and theologically difficult. Free will was the central issue of his debate with the Northern Humanist, Erasmus.

56. Pojman, 115–116. Many Christian philosophers and philosophical theologians seem to me often to forget that for Kierkegaard, there are clear logical implications on Lutheran and more broadly internalist or Christian witness-evidentialist premises, why faith is not a form of knowledge in the philosophical sense. They follow a passionate appropriation model of faith, yet from Kierkegaard's perspective, and in this instance also from a purely philosophical position, they conflate the agent's affectively-conditioned appropriation of scripture with their meeting a basing requirement for propositional faith. While Lessing says that he cannot honestly make the leap required to cross the ugly broad ditch, Kierkegaard tells us that he makes it, but also that the mystery or paradox of pronouncing subjective passions as the path to highest truth must remain unresolved but explicitly acknowledged. Apparently, though, it is 'resolved' in the minds of many contemporary Protestant Christian philosophers simply by going *unacknowledged*. The mutualist version of exclusivism proliferates religious "truth" and "knowledge." It allows Kierkegaard's move the Pojman points out, from faith to truth, but does not seem to notice that it proliferates truths and knowings at the same time. The idea of religion-specific knowledge in the face of religious contrariety is a difficult concept, indeed. So it is unclear to me if the mutualist is just saying that exclusivists have an intellectual right to say or think that they know all kinds of religion-specific theological claims, (e.g., that God is triune, or the Jesus is God), or actually saying that the Christian, the Jew, and the Muslim, just for starters, actually *have* contrary, religion-specific knowledge. This multiplication of 'knowings' with contrary propositional content is the cost of reducing truth to faith-based belief,

and not letting it serve its expected normative function as an independent corrective of belief.

57. Compare Grube (2015), 421.

58. Knitter (2004, 25). This is why for Knitter, "Doing comparative theology is not an alternative to the theology of religions but should be an integral part of it, preventing us [i.e., theologians] from aprioristic and apodictic judgments so that we can arrive at our various positions cautiously and tentatively, always open to critical objections and potential revisions" (29). Compare Neville 2018 on the value to theology of comparative methods and sincere dialogue.

59. Rather than identify this first bridge with Hick's transcategorical Real in Itself, a philosophical approach might be exemplified by James' "religious hypothesis" or by Ian Barbour's Dialogue model, where methodological parallels between theological and scientific reasoning are developed, and "limit questions" that science raises but does not answer are ones that each person might blamelessly answer for themselves using their own religion's concepts. Many who build such a bridge argue for a simpler, common faith and this sometimes finds expression in deism, humanism, or New Age spiritualism as well, so this sort of bridge is broadly inclusive.

60. Every Abrahamic religion has a mystical sub-stream. The Christian medieval work, *The Cloud of Knowing* has it that, "Whoever hears or reads about all this, and thinks that it is fundamentally an activity of the mind, and proceeds then to work it all out along these lines, is on quite the wrong track. He manufactures an experience that is neither spiritual or physical." Apophatic perspectives deserve their due, but in defense of positive theology also (because I have criticized only exclusivist apologetics), the Hindus acknowledge multiple *margas* or paths for virtuous expression, a more scholarly and systematic mode of study being one of them. If I am one blind person and you another, we each need to determine a method for determining the presence we feel, but that method may not be the same.

61. For discussion see Sands, 183. I think Sands is right to see a close complementarity between pragmatist and virtue theoretic approaches in philosophy of religion.

62. William James, *Varieties,* 21. For example, when Teresa of Avila was questioned by Church authorities over whether or not her mystical visions were veridical, or a sign of heresy or witchcraft, her life was in great danger. She could do no better than give evidence of the profoundly positive effects of her visions over her moral actions, and faith. In her case this argument was successful, and she was canonized St. Teresa in the early seventeenth century, forty years after her death.

63. On "friendly" versus "unfriendly" theism and atheism, see Greco 2008, and Kraft and Basinger, 2008. Numerous authors who argue in favor of "friendly theism" and "friendly atheism" support it through epistemic humility, against the non-reciprocating "unfriendly" versions of each that tend to predominate in the polemical discourse of our present-day 'culture wars' over reason and faith, science and religion. Kitcher's term "soft" atheism and its contrast with the hard and aggressive ('miltant modern') atheism that he rejects, strongly overlaps.

64. See Karen Armstrong's *A History of God* for an insightful discussion of the slow development of monotheism and its lasting effects. My point is that religious absolutism and universalism are different things, and that claiming that God as described in a particular putative revelation is "*the* one and true god," presupposes

a background of competition like that between Moses and the magician of Pharaoh (who, not incidentally, could also perform genuine miracles or magic). It suggests a quite different and far less rationally compelling response to religious contrariety than should logically follow from the divine attributes of a universally loving and just god.

65. Knitter sees Griffiths's mutualist exclusivist stance as vaguely drawing upon the valid Hegelian/Marxian insight that the search for truth works dialectically through the clash of opposing ideas. But on closer inspection it is not hard to see how exclusivism militates against dialectics. The analogy between philosophical dialectics and "polemical apologetics" Griffiths recommends is a weak analogy.

66. This is what J. R. Hustwit (2014) terms a *discontinuity* or a *warfare* model of the relationship between religions. Hustwit writes that to deny (IGR) requires both to privilege one's own experiences and "to fail to extend this charity [symmetrically] to others and/or to overlook the fact of foundation for one's own beliefs. Either way, without evidence that the cognitive faculties of Christians are superior to Jain, Hindus, and Buddhists, the warfare model is, at best, guilty of serious inconsistency" (36). A Conflict or *warfare* model of the relationship is *one way* to try to motivate rejecting (IGR). But an Independence or *discontinuity* model appears to try an end-run around (IGR) rather than claiming an intellectual unique right to deny it outright. The logical-inconsistencies are equally apparent here, however. Hustwit seems correct that "the discontinuity model results in a superficial tolerance of other religions because genuine revelation is not a competitor, so there is no need for explicit hostility. However, the inclination towards dialogue is non-existent in a discontinuity model. One finds, at best, a cool indifference toward religious diversity" (36). This description of *discontinuity* reflects the mutualist perspective of Griffiths and others quite well, and depending on one's interpretation of Barth, he is sometimes placed in this camp as well.

67. Steve Clarke (2012) refers to interventionist exclusivism: when a group aims for conversion of non-believers by love or by force. Clarke notes, "The benefits of coercion for the interventionist salvific exclusivist are not exhausted by opportunities to make additional conversions. The interventionist salvific exclusivist is in competition with other religions, many of which have an interest in making apostates of the followers of her religion. If believers in these other religions are also [interventionists] then all things being equal, they will be as motivated as she is to make conversions" (211).

68. For context, we might note that Barth's influence was greatest in what we might take as first-wave post-liberal Protestant apologetics. While he was German, he became influential in Protestant thought in the United States, not long after the term "fundamentalism" was introduced into public discourse with the publication between 1910 and 1915 of *The Fundamentals: A Testimony to the Truth* by the Bible Institute of Los Angeles. Whether Alvin Plantinga's view is an explicit example of it single-religion exclusivism is up for debate, as his treatment of proper basicality pushes him in a plural-religion or mutualist exclusivist direction.

69. Plantinga I take it must be a particularist exclusivist since warrant or reliability, unlike internalist justification, cannot be true of incompatible beliefs, or belief understood on a bivalent understanding of truth for the religious domain.

70. "This happens with arguments, as also elsewhere, through a certain likeness between the genuine and the sham." Aristotle, *On Sophistical Refutations*, 164a20.

71. Griffiths 2001, 159.

72. Hick, *The Interpretation of Religion*, 2nd ed., 235. Hick continues, "Let us avoid the implausibly arbitrary dogma that religious experience is all delusory except with the single exception of the particular form enjoyed by the one who is speaking." Discussed in Adamo, "One True Ring or Many?" 145–146.

73. Hick is a highly influential philosophical theologian, and it is plausible to conceive Griffiths and other mutualist exclusivists as trying to accommodate his Golden Rule by conceding to John Hick that those who experience the world religiously cannot "reasonably claim that our own form of religious experience, together with that of the tradition of which we are a part, is veridical whilst the others are not" (235).

74. J. R. Hustwit (2014, 36–37) understands (IGR) as asserting, "that we ourselves believe there is a right relation between our own experience and our religious beliefs, and there is no rational reason to deny this relation to others." This is why (IGR) militates against bivalence and peer denial. Indeed, Hick's use of it comes in the service of rebutting religious exclusivism and supporting a still realist, but pluralist alternative. But the mutualist exclusivists as I understand them are endorsing (IGR) while expressing their own indifference to difference. They still hold that there is no *religious* value in other traditions, and nothing to be learned through dialogue. The question is, when one takes mutualism seriously, whether one can consistently hold this.

75. In terms of Ian Barbour's influential taxonomy of models of the relationship between religion and science (Conflict, Independence, Dialogue and Integration), the linguistic and post-modern turns (perhaps as exemplified in Wittgensteinian fideism) push away from Conflict and toward Independence. But in these same terms, mutualist exclusivists are accepting most of the *premises* for such a turn, while somehow claiming that it is logically consistent with maintaining almost unchanged the attitudes toward religious aliens and asymmetric trait-ascriptions of the earlier, 'naïve' particularist stance. All that has changed, it appears, is the apologetic strategy, through the addition of a purportedly strong positive apologetic in mutualist ethics / epistemology. This is why I would say that mutualist exclusivism is strongly analogous to the a kind of moral (or cognitive) relativism that would assert, 'All morals (or beliefs) are relative to culture, but *within* each culture, wrong and right (or false and true) are absolutely clear, and beyond criticism.' Obviously, this view is one-sided and seems to be a refutation of facts, since in real life sub, intra, and inter-cultural change is an ongoing process.

76. Another way to put the question is, "How one can assent to moral / epistemic mutualism, yet not go on to endorse *religious* mutualism in any one of Knitter's multiple senses?"

77. Margalit, "The Ring," 152.

78. Garrett Green, 1995, 474.

79. Gellman, 402.

80. Knitter, 186.

81. In attributing mutualism to Griffiths and others who defend exclusivist attitudes using neutral "home" and "alien" terms, I want to be clear that I am not using the term in Knitter's sense (I came upon Knitter's work very lately). In discussion not only of Knitter's "bridges" but also of our own approach, I take inclusivism and exclusivism as exhaustive of the possibilities, with "pluralism" just being a strong form of inclusivism. Various taxonomies would argue for more categories, but it is appropriate for someone trying to stay neutral to questions about realism or non-realism about religious language, and the inclusivist/exclusivist distinction is simply enough to allow this.

82. The principled version of ethical egoism, championed by Adam Smith, holds that pursuing our individual self-interest is our goal, but that this pursuit of our own individual goods also maximizes the greatest good overall. As if by an invisible hand, our each promoting our own individual interests or happiness works to maximize happiness overall. Unprincipled ethical egoism also advises acting self-servingly, but it makes no such claim about a collective good being promoted by egoistic actions.

83. Mill, *On Liberty,* Chapter 1.

84. As Bob Plant (2011, 177) writes, "Wittgenstein's remarks on religious and magical practices are often thought to harbour troubling fideistic and relativistic views. Unsurprisingly, commentators are generally resistant to the idea that religious belief constitutes a 'language-game' governed by its own peculiar 'rules', and is thereby insulated from the critical assessment of non-participants. Indeed, on this fideist-relativist reading, it is unclear how mutual understanding between believers and non-believers (even between different sorts of believers) would be possible." While many (especially exclusivist) theologians explicitly or implicitly do embrace adopt this very radical combination of fideism and relativism, Plant argues that it is not the best way to read Wittgenstein's remarks of religious belief. Still, Kierkegaard's influence on Wittgenstein's lectures was profound, and it is difficult *not* to read Kierkegaard as endorsing this combination. Genia Schönbaumsfeld (2009, 131) interestingly argues that what the two thinkers have in common, however, is an attempt to go beyond the dichotomy of ways to treat faith either "as a 'propositional attitude' on the one hand or as a mere 'emotional response' with no reference to the 'real world' on the other."

85. The appeal to supernatural or final causes as trumping any and all philosophical and scientific standards of epistemic risk does not provide an avenue for by-passing inductive normativity as based on shared, observable proximate causes. It always carries the rider, 'in the home religion but not others,' which is itself an asymmetry that demands neutral criteria if not to be seen as but an article of faith. This is a retreat from reason and accountability for faith-based commitments. Such theologically cast, religion-specific appeals to final causes as discounting shared, neutral evidence, are inevitably claims that 'the pattern stops here'; but doing so marks it as an authority-based claim or a fideistic article of faith. This objectively, i.e., in the shared natural and social world we inhabit, increases the alethic and epistemic (and potentially also, moral) riskiness of the faith ventures based on such assumptions. One can say that 'metaphysics is first philosophy,' but from the interest of neutrality where truth claims

need to be justified and not simply assumed, this as I argue is descriptively an instance of *testimonial authority assumption,* a clear marker of religious fideism.

86. Walter Sinnott-Armstrong (2009) provides a poignant example of these real-world consequences, and of tensions regarding them cannot be ignored because they deeply affect the life of many churches. His case is that of Bishop Carlton Pearson, a graduate of Oral Roberts University who ran a Tulsa, OK-based evangelical megachurch. The website description of Bishop Pearson is from http://www.bishop-pearson.com/about-us. Thanks to Walter for bringing this case and his use of it in his book to my attention. As an update, Pearson's spiritual journey and the reactions it continues to provoke are portrayed in the outstanding docudrama, *Come Sunday* (2018).

87. See Fricker, M. (2007) *Epistemic Injustice: Power and the Ethics of Knowing.* Consistent with work on epistemic injustice, I hold that attitudes and beliefs about others can wrong others. But this claim is not uncontroversial. For recent work on this question of doxastic responsibility and its limits, see the journal special edition edited by Rima Basu and Mark Schroeder (2018a), and their paper "Epistemic Wronging" (2018b), which (like Axtell 2013) appears to defend Susan Haack's (1997) moral-epistemic "overlap" account.

88. Griffiths, 1994, 32.

89. What psychologists Kathleen Kennedy and Emily Pronin argue in their recent article, "Bias Perception and the Spiral of Conflict," seems to apply. They argue that reciprocally aggressive and competitive behavior, as seen in cases of spiraling conflict, typically roots in "people's inclination to perceive others as biased—particularly others who disagree with them." This inclination "can initiate this conflict spiral, as well as fuel it and prevent its resolution." What their studies demonstrate is "that people's perceptions of their adversaries as biased leads them to act conflictually toward those adversaries. That conflictual action, in turn, is perceived by its recipients as a sign of bias, thereby leading those recipients to respond conflictually, as the spiral continues" (2012), 406.

90. Christian inclusivists often cite 1 Timothy 4:10: "For it is for this we labor and strive, because we have fixed our hope on the living God, who is the Savior of all men, especially of believers"; also 2 Peter 3-9: "The Lord is not slow about His promise, as some count slowness, but is patient toward you, not wishing for any to perish but for all to come to repentance; also 1 John 2:2: "and He Himself is the propitiation for our sins; and not for ours only, but also for those of the whole world." See Aydin (2004) for similar inclusivist interpretation of the Hebrew Bible and even the Quran, despite its many exclusivist passages.

91. The conclusion of Ramelli's study of Church history is, "The case against Origen compels not, and the arguments adduced against *apokatastasis* are largely weak. Justinian's argument from the supposed symmetry of the eternal punishment and eternal life is demonstrably invalid" (S. Nemes 2015, Review of Ramelli). See Ramelli (2013) for a theological defense of the orthodoxy of *Apokatastasis*, and Wessling (2019) for discussion. For overlapping theological work, see Fringer and Lane (2015) and Gibberson (ed.) 2016.

92. Reflecting on the similarities between the naturalistic faith of John Dewey and the supernaturalistic orientation of William James, John Bishop (2016) writes, "Both Dewey and James defend models of faith with a view to advancing the idea that authentic religious faith may be found outside what is generally supposed to be theological orthodoxy. Furthermore, they suggest that 'un-orthodox' faith may be *more* authentic than 'orthodox' faith. 'The faith that is religious,' says Dewey, '[I should describe as] the unification of the self through allegiance to inclusive ideal ends, which imagination presents to us and to which the human will responds as worthy of controlling our desires and choices'" (*A Common Faith* 1934, 33).

93. On the present view, the *overdetermination* of religious choices or actions by numerous evolutionary, affective, and social causes is only the flip side of the problem of the *underdetermination* of faith-based belief by evidence, that is, of the *fideistic minimum* present in all faith traditions. Under and overdetermination are *paired* theses. Therefore, the multifarious causes of violence are perhaps not as unanalyzable as Cassam suggest, and I propose that we see *overdetermination theory* as itself an important part of what Cassam terms the epistemology of terrorism and counter-terrorism. Understood as a study of *contributory* causes, overdetermination theory tied to scales for fideistic orientation can yet provide an epistemological footing for optimism about the continued improvement of our ability to predict behaviors and to suggest when intervention of some kind might be appropriate.

94. As children of time, we deserve respect for background beliefs and for many other effects of culture. Guidance must be consistent with psychological acknowledgment of pragmatism about reasons and of the ecological rationality of human agents. I would not presume to say that belief may never be permissibly responsive to non-epistemic reasons. We must not forget that we rightly reason holistically, and that as creatures of time as well as of place, we inevitably 'live forward.' Looking backward, as Montaigne correctly says, is much more difficult for us, and this is where philosophy and the sciences help the most. We simply do not know, prior to careful reflection and honest dialogue with others, the 'real' causes for our beliefs. We need not agree with a broad skepticism that insists that 'ignorance of our ignorance is the death of knowledge,' in Whitehead's phrase. But again, what consequences to draw from the epistemic location problem are by no means clear-cut.

95. My paper "From Internalist Evidentialism to Virtue Responsibilism" argued that the norms that inform an ethic of belief are typically more diachronic than synchronic, and that guidance-giving takes place in the context of ecological rationality, not ideal agency where the *order* of acquired evidence should make no rational difference as all. Note that the objections I present to Feldman and Conee's explicitly *epistemic* evidentialism are meant to be complemented by my direct response (2018) to the over-weaning *moral* evidentialism of Scott Aikin and Rob Talisse (2018). Both parties I think misapply the *Rational Uniqueness Thesis* to the epistemology of controversial views.

96. See Carter (2017) and Bondy and Carter (eds.) 2019. To accommodate the unlivability objection to principled agnosticism, Carter expands the connotation of "agnosticism" to include the sub-doxastic attitude of 'suspecting that,' when

conditions are right. But in this prescription, much like Feldman, there is still assumed a single right response to revealed peer disagreement among controversial views: agnosticism. Like Feldman it appears that Carter's categories of doxastic attitudes are still essentially treated deontologically, since they line up with epistemic duties or entitlements. These are things denied by permissivists like myself. I take epistemic and pragmatic reason, and again, the rational and the social, to be artificially dichotomized in accounts that treat guidance in this way. Recognition of the collapse of the fact-value dichotomy is advantageous to the epistemology of controversial views. Until we dichotomize the rational and the social our dependency on epistemic and doxastic luck is not (or not so) troubling. But much of what I take to be best work on the epistemology of disagreement is on the permissivist side. See especially the work of Thomas Kelly, and Matthew Kopec and Michael Titelbaum.

97. Sometimes contingency or variability arguments are described as arguments from *evidentially irrelevant causes of belief,* or simply as *debunking arguments*, on assumption that they threaten to explain the etiology of these beliefs in a way that has nothing to do with their likelihood of being truth. I doubt this approach, since I doubt the rational-social dichotomy on which it is based. On the other extreme are dogmatists and phenomenological conservatives who have also taken some interest in the epistemic location problem, but who use "parity" and other sorts of arguments, often authority-based, to argue that evidential or environmental luck is no concern to well-founded beliefs. For some, 'seeming is believing,' and the seriousness of the problem finds no foothold.

98. See Booth (2011) in support of the separate projects idea, the 'divorce' between the theory of rationality and the analysis of knowledge earlier proposed by Richard Foley.

Chapter 6

The Pattern Stops Here?

Counter-Inductive Thinking, Counter-Intuitive Ideas, and Cognitive Science of Religion

"No. There it will break down. . . . No Induction. Terror. That is, as it were, part of the substance of the belief."[1]

—Ludwig Wittgenstein, *Lectures on Religious Belief*

WHAT IS MEANT BY "SCIENCE OF RELIGION"?

Cognitive science of religion (hereafter CSR) is a relatively new field of research, at this writing about 25 years old.[2] CSR has been a source of interest by religious and non-religious academics alike, with some of its biggest conferences held at religiously affiliated colleges.[3] Justin Barrett defines CSR as an attempt to scientifically account for patterns of social expression often deemed religious. Dimitris Xygalatas defines CSR as an empirically based study of mental capacities and processes that underlie recurrent patterns of religious thought and behavior. As an experimentally focused human science, CSR researchers frame specific hypotheses that allow for testable predictions. These hypotheses might concern psychological and evolutionary mechanisms of belief formation, maintenance, and revision. They might concern cognitive or evolutionary explanations for why religious beliefs and practices emerge and persist, based on dynamics of ordinary cognition.

In the 2013 inaugural issue of the *Journal for the Cognitive Science of Religions* the editors lay out some of the core questions CSR studies: "How are religious concepts generated, acquired, represented and transmitted?" and "What are the cognitive structures governing and constraining these processes, and how have these structures been shaped?" CSR researchers, they write, "aim to shed light both on the proximate psychological mechanisms underpinning religious belief and behaviour, and on the ultimate evolutionary forces that sustain religious representations."[4]

In these respects, CSR remains consonant with Hume's approach in his *The Natural History of Religion,* which sought a fuller understanding of religious expressions by distinguishing two different questions, that concerning the reasonableness of religious credences, and that concerning their etiology or causal origins:

> As every enquiry, which regards Religion, is of the utmost importance, there are two questions in particular, which challenge our principle attention, to whit, that concerning its foundation in reason, and that concerning its origin in human nature.[5]

While no doubt steeped in theory, CSR as I understand it takes no stance on the question of realism or non-realism about religious use of language. As a science, CSR concerns itself with the second of Hume's questions—origins in human nature, and not either with the first question about rationality or justification, or with questions of metaphysics. It assumes no necessary incompatibility of the CSR literature with theism. Questions of its implications for debates over religious realism or anti-realism, and for the existence of supernatural occurrences, are questions that go beyond science proper. But issues that are beyond the scope of science to investigate directly are often pursued by philosophers, theologians, or others who might draw from CSR research.

Helen De Cruz, a philosopher, asks, "Does the second question have an impact on the first, i.e., does the causal, psychological origin of religion have an impact on the reasonableness of religious beliefs?"[6] The short answer is that they may, but that normative issues like those about reasonableness and justification are basically philosophical rather than scientific questions. Secular and religious thinkers who debate the force of etiological challenges to the well-foundedness of religious beliefs would do well to be empirically informed, but these debates are carried on beyond the boundaries of science. So also, whether serious de jure and de facto challenges arise *from* CSR is not itself a question *for* CSR, for the simple reasons that these are moral, epistemological, and metaphysical questions.[7] CSR researchers typically hold that CSR is committed to no position theological or a-theological on the existence of divine or supernatural forces.[8] CSR is concerned with naturalistic explanation, and so with the causal mechanisms or processes underlying visible manifestations of religion. But as Justin Barrett puts it, CSR is *methodologically* a-teleological in its approach to causes; it is neutral to and not eliminative of another whole order of causes asserted by theologians as higher or deeper.[9]

Robert McCauley writes in "Cognitive Science and the Naturalness of Religion" that his approach to religious phenomena finds the persistence of religion attributable to "the cognitive naturalness of religious ideas, i.e. attributable to the readiness, the ease, and the speed with which human minds acquire and process popular religious representations."[10] CSR seeks explanations of cultural phenomena in terms of acquisition, representation and transmission involving cognitive capacities. These evolutionary and cognitive approaches display less interest in study of cultural differences, but need not exclude them.

Before framing the main thesis for this final chapter, we need to say more about how, in the present study, evolutionary and cognitive approaches are connected with the previous chapter's focus on comparative fundamentalism. Barrett and McCauley both recognize the need for balance between the particular and universal (or generic) in the study of religious ideas. How ideas transfer also needs to be balanced in this way. There is no simple answer as to whether to study religion or *religions.* One aim of CSR to which I hope this chapter will contribute is to disentangle the relationship between cognition and culture in religious representations. But Justin Barrett seems correct that even within CSR there has been something akin to a nature–nurture debate.[11]

The nativist strand in this debate strips away cognitive specificity to explain the propensity for religious credences in terms of a universal cognitive architecture. The nativist is the universal side—what is universal to the human condition. As an example, researchers in CSR sometimes apply dual—processing models of thought drawn from social psychology and neuroscience. We all share the features of the "old" mind and depend heavily its intuitive, heuristic Type 1 reasoning. This type of reasoning is fast and frugal, so we are naturally hesitant to "de-couple" from it. Our reliance on it many times that we should have employed some slower and more methodical dispositions of Type 2 explains many deviations with normatively correct reasoning. At the nurturist end of this debate, emanating mostly from social psychology and cultural anthropology, we find a different emphasis: one that highlights religious specificity, as studied through ritual and community, culturally conditioning of belief, and the politics of identity. These interests in general cognitive explanation and studies of more ethnographically specific levels of description are each legitimate, and necessary for the development of the field. Numerous scholars are combining aspects of each, but balancing them theoretically remains a challenge for researchers. There are many reasons why.

According to researchers focusing on what is universal in our cognitive architecture, too much emphasis on differences in religious belief and practice is seen as an unwarranted impediment to inquiry. Todd Tremlin writes,

> Among the roadblocks to a scientific study of religion is the long—standing view that religious thought is somehow unlike other kinds of thought, and that

it therefore cannot be explained in the same way that ordinary ideas can be. . . . Another traditional misconception of religious studies is that the tremendous diversity within religion found around the world makes it impossible either to generalize about human religiosity or to construct a single explanatory theory.[12]

CSR does not approach religion as an evolved adaptation or as employing cognitive architecture specialized for the acquisition of religious behavior. Rather than there being any special module for religiosity, many CSR researchers share the by-product thesis: that thesis that religious ideas arise as a by-product of cognitive modules and mechanisms that also have quite unrelated adaptive functions. Robert McCauley understands religious ideas as resting on normal mental structures and processes. The processes on which CSR has focused most, ToM (theory of mind) and HADD (hyperactive agency detective device), are the ones originally evolved to serve different though functionally related purposes.[13]

Comparative fundamentalism (CF) primarily comes out of religious studies and subfields like comparative religious ethics. Scholars in these fields might worry that too much emphasis on generic processing and evolutionary explanations might be an impediment to studying the religious behavioral patterns and social dynamics they are most interested in. So as we continue to develop our inductive risk toolkit, this chapter will propose specific ways through which this general-specific contrast between CSR and Religious Studies can be mediated, and CSR and CF more closely connected with each other. There might be numerous ways in which the general and specific might be balanced in CSR research. But I will argue that philosophy of luck as developed in the first two chapters, and religious fideism and counter-inductive thinking as studied in the third and fourth chapters, both raise pertinent questions that CSR can best address. These same concerns with strong fideism and its demonstrable connections with counter-inductive thinking can also bring CSR and CF into closer connection with each other.

VAINIO'S CHRISTIAN PHILOSOPHIC APPROPRIATION AND CRITIQUE OF CSR

Epistemology and ethics are fields that prescribe norms of thought and action. Cognitive and social psychology help explain the mechanisms that cause us to deviate either consciously or unconsciously from normative principles of logic or ethics, and in some cases to flout them more or less predictably. These sciences are in turn informing what Jack Lyons and Barry Ward call the "new critical thinking," by which they mean a pedagogy that does not only study formal reasoning and informal fallacies, but also recognizes that "many of our mistakes are not caused by formal reasoning gone awry, but by our bypassing it completely. We instead favor more comfortable, but often unreliable, intuitive methods."[14]

My point is that only by more closely aligning philosophical normativity with psychological study can we hope to improve *real world* critical thinking, as is crucially necessary to address many problems that we face. A growing number of theologians and religious philosophers would agree. Empirically informed religious thinkers like Olli-Pekka Vainio in his recent book, *Disagreeing Virtuously: Religious Conflict in Interdisciplinary Perspective* (2017) are well aware of the impact of biases and heuristics on human cognition, and are as interested as any secular philosopher in the implications of the human sciences for religious epistemics. Vainio acknowledges that "quite a large amount of our religious cognition is channelled through Type 1 cognitive processes. Even if this does not automatically cause massive suspicion, it may cause theological problems within religious systems."[15]

Following upon his earlier study of the variety of forms of fideism, Vainio's approach in *Disagreeing Virtuously* emphasizes that "the problematic elements of religion are usually those that are shared by every human being, regardless of their worldview. If there's something that we should worry about, it is the dynamics to create and enforce ingroup/outgroup distinctions, be they religious or secular."[16] Subject to these qualifications, Vainio is interested in defending virtuous disagreement among religious adherents, and between the religious and non-religious. So Vainio takes a pro-attitude toward interdisciplinary dialogue between theologians, philosophers, and psychologists over the effects of psychology on what he calls people's different doxastic policies or theological methods. He aims to improve the dialogue between these parties by developing a "dynamic view" of disagreement informed by the human sciences, on the one hand, and virtue theory on the other.

I highly admire Vainio's approach in *Disagreeing Virtuously,* and how this Christian thinker appropriates CSR to help explain religious violence and to defend toleration and the importance of continuous dialogue across traditions. Since we have both developed virtue-theoretic accounts of doxastic responsibility, there is a good deal of common ground in our projects in philosophy of religion. This said, I will take issue with three specific positions Vainio takes, and discussing these will lead us afterwards to want to look more carefully at so-called "debunking" explanations, and at the relationship between more qualified de jure and more sweeping de facto challenges.

Firstly, while Vainio's book provides many rich thick descriptions of the role of particular intellectual and moral virtues in a religious life, he defends the reasonableness of the exclusivist response to religious multiplicity on one of the few pages where he engages it directly. I will not here repeat the problems raised for that response in this book. But I will briefly respond that Vainio's endorsement of reasonable or virtuous exclusivism is logically inconsistent with the account he gives of the virtues.

Secondly, I will defend CSR against Vainio's charge that there is a standard model in CSR that applies dual-process theory in a reductive way, treating religious phenomena largely or wholly as emanations of Type 1 thinking, with all its flaws. This issue will open out into a broader discussion of the relationship between de jure and de facto challenges, their different intended targets, and the conditions under which the presence of a plausible and sufficient naturalistic explanation of a phenomena is sufficient grounds to slide to the stronger de facto challenge. With this latter topic, I will also be able to develop some of the parallels between my approach in this book, and Hume's approach to miracles.

Thirdly, I will take issue with how Vainio treats religious diversity that arises from the same or similar belief-forming functions. Vainio asks whether NERBs—naturalistic explanations of religious beliefs—present any very direct challenge to the attitude of religious exclusivists. But his argument that they do not present a serious challenge relies upon a sense of exclusivism ("open" doctrinal exclusivism) far weaker than the salvific exclusivism we have seen numerous examples of. So his answer I will argue comes too easily, since NERBs challenge naturalistically unsupported asymmetries in trait-ascription, and there are far more of these in full-blooded salvific exclusivism. I will argue that NERBs pose a special challenge where the *same* belief—formation method manifests in the form of religious diversity, and another where this method manifests in infallibilist beliefs and exclusivist attitudes, which set each against the others as competitors for one true path to truth and/or salvation.[17]

The first issue concerns Vainio's description and dismissal of what he perceives as a standard model in CSR, a model he says aims to associate all or most religious thinking with Type or System 1 processing. Part of his complaint regards CSR's studies of "theological incorrectness," and its primary focus on "popular religiosity."[18] This exhibits, he thinks, a disregard for how religious thinkers engage Type or System 2 reasoning, reflecting deeply on their beliefs and their causes, and improving their epistemic standing with respect to them. Vainio cites Justin Slone's book *Theological Incorrectness: Why Religious People Believe What They Shouldn't* (2004) as indicative of this distortion of religious views. "It is not clearly the case that religious believers are not engaging in higher and refined forms of cognition, or that theologian's ideas are systematically disregarded." This reductive image of CSR that Vainio thinks is the standard model is one where "religion is almost purely a matter of type 1 cognition," and where type 2 cognition (theology and philosophy) functions as "*post hoc* rationalizations of fundamentally irrational folk beliefs."[19] Vainio is more generally concerned that "CSR writers have different views about the religious relevance of their theories, but negative relevance is often simply assumed without further argument."[20] When researchers like the ones Vainio cites describe religious beliefs or behavior as irrational, isn't it because they are already assuming the de facto view that religious beliefs are untrue? By contrast, Vainio argues that even if people may not always be virtuous in belief-acquisition, they can and typically do become so in the course of second-order reflection; this reflection, he points out, often works to raise their interest in and conformity with more systematic theological thinking.[21]

There are clearly some valid points here, and the line between CSR or any science and a realist or antirealist metaphysic concerning their subject matter, ought to be maintained. We can agree that how study of group biases applies to religious identity, teachings, and dynamics is an open question. But while there might well be examples of it, most CSR integration of dual-process cognitive theory does not appear to beg these questions, or to make for a valid target for Vainio's criticism. Aggressive atheists or "debunkers" might appropriate CSR data for their own arguments; CSR researchers might not feel themselves bound by the "methodological agnosticism" taught to religious studies majors. But among CSR researchers in the field today I doubt that there are many examples of the reductive stance Vainio describes. As a prime example, McCauley's CSR applies dual-process cognitive science, yet it clearly allows the reflective, "slow" thinking that Vainio calls upon religious adherents to apply to their beliefs. The explicit religious credences adopted and transmitted by the religious, McCauley argues, are generally those in line with what is maturationally natural. We only need common or universal human cognitive architecture to explain why maturationally natural ideas, when processed through domain-specific modules or belief-forming functions, become especially appealing options for adoption and transmission across time. Evolutionary perspectives draw on universal causes rather than proximate environmental ones, but more reflective thinking may always be applied to one's beliefs, *however* acquired.

Type 1 processing is sometimes related to automaticity. Automaticity is rapid and effortless cognition that operates without conscious awareness or deliberative control. But these faculties are not always unreliable, nor do they threaten a credit theory of knowing. Clea Rees and Jonathan Webber's "Automaticity in Virtuous Action" (2014) develop the specific contributions of automaticity for moral and intellectual virtue. The automaticity and/or heuristic aspects of our thinking often support, rather than just threaten, the development of habits and dispositions of critical thinkers. I relatedly argue elsewhere (2017c) that autonomous processing can be supportive of the virtues, but also that heuristic reasoning becomes unreliable when what West,

Toplak, and Stanovich (2008) term "fluid rationality" or higher-order critical reasoning dispositions are instead called for in one's epistemic context or problem-situation. Persons who lack the ability for sustained de-coupling will fail reasoning tasks that the engagement of their fluid rationality would allow them to succeed with. Of course, the normal development of the critical reasoning dispositions of fluid rationality involves recognizing and applying inductive norms (causal reasoning, generalization, and analogy).[22]

The philosophical and theological implications of dual-process theory, or the ecological nature of human cognition, are certainly debatable. I believe there are strong normative implications that both fields have yet to fully come to grips with. While it is a bit of a digression, let me add a suggestion about how theologians and philosophers can at least better recognize these normative implications. This suggestion is especially of value if the disputants are talking past one another. I suggest taxonomizing issues about naturalism and normativity by crossing the distinctions between the *etiological* and the *axiology*, and between the *deep* (ancient; general) and the *shallow* (acquired; learned; normative). What I have in mind is one dimension running between that which is buried *deep* or only *shallow* in the human psyche, and the other dimension running between the *etiological* (order of causes) and the *axiological* (order of values).

Thinking in maturationally natural ways is etiologically deep, but typically axiologically shallow, since its specific content is conditioned and filtered by culture. Thinking in maturationally natural ways draws attention to propensities of mind that are etiologically deep because rooted in our "old mind," in "online" cognition; but it is axiologically shallow because it draws norms from culture, and often refuses or is in tension with logical and epistemological norms. Reasoning and the acquired critical thinking dispositions are just the opposite. They are axiologically shallow, and have the characteristic McCauley attributes to the "practiced natural." These norms are correctives to biases where they intrude on inquiry. We have to value and habituate ourselves to critical reasoning skills, and habituation is a matter of practice; this does not come easily or naturally, and until internalized as good habits of thought there may be much psychological resistance to them.

The upshot for our present discussion is that CSR's concern with universal cognitive architecture is a concern for *etiologically deep* sources of religious ideas, and not with what is *etiologically shallow* in the sense of ideas acquired along with culture, or corrected religion-specific theologies or rituals. This contrast, additionally, should not raise flags that religion is being denied recognition as a source in people's lives or core *values*. That would be a claim about *axiology*. Facility with theological reasoning, and the ability of some not to stray as others do from the content and norms of theological correctness within a tradition may be well and good for the individual. But this is a different question than that of belief-acquisition and transfer. Ideally, my taxonomy enables clearer location of the points of contention in the debate

Table 6.1   Organization of the Philosophical Implications of Dual-process Theory

	Deep	*Shallow*
Etiologically	• Mere behaviors • Type 1 processing • Heuristic thinking of the old mind • Appeal of maturationally natural ideas	• Intentional actions • Type 2 processing • Self-conscious employment of a doxastic strategy • Fluid rationality and critical thinking dispositions
Axiologically	• Pro-social moral emotions • Anti-social emotions/*Thanatos* or other recurrent regressive values • Self-interest; ingroup–outgroup dynamics	• Societal expectations and assigned social roles • Culturally recognized virtues and vices • Posited universal moral principles or rights. • Evolved scientific and disciplinary norms

over CSR, such as debate over availability of NERBs for beliefs in different domains, and their implications in particular for how we understand religious differences. Table 6.1 includes some brief examples of how this classification works.

The organization of issues according to this taxonomy also allows us to parse concerns about safety, sensitivity, and epistemic risk (chapter 2). It is not enough to rebut etiological challenges based on CSR research as Vainio does by pointing out how people may improve their theological reasoning within the faith-tradition in which they are raised. The question of safe and sensitive belief-acquisition is an externalist concern, and this is why the *post hoc* use of reason to defend or extend beliefs acquired on another basis is indeed philosophically significant, as we have previously argued. Those processes which are maturationally natural can be anticipated to continue to impact thought and culture, widely construed, even if they are not reliable processes in the sense of giving rise to beliefs that are truth-apt. One might correctly say that this is true for the full range of our controversial views, if it is true at all. But the self-reflection of a religious agent subsequent to an act of testimonial authority assumption will not very directly affect the *external* concerns with safety and sensitivity on which etiological challenges may be based. It cannot, because these are not even in the same ballpark: No appeal to theological systematization and reflection within a faith-tradition has the power to later transform intervening or environmental veritic luck into benign evidential luck. Etiological challenges as framed by philosophers instead need to be met with *specific* reasons why the good religious luck in the etiology of a belief is benign rather than malign. Then the debate can truly be engaged. But to treat theological reflection as upgrading positive epistemic status, or as a sufficient demonstration of the agent's intellectual virtue, would be to assume that internal cogitations negate externalist concerns with veritic luck. That, I take it, is logically precluded by the external and modal status of veritic luck.

The second concern I raised above is the position Vainio takes on how NERBs are related to recognized religious diversity. He makes the blanket claim that

> NERBs do not bring anything new that would dramatically change the situation. We already knew that diversity existed; suggesting a cognitive mechanism that brings about diversity does not alter the basic premises of the solutions that Christian theologians have already suggested in the course of history.[23]

Cognitive science of religions raises an interesting philosophical question: If we are able to tell a plausible naturalistic story about how religiosity emerged in the course of human evolution, have we provided a debunking account, one that reveals the true nature of religion as something produced by impersonal forces of evolution? Vainio insists not, and this is consistent with our own non-reductionist view. Truth-tracking and fitness-tracking functions of belief are not identical, but neither are they mutually exclusive categories. Vainio may be right that "throughout their history, theistic religions have formulated answers that take into account the diversity of religions in a way that reflects their core beliefs." According to the author, "contemporary CSR provides nothing that would make religious noncognitivism or anti-realism more plausible than they were before."[24]

To support this conclusion, Vainio has his readers focus on a peculiar claim made by Barrett: that if NERBs produced religious uniformity among humans, this might actually be a ground for antirealist. Vainio then reasons:

> For Barrett, NERBs combined with the *unity* of religions and worldviews would count against theological realism. In order for NERBs to acquire their debunking power, we would need a uniform belief—formation process that produces demonstrably false beliefs, not supported by epistemic arguments. So if NERBs plus uniformity would be more problematic for exclusivists, we can conclude that NERBS plus diversity does not have an immediate effect on the evidential force of the exclusivist claims. Therefore, the debunking thesis fails.[25]

Vainio's inference regarding the combination of NERBS and religious diversity, and his subsequent dismissal of their relevance to exclusivist responses to religious multiplicity, seems far too quick. I will argue that it is quite unsound: The relationship between NERBS and religious diversity is neither so uniform nor as settled as Vainio here asserts. Let me explain why.

Firstly, the application of NERBS likely does not require Barrett's somewhat quirky claim in the first place. Vainio might just be trying to argue on Barrett's premises, but imagining exclusivism—even doctrinal exclusivism—together with complete uniformity of belief makes no sense to me. Who would these exclusivists be excluding? For on this scenario there are no nonbelievers, and the uniformity of belief guarantees that there is only one set of beliefs that humans in fact adopt. Secondly, even assuming Barrett's claim that NERBs plus uniformity of religious belief provides the strongest case for anti-realism about religious belief, Vainio ignores an important detail in Barrett's argument: that "beliefs about God's, souls, and the rest would likewise be more suspect if it were discovered that *no matter the information available*, the mind used it to arrive deterministically at such beliefs" (italics added for emphasis).[26] This rider makes the conditions under which uniform belief would invite skepticism still more hyperbolic. How would we ever discover if this odd counter-factual condition, no matter the information available, were met? This again makes doubtful Vainio's unusual view that contrariety somehow *reduces* the plausibility of fictionalism or anti-realism in that domain. As a general point, it increases it. Finally, Vainio's conclusion appears overdrawn because there are clearly conditions where a belief-forming cognitive mechanism that gives rise to diverse outputs should motivate skepticism about the epistemic status of *all*, not just some of the generated beliefs. Our study focuses not on religious truth and knowledge, but on doxastic responsibility and the intellectual viciousness of counter-inductive thinking. Still, we should not shy away from direct examination of the relationship between de jure and de facto challenges.

This relationship between the two types of challenges, which some recent collections in CSR contain interesting papers on, will be the focus of the next section. But throughout the course of this book we have been concerned with doxastic methods that generate sharply *asymmetric* moral, epistemic, and theological trait-ascriptions. We termed the production of contrariety through symmetrical proximate causes as the main generator of what we earlier termed *enemy in the mirror effects* (EME). So I do think that religious contrariety generated under unsafe or counter-inductive doxastic methods has an immediate effect on the evidential force of the exclusivist claims. The question, "Are any of them better off?" naturally arises from our Etiological Symmetry thesis (in chapter 2) plus the multiplicity or diversity it produces. This goes quite some distance, we have held, to explaining why exclusivist responses to religious multiplicity are far more common in testimonial traditions like those of the Abrahamic religions, than, for instance, in mystical or meditational practice–oriented traditions.[27] Their mirrored vice/bias charges directed at faith-based belief in all alien faith communities makes considerably worse their case for being epistemologically or alethically better off than others.

When the attitude exhibited by a religious exclusivist or recommended by an apologist is the attitude we would say that a biased individual *would* exhibit, we have the phenomena that we have called bias-mirroring. I take it that the exclusivist cannot plausibly deny this of exclusivists either of the home religion or of an alien one. But now the question becomes, in an inference to the best explanation, does the self-exception cast in theological terms of divine plan, or the NERB, provide the better explanation? Following the Diversity Principle as a major norm of inductive reason, more diverse evidence is normally stronger than less diverse evidence. If the majority of religions, those not of the purported true faith, are well-explained by the NERB, there is an inductive presumption that describing one's own religion as the lone exception to naturalistic explanation does not of itself insulate one from the challenge. In the case of explanations involving identity bias one would think rather that religious exclusivism *invites* uniform application, since self-exemption from causes that regularly lead to false religious beliefs is close to the very definition of exclusivism. The more numerous the self-exemptors, the more likely that all are shaped by the same causal factors. Applying the diversity principle rebuts Vainio's argument, and indicates that the strength of NERBs to motivate debunking explanations is a question of their inductive strength. The New Problem is then a problem for Vainio insofar as it shows that when religious exceptionalism partakes of counter-inductive thinking, the alternative naturalistic explanation gains considerable strength.[28]

Vainio is probably right that the theological liberalism of a generation ago, perhaps exemplified in John Hick's neo-Kantian *ding-an-sich* "tried to universalize everything in monistic fashion," while contemporary revisionism, in adopting more aspects of postmodernism, steps away from such essentialism and instead acknowledges genuine particularity. Liberal and conservative theologians might agree on this, though responses to multiplicity or related issues divide them. But we can add support to our response to Vainio by relating another recent discussion of the reach and limitations of so-called evolutionary debunking arguments. According to P. E. Griffiths and John Wilkins (2013), "Evolutionary debunking arguments suggest that the evolutionary origins of our cognitive faculties should undermine our confidence in the beliefs which those faculties produce."[29] Evolutionary adaptions may produce beliefs that in some domains are truth-apt, and in other domains are not. So it is incumbent on evolutionary debunking arguments that they have resources to distinguish specific classes of belief for which the skeptical argument has force, and other beliefs for which it does not.

On the third point of contention, Vainio defines exclusivism in terms of its doctrinal, not its salvific sense. Many soteriological exclusivists are not also doctrinal exclusivists, and so can allow that there may be religious truths to be found outside the home religion. Exclusivism in the doctrinal sense is only about religious truth-possession, and so his "open exclusivism," is a watered down version of what most self-described exclusivists hold.[30] This has an important implication for how Vainio treats NERBs. When he asks whether NERBs present any very direct challenge to the attitude of religious exclusivists, he presents exclusivism differently than when it implicates the further explanatory asymmetries of religious *value* and of culpability for unbelief that salvific exclusivism ascribes to religious aliens.[31] I see NERBs as challenging asymmetries not supported by relevant difference reasoning. Salvific exclusivism attributes many more relevant differences to religious insiders and outsiders than does doctrinal exclusivism. It most notably includes that religious aliens' lack value in God's eye, and that they are morally culpable for not having taken up the one salvific religious identity. Essentially it is about people and their actions, not just about truth taken abstractly. Until Vainio takes up the harder case of salvific (or soteriological) exclusivism, I remain unconvinced by his treatment of NERBs and his conclusion that they raise no new worries for exclusivists. Moreover, I suspect that many of the intellectual virtues Vainio so nicely develops in his book, for instance "open-mindedness," "maintaining a critical attitude and public conversation," "virtuous tolerance" or the idea that inter-religious dialogue has to express intellectual virtues, are either rejected outright or implicitly violated in salvific exclusivism.[32]

Under what specific conditions might evolutionary explanations "debunk" belief? This is a question that Griffiths and Wilkins ask, but that Vainio's discussion seems to miss due to the blanket response he makes, that NERBS can never really suggest any new challenges that theologians have not already thought about and responded to. The authors employ the helpful concept of a "Milvian Bridge" for domains in which natural selection will favor the production of truth-apt beliefs. They argue that "there is a Milvian Bridge connecting true commonsense beliefs to evolutionary success," while "no Milvian Bridge links true religious beliefs to evolutionary success." What the authors mean is that in the one domain but not the other, it is plausible to link true belief with pragmatic success, that is, to see evolutionary success as grounds for attributing truth.[33] So as the authors seem right to point out,

> It is an error to contrast truth-tracking with fitness tracking because this treats complementary explanations at different levels of analysis as if they were rival explanations at the same level of analysis. . . . "Fitness-tracking" is not an alternative to 'truth-tracking' because truth-tracking is a property at a lower level of explanation. . . . It makes sense to ask if a trait is an adaptation for respiration, or for foraging, or for something else. It makes no sense to ask if a trait is an adaption "for fitness," since that is simply to repeat the definition of an adaptation—a trait that evolved because it enhanced fitness.[34]

So evolutionary debunking arguments that work on universal causes have no force on everyday commonsense ideas, or arguably on beliefs obtained through scientific reasoning. But etiological challenges based on an unusual proximate mechanism, like brainwashing, might challenge particular beliefs. Evolutionary debunking may, however, have more force against moral beliefs or religious beliefs, again either by domain or by individuated belief. The success of debunking is tied to its ability to target an over-strong realism about the domain to which the target belief belongs. Religious beliefs, the authors conclude, "emerge as particularly vulnerable to evolutionary debunking arguments. . . . Current evolutionary theory really does support the view that human beings would have religious beliefs even if all religious beliefs were uniformly false." But, they continue, "debunking is not disproving. If there are independent reasons for religious belief, their cogency is not removed by the fact that religious beliefs have evolutionary explanations."[35] This seems to be a more sound way to approach the special concern that the combination of NERBS plus religious diversity raises. But the relation between our de jure challenge (to the reasonableness of the exclusivist attitude), and a more widely cast de facto challenge (to beliefs acquired on the basis of testimonial authority assumption) invites a more direct discussion.

DE JURE AND DE FACTO CHALLENGES: HOW RELATED?

Challenges to a belief can take multiple forms. The literature on so-called debunking unfortunately equivocates somewhat between an argument that casts doubt on the *doxastic responsibility* (moral and intellectual virtue) of the agent in coming to hold or maintain the belief, and an argument that casts doubt on the *truth* (or candidacy *for* truth) of what the agent asserts.

If "debunking explanation" is defined as covering both de jure and de facto challenges, as it seems to be in the literature, it is not a very helpful term. While I will not use this term, the relationship between de jure and de facto challenges is indeed an important question.[36] Philip Kitcher's work should be mentioned in this connection. Kitcher's Terri Lectures make solid points about the *symmetry - of - generation thesis* (thesis (ES) in Chapter 2). Recall that etiological symmetry holds wherever the proximate grounds behind beliefs are of the same general type. I see myself as close to Kitcher on this, as well as on his articulation of different models of faith with varying degrees of rational respectability (and also on his clear, strong response to Dawkins, Sam Harris, and other "militant modern atheists").

However, Kitcher does not develop the further connections that interest us here: how asymmetry of content—strong and even polarized contrariety—*flows from etiolog*ically symmetrical processes, especially in testimonial faith-traditions.[37] Following upon my response to Vainio in the previous section, my thesis is that the *combination* of etiological symmetry and content contrariety is what we need to pay the most attention to. If this combination is quite epistemically significant, it is because it exhibits the clearest indicators of counter-inductive thinking. But notice also that it is combinations of this sort that also raise the plausibility of moving from judging some claims in the domain as untrue while allowing that others are possibly true, to judging it more likely that all of them are untrue. The debate over miracle claims is a debate where this dynamic of movement from a de jure to a de facto challenge is ever-present, so we can develop our thesis further by briefly comparing it with Hume on miracles.

Hume on Miracles

In certain respects, my project's concern with the explanatory asymmetries that power apologetics for religious exclusivism also parallels the Humean critique of miracles. The relationship between de jure and de facto challenges might be illuminated through this parallel, so let us make a brief digression. Hume did not overgeneralize in the way that presents religious beliefs as *en toto* rational or irrational. There are different possible bases for belief, through reasoning, experience, testimonial transfer, etc. Hume's argument starts from an epistemic focus on the reasonableness of belief in miracles on the basis of testimony; it focuses on the rational credibility of such claims for the recipient of testimony about a miracle event, not for someone who purportedly experienced such an event first-personally. The New Problem's challenge to sharply asymmetrical trait-ascriptions basically parallels this. In both cases this is an epistemological argument, or what we have called a de jure challenge.

But notice that Hume's argument also has potential, whether Hume pushed this line or not, for denying the very *existence* of miracles—a stronger de facto argument. The de facto argument concerning miracles, suggested but not fully developed by Hume, holds that while it is logically *possible* that most miracle claims are false while some smaller number of them are true—say the miracle events recounted just in religion x's sacred narratives, uniquely—it is far more *probable* that all of them are false. Somewhat relatedly, in psychology if you design tests to look for an effect but in repeated studies do not observe it, this is good evidence that there *is no such effect*. This is no mean appeal to ignorance, but takes place through the search for evidence, and by deducing observable consequences from working hypotheses. Moving from absence of evidence to evidence of absence thus seems be part of abductive reasoning; the epistemic import of lack of empirical evidence depends upon context, and by no means is always fallacious.[38]

Hume's argument regarding miracles also has versions which draw attention to the counter-inductive nature of miracle claims. This comes in two ways: in his analysis of testimonial sources of such claims, and in the alternative psychological explanation he offers of why miracle claims are often persuasive for recipients of the testimony.[39] About the first he writes, "When anyone tells me, that he saw a dead man restored to life, I immediately consider with myself, whether it be more probable, that this person should either deceive or be deceived, or the fact, which he relates, should really have happened." Belief based on human testimony varies with people's experience. "Where this experience is not uniform on any side, it is attended with an unavoidable contrariety in our judgments, and with the same opposition and mutual destruction of opposites as with every sort of evidence."[40] To respect inductive norms concerning the reception of testimony, Hume thinks that we should always reject the miracle claim unless the falsehood of the testimony would be more miraculous than the breach of a causal regularity. Hume's own skepticism about the principle of induction has often been cited against him where he purports to say that the violation of a law of nature must be highly improbable. But Hume does not rely on his epistemological argument alone; he offers multiple supporting psychological explanations, explanations that people are motivated thinkers, and are driven by "the passion of *surprise* and *wonder,* arising from miracles," leading to their being too easily persuaded on the basis of vivid or eloquent testimony.[41] My point is not that these alternative psychological explanations are correct, but only that the better supported one takes them to be, and the closer their fit with the epistemological considerations, the more philosophically motivated would be the assent from a de jure to a de facto challenge to miracles.[42]

With regard to etiological challenges, it might be suggested that judging the ground for a belief to be not just inductively weak, but positively *counter-inductive*, provides just the kind of criteria that might validate assent to the stronger, "debunking" sort of challenge. If so, this may be because what we find salient in such cases is not just failure of *safety*, but of *sensitivity*. Sensitivity demands that if p had been false then the agent in question would not have believed p on the basis on which she actually believes p. Helen De Cruz comments that when people apply maturationally natural doxastic methods, the beliefs they acquire are often insensitive. This occurs if they "would believe it even if God did not exist—making their belief veritically lucky."[43] This is as much to say that sensitivity failure, as distinguished from safety failure, engages more directly the *truth-aptness debate.* Now, it stands to reason that this may be so for particular beliefs, or for whole domains of belief/opinion.[44] If this is correct then sensitivity failure also serves to show when and how far the door is open for a skeptical de facto, in addition to a responsibility / rationality focused de jure challenge.

The Religious Credence Thesis: Another
Sort of Debunking Argument?

How should we understand the relationship between de jure and de facto challenges? If these two objections are independent of one another then the philosophical success of one of these challenges does not guarantee the success of the other. So as a quick example of different views of how they relate, it is quite common among nontheists to combine a de jure objection that theism is epistemically unacceptable with agnosticism about the de facto objection that theism is false.[45] Principled agnostics tend to think that this gives their position the upper hand against atheists who may take de facto challenges to fall out of de jure challenges to the epistemic *standing* of some target beliefs or attitudes. Among theists, Alvin Plantinga, describes a "proper" de jure objection as a de jure objection that cannot be shown to implicitly depend on a de facto objection. In *Warranted Christian Belief,* Plantinga argues that there are no de jure objections that do not implicitly depend on a de facto objection, that latter being seen as one the theist can easily reject. John Bishop and Imran Aijaz (2004) reply that this strong dependence Plantinga asserts is too quick, and that the externalist epistemology that Plantinga appeals to, fails to justify the categorical rejection of de jure challenges to Christian belief. More positively, however, moderate religious fideism has the resources to "constrain" strong fideism by retaining some conditions for proper de jure challenges. Understanding faith as *doxastic venture,* as did Mill and James, is consistent with moderate religious fideism, Bishop and Aijaz argue, but not with a view like Plantinga's where "certain belief" and knowledge are self-attributed by the faithful. A doxastic venture account explains how a plurality of religious faith ventures arises, and the moral and epistemic limits of our right to them. But "doxastic" venture is used loosely here, since the authors do not want to beg the normative question about whether faith is rightly understood as a certain kind of propositional attitude. Some of what we call doxastic ventures may be sub-doxastic so long as it one's attitude toward faith-propositions is able to serve its normal function in practical reasoning.[46]

While developing a narrowly targeted, proper de jure objection is the main approach we have pursued, CSR has little truck with de jure challenges, since these deal with questions of epistemic guidance and of the ethics of belief. CSR can proceed in simple suspension of de facto questions about the existence of God. But there is a second kind of de facto challenge on the table that CSR research might support. This is a challenge not to the positive epistemic standing of given religious beliefs, nor is it directly a challenge to the existence of God. It is a challenge to the correctness of a description of religious "avowals" (for example, creedal confessions) as "beliefs" in the first place.

This sort of "debunking" argument may seem highly revisionary because it challenges the self-understanding of those engaged in religious discourse, insofar as that self-understanding is overtly realist about religious language. Hence this kind of challenge is more closely aligned with fictionalist or non-cognitivist views about the aims of religious discourse. But for us it suggests further options for how best to understand the relationship between de jure and de facto challenges. Let us call this form of de facto challenge a challenge to status as an epistemic *state*, and we can look at how it draws directly upon work in CSR. But to provide background I will first digress onto Wittgenstein's *Lectures on Religious Belief*, before turning directly to the arguments of Neil van Leeuwen, who best presents this type of challenge.

In the epigraph for this chapter, from Wittgenstein's *Lectures on Religious Belief*, we read, "No. There it will break down. . . . No induction" (56). Wittgenstein's passage I interpret as connecting both with a) our methodological approach emphasizing the centrality of counter-inductive thinking in strongly fideistic conceptions of faith; and b) our analysis of logical and moral faults of the exclusivist response to religious multiplicity. The exclusivist is always claiming that an inductive pattern, however strong it may be, "breaks down" in their own case, usually because of their unique relationship with God. The pattern we apply to all others (whether the "we" is a neutral observer or a committed exclusivist), a pattern of producing many false beliefs, breaks down *in our own case:* This is the exclusivist's purport. The reliability of our own testimonial tradition is wholly dependent upon its truth, but since exclusivists of every faith claim truth for themselves, the pattern-breaking reliability of a single testimonial tradition is still asserted in the face of inductive logic. "No induction. Terror" clearly suggests violation of inductive norms. The only way it is not a violation is that the refusal of the demand suggests that religious language plays a quite different language game altogether, a game where "truth" loses all of its shared meaning. In the space of epistemically good reasons, the "No induction" demand itself demands justification. Not providing a positive response to it is to leave reasonableness, so long as reasonableness calls upon rational accountability, or the giving and asking for reasons.

Wittgenstein's *Lectures on Religious Belief* perhaps equivocates between descriptive and prescriptive fideism. I take it as primarily descriptive of how faith-based avowals often functions. But what has become known as Wittgensteinian fideism is weakly prescriptive as well. His claim about the distance between scientific and faith-based practice (which is fitted together with his picture theory of meaning) seems to instill an Independence model of the relationship between science and religion. Most theologians influenced by the Wittgensteinian view are not proponents of a Conflict, but of an Independence model. But let us back up and consider Wittgenstein's passage more closely on its own terms; although he was not specifically concerned with our special focus, his work can still help us illuminate aspects of fideistic thinking. Commenting on the contrast of religious and scientific practice, he writes, "A religious belief might in fact fly in the face of" a forecast based upon objective reasoning. In the face of an objective inductive pattern, Wittgensteinian fideism describes the faith-based believer in the Day of Judgment as asserting, "No. There it will break down. . . . No induction. Fear. That is, as it were, part of the substance of the belief."[47] As a historical side-note, Wittgenstein read and appreciated Kierkegaard, who held a strong version of prescriptive fideism, claiming that genuine faith *should not* be based upon "objective reasoning."

This is why there is a mismatch but not a *contradiction* between a) the traits of factual belief as we understand it in everyday and scientific thinking, and b) what the religious adherent regards as their belief that a prophesied event, like the Day of Judgment, will indeed occur. Wittgenstein is focusing on the (mis)communication between the Day of Judgment believer and another person who does not believe it. "These controversies look quite different from any normal controversies. Reasons look entirely different from normal reasons."[48] He goes on to comment, "In a religious discourse we use such expressions as: 'I believe that so and so will happen,' and use them differently to the way we use them in science. . . . [T]here is this extraordinary use of the word 'believe.' One talks of believing and at the same time one doesn't use 'believe' as one does ordinarily."[49]

Together with Wittgenstein's broader account of disparate language games with little commensurability between them, these passages go some distance in explaining Wittgenstein as articulating an Independence model of the relationship between scientific and religious thought. Vainio and others point out that there has been a "slide to 'Wittgensteinian fideism' in narrative theology." But logically, this means accepting more of an Independence model of faith and reason. The question becomes whether the insulation of beliefs from evidential challenge which Independence affords does not come at the cost of ceding historical claims ("propositions") to evidence-based objective reasoning. This is why charges of relativism regularly attend critical examination not only of particularist exclusivism, but also of any conception of religious language games that insulate religious assertions from the need for rational justification.

Following this line of thought there is a kind of cognitive dissonance that we would expect to arise for agents in such a situation of prescribed certainty that events, such as miracle events in a purported special revelation, in fact transpired. This is because to make an act of faith the basis for certainty about truths of an historical order invites all the oddities that Kierkegaard drew attention to, and for which his own response was to abandon objective reasoning in favor of embracing the paradoxical idea of "truth as subjectivity." Evidences are conditional, but truth-qua-faith is prescribed to be unconditional. Religious truth does not require or perhaps even desire evidence in the objective sense, but the credence is still a belief with a historical/factual content.[50]

Since these deep thinkers, Lessing, Kierkegaard, Barth, Wittgenstein, and many others all point to this cognitive dissonance through metaphors like "ditch," "chasm," etc., let us give a more definite terminology to this important problem where logic and psychology clash. Let us define *State and Standing Tension Effects* as follows:

> (SAST) The effects (reported or indicated) of unresolved tension in an agent's thought process brought on by a combination of:
>
> a) the underdetermination of historical evidence for a justification of faith, and
>
> b) the overdetermination by multiple trait-dependent factors for taking purported special revelation to supply well-grounded historical/empirical beliefs.[51]

A philosopher who develops this area of concern between psychology and epistemology is Neil van Leeuwen. In his papers, "Do Religious 'Beliefs' Respond to Evidence?" (2017) and "Religious Credence is not Factual Belief" (2014), the author argues that "psychology and epistemology should posit distinct cognitive attitudes of religious credence and factual belief, which have different etiologies and different cognitive and behavioral effects."[52] Leeuwen more specifically argues that religious credence[53] and factual belief have distinctive properties of their own: "[F]actual beliefs (i) are practical setting independent, (ii) cognitively govern other attitudes, and (iii) are evidentially vulnerable. By way of contrast, religious credences (a) have perceived normative orientation, (b) are susceptible to free elaboration, and (c) are vulnerable to special authority. Leeuwen's term "credence" does not *require* a doxastic interpretation, and it captures the mood of faith in following what one takes to be doxastic requirements.[54]

I think Leeuwen is correct that "when we talk about differences in 'beliefs,' we tend to focus on differences in *contents,* without considering the possibility that we are lumping distinct *attitudes* under this one word."[55] The support he offers for this claim draws upon differences between cognitive and conative attitudes, where the former represent how situations *are or might be*, while the latter represent how the agent would like things to be, or how things *should be made to be*. Using this distinction, it becomes problematic to say that things on William James' faith-ladder, where there is a shift from what ought to be to what is, rightly constitute "beliefs." James indeed urged us to recognize the mood of faith in our faith ventures. While astute on that matter, James never seems to have questioned that these were *doxastic* ventures; he routinely traffics in the language of religious *beliefs*. Whether it is even possible to intentionally follow Kierkegaard's prescription and acquire a belief one judges not to be sufficiently supported by one's evidences, has been recently debated between Andre Buckareff (2005) and John Bishop (2005). For our study, the important point is that this problem must lead one to acknowledge what kinds of evidence might support non-doxastic alternatives to a simple "belief" characterization of faith commitments.[56] Looking to actual doxastic practice among the religious returns us to *SAST effects*. The logical tensions between fideism and the evidential grounding normally expected of historical beliefs tend to be ignored when the model of faith that is adopted involves any kind of prescribed certitude, or prescribed absence of doubt. This prescription makes the will primary in acquiring or maintaining religious commitments. Prescribed certainty appears suspiciously oxymoronic. But the logical tensions between affective grounds and historical belief cannot be fully repressed. They have psychological effects, which Leeuwen supplies empirical evidence of, and which we have described as involving observable *SAST effects*.

In this connection, Leeuwen's analysis might be seen as a different and more subtle form of debunking, a *de facto* form that draws more upon logical and philosophical than evolutionary grounds. But as Leeuwen points out, illusory self-attributions of belief, which are certainly possible, are harder to investigate when philosophy and cognitive science both tend to assume that belief "is a single cognitive attitude type and that variation in behavioral effects of different beliefs is due to variation in contents" (706). Leeuwen's strongest thesis, and one that he suggests should guide further psychological and epistemic inquiry, is:

(RCT) *Religious Credence Thesis*: psychology and epistemology should posit distinct cognitive attitudes of religious credence and factual belief, which have different characteristic etiologies (how they're formed and revised) and different forward effects (downstream consequences).

I am not here endorsing this thesis, but the basic distinction between belief and credence clearly connects with some aspects of our approach through philosophy of luck. It also suggests an interesting motivation for a de facto challenge that might either complement or compete with the de jure-focused treatment I gave to the New Problem. What we earlier described as *SAST effects* addresses the same mismatch of belief and evidence. Both Leeuwen's approach and my own have potentially strong implications for religious epistemics. Philosophers of religion have often described it by saying the phenomenology is one of "believing in" rather than "believing that." Kierkegaardian truth-as-subjectivity is over-against objective reasoning, but the "gulf" or "chasm" thus created cannot simply be denied. Prescribed certainty can engender a kind of cognitive dissonance when the prescription to have faith talks to the heart, yet faith is supposed to be held propositionally.[57] The resulting mismatch of belief and evidence invites confabulation on the part of agents, so that strong fideism is a prime area for study of confabulatory explanations.

The religious normally self-ascribe beliefs to themselves, yet the model of faith at work is often one that also identifies genuine faith with heart-felt avowal. This challenges any simple assumption that religious avowals are cognitive utterances. Before judging belief-attribution as appropriate or somewhat illusory in the religious domain, Leeuwen wants us to note examples of conflations in pre-theoretical speech. Historical examples he discusses are "jade" and "hysteria"; both terms once lumped together as phenomena that moderns have learned to more carefully distinguish. Leeuwen thinks there is an analogy with the catchall term "belief." He is at least correct that good science depends on recognizing distinct phenomena as distinct, and that we need more clarity about "belief" and its close cousins. A related point I would emphasize is that if the belief/credence or doxastic/sub-doxastic distinction is indeed looming larger today in philosophy of religion and in cognitive science of religion, it may be because our descriptive fideism has led us to better recognize the way people can conflate these.

Another thing my analysis adds to Leeuwen's is that "prescribed belief" and "prescribed certitude," due to their implicit strong voluntarism, are useful markers of credence rather than belief. The argument here, as in our own de jure approach, has much to do with the strengths of analogies, and the conditions for reasonably drawn disanalogies. Etiological symmetries and asymmetries; psychological states of belief and of affective credence; epistemic and pragmatic reasons: each of these pairs point to what credences are *if* they are not beliefs; these pairs do not merely point to what kinds of evidence there is for some target religious proposition.[58] Motivated reasoning—directional thinking—leads to the question of what religious credences are, and not just what levels of total evidence there are for different religious propositions.[59] Motivated reasoning or directional thinking leads to these paradoxes of pre-scribed certainty. Predictably, people try to steer clear of these paradoxes by denying or "sinking the fact" of directional thinking in the acquisition and maintenance of their beliefs in the religious domain.[60]

No greater moral dissonance is aroused in an individual than by a perceived demand of faith that the individual make what Kierkegaard famously termed a "teleological suspension of the ethical." This term is tantamount to Abraham's perceived duty to follow the will of God for a ritual sacrificing of his son Isaac, against all "universal" ethical reasoning. A perceived divine command is answered by the knight of faith. The "particular," suspends and then overrides natural sentiments and universal principles; one's duty is not to think or to question, but to make oneself the vessel of God's will even where its rationality or morality is something of a complete mystery. The moral dissonance thus aroused when the perceived demand of God seems at odds with universal moral thinking, such as a parent killing his or her own child, or a loving god demanding blood, cannot but affect the individual's psyche. This is perhaps why Kierkegaard, that great lover of paradox, gave us such a rich reflection on Abraham as an exemplar of faith, and on why says he that he both admired and abhorred his action in preparing for this sacrifice. But SAST effects and Leeuwen's Religious Credence Thesis focus attention directly not on ethical choices and ensuing moral dissonance, but rather on its epistemological correlate, religious avowals on fideistic motivations, or what I propose to call "teleological suspension of the logical," or "teleological suspension of the epistemological."

In summary, while I remain skeptical of any sweeping, highly revisionary account of religious seemings as non-doxastic that Leeuwen's Religious Credence Thesis introduces, I still want to heed his warnings against accepting belief-talk uncritically.[61] Faith venture should be understood as potentially referring to doxastic *or* to sub-doxastic commitments. Leeuwen's thesis and the empirical support that he offers for it substantially broadens our understanding of de facto challenges and their relationship to our more restricted de jure argument focused just around exclusivist responses to religious multiplicity. While it might seem natural to associate (RCT) with a sweeping de facto argument, in fact Leeuwen's account throws a strong light on what he terms "extremist credence." Extremist credences "are vicious because they are not responsive to evidence and they have unrestricted downstream consequences on thought and action."[62]

It is these cognitive attitudes that display the strong mismatch we find in *SAST effects*. Leeuwen defines extremist credences as ones that are allowed to be "behavior-guiding," and to have "wide cognitive governance," yet without acknowledging evidential vulnerability: "As the practical setting of religious credence expands to cover more and more of an agent's life, without also acquiring evidential vulnerability, the agent tends toward extremism, which is vicious."[63] In summary, this passage I think locates a key target of Leeuwen's argument, similar to our own, as what we have termed strong fideism and the teleological suspensions of the ethical, logical, and epistemological that it regularly generates.

Counter-Inductive Thinking and Minimally Counter-Intuitive Teachings: How Related?

As we noted earlier, comparative fundamentalism and CSR have not been closely connected, and CSR is sometimes criticized for neglecting the particularities of practices and beliefs that interest those in religious studies. It is of course such particularities that claims to religious uniqueness are premised upon. Robert McCauley's response to the question of balance raised earlier is that CSR's focus on popular religiosity and the appeal of maturationally natural ideas is well suited "to redress an imbalance in religious studies—an imbalance in favour of the particular over the general and the interpretive over the explanatory."[64]

McCauley and other cognitivists take popular representations of the supernatural to be culturally successful *because they trigger and are processed by intuitive systems.* By their focus on what I call the etiologically deep, they tend to ignore *directional thinking.* McCauley shares James' claim that theological systems are secondary constructions, but he is quite critical of what he perceives as James' over-emphasis on faith tendencies as emotionally engaged. Also, James focused on experience, mostly of the exceptionally faithful, while McCauley focuses on evolutionary mechanisms and their manifestation in popular religiosity. While CSR's focus is certainly valid, I worry that the cognitivist approach tends to jettison Mill's and James' interests in individual temperament and the role of emotions and value religious faith ventures. James is certainly correct that there is constant movement between belief and value during assent up the "faith ladder." Also, the role of directional thinking in generating religious contrariety is central to our earlier critique of fundamentalism, and to any de jure or responsibility-focused approach such as we have taken in this book.

But there may be grounds for rapprochement between the more cognitivist and comparative approaches in the study of religion. There may be specific research projects that call upon both, and require their broader integration. This is what I think we discover when we pose a question about the relationship between McCauley's interest in the universal appeal of "minimally counter-intuitive" ideas, and our own interest in people's differential predilection to indulge in "counter-inductive" thinking. Let us explore this relationship more methodically. CSR tells us that there is a correlation between "minimally counter-intuitive" ideas arising from maturationally natural processes, and the beliefs/credences that people find the most memorable, "live," or appealing.[65] Does this attractiveness of ideas that are "just weird enough" suggest that there could be a more direct relationship also between Type 1 or maturationally natural processing and counter-inductive thinking? In other words, does the attractiveness of counter-intuitive or counter-schematic religious ideas for some agents predict a pattern of counter-inductive *inference* in the religious domain? I believe so, and will here argue that this connection between CSR's focus on counter-intuitive *content* with our own focus on violation of inductive norms in one's mode of inference and explanation has the potential to expand CSR's focus by connecting it in various ways with religion and philosophy of luck/risk as articulated in part I.

A propensity for counter-inductive thinking may be only one instance of negative attitudes toward reason carried in one's model of faith. Emil Brunner, an influential Lutheran post-liberal, for example claims that "the teaching of the gospel and the theory of progress are irreconcilable opposites."[66] This is a conflict model of the relationship between faith and reason. It may relatedly be suggested that a combination of CSR's religious idea-focused approach and our own explanation-focused approach both diagnose "ironic" rationalizations of religious exceptionalism. The example we have used is Barth's irony that God faults all religion, yet chooses Christianity to be the root of revelation, and Christians alone to rightly award themselves "the prize." But this extends more generally to scriptural passages where God's irony shows through a) in disdaining the evidence-demanding "doubting Thomas"; b) in choosing to convey highest wisdom or revelation through those who seem weakest; or c) in choosing a divine plan where the meek shall eventually inherit the earth; or d) in purposefully making true saving revelation appear as "foolishness to the Greeks," etc.[67] Are highly ironic religious narratives such as these perhaps *more* credible to individuals whose model of faith is more than just moderately fideistic? If so, is this perhaps because these ironies, connected with minimally counter-intuitive ideas on the one hand and discovery of truth through counter-inductive inference on the other, coheres with their own strongly anti-rationalist theological method?

CSR is seeing innovations that allow investigators better access to people's actual and/or implicit religious beliefs and attitudes. For example, interest has been drawn to covert and implicit measures of religiosity, in addition to explicit measures like: self-reports; source monitoring tasks; partially structured measures using responses to short narratives; consistency between explicitly and implicitly held religious beliefs; and theological correctness or distance between theologically correct belief and popular religiosity.

Attempting to find measures for "religiosity" in some general sense is not as useful for connecting CSR with philosophy of religion, as are more specific measures for counter-inductive thinking and what I term bias-mirroring. From a descriptive or scientific perspective, the etiology of belief in religious faith-traditions is symmetrical until proven otherwise. But asymmetric trait-ascriptions can still be studied simply as bias-*like*, since methodological neutrality limits do not license psychologists to "reduce" ironic narratives to tropes, or theologically-case asymmetric religious trait-ascriptions to known social bias. It does license them to study how people's self-reported responses to religious multiplicity *mirror* known cognitive and social biases. Let's call this a *bias-mirroring effect* (BME). As the New Problem in chapter 2, and the articulation we gave to descriptive fideism in chapters 3 and 4 worked to show, strong fideists to a significant extent mirror one another in their mode of belief-acquisition, and in the ways that they maintain their uniqueness and superiority. Some of the best evidence for the mirroring of social biases among test subjects might be the extent to which they *attribute* bias to religious aliens in order to buttress their uniqueness and to explain the falsity of contrary beliefs and the culpability of others in holding them. Bias-mirroring effects are in evidence wherever we find test subjects responding in ways that a biased individual *would* think or judge.

It has been proposed that CSR's studies of minimally counter-intuitive ideas and their psychological appeal can be approached philosophically from its connection with epistemic risk and with how religious agents weigh or fail to weigh this risk. If there is such a connection between counter-intuitive content of appealing ideas and counter-inductive thinking as a matter of strength of fideistic orientation, then religious epistemics must study the implications of these and other empirical studies. This also reinforces the point that in CSR there is no either/or choice between an explanatory approach focused on general cognitive mechanisms and an approach through comparative study of fideistic orientation. Cognitivists remain interested in studying the "doctrinal mode of religiosity," and my suggestions for more integration between CSR and religious studies are made in the spirit of Jesper Sorensen's claim that cognitivist theories enable "more precise historical (and ethnographic) descriptions as well as facilitate comparative historiography."[68]

The best way to look for these connections between the counter-intuitive and the counter-inductive is to utilize our inductive risk toolkit to pose some new questions at this intersection. Table 4.2 codifies a number of these suggestions including how best to scale *fideistic orientation* along a spectrum from weaker to stronger. Philosophers might interact with cognitive psychologists in designing related tasks, and honing the hypotheses that motivate them. The two kinds of *tasks* outlined on this table—Inductive Risk and Source Monitoring—are easy-enough to define. Inductive Risk tasks are tasks with making inferences from inductive evidence. Source monitoring tasks ask test subjects to interpret the meaning of provided testimony, to assess the trustworthiness of a testimonial source, and to distinguish empirical from narrative meaning. The two kinds of *effects* outlined on the table—Bias Mirroring and SAST—are ones that I suggest can best be studied in self-reporting surveys about their own doxastic methods, after they have been *primed* in ways that make them sensitive to these problems in other people's (for instance, religious outsiders') doxastic methods.[69] Some of the other questions on the chart highlight how philosophers best interact for the sake of this research program with social psychologists concerned with religious radicalization, or with comparative religious studies scholars.

My proposal for balancing the general and the particular in the scientific study of religion is also in a sense a proposal for bringing philosophy and psychology of religion closer together. Trying to develop specific scales for the just-described observable effects would be a collaborative project that goes well beyond the scope of this book. But McCauley and other CSR researchers often call for new questions at the interfaces of philosophy and psychology. Table 6.2, with which we can draw this chapter to a close, aims

Table 6.2 CICI: Some Key Questions for Research on Relationships between the Appeal of Counter-Intuitive Ideas and the Penchant for Counter-Inductive Thinking

Inductive Risk Tasks	**Tasks with Inductive Evidence and Inference**[72]
a) Tasks on fluid rationality and critical reasoning dispositions	What are the studyable relationships between the *natural asymmetry* of causal explanation and the way that asymmetries are ascribed and causal inferences made by people in the religious domain?
b) Rationalism-Fideism Scale	Does the attractiveness of counter-intuitive or counter-schematic ideas or evidence for some agents predict a pattern counter-inductive *inference* in the religious domain?
c) Fundamentalist Orientation Scales	Does strongly fideistic orientation correlate with heightened counter-intuitive, counter-schematic, counter-inductive, and counter-evidential thinking?[73]
	What is each tested person's orientation on a rationalistic-to-fideistic spectrum? How can their *specific* theological method be described?
	How might strong fideistic orientation be measured with markers of the person's inductively risky beliefs or doxastic strategies?
	Is cognitive risk-taking prescribed by the agent's theological method? Is the need for objective evidence of one's religious beliefs accepted or rejected?
	How can religious orientation scales be made more comparative? How can psychologists study similarities among Abrahamic religions? What are the markers of fideistic *testimonial authority assumption*?
	In what domains or with what priming does inductive norm violation most often occur? How do counter-inductive inferences protect assumptions of religious uniqueness and superiority?
Source Monitoring Tasks	**Tasks of interpreting the meaning of provided *testimonial or other sources of claims***
a) Assessment of claims & sources of claims	How do religious and non-religious subjects differ in how reliably they are able to monitor claims and sources of claims?
b) Assessment of narrative vs. simple testimonial intent	Do religious subjects differ from others in how reliably they track inner vs. outer sources of experience?
c) Assessment of authority of the written word, or expertise in different domains	How *trait-dependent* are these and other inferences people make from their purported religious experiences?
	How reliably do they track differences between simple and narrative testimony? For example, how reliably do they track imaginary elements, and author intent?

(Continued)

Table 6.1 (Continued)

How reliably do they recognize non-literal passages within longer testimonial tracks?

Are people more likely to attribute reliability and inerrancy to a written text, in contrast with non-written forms of testimony?

How do assumptions about religious authority or expertise bear upon what religious ideas are treated as inerrant?

Do people attribute expertise uncritically or in minimally truth-apt domains where expertise is doubtful?

Are ambiguous/mysterious/ironic religious texts/teachings preferred and found persuasive (the Guru effect)?

Indicators of religious subjects mirroring what they concede biased persons would say or do.

Do religious and non-religious subjects differ in likelihood of absolutizing ethics, or culture-specific mores? In advocating express moral paternalism?

Do religious and non-religious subjects differ in mirroring epistemic or ontic injustice toward outgroupers?

How do religious and non-religious subjects differ in how they mirror group biases (for instance, ingroup–outgroup bias, group polarization)?

Is there more willingness among religious persons to risk others by submitting them to the ingroup's moral dictates? How is the exposure of others to moral risk rationalized?

How do religious and non-religious subjects differ in how they mirror personal biases (for instance, myside bias, belief bias, assimilation bias, false consensus, pluralistic ignorance)?

Does the religious subject's response to religious multiplicity rely on peerhood denial through theologically cast discrediting mechanisms?

Does the religious subject's response to religious multiplicity rely on "easy closure" inferences to support the falsity of all beliefs inconsistent with the home religion, or to support the reduction of complex multiplicity to simple contradiction and truth versus falsity?

Does the religious subject mirror belief bias and myside bias more so than non-religious subjects? Is this mirroring more pronounced as the subjects studied move up the scale of fideistic orientation?

Bias-Mirroring Effects
a) Ethnocentrism
b) Group biases
c) Interpersonal biases

SAST (Epistemic State and Standing Tension) Effects a) Pressure on epistemic standing of beliefs/judgments b) Slippage between models, and logical coherence faults	***Indicators of religious subjects having unresolved mismatches, for example, mismatches between explicit and implicit, or between religious credences and evidence/belief, etc.*** When a task shows the religious subject that a (or preferably her own) doxastic strategy is epistemically risky, does she display expected contingency anxiety? Does she show marks of tension between asserting a religious absolutism and the cultural contingencies of religious identity? If so, how does this come with willingness for belief revision? If not, is the absence of contingency anxiety associated with marks of cognitive dissonance? Of confabulatory explanation? Are there indicators of religious subjects' cognitive attitudes as fitting profiles of alief rather than belief, conative rather than cognitive attitudes, etc.? Is there observable "slippage" in the subject's responses between emotional/affective responses and assertion of cognitive truth claims? Is there observable "slippage" between the agent's espousal of an Independence model and a Conflict (or Warfare) model of the relationship between reason and faith? Does priming the subject for SAST effects increase her willingness to compensate with a higher reliance on a Conflict (Warfare) model of the relationship between faith and reason? Under what priming or assigned tasks do we observe religious subjects violate inductive norms, or express a willingness for teleological suspension of the logical, or the epistemological?

Tasks for measuring attitudes toward inductive risk include religious versions of tasks and the well-known assimilation bias: the tendency to favorably interpret and evaluate information that supports their existing beliefs (Jong, 69). They might include covert measures of belief that x, where x accords or breaks with inductive norms. There are numerous relations between counter-intuitive, counter-evidential, counter-schematic ideas, and counter-inductive thinking or inference. While I have focused only on the latter, counter-schematic ideas are absurd, and potentially a test of weak inductive inferences: causal, generalizing, or analogical/disanalogical.

to provide some slightly more formal questions reflecting our approach. Since we primarily motivate it as an investigation of possible correlations between the Appeal of Counter-Intuitive Ideas and the Penchant for Counter-Inductive Thinking, I will give this research program the simple acronym, *CICI*.

PART TWO CONCLUSION

Part II of this book developed implications and applications of part I's focus on problems of religious luck/risk. It did so by recasting many of the problems regarding luck-leaning asymmetric religious-trait ascriptions into more formal terms of assumed moral and epistemic risk. Inductive risk emerged as a central concept in this study, and as a concept that helps operationalize problems of lucky belief, luckily true belief, and moral risk attending doxastic faith ventures. We gave fullest development to why there may be strong correlations between inductively risky cognitive strategies and religious fideism, what implications such correlations might have, and what sorts of reasoning tasks and self-reporting questions might be assigned to subjects of psychological experiments to test for these correlations and others involving specific religious orientation and disposition to violate inductive norms.

Chapter 3 more specifically elaborated how religious contrariety arises on the basis of etiological symmetries. It examined the *enemy in the mirror* phenomenon where multiple groups, while arising on a similar basis at least in terms of proximate causes, come to similarly absolutistic stances where unfriendliness toward religious outsiders is typical, and may even be taken as theological correctness. Uniqueness of content or standing with the divine is emphasized, and etiological symmetry and its epistemological implication is ignored. The emergence of the enemy in the mirror can be predicted to arise in testimonial traditions which promote strongly fideistic models of faith. A research program to examine fideistic orientation and its relation to epistemically risky doxastic strategies is one of potentially numerous research programs on which philosophers and psychologists might work collaboratively.

Chapter 4 took up the matter of the limits of reasonable disagreement more directly, describing and critiquing both forms that salvific exclusivism can take, particularist exclusivism and mutualist exclusivism. Since mutualist exclusivism aims to get around powerful objections to the reasonableness of particularist or religion-specific exclusivism, that chapter developed a dilemma and other direct arguments to challenge it.

Chapter 5 presented a critical examination of the logical coherence of the two forms of religious exclusivism, religion-specific, and mutualist. Picking up where the Exceptionalist Dilemma of the New Problem in chapter 2 left off, but utilizing more of the Inductive Risk Toolkit developed in the intermediate chapters, I explained why post-liberal theologians have turned toward mutualist exclusivism when they try to defend the rationality or reasonableness of the two things that have been the focus of this book: exclusivist responses to religious multiplicity, and radically asymmetric religious trait-ascriptions. It was argued that mutualist exclusivism on closer examination implies its own contradiction, and so is conceptually incoherent. I also argued that in its practical consequences it tends to produce the enemy in the mirror, and to mirror all manner on known biases by rejecting genuine interfaith dialogue in favor of polarized and polemical apologetics. So not just the logical coherence, but the moral and theological adequacy of mutualist exclusivism were also directly challenged.

Chapter 6 then examined themes in CSR, and suggested a substantial fusion of concerns with counter-intuitive ideas (an assessment of content) and counter-intuitive thinking (an assessment of patterns of inference). We asked whether McCauley's study of the appeal of maturationally natural ideas, including those that have some degree of counter-*intuitiveness*, can be connected with observable counter-*inductive* propensities in their patterns of *inference*. I argued that philosophy of luck/risk allows us to investigate the many connections between strong or counter-inductive fideism and the counter-intuitive ideas of popular religiosity. I have argued that a proper de jure objection to the well-foundedness of belief and to the doxastic responsibility of the agent can at the least be made when the target of the de jure challenge is specific beliefs, attitudes, or doxastic strategies. Since our account is agent focused and, as pragmatist, holds an understanding of epistemology as a theory of inquiry and agency, we did not target theism generally. Theism, deism, pantheism, and many other conceptions of godhead may be associated with texts considered scriptural, but we have explored how especially important the concept of special revelation is in the testimonial traditions, especially those of the Abrahamic family of religions. And we argued that the testimonial authority assumption takes many different, culturally specific forms, but is clearly one of multiple markers of fideistic orientation. Such a restricted target as my own does not presuppose the truth or falsity of theism, and is methodologically agnostic about putative special revelations. If it is judged by the reader that my approach goes beyond neutrality to overt skepticism about purported special revelation, then the reader will associate it with the many European and American Enlightenment-era *philosophes*. This need and should not depend on the falsity of something so broad as what James calls "the religious hypothesis," though the relationship between de facto and de jure objections is an interesting and timely project that Leeuwen's credence theory, philosophers of religion, CSR researches and theologians concerned with luck-free theologies should all pursue. I introduced my own collaborative research program, *CICI* that gives reason to think there are important hypotheses to be pursued at the intersection of CSR research on the popular appeal of counter-intuitive ideas, and research focused on counter-inductive thinking, as our inductive risk theory proposes. McCauley is always inviting new questions to spur further developments in CSR, and in answer to this we concluded with a list of more specific questions that allow us, a) to give more detail to the proposal for a new scale for religious orientation that focuses on characteristics of counter-inductive thinking as a key indicator of strongly fideistic orientation; b) to more specifically connect CSR with philosophy of luck, with problems of religious luck, and with the hypothesis of descriptive fideism; c) to develop all of these as a contribution to the advancement of the field of comparative fundamentalism; and d) to try to balance in this proposed research program the powerful generalism of the cognitive approach with the careful attention to trait-dependent individual and group differences, including differences in doxastic methods, that is so important in philosophy and social science as well as in theology.

BOOK CONCLUSION

The explanatory relevance of measures of inductive risk connects it with cognitive and social psychology of religion, while its normative relevance connects it with epistemology of testimony, the epistemic significance of disagreement, and the ethics of belief. The chapters of part II have developed both sides of our inductive risk account, while trying to keep them properly separated.

On the normative side, the major theme of the book has been the limits of reasonable disagreement, and how these limits are surpassed in responses to disagreement or to religious diversity where one or more of the disputants rely explicitly or implicitly on counter-inductive thinking to judge matters of religious truth. We have argued for the intellectual and moral inadequacy of the exclusivist response to religious multiplicity, and insisted that at the very least, its theological adequacy cannot be affirmed by theologians apart from these other two. We have emphasized that given the plurality of models of faith that the religious employ, a person's inherited model of faith should be the first, and not the last thing given critical attention by responsible believers. We therefore more constructively discussed moral and epistemic virtue, and how appealing to virtue-based conceptions of moral and doxastic responsibility suggests a good deal of common ground between religionists and secularists, and a basis for dialogue.

Problems of religious luck can be debated in a lot of different ways, and I have tried to advance this debate rather than arguing that it must play out in one specific way in philosophy of religion. So we have tried to stay neutral with respect to certain debates about religious realism, so as to produce a proper de jure arguments against exclusivist attitudes to religious multiplicity, and against theologically cast, but bias-mirroring asymmetric trait-ascriptions to religions insiders and outsiders. I have not assumed that belief may never be permissibly responsive to non-epistemic reasons, and I reject one-size-fits-all answers to the question of how a person should reasonably respond to genuine peer disagreement. Since our focus has been on the *limits* of reasonable disagreement, we have not said a great deal positively in support of a permissivist ethics of belief, although we have situated our account in close proximity to pragmatism and to Rawlsian reasonable pluralism.

The inductive risk account might be consistent with different accounts of the ethics of belief, and of proper philosophical guidance. But my own pragmatism leads me to view as permissible all such religious faith ventures as do *not* centrally "aggravate" problems of religious luck, to go back to Zagzebski's original paper. I have on these issues basically taken a Rawlsian, broadly permissivist view, while developing with Bishop and Aijaz the important idea that recognition of a right to moderately fideistic assumptions is the most philosophically sound and practically effective way to constrain strongly fideistic faith ventures. In this way also, the book does not just explain how to present a proper de jure objection; it also suggests how to *answer* such an objection when its target is sweepingly broad (for instance, alleging the irrationality of all theistic belief), or when the objection is only belief and not *agent* focused.

I had earlier thought to conclude this book with reference to William James's famous 1896 Preface to *The Will to Believe and Other Essays in Popular Philosophy,* where he writes,

> [I]f we are empiricists, if we believe that no bell in us tolls to let us know for certain when truth is in our grasp, then it seems a piece of idle fantasticality to preach so solemnly our duty of waiting for the bell. Indeed we *may* wait if we will,—I hope you do not think that I am denying that—but . . . in either case we *act*, taking our life in our hands. No one of us ought to issue vetoes to the other, nor should we bandy words of abuse. We ought, on the contrary, delicately and profoundly to respect one another's mental freedom: then only shall we bring about the intellectual republic.[70]

The Preface ends with James's prescription that we "live and let live" in spiritual or secular experiments of living, tolerating them so long as they are tolerant themselves. As a permissivism there is no duty to tolerate the intolerant, and the logical coherence of pluralism is clearly decreased, not increased, by the notion of toleration of anti-pluralism *without limit*. But there is keen recognition in James's view that religious and philosophical overbeliefs serve positive functions personally and socially, and that in them "the negative, the alogical, is never wholly banished." Thus I agree strongly with James's permissivist recommendation to value and support that "spirit of inner tolerance without which all our outer tolerance is soulless, and which is empiricism's glory."[71] But I will make one qualification of this claim, to say instead that rational support for a spirit of inner tolerance is *empiricism's conclusion,* and *God's glory.*

NOTES

1. Ludwig Wittgenstein, *Lectures on Religious Belief.* Reprinted with permission of University of California Press.

2. Philosophers since Thales and Xenophanes have offered insight into religious psychology, sometimes contrasting the poets and priests who employed *mythoi* to explain events, and natural philosophers who by employing *logoi* gave impetus to Greek science. Some of the ancients, like Hippocrates, the father of medicine, criticized the philosophers *along with* the poets and priests, contrasting all of them with his more empirical approach to the causes and treatment of disease. But the turn from myth and supernaturalism at the dawn of philosophy in the Greek tradition needn't be thought of as pitting science and faith, Enlightenment-mode thinking versus irrationalism. CSR seemingly draws as easily from counter-Enlightenment thinkers like Montaigne, Pascal, James, as it does from Enlightenment mode thinkers like Lessing, Locke, Hume, Kant, and Voltaire.

3. Adam Green (2013, 417) for example writes that, "the cognitive science of religion can actually be used as a tool when doing theology from within the perspective of a faith tradition. It can, in effect, help to clarify religious doctrine from the inside."

4. D. Xygalatas and R. McKay, "Announcing the *Journal for the Cognitive Science of Religion,*" 1.

5. Hume, *Natural History of Religion,* Introduction. Compare what James calls the "intellectual operations" related to religion (*Varieties,* 433) include primarily those that of our overbeliefs, those of philosophy, and those of a science of religion. Graham Wood (2011, 734) notes, "as Hume's famous distinction makes clear, there is an important difference between the reasons for religious belief and the causes of religious belief."

6. We will engage them more later, but they are strictly speaking limit questions for science, if we are not to conflate science and values, description and naturalistic explanation with endorsement of a strongly naturalistic metaphysics. The explanatory scope of CSR falls well short of deciding such things as the reality of miracles. Theistic and atheistic worldviews, and spiritualist and materialist metaphysics are in the domain of controversial views, whereas science and religious studies are methodologically "agnostic" or neutral on questions of religious metaphysics. They may still be a source of well-grounded empirical premises that might be used in arguments that

aim to establish a metaphysical conclusion. This may be a simplistic answer, but for our study we will hold tightly to the neutrality of CSR to questions metaphysical.

7. To reiterate, *de facto objections* state that purported force f likely does not exist, or that the claim that p is likely false *rather than* true. De jure *objections* state that force x is explanatorily spurious or superfluous, or that the claim that p, whether true or not, is rationally or morally deficient. The epistemological use is typically that the claim that p lacks positive epistemic standing, on account of its being epistemologically unjustified/unsafe/insensitive, etc. This mildly generalizes Plantinga's description. Focusing only on "Christian belief" he writes, "*De facto* objections are relatively straightforward and initially uncomplicated: the claim is that Christian belief must be false (or at any rate improbable), given something or other we are all alleged to know. *De jure* objections, by contrast . . . are much less straightforward. The conclusion of [a *de jure*] objection will be that there is something wrong with Christian belief—something other than falsehood—or else something wrong with the Christian believer: it or she is unjustified, or irrational, or rationally unacceptable, in some way" (*Warranted Christian Belief,* ix). I am treating *de jure* challenge, and the concept of reasonableness more generally, as something that can be framed so in terms open to any or all of the three kinds of "adequacy" objections: epistemological, ethical, and theological. The overlap in these approaches strengthens is appropriate to the dialectical setting where disputants may not have a lot of common ground; they need multiple modes of criteria in order to assess the normative force of a *de jure* challenge, and the three-pronged approach supplies this.

8. Philosophers, theologians, and others can talk about CSR as having implications that support or undermine the rationality of belief, or support or undermine the truth-aptness of theistic beliefs, but these issues are not scientific. Truth-aptness is closely connected with sensitivity, since the sensitivity principle imposes a modal constraint on true belief: if the proposition believed were false, one would not believe it. Sensitivity, for those who would defend it as a condition on justification or knowledge, requires is that one would not believe P by the same method were P false.

9. Theologians often posit final in addition to efficient causes, or they take natural laws discoverable scientifically as "secondary" causes, with "primary" causes standing beyond or before them. To the extent that the "final" or "primary" causes are understood to be consistent with natural law (as contrasted, say, with the view that God controls all things directly), these faith-based tenets are part of an Independence rather than a Conflict model of the relationship between religion and science. Their problem is not direct tension with discoverable facts, but mainly their apparent unfalsifiability and superfluous nature from the scientific point of view. These concerns are taken here as ones for philosophers and theologians; while they are material in understanding *de jure* and *de facto* challenges, CSR as an empirically-oriented science can proceed neutrally to them. For better or worse, religious studies scholars usually refer to this as methodological agnosticism.

10. McCauley 2010, 779.

11. The debate is more broadly recognizable even in the contrasting focus on "religion" (CSR favors the singular term) versus "religions" (for instance the hermeneutic study that calls itself "theology of religions").

12. Tremlin, *Minds and Gods* (2010, 9.)

13. This suggests to me that religious exclusivism may be a special expression of other, well-recognized sorts of us—of them separations, in that despite the unique content of the beliefs, they are produced by many of the same processes. What is different is the metaphysical explanation, but ideas are maintained and passed on which have social evolutionary advantages that others do not.

14. Jack Lyons and Barry Ward, *The New Critical Thinking,* Introduction. As articulated earlier by Paul Thagard, "Attempts to improve inferential practice need to consider psychological error tendencies, which are patterns of thinking that are natural for people but frequently lead to mistakes in judgment." Philosophical rationalism tends to lead philosophers to conflate thinking and reasoning, but, for instance, "It would be highly misleading to depict motivated inference as a sort of fallacious argument akin to wishful thinking, of the form: I want X, therefore X is true. . . . Motivated inference is more complex than wishful thinking because it involves selective recruitment and assessment of evidence based on unconscious processes that are driven by emotional considerations of goals rather than purely cognitive reasoning" (2011, 156).

15. Vainio 2017, 94.

16. Vainio, 112.

17. Vainio anticipates a potentially strong *de facto* objection even against theological adequacy of such a view, since by the theist's own account of divine attributes, God should not be a deceiver. Theologically, a method of belief formation that resulted in a great deal of false positives would be, at the least, inefficient. Morally, it raises all kinds of problems like those of non-culpable nonbelievers, and intellectually, it puts human beings in a terrible epistemic position. This is why Visala and Leech describe such a scenario as a deceiving god scenario, and why they develop a deceiving god argument (*Deus deceptor*), in that "it seems that God is responsible for creating a set of cognitive processes that, for the most part, prevent real knowledge of spiritual reality, while allowing multiple false conceptions to develop freely" (2011, 95). Religious rationalists like Descartes would be rolling over in their graves at the reliance on an assumption that God is a deceiver. There are some theological responses intended to support exclusivism. Vainio thinks that from a Molinist perspective, one can consistently claim that because God has middle knowledge, he can set apart those who would not believe in any possible world. "These individuals (i.e., those who are not elected) are then located in a time and place for Christian faith are nonexistent or rare." Also possible he thinks is a sterner Calvinist response: "God wishes to save only those whom he has elected from *massa perditionis."* On both scenarios, the saved must be few, and those justly condemned outnumber them massively. Limited atonement is very controversial, both morally and as a biblical interpretation. It is biblical enough if one is literalist about Revelations 7, which says the 144,000 are to be saved, which, if one does the math against the 7 billion estimate of humans that have ever lived, comes out to $(144000/7000000000) \times 100 = 0.002\%$. For literalists, then, 99.998% of the population goes to hell. More importantly, in his subsequent treatment of NERBs, Vainio conflates the distinction between *de facto* and *de jure* objections, a distinction we have made efforts to carefully delineate. It is

not my point to go back to moral and theological critique, but my earlier thesis stands that it is a radically fideistic account that separates theological qua biblical adequacy from moral and epistemological concern, as both of these response to the *Deus deceptor* argument appear to do.

18. Barrett's account suggests that religious traditions are more or less coincidental conglomerates of cognitively optimal concepts, possibly epiphenomena without causal effect. "[P]psychologist Justin Barrett has demonstrated that, when performing under pressure, people tend to make inferences that are often in sharp contrast to their explicitly held theological convictions, and instead fall back on intuitive ideas. This distinction between explicitly held theological ideas and implicit theological incorrectness highlights the question whether we can understand behaviour by reference to the teachings of religious systems" (J. Sorensen, 2005, 476).

19. Vainio, 83. Vainio utilizes studies in cognitive science of religion, but also criticizes the reductive spirit of many of its practitioners, or at least of the non-scientists who try to use it as grounds for religious skepticism. He complains, for example, that "the cognitive science of religion has concentrated almost solely on religion as a product of type I cognition. This tends to distort the religious reality the theories are trying to depict and explain. It is not clearly the case that religious believers are not engaging in higher and refine forms of cognition, or that theologians ideas are systematically disregarded. . . . The image that a casual reader gets is that type II cognition (theology and philosophy) are *post hoc* rationalizations of fundamentally irrational for beliefs. However, if we investigate, we see immediately how odd and *ad hoc* this claim is. The same dialectic also pertains to scientific theories and philosophical arguments as they supervene on folk beliefs and try to control and refine them" (83).

20. However, Vainio seems to miss that unlike the ideal of psychology that reductive eliminativism upholds, many theorists in CSR today like Jong and McCauley are explanatory pluralists, holding that "theories at different levels can co-evolve and mutually influence each other, without reduction of the higher-level theory to the lower-level one." Schouten and de Jong (2012), Introduction.

21. Cleveland's *Disunity in Christi* is far less concerned than Vainio with the implications of these psychological studies for religious epistemics, but in more practically concerned with their implications for the prospects of Christian unity. For example she discusses the implications of the study of *group polarization* for religious philosophy. Studies suggest that people reason better in groups when there is diversity of opinion, and willingness to voice dissent and the reasons for it. On the other hand, "In the absence of diverse influences, homogenous groups tend to adopt more extreme and narrow-minded thinking as time passes." This is so even though, as Cleveland notes, churchgoers today to an unprecedented degree tend to 'shop' for the church and community that express their values. Indeed, those who "exit adolescence without interacting across cultural lines can easily evolve into churchgoers who continue to maintain these divisions in culturally homogenous churches. Ultimately, homogeneity within churches lives on while meaningful cross-cultural and cross-ideological interactions are limited" (Cleveland 2013, 26–27).

22. See my "Thinking Twice about Virtue and Vice" (2017c). I there argue that credit theories can treat many cases of cognitive success through heuristic cognitive

strategies as credit-conferring, It depends on whether the heuristic strategy of inquiry (described at the right level of generality to address the "Generality Problem") is reliable in that type of epistemic situation/domain. This all bears on the philosophical implications of dual-process theory, arguing that the ecological nature of human cognition has strong normative implications for epistemology, including virtue epistemology. A genuine convergence between virtue epistemology and dual-process theory is called for, while acknowledging that this effort may demand new and more empirically well-informed projects on both sides of the division between Conservative virtue epistemology (including the credit theory of knowing) and Autonomous virtue epistemology (including projects for providing guidance to epistemic agents). See also Church and Samuelson (2014) for a similar attempt to reconcile virtue theory and dual-process theory/ecological rationality. Our papers both respond directly to the situationist challenge to virtue epistemology, and I also respond there to the "Trade-off Dilemma" of John Doris, and Lauren Olin and their "vicious minds" hypothesis. See Keith Stanovich (2011), West, Toplak and Stanovich (2008) for an introduction to dual-process theory, and philosophers such as Nancy Snow (2006; 2009) and Holly Smith (2015), Table 1 reflects further ideas about philosophy and current cognitive science.

23. Vainio (2017), 98.

24. Vainio (2017), 99.

25. Vainio (2017), 99.

26. Barrett (2011, 150–151), quoted by Vainio (2017, 98).

27. Mahmut Aydin (2004) emphasizes this about the Abrahamic religions in particular, that the main cause of enmities, conflict and hatred "is to be found in the way believers so exaggerate their differences that they forget their common core" (235). He reminds us that taking other religions' beliefs as contradictory rather than contrary is a *choice* dependent on such exaggerations. On the ancient South Asian parable of the *Blind Men and the Elephant,* retold by the Sufi mystic Rumi, had the men been given sight on their partial views of the Absolute, 'they would have found there were no contradictions between their words.' Aydin argues that not just for Rumi, but in the Hebrew bible and also on Quranic ground, "There is a taste of Divine Being in the heart/soul of every religious community" (224).

28. Unreliability can be cast at a level of more proximate causes, as we saw from contingency arguments in Chapter 2. That religious beliefs conflict, and that most religious believers themselves attribute falsehood to most religious beliefs, would seemingly be enough to establish unreliable mechanism if beliefs all rooted in a single source. Yet of course conformist fideists—those who assume the special authority of the home religion's testimonial tradition—typically deny that their belief uptake is grounded in the *same* mechanism or doxastic method as those that produce all those beliefs they judge false. The level of generality at which (ES) describes the doxastic strategy (belief-forming function) they would hold to be too wide. But if plausible relevant difference reasoning is not forthcoming to support this reply, the position threatens to give up philosophical response, and to collapse into merely negative apologetics.

29. Griffiths and Wilkins 2013, 143. On evolutionary debunking and moral and religious beliefs, see also M. Bergmann and P. Kain (eds.) (2014), *Challenges to Moral and Religious Belief: Disagreement and Evolution.* D. Enoch and E. Guttel

(2010) also argue that we need a more nuanced understanding of the philosophical significance of debunking explanations. D. Leech and A. Visala (2012) nicely distinguish evolutionary from co-evolutionary and from cognitive explanations among naturalistic explanations of religion.

30. Vainio, 96–97. I want to thank John Bishop for comments on a draft paper that steered me to focus on soteriological exclusivism as the more interesting target of philosophical interest. This is supported further by the fact that Griffiths (2001) defends mutualist salvific exclusivism, while interestingly enough finding doctrinal exclusivism unsustainable. Griffiths also makes use of the open/closed exclusivism distinction (see also Marbaniang 2010, who says that fundamentalist faith evinces three epistemic conditions: unconditional subjection to authority, existential identity, and closed exclusivism, and also absolutist ethics and a utopian eschatology), but I find the open/closed distinction vague in its meaning and application to individuals. On the other hand, McKim (2012) supplies very detailed treatment of the overlaps and differences between doctrinal and soteriological exclusivism, and cogent critiques of both forms.

31. Vainio's characterization of exclusivism is suspect, since his account of it leaves out no moral requirements on heaven and the religion-specific cognitive components the salvific exclusivist insists upon. Salvific exclusivism is not "open" in the way that doctrinal exclusivism logically may be. For instance, escapism or potential universal salvation looks good from a perspective of moral theology, but in Paul's treatment of works of the flesh for instance, he insists that "those who do such things will not inherit the kingdom of God" (Galatians 5:22–23). Also, without the stronger salvific exclusivist riders, Jesus could have served to redeem human sin, *regardless* of whether his life and teachings were actually remembered and honored, or he was forgotten.

32. For example, "Because of our cognitive biases, we often have a comfortable default position, which resists change. An open-minded person is able to transcend this . . . open-mindedness entails that we must sometimes remain in a state of uncertainty" (158). Everyone probably thinks of themselves as open-minded, but under the supplied description this is not something most exclusivists endorse or live up to, as least as I read them, since the models of faith they adhere to call explicitly for resistance to change, and for conceiving faith as immune to standing intellectual uncertainty, or momentary wavering into doubt.

33. "We call an argument which links true belief with pragmatic success a "Milvian bridge" (recalling how Constantine's victory in the battle by that name was traditionally ascribed to the truth of his Christian beliefs, and the falsity of his enemies' beliefs). . . . Milvian bridge: X facts are related to the evolutionary success of X beliefs in such a way that it is reasonable to accept that and act on X beliefs produced by our evolved cognitive faculties" (134). But at the same time, Griffiths and Wilkins take those would-be debunkers of religious belief to task who simply dichotomize between truth-tracking and fitness tracking in order to argue that the evolutionary fitness of religious beliefs is wholly independent of truth. The idea of domains where there is or is not such a "bridge," nicely corrects for the dichotomizing tendency Vainio alleges to find in CSR.

34. Griffiths and Wilkins 2013, 136–137. Note that this author, Paul E. Griffiths is not Paul I. Griffiths, the Christian thinker whose apologetics for exclusivism we previously critiqued.

35. Griffiths and Wilkins, 144. See also Griffiths and Wilkins 2010.

36. "If the explanation shows *either* that X's belief in the claims P is due to an unreliable mechanism *or* that X would have been likely to believe the claims P whatever their truth—value, then X's beliefs do not amount to knowledge." (Pigden, "Subversive Explanations" (2013), 147; see also Nola's "Do Naturalistic Explanations of Religious Beliefs Debunk Religion?" in the same volume).

37. This idea about asymmetry of content (religious multiplicity or diversity) manifesting out of symmetry of process of belief-uptake does not seem to have been carried out by Kitcher, but I would argue that it is complementary with Kitcher's articulation of a naturalistic and humanistic worldview. Kitcher's humanism allows the reasonableness of alternative religious orientations. I agree with Kitcher most when he targets his criticism on the Belief Model of faith, while allowing reasonable agents other models that do not so much incite bigotries or religious intolerance, or conflict with science.

38. In the laboratory setting, with variables controlled as far as possible, and auxiliary conditions are adequately independent, if the hypothesis predicts something and it is not observed, it simply is not there. In science there are few quick kills, and tenacity can be a personal virtue where synchronic theory virtues do not supply a definitive choice among competing theories; adjustments to auxiliary assumptions or tweaks to the hypothesis might work, but if *ad hoc* adjustments continue to be made this tends to rob the hypothesis of its testable empirical content rather than increases it as is what happens in progressive research programs of any kind (Imre Lakatos). And what, after all, is more *ad hoc* than, in response to a call for explanation of an asymmetrical ascription of good religious luck, explaining it in terms of another? But it may be different in religion because the singular proposition, "God exists" is not *expected* to be verifiable by the five senses. If I tell you, "I have a green genie in my briefcase," and my class then dissects my briefcase and no one finds any trace of it, it will not help that I tell my class, "It is an invisible green genie." Unless highly credulous, they will be green genie atheists, not green genie agnostics. Ditto with what you think about weapons of mass destruction under Saddam Hussein Iraq: holding out that there *might* be WMDs there naturally-enough gave way to overt skepticism, given the strong but failed efforts to locate them. How different is it with evidencing theistic claims, or classes of supernatural event claims, such as miracles? Does absences of evidence ever legitimately become evidence of absence? I have no definite thesis on this, but the inference would seem to be much sounder if there is also a naturalistic story to tell about how these beliefs arise in people, and would arise, even if they are not true.

39. Later Enlightenment figures who were skeptical of special revelation took this from Hume. Thomas Paine wrote that "It is revelation to the first person only, and hearsay to every other, and consequently [these others] are not obliged to believe it." Paine (1967) [1776], 292–293.

40. All Hume quotes are from *Enquiry,* Section 10, 'Of Miracles.'

41. The performance of miracles as proof of divine connection is often demanded by characters in Abrahamic narratives. The performance of miracles for the

confirmation of faith is a repeated trope, though attitudes vary from ecstatic reception to being critical of a 'Doubting Thomas' for his unfaith, and from prophets pleased to show God's power through them, to prophets who refuse to perform them precisely when others ask or demand it of them as proof. Historical-critical methods point to another and more subtle form of persuasion. They raise concerns about *prefiguration* in miracle stories. For example, Jesus in some gospel accounts repeatedly does things that the intended readership would recognize as the fulfillment of older Jewish prophesy of a coming messiah. This suggests a persuasive intent on the part of the authors; for New Testament readers may be seen as the most significant of Jesus' miracles. Events that (whether through conscious prefiguration or not) confirm an older prophesy function to legitimize the narrative of a new covenant with God, and they add an intellectual element to the ever-present persuasive role in miracles in instilling faith.

42. I am not here offering a full account of the relation between the *de jure* and *de facto,* either in regards to miracle claims, or to luck-leaning asymmetric religious trait-ascriptions. I can just summarize some of the questions to ask. One is, 'Under what conditions does absence of evidence comport to rationally sufficient evidence of absence?' On the one hand, there is the appeal to ignorance *fallacy.* On the other hand, we know that in science and everyday life, absence of evidence after careful and prolonged efforts at inquiry, and especially under controlled conditions where we do our best to eliminate hidden variables, *does* typically comport to evidence of absence.

43. De Cruz, "the relevance of Hume's natural history of religion for cognitive science of religion." *Res Philosophica.*

44. The epistemological literature agrees Dani Rabinowitz that, "In some cases sensitivity is the more stringent condition, while in others safety is. . . . [T]he following pair of conditionals are false: If S safely believes P then S sensitively believes P; If S sensitively believes P then S safely believes P. The logic of these conditionals makes explicit the respects in which safety is similar to and different from the sensitivity condition." "The Safety Condition on Knowledge," Internet Encyclopedia of Philosophy. Accessed from http://www.iep.utm.edu/safety-c/, June 10, 2018. Part of what I am saying connects sensitivity failure to truth-aptness considerations is supplied by understanding that the scope of the sensitivity condition does not extend to necessary truths or to knowing the falsity of radical skeptical scenarios. The condition is thus limited to, but also especially illuminative of, rational justification for "contingently true propositions." These points hold whether sensitivity is a necessary condition on knowing or not (as a virtue epistemologist, I think an aretaic conditions serves better, but that sensitivity *concerns* are nevertheless important especially in regard to environmental epistemic luck). The insensitivity of belief and cognitive overdetermination, in the form of what John K. Davis calls trait-dependent belief, are also linked. I develop these connections further in Axtell, 2019.

45. Brian C. Barnett (2019) provides a strong discussion of the debate. He also supports the conclusion that Plantinga's General Reduction Argument fails, and therefore that "theists must deal with each *de jure* objection one at a time, and independently of the *de facto* objection" (14). An example of skeptical evidentialists who make quite sweeping *de jure* objections to theistic belief, see Todd Long (2010). By contrast I think that a sweeping *de facto* objection (for instance, that that are no sound miracle claims, or no special revelations) is better motivated than a claim that

everyone must be irrational who believes such a thing. I believe many Enlightenment thinkers (for example Thomas Paine, or Voltaire) made both *de jure* and *de facto* claims, but did not confuse them in the ways that modern-day impermissivism will drive one to do. On this view one might possibly still move from the one kind of argument to the other, but not without a clear argument: *de jure* and *de facto* arguments are to be constructed with as much independence from one another as they can, *unless* one is quite explicitly trying to argue for an entailment. Entailment from *de jure* to *de facto* might be exampled in one's arguing the 'mutual destruction' of miracle claims in different religions. It is possible that the one's we have studied as ill-founded but others are well-founded, but it is more likely that they are all false claims, not just some. Entailment from *de facto* to *de jure* might be exampled in the "unfriendly" inference from there is no proof positive for God's existence, all people are "irrational" who believe that God exists. These are just schematic examples.

46. Bishop and Aijaz's account is clearly closest to my own, and I develop a character-focused and neo-Jamesian permissivism in Axtell 2015 and Axtell 2019. Bishop and Aijaz's (2004) aims "(1) to argue that Alvin Plantinga's Reformed epistemology does not provide a categorical affirmative answer to the 'de jure question' about Christian belief; (2) to argue that—on the assumption that our total independent evidence leaves it open whether Christian belief is true or false—a categorical affirmative answer to the de jure question requires defending doxastic venture in favor of Christian belief; and (3) to suggest that PRE's appeal to epistemological externalism may play a significant role in defending the epistemic propriety of doxastic venture in favor of Christian belief. On (3), the authors were correct to concede to Buckareff (2005) that a venture of faith might sometimes be sub-doxastic, so long as "full practical commitment" can still be made to faith-propositions without actual belief. For further debate with Bishop and Aijaz's thesis, see Griffeon 2015.

47. Wittgenstein, 56.

48. Wittgenstein continues, "What we call believing in a Judgement Day or not believing in a Judgement Day—The expression of belief may play an absolutely minor role. If you ask me whether or not I believe in a Judgement Day, in the sense in which religious people have belief in it, I wouldn't say: 'No. I don't believe there will be such a thing.' It would seem to me utterly crazy to say this. And then I give an explanation: 'I don't believe in . . .', but then the religious person never believes what I describe. I can't say. I can't contradict that person" (57). "In one sense, I understand all he says—the English words 'God,' 'separate,' etc. I understand. I could say: 'I don't believe in this,' and this would be true, meaning I haven't got these thoughts or anything that hangs together with them. But not that I could contradict the thing."

49. Wittgenstein, 57, 59.

50. "Here we are distinguishing between the views of those who think that they need not rest on the evidential basis and those who hold the far more radical belief that faith needs neither evidences nor the facts themselves" (Gary Habermas, 1991).

51. Overdetermination theory is still a largely unexplored approach in debates over the basing relationship. But it is motivated by the holistic nature of people's reasoning about worldview beliefs, and under conditions of uncertainty and other pragmatic constraints, as Rawls alerted us to. It is motivated also, we have now seen, by some

specific psychological studies, research that illuminates how trait-dependent judgment contributes to psychographic contrariety. See Axtell 2019 for development.

52. A further paper by Leeuwen (2007) argues that self-deception does not typically result in "belief" but in "avowed belief." Since CSR is interested in popular religiosity and theological incorrectness, there are some rich CSR connections here as well, and Leeuwen develops them to a degree.

53. This language, though, might be confusing, since many epistemologists of internalist and probabilist orientation use "credence" as an evidence-based confidence level, such as .6. Compare Lara Buchak (2014), who nicely tries to mediate what she sees as two robust traditions that dealing with doxastic attitudes. In our terms, the one tradition focuses on the etiologically and axiologically deep (Leeuwen), while the other, the probabilistic tradition, focuses on the shallow side of Table 1. Still, Leeuwen and Buchak might both endorse what Carter, Jarvis, and Rubin (2016) refer to as "doxastic state pluralism," and I accept this latter as an essential aspect of the epistemology of controversial views.

54. Leeuwen's distinction seems related to the better-known distinction between "sensory" and "emotional" experience. On the latter, Foresman, Fosl and Watson (2017) note that many of our beliefs are formed on the basis of both kinds of experience. They remind us of Montaigne's claim "What we see and hear when we are transported with emotion we neither see nor hear as it is." Some thinkers and traditions disparage emotional experience as evidence in epistemic or critical matters, while others (James, for example) champion it. Realistically, "even if we are suspicious of the role emotional experience plays in reasoning we cannot completely eradicate it" (234). For Foresman et al., it is important first that we distinguish them rather than conflating them, and then that we assess carefully: "*Emotional experience* refers to our affective impression of all those things that are brought into our perception through our senses. . . . There are a number of similarities between these two types of feeling [sensory and emotional]. First, both happen independently of our *wills*; . . .Secondly, both kinds of feeling happen largely independently of conscious, critical *judgments* we make about them. . . . Despite the similarities between sense experience and emotion, there are strong reasons for distinguishing them . . . [including that] the content of sense experience is about a different type of reality from emotions. Experience seems to direct our attention to something *outside* of ourselves, which may or may not be presented to us accurately. . . . The content of our emotions, however, seems to be about something quite different. For the most part, the content of emotions seems to be to something *inside us*" (222).

55. Leeuwen 2014, 698.

56. Buckareff (2005) argues that faith is best conceived of as a *sub-doxastic* venture, and that "Bishop fails adequately to show that faith in the face of inadequate epistemic reasons for believing is, or can even be, a uniquely *doxastic* venture." Bishop (2005) responds that "it is indeed impossible intentionally and directly to acquire a belief one judges not to be supported by one's evidence. But Jamesian doxastic venture does not involve any such direct self-inducing of belief: it is rather a matter of an agent's *taking* to be true in practical reasoning what she *already*, through

some 'passional,' non-epistemic, cause, *holds* true beyond the support of her evidence." Eklund (2014) updates this debate.

57. At least where we are focusing on problems with theological methods on which having faith mean *believing the factual truth* of narrative events in scripture, the foremost problem is that agents may actually be conflating cognitive states if the states they self-report having are emotionally-charged or held above challenge or serious revision.

58. Leeuwen's project like my own is not well-aided by the generic scales of religiosity and spirituality the psychologists have often applied, but suggests a need for more detailed scales, informed by theory. But cognitive scientists already recognize that avowals cannot simply be taken at face value. Studies of differences between explicit measures of religiosity such as self-reports and implicit measures throw some light on that subject. This firstly goes to the question of whether one *can* believe theological claims that they may not actually understand. It secondly goes to the CSR distinction between times when "theologically correct" beliefs are maintained to people, and times when they tend to slide back into theologically incorrect" assertions, for example, in more "freely elaborated" or anthropomorphic claims about godhead.

59. Van Leeuwen writes that "This theory locates religious credence and factual belief in relation to other cognitive attitudes, like fictional imagining, hypothesis, acceptance in a context, and assumption for the sake of argument," and he argues that "religious credence has key features in common with these latter attitudes that that distinguish them from factual belief" (2014, 699). Among these features that religious credence shares with fictional imagining and other secondary cognitive attitudes is that that they are not typically held to "norms of truth and evidence" (712).

60. Does being self-deceived that p entail believing that p? Leeuwen cites Robert Audi for this revisionary claim that Leeuwen himself rejects. But he defines avowal as "a tendency to affirm verbally (both privately and publicly) that lacks normal belief-like connections to non-verbal actions" (2007, 419). My account is neutral on this debate and on the question of whether or not a bias, for instance ethnocentrism, involves believing certain things to be true. I hope my use of "avowal" as a general term that could be cognitive *or* non-cognitive, doxastic or sub-doxastic, does not confuse my description of Leeuwen's views.

61. After all, the models of faith that most highly insist upon "belief" but exhibit the Epistemic Tension are also the models of faith that support a Conflict model of the relationship between faith and reason. Proponents of Conflict, whether of the biblical literalist or aggressive atheist sort, agree that religions make overt empirical truth claims; the only question is whether these claims are factually true or not. Conflict is to be avoided where possible, and Leeuwen's proposed distinction is a step in that direction.

62. Leeuwen 2014, 711.

63. Leeuwen 2014, 713.

64. McCauley and Whitehouse, 2. Compare Sorensen: "We need to address the universal questions raised above and this cannot be done by means of localised interpretations. Further, explanatory theories not only enable us to address such general questions but also to fertilise local interpretations by supplying a more solid

terminological grounding and presenting new potential lines of enquiry. All interpretations are theory-dependent and the more explicit the theories are, the better.
Thus the cognitive science of religion does not reject the role of interpretation in the
academic study of religion, but merely attempts to right an unbalance by insisting
on the necessity of explanatory theories" (2005, 467). Sorensen insists that public
representations are only one side of the coin, and that "keeping universal cognitive
mechanisms in mind can help historians avoid historical exoticism, in the same way
as it helps anthropologists avoid cultural exoticism."

65. This idea together with some aspects of HADD are anticipated in Hume's
observation that, "we have a strong disposition to read mentality into what is not
really mental. Thus, we tend to treat these unknown causes as agents to be appeased"
(Hume 1993, 141).

66. Brunner 1937, 155. See Blanshard for critical commentary.

67. Perhaps extending from Paul (1 *Corinthians* 1:23), the strong fideism of Tertullian informed his ironic claim, "The most ignorant peasant under the Christian
dispensation possesses more real knowledge than the wisest of ancient philosophers"
(*Apologeticus*).

68. Sorensen 2005, 487–488.

69. For example with SAST Effects, priming a subject might be on the lines of
Leeuwen's point (2014) that cognitive attitudes are attributed to what is "evidentially
vulnerable" and subjection to "general cognitive governance." Test subjects can be
primed to acknowledge this with respect to other people's beliefs, before being asked
about their own. If their reports about their own faith-based precepts are revealed by
subsequent self-reports to be evidentially *in*vulnerable and to *lack* general cognitive
governance characteristic of belief, then the subject is displaying SAST Effects.

70. James, the 1896 Preface to James' *The Will to Believe and Other Essays in
Popular Philosophy*.

71. This, despite how often members of both groups—epistemologists and
theologians—seem to unite in principled opposition to James spirit of inner tolerance.
Decades later, James would respond to his critics, secular and theistic, who accused
him of 'preaching reckless faith': "I have preached the right of the individual to
indulge his personal faith at his personal risk. I have discussed the kinds of risk; I have
contended that none of us escape all of them; and I have only preached that it is better
to face them open-eyed than to act as if we did not know them to be there." Quoted in
Bruce Kuklick's introduction to James's *Pragmatism* (1907, xv). While I do not find
James's version of permissivism is adequately risk-averse (see Axtell 2018 for my
critique, and compare Aikin and Talisse 2018) I think this permissivism-with-teeth is
on the right track.

Bibliography

Adamo, Christopher. "One True Ring or Many?: Religious Pluralism in Lessing's *Nathan the Wise*." *Philosophy and Literature* 33, no. 1 (2009): 139–149, doi: 10.1353/phl.0.0048.

Adams, Robert M. "Kierkegaard's Argument against Objective Reasoning in Religion." In *Philosophy of Religion: An Anthology*, 3rd ed., edited by Louis P. Pojman, 408–418. Belmont, CA: Wadsworth Publishing, 1998.

Aijaz, Imran and John Bishop. "How to Answer the 'de Jure' Question about Christian Belief." *International Journal for Philosophy of Religion* 56, no. 2–3 (2004): 109–129.

Aijaz, Imran. "Traditional Islamic Exclusivism – A Critique." *European Journal for Philosophy of Religion* 6, no. 2 (2014): 185–209.

———. "Some Ruminations about Inculpable Non-belief." *Religious Studies* 49, no. 3 (2013): 399–419.

———. "Belief, Providence and Eschatology." *Philosophy Compass* 1 (2008): 231–253.

Aiken, Scott and Robert B. Talisse. *Why We Argue, and How We Should.* London: Routledge, 2013.

Aiken, Scott and Robert B. Talisse. "The Will-to-Believe is Immoral." In *William James, Moral Philosophy, and the Ethical Life: The Cries of the Wounded*, edited by Jacob Goodson, 143–160. Lanham, MD: Lexington Books, 2018.

Alexander, David and Daniel M. Johnson. (eds.) *Calvinism and the Problem of Evil.* Harrison, NY: Pickwick Publishing, 2016.

Alimi, Eitan Y., Charles Demetriou, and Lorenzo Bosi. *The Dynamics of Radicalization: A Relational and Comparative Perspective.* Oxford: Oxford University Press, 2015.

Altemeyer, Bob and Bruce Hunsberger. "A Revised Religious Fundamentalism Scale: The Short and Sweet of It." *International Journal for the Psychology of Religion* 14, no. 1 (2004): 47–54.

Amesbury, Richard. "Fideism." In *Stanford Encyclopedia of Philosophy*, edited by Edward N. Zalta, Stanford, CT: Metaphysics Research Lab at Stanford University, 2007. http://plato.stanford.edu/entries/fideism/.

Anderson, Mark B. "Molinism, Open Theism, and Soteriological Luck." *Religious Studies* 47, no. 3 (2011): 371–381.

Anderson, Pamela S. "Postmodern Theology." In *The Routledge Companion to Philosophy of Religion*, edited by Chad Meister and Paul Copan, 569–581. New York, NY: Routledge, 2007.

Aristotle. *On Sophistical Refutations*, translated by W. A. Pickard-Cambridge. e-Books@Adelaide. Adelaide, Australia: University of Adelaide, 2015. https://ebooks.adelaide.edu.au/a/aristotle/sophistical/.

Armstrong, Karen. *A History of God: The 4,000-Year Quest of Judaism, Christianity, and Islam*. New York, NY: MJF Books, 2015.

———. *The Case for God*. New York, NY: Anchor Books, 2013.

———. *The Battle for God: Fundamentalism in Judaism, Christianity and Islam*. New York, NY: Knopf/HarperCollins, 2000.

Audi, Robert. "The Ethics of Belief and the Morality of Action: Intellectual Responsibility and Rational Disagreement." *Philosophy* 86, no. 335 (January 2011): 5–29.

Axtell, Guy. "Well-Founded Belief and the Contingencies of Epistemic Location." In *Well-Founded Belief: New Essays on the Epistemic Basing Relation*, edited by P. Bondy and J.A. Carter. Oxford: Oxford University Press, forthcoming, 2019.

———. "William James on Pragmatism and Religion." In *William James, Moral Philosophy, and the Ethical Life: The Cries of the Wounded*, edited by Jacob Goodson, 317–336. Lanham, MD: Lexington Books, 2018.

———. "Thinking Twice about Virtue and Vice: Philosophical Situationism and the Vicious Minds Hypothesis." *Logos & Episteme* 8, no. 1 (2017): 7–39, doi:10.5840/logos-episteme2017811.

———. "Possibility and Permission? Intellectual Character, Inquiry, and the Ethics of Belief." In *William James on Religion*, edited by S. Pihlstrom and H. Rydenfelt, 165–198. London: Palgrave Macmillan, 2013.

———. "From Internalist Evidentialism to Virtue Responsibilism: Reasonable Disagreement and the Ethics of Belief." In *Evidentialism and its Discontents*, edited by Trent Dougherty, 71–87. Oxford: Oxford University Press, 2011.

———. "Recovering Responsibility." *Logos and Episteme* 3 (Fall, 2011): 429–454.

———. "Review of Robert C. Roberts and W. Jay Wood *Intellectual Virtues*." *Ethics* 119, no. 2 (2009): 377–382.

———. "Blind Man's Bluff: Plantinga's Apologetic Stratagem." *Phil. Studies* 30, no. 1 (2006): 131–152.

———. "Teaching James's 'The Will to Believe.'" *Teaching Philosophy* 24, no. 4 (2001): 325–345.

Aydin, Mahmut. "A Muslim Pluralist: Jalaluddin Rumi." In *Myth of Religious Superiority: Multifaith Explorations of Religious Pluralism*, edited by P. Knitter, 220–236. Maryknoll, NY: Orbis Books, 2004.

Baker-Hytch, Max. "Religious Diversity and Epistemic Luck." *International Journal for Philosophy of Religion* 76, no. 2 (2014): 171–191.

————. "Testimony amidst Diversity." In *Knowledge, Belief, and God: New Insights in Religious Epistemology*, edited by Matthew A. Benton, John Hawthorne, and Dani Rabinowitz. Oxford: Oxford University Press, 2018. doi:10.1093/oso/9780198798705.003.0010.

Baldwin, Erik and Michael Thune. "The Epistemological Limits of Experience-Based Exclusive Religious Belief." *Religious Studies* 44, no. 4 (2008): 445–455. doi: 10.1017/S0034412508009530.

Ballantyne, Nathan. "De-Biasing Biased Thinkers (Including Ourselves)." *Journal of the American Philosophical Association* 1, no. 1 (2015): 141–162.

————. "Does Luck Have a Place in Epistemology?" *Synthese* 191, no. 7 (2014): 1391–1407.

————. "The Problem of Historical Variability." In *Disagreement and Skepticism*, edited by D. Machuca, 239–259. New York, NY: Routledge Press, 2013.

Barnett, Brian C. "A Probabilistic Defense of Proper De Jure Objections to Theism." *Religious Studies*, forthcoming, 2019.

Barrett, Justin L. *Cognitive Science, Religion, and Theology: From Human Minds to Divine Minds*. West Conshohocken, PA: Templeton Press, 2011.

Barth, Karl. *Church Dogmatics, Volume 1*. Peabody, MA: Hendrickson Publishers, 2010.

Basinger, David. *Religious Diversity: A Philosophical Assessment*. London: Routledge Press, 2002.

Basu, Rima and Schroeder, Mark (eds.) "Can Beliefs Wrong?" special edition, *Philosophical Topics* 46, no. 1 (2018a).

Basu, Rima and Schroeder, Mark. "Epistemic Wronging." In *Pragmatic Encroachment in Epistemology*, edited by Brian Kim and Matthew McGrath. London: Routledge, 2018b.

Bergmann, Michael and Patrick Kain. (eds.) *Challenges to Moral and Religious Belief: Disagreement and Evolution*. Oxford: Oxford University Press, 2014.

Biddle, Justin B. "Inductive Risk, Epistemic Risk, and Overdiagnosis of Disease." *Perspectives on Science* 24, no. 2 (2016): 192–205.

Biddle, Justin B. and Rebecca Kukla. "The Geography of Epistemic Risk." In *Exploring Inductive Risk*, edited by Kevin C. Elliot and Ted Richards, 215–238. Oxford Scholarship Online. *111* Oxford: Oxford University Press, 2017. doi:10.1093/acprof:oso/9780190467715.001.0001.

Bishop, John. "Trusting Others, Trusting in God, Trusting the World." In *Religious Faith and Intellectual Virtue*, edited by Lauren F. Callahan and Timothy O'Connor, 159–173. New York, NY: Oxford University Press, 2014.

————. "How a Modest Fideism May Constrain Theistic Commitments: Exploring an Alternative to Classical Theism." *Philosophia* 35, no. 3–4 (2007a): 387–402.

————. *Believing by Faith: An Essay in the Epistemology and Ethics of Religious Belief*. New York, NY: Clarendon Press, 2007b.

————. "On the Possibility of a Doxastic Venture: A Reply to Buckareff." *Religious Studies* 41, no. 4 (2005): 447–451.

Blanshard, Brand. *Reason and Belief* (The 1970 Gifford Lectures). London: George Allen & Unwin, 1974. https://www.giffordlectures.org/books/reason-and-belief/.

Bogardus, Tomas. "The Problem of Contingency for Religious Belief." *Faith and Philosophy* 30, no. 4 (2013): 371–392.

Bondy, Patrick and Duncan Pritchard. "Propositional Epistemic Luck, Epistemic Risk, and Epistemic Justification." *Synthese* (2016): 1–10. https://doi.org/10.1007/s11229-016-1262-2.

Booth, Anthony and Rik Peels. "Why Responsible Belief Is Permissible Belief." *Analytic Philosophy* 55, no. 1 (2014): 75–88.

Bortolotti, Lisa and Matthew Broome. "A Role for Ownership and Authorship in the Analysis of Thought Insertion." *Phenomenology and the Cognitive Sciences* 8, no. 2 (2009): 205–224.

Bortolotti, Lisa. "Stranger than Fiction: Costs and Benefits of Everyday Confabulation." *Review of Philosophy and Psychology* 9 (2018): 227–249. https://doi.org/10.1007/s13164-017-0367-y.

Brady, Michael S. and Miranda Fricker. (eds.) *The Epistemic Life of Groups: Essays in the Epistemology of Collectives.* Oxford: Oxford University Press, 2016.

Brague, Remi. "The Concept of the Abrahamic Religions, Problems and Pitfalls." In *The Oxford Handbook of the Abrahamic Religions*, edited by Adam J. Silverstein and Guy G. Stroumsa. Oxford: Oxford University Press, 2015. doi:10.1093/oxfordhb/9780199697762.013.5.

Breyer, Daniel. "Reflective Luck and Belief Ownership." *Acta Analytica* 25, no. 2 (2010): 133–154.

Breyer, Daniel. "Ownership, Agency, and Defeat." *Acta Analytica* 28, no. 2 (2013): 253–256.

Breyer, Daniel and John Greco. "Cognitive Integration and the Ownership of Belief: Response to Bernecker." *Philosophy and Phenomenological Research* 76, no. 1 (2008): 173–184.

Brunner, Emil. *The Divine Imperative.* Cambridge: Lutterworth Press, 2003.

Buchanan, Allen. "Political Liberalism and Social Epistemology." *Philosophy and Public Affairs* 32, no. 2 (2004): 95–130.

Buchak, Lara. "Belief, Credence, and Norms." *Philosophical Studies* 169, no. 2 (2014): 285–311.

Buckareff, Andrei and Allen Plug. "Escapism, Religious Luck, and Divine Reasons for Action." *Religious Studies* 45, no. 2 (2009): 63–72.

Buckareff, Andrei. "Can Faith be a Doxastic Venture?" *Religious Studies* 41, no. 4 (2005): 435–445.

Callahan, Laura F. and Timothy O'Connor. (eds.) *Religious Faith and Intellectual Virtue.* New York, NY: Oxford University Press, 2014.

Carroll, Thomas D. "The Traditions of Fideism." *Religious Studies* 44, no. 1 (2008): 1–22.

Carter, J. Adam, Benjamin W. Jarvis, and Katherine Rubin. "Belief without Credence." *Synthese* 193, no. 8 (2016): 2323–2351.

Carter, J. Adam. "On Behalf of Controversial View Agnosticism." *European Journal of Philosophy.* (2018): 1–13. https://doi.org/10.1111/ejop.12333.

———. "A Modal Account of Luck Revisited." *Synthese* 194, no. 6 (2017): 2175–2184.

Cassam, Quassim. "The Epistemology of Terrorism and Counter-Terrorism." In *Philosophy*, special edition. Cambridge: Cambridge University Press, forthcoming, 2018.

Christiansen, David. "Disagreement and Public Controversy." In *Essays in Collective Epistemology*, edited by Jennifer Lackey, 142–163. Oxford: Oxford University Press, 2014.

Christiansen, David and Jennifer Lackey. (eds.) *The Epistemology of Disagreement: New Essays*. Oxford: Oxford University Press, 2013.

Church, Ian M. and Robert J. Hartman. *The Routledge Handbook of the Philosophy and Psychology of Luck*. London: Routledge Press, 2019.

Church, Ian M. "Getting 'Lucky' with Gettier." *European Journal of Philosophy* 21, no. 1 (2013): 37–49.

Clarke, Steve. "Coercion, Consequence and Salvation." In *Scientific Approaches to the Philosophy of* Religion, edited by Y. Nagasawa, 205–223. New York, NY: Palgrave Macmillan, 2012.

Clary, Erik M. "Theology of Religions in Flux: On Paul Knitter's Soteriological Shift Culminating in Mutualism." *Trinity Journal* 31, no. 2 (2010): 243–263.

Cleveland, Christena. *Disunity in Christ: Uncovering the Hidden Forces that Keep Us Apart*. Westmont, IL: IVP Books, 2014.

Coffman, E. J. *Luck: Its Nature and Significance for Human Knowledge and Agency*. London: Palgrave Macmillan UK, 2015.

Cohen, G. A. "Paradoxes of Conviction." In *If You're An Egalitarian, How Come You're So Rich?*, edited by G. A. Choen, 7–19. Cambridge, MA: Harvard University Press, 2000.

Condorcet, Marquis de. "Outlines of an Historical View of the Progress of the Human Mind." (Translated from the French.) (Philadelphia: M. Carey, 1796). August 14, /2018. http://oll.libertyfund.org/titles/1669.

Cowan, Steven. "Molinism, Meticulous Providence, and Luck." *Philosophia Christi* 11, no. 1 (2009): 156–169.

Craig, William L. "'No Other Name': A Middle Knowledge Perspective on the Exclusivity of Salvation through Christ." *Faith and Philosophy* 6, no. 2 (1989): 172–188.

———. "Middle Knowledge and Christian Exclusivism." *Sophia* 34, no. 1 (1995): 120–139.

Davis, John K. "Faultless Disagreement, Cognitive Command, and Epistemic Peers." *Synthese* 192, no. 1 (2015): 1–24.

———. "Subjectivity, Judgment, and the Basing Relationship." *Pacific Philosophical Quarterly* 90, no. 1 (2009): 21–40.

Davison, Scott. "Salvific Luck." *International Journal for Philosophy of Religion* 45, no. 2 (1999): 129–137.

Dawkins, Richard. *The God Delusion*. Boston, MA: Mariner Books, 2008.

Dawes, Greg. and James Maclaurin. (eds.) *A New Science of Religion*. New York, NY: Routledge, 2013.

Dawes, Gregory and Jonathan Jong. "Defeating the Christian's Claim to Warrant." *Philo* 15, no. 2 (2012): 127–144.

D'Costa, Gavin. "The Impossibility of a Pluralist View of Religions." *Religious Studies* 32, no. 2 (1996): 223–232.

De Cruz, Helen. "Divine Hiddenness and the Cognitive Science of Religion." In *Hidden Divinity and Religious Belief*, edited by Adam Green and Eleonore Stump, 53–68. Cambridge: Cambridge University Press, 2015.

———. "The Relevance of Hume's Natural History of Religion for Cognitive Science of Religion." *Res Philosophica* 92, no. 3 (2015): 653–675.

———. "The Enduring Appeal of Natural Theological Arguments." *Philosophy Compass* 9, no. 2 (2014): 145–153. doi:10.1111/phc3.12105.

Diller, Jeanine and Asa Kasher. (eds.) *Models of God and Alternative Ultimate Realities.* Heidelberg, Germany: Springer Netherlands, 2013.

DiPaolo, Joshua and Robert M. Simpson. "Indoctrination Anxiety and the Etiology of Belief." *Synthese*, 193, no. 10 (2016): 3079–3098. doi:10.1007/s11229-015-0919-6.

Douglas, Heather. "Inductive Risk and Values in Science." *Philosophy of Science* 67, no. 4 (2000): 559–579.

Dulles, Avery. "The Problem of Revelation." *Proceedings of the Catholic Theological Society of America* (1974): 77–106. https://ejournals.bc.edu/ojs/index.php/ctsa/article/view/2791/2420.

Dutton, Kevin and Dominic Abrams. "What Researchers Say about Defeating Terrorism." *Scientific American Mind.* https://www.scientificamerican.com/article/what-research-says-about-defeating-terrorism/.

Eklund, Dan-Johan. "Is Non-evidential Believing Possible? John Bishop on Passionally Caused Beliefs." *Religious Studies* 50, no. 3 (2014): 309–320. https://doi.org/10.1017/S0034412513000516.

Elliot, Kevin C. and Ted Richards. *Exploring Inductive Risk: Case Studies of Values in Science.* Oxford: Oxford University Press, 2017.

Enoch, David and Ehud Guttel. "Cognitive Biases and Moral Luck." *The Journal of Moral Philosophy* 7 (2010): 1–15.

Engel Jr., Mylan. "Epistemic Luck." *Internet Encyclopedia of Philosophy.* http://www.iep.utm.edu/epi-luck/.

———. "Is Epistemic Luck Compatible with Knowledge?" *Southern Journal of Philosophy* 30, no. 2 (1992): 59–75.

Euben, Roxanne. *Enemy in the Mirror: Islamic Fundamentalism and the Limits of Modern Rationalism.* Princeton, NJ: Princeton University Press, 1999.

Fantl, Jeremy. *Limitations of the Open Mind.* Oxford: Oxford University Press, 2018.

Foresman, Galen, Peter Fosl, and Jamie C. Watson. *The Critical Thinking Toolkit.* London: Wiley-Blackwell, 2017.

Fraser, Rachel. "Testimonial Pessimism." In *Knowledge, Belief, and God: New Insights in Religious Epistemology*, edited by Matthew A. Benton, John Hawthorne, and Dani Rabinowitz, 203–227. Oxford: Oxford University Press, 2018.

———. "The Pragmatics and Epistemology of Testimony." Podcast of the Moral Sciences Club, University of Cambridge. Cambridge, Recorded May 16, 2017. https://sms.csx.cam.ac.uk/media/2481645.

Freedman, Karyn L. "Testimony and Epistemic Risk: The Dependence Account." *Social Epistemology* 29, no. 3 (2015): 251–269. doi:10.1080/02691728.2014.884183.

Fricker, Miranda. *Epistemic Injustice: Power and the Ethics of Knowing.* Oxford: Oxford University Press, 2007.

Fringer, Rob A. and Jeff K. Lane. *Theology of Luck: Fate, Chaos, and Faith.* Kansas City, MO: Beacon Hill, 2015.

Gellman, Jerome. "In Defence of a Contented Religious Exclusivism." *Religious Studies* 36, no. 4 (2000): 401–417.

Giberson, Karl H. (ed.) *Abraham's Dice: Chance and Providence in the Monotheistic Traditions.* Oxford: Oxford University Press, 2016.

Goldman, Alvin I. "Epistemics: The Regulative Theory of Cognition." *Journal of Philosophy* 75, no. 10 (1978): 509–523.

Greco, John. "Friendly Theism." In *Religious Tolerance through Humility,* edited by J. Kraft and D. Basinger, 51–60. Burlington, VT: Ashgate, 2008.

Green, Adam. "Cognitive Science and the Natural Knowledge of God." *The Monist* 96, no. 3 (2013): 399–419.

Green, Garrett. "Challenging the Religious Studies Canon: Karl Barth's Theory of Religion." *The Journal of Religion* 75, no. 4 (1995): 473–486.

Griffiths, Paul E. and John Wilkins. "Evolutionary Debunking Arguments in Three Domains: Fact, Value, and Religion." In *A New Science of Religion,* edited by G. Dawes and J. Maclaurin, 133–146. London: Routledge, 2013.

Griffiths, Paul and John Wilkins. "When Do Evolutionary Explanations of Belief Debunk Belief?" *Phil Sci Archive,* 2010. http://philsci-archive.pitt.edu/5314/ (accessed November 2017).

Griffiths, Paul J. *Problems of Religious Diversity.* Hoboken, NJ: Wiley-Blackwell, 2001.

———. "Why We Need Interreligious Polemics." In *First Things* 44 (1994).

———. *An Apology for Apologetics: A Study in the Logic of Interreligious Dialogue.* Eugene, OR: Wipf and Stock, 2007.

Grube, Dirk-Martin and Walter Van Herck. (eds.) *Philosophical Perspectives on Religious Diversity: Bivalent Truth, Tolerance, and Personhood.* London: Routledge, 2018.

Grube, Dirk-Martin. "Justified Religious Difference: A Constructive Approach to Religious Diversity." *International Journal of Philosophy and Theology* 76, no. 5 (2015): 419–427.

———. "Justification Rather Than Truth: Gotthold Ephraim Lessing's Defence of Positive Religion in the Ring-Parable." *Bijdragen International Journal of Philosophy and Theology* 66, no. 1 (2005): 357–378.

Gschwandtner, Christina. "Philosophical Reflections on the Shaping of Identity in Fundamentalist Religious Communities." *International Journal of Philosophical Studies* 24, no. 5 (2016): 704–724.

Habermas, Gary R. "An Appraisal of the Leap of Faith.' *LBTS Faculty Publications and Presentations* (1991): 398. http://digitalcommons.liberty.edu/lts_fac_pub s/398.

Haack, Susan. "'The Ethics of Belief' Reconsidered." In *The Philosophy of Roderick M. Chisholm,* edited by Lewis E. Hahn, 129–144. Chicago, IL: Open Court, 1997.

Haidt, Jonathan. *The Righteous Mind: Why Good People Are Divided by Politics and Religion.* New York, NY: Vintage Books, 2012.

Hales, Steven and Jennifer A. Johnson. "Luck Attribution and Cognitive Bias." *Metaphilosophy* 45, no. 4–5 (2014): 509–528.

Hanson, Delbert J. *Fideism and Hume's Philosophy.* Bern, Switzerland: Peter Lang International Academic Publishers, 1993.

Harman, Gilbert. "Knowledge, Reasons, and Causes." *Journal of Philosophy* 67, no. 21 (1970): 841–855.

Hartman, Robert J. *In Defense of Moral Luck: Why Luck Often Affects Praiseworthiness and Blameworthiness.* London: Routledge, 2017.

———. "How to Apply Molinism to the Theological Problem of Moral Luck." *Faith and Philosophy* 31 (2014): 68–90.

———. "Involuntary Belief and the Command to Have Faith." *International Journal for Philosophy of Religion* 69, no. 3 (2011): 181–192.

Hempel, Carl G. "Science and Human Values." In *Aspects of Scientific Explanation and Other Essays in the Philosophy of Science*, 81–96. New York, NY: The Free Press, 1965.

Herman, David. *Storytelling and the Sciences of Mind.* Boston, MA: MIT Press, 2013.

Hick, John. *The Interpretation of Religion: Human Responses to the Transcendent, Second Edition.* New Haven, CT: Yale University Press, 2005.

———. "The Epistemological Challenge of Religious Pluralism." *Faith and Philosophy* 14, no. 3 (1997): 277–286.

Hirstein, William. *Brain Fiction: Self-Deception and the Riddle of Confabulation.* Denver, CO: A Bradford Book, 2005.

Hood Jr., Ralph W., Peter C. Hill, and W. Paul Williamson. *The Psychology of Religious Fundamentalism.* New York, NY: Guilford Press, 2005.

Howard-Snyder, Daniel and Paul K. Moser. (eds.) *Divine Hiddenness: New Essays.* Cambridge: Cambridge University Press, 2002.

Howell, Robert J. "Google Morals, Virtue, and the Asymmetry of Deference." *Noûs* 48, no. 3 (2014): 389–415.

Hume, David. *Dialogues and the Natural History of Religion*, edited by J. Gaskin. Oxford: Oxford University Press, 2009.

Hunt, David. "Middle Knowledge and the Soteriological Problem of Evil." *Religious Studies* 27, no. 1 (1991): 3–26.

Hustwit, J. R. *Interreligious Hermeneutics and the Pursuit of Truth.* Lexington, KY: Lexington Books, 2014.

Ichikawa, Jonathan J. and Steup Matthias. "The Analysis of Knowledge." In *The Stanford Encyclopedia of Philosophy*, edited by E.N. Zalta. Stanford, CT: Metaphysics Research Lab at Stanford University, 2018. https://plato.stanford.edu/entries/knowledge-analysis/ (accessed 2018).

James, William. *The Will to Believe and Other Essays in Popular Philosophy.* Cambridge, MA: Harvard University Press, 1979.

———. *Pragmatism.* Indianapolis, IN: Hackett Publishing Co., 1981.

———. *The Varieties of Religious Experience.* New York, NY: Dover Publications, 2002.

———. *Some Problems of Philosophy.* Cambridge, MA: Harvard University Press, 1979.

Jensen, Alex, Valerie J. Chock, Kyle Mallard, and Jonathan Matheson. "A Review of Linda Zagzebski's *Epistemic Authority*." *Social Epistemology Review and Reply Collective* 6, no. 9 (2017): 29–34.

Jones, James W. "Religion and Violence from a Psychological Perspective." In *The Oxford Handbook of Religion and Violence*, edited by Michael Jerryson, Mark Juergensmeyer, and Margo Kitts, 385–396. Oxford: Oxford University Press, 2013.

Jones, Russell E. "Escapism and Luck." *Religious Studies* 43, no. 2 (2007): 205–216.

Jong, Huib Looren de. "Introduction: A Symposium on Explanatory Pluralism." *Theory and Psychology* 11, no. 6 (2001). http://journals.sagepub.com/doi/abs/10.1177/0959354301116001.

Juergensmeyer, Mark. *Terror in the Mind of God: The Global Rise of Religious Violence*. Berkeley, CA: University of California Press, 2003.

Kant, Immanuel. "The End of all Things." In *Perpetual Peace and other Essays*, translated by Ted Humphrey, 93–102. Indianapolis, IN: Hackett Publishing Co.

Katzoff, Charlotte. "Religious Luck and Religious Virtue." *Religious Studies* 40, no. 1 (2004): 97–111.

Kelly, Thomas. "Evidence Can Be Permissive." In *Contemporary Debates in Epistemology, 2nd Edition*, edited by Matthias Steup, John Turri, and Ernest Sosa, 298–311. Hoboken, NJ: Wiley-Blackwell, 2013.

———. "Disagreement, Dogmatism, and Belief Polarization." *Journal of Philosophy* 105, no. 10 (2008): 611–633.

Kennedy, Kathleen A. and Emily Pronin. "Bias Perception and the Spiral of Conflict." In *Ideology, Psychology, and Law*, edited by Jon Hanson, 410–446. Oxford: Oxford University Press, 2012.

Kidd, Ian J. "Charging Others with Epistemic Vice." *The Monist* 99, no. 3 (2016): 181–197.

———. "A Phenomenological Challenge to 'Enlightened Secularism.'" *Religious Studies* 49, no. 3 (2013): 377–398.

Kierkegaard, Søren. *Concluding Unscientific Postscript to Philosophical Fragments, Volume 1*, edited and translated by Edna Hong and Howard Hong. Princeton, NJ: Princeton University Press, 1992.

———. *Philosophical Fragments*, edited and translated by Edna Hong and Howard Hong. Princeton, NJ: Princeton University Press, 1985.

———. *Fear and Trembling*, translated by Alastair Hannay. London: Penguin Classics, 1986.

Kitcher, Philip. *Life after Faith: The Case for Secular Humanism*. New Haven, CT: Yale University Press, 2015.

———. "Militant Modern Atheism." *Journal of Applied Philosophy* 28, no.1 (2011): 1–13. doi:10.1111/j.1468-5930.2010.00500.x.

Knitter, Paul. (ed.) *The Myth of Religious Superiority*. Maryknoll, NY: Orbis Books, 2004.

———. *Introducing Theologies of Religions*. Maryknoll, NY: Orbis Books, 2002.

Knobe, Joshua and Bertram F. Malle. "Self and Other in the Explanation of Behavior: 30 Years Later." *Psychologica Belgica* 42, no. 1–2 (2002): 113–130.

Kopec, Matthew and Michael Titelbaum. "The Uniqueness Thesis." *Philosophy Compass* 11, no. 4 (2016): 189–200.

Kraft, James. *The Epistemology of Religious Disagreement: A Better Understanding.* London: Palgrave Macmillan, 2012.

Kvanvig, Jonathan L. "Jonathan Edwards on Hell." In *Jonathan Edwards: Philosophical Theologian*, edited by Paul Helm and Oliver Crisp, 1–12. London: Routledge, 2003.

Lackey, Jennifer. "Experts and Peer Disagreement." In *Knowledge, Belief, and God: New Insights in Religious Epistemology*, edited by Matthew A. Benton, John Hawthorne & Dani Rabinowitz, 228–245. Oxford: Oxford University Press, 2018.

———. "Taking Religious Disagreement Seriously." In *Religious Faith and Intellectual Virtue*, edited by Lauren F. Callahan and Timothy O'Connor, 299–316. New York, NY: Oxford University Press, 2014.

Leeuwen, Neil Van. "Do Religious 'Beliefs' Respond to Evidence?" *Philosophical Explorations* 20, no.1 (2017): 52–72.

———. "Religious Credence is not Factual Belief." *Cognition* 133, no. 3 (2014): 698–715.

———. "The Product of Self-Deception." *Erkenntnis* 67, no. 3 (2007): 419–437.

Lewis, Thomas A. *Why Philosophy Matters for the Study of Religion – and Vice Versa.* Oxford: Oxford University Press, 2015.

Lightfoot, Cynthia. *The Culture of Adolescent Risk-Taking.* New York, NY: Guilford Press, 1997.

Liht, José, Lucian G. Conway, Sara Savage, and Weston White. "Religious Fundamentalism: An Empirically Derived Construct and Measurement Scale." *Archive for the Psychology of Religion* 33, no. 3 (2011): 299–323.

Lindbeck, George. "The Gospel's Uniqueness: Election and Untranslatability." *Modern Theology* 13, no. 4 (1997): 423–450.

Lefebure, Leo D. *Revelation, the Religions, and Violence.* Maryknoll, NY: Orbis Books, 2000.

Locke, John. *The Second Treatise of Government and a Letter Concerning Toleration.* Mineola, NY: Dover Publications, 2002.

Long, Todd R. "A Proper *de jure* Objection to the Epistemic Rationality of Religious Belief." *Religious Studies* 46, no. 3 (2010): 375–394. Cambridge, MA: Cambridge University Press. doi:10.1017/S0034412509990382.

Longino, Helen E. "The Epistemic Life of Groups: Essays in the Epistemology of Collectives." *Australasian Journal of Philosophy* 96, no. 2 (2018): 401–404.

———. "Feminist Epistemology at Hypatia's 25th Anniversary." *Hypatia* 25, no. 4 (2010): 733–741.

Lyons, Jack and Barry Ward. *The New Critical Thinking: An Empirically Informed Introduction.* London: Routledge, 2017.

Maitzen, Stephen. "Divine Hiddenness and the Demographics of Theism." *Religious Studies* 42, no. 2 (2006): 177–191.

Malle, Bertram. "Attributions as Behavior Explanations: Towards a New Theory." University of Oregon, 2003 (unpublished manuscript, Copyright by Bertram F. Malle).

Marbaniang, Domenic. "Religious Fundamentalism and Social Order: A Philosophical Perspective." *Religious Fundamentalism* (2010). (unpublished conference paper). https://philpapers.org/rec/MARRFA-4.

———. "Anatomy of Religious Violence." *Basileia* 1, no. 1 (2008): 20–24.

Margalit, Avishai. "The Ring: On Religious Pluralism." In *Toleration: An Elusive Virtue*, edited by David Heyd, 147–157. Princeton, NJ: Princeton University Press, 1996.

Margolis, Joseph. *The Truth about Relativism.* Oxford: Blackwell Publishers, 1991.

Marsh, Jason. "Do the Demographics of Theistic Belief Disconfirm Theism? A Reply to Maitzen." *Religious Studies* 44, no. 4 (2008): 465–471.

Mathewes, Charles, Matthew Puffer, and Mark Storslee, (eds.) "Comparative Religious Ethics." *Critical Concepts in Religious Studies.* London: Routledge, 2016.

Mawson, T. J. "Mill's Argument against Religious Knowledge." *Religious Studies* 45, no. 4 (2009): 417–434.

McAdams, Dan P. *The Stories We Live By: Personal Myths and the Making of the Self.* New York, NY: The Guilford Press, 1997.

McCain, Kevin. "The Virtues of Epistemic Conservatism." *Synthese* 164, no. 2 (2008): 185–200.

McCauley, Robert. *Philosophical Foundations of the Cognitive Science of Religion: A Head Start.* London: Bloomsbury Publishing, 2017.

———. *Why Religion is Natural and Science is Not.* Oxford: Oxford University Press, 2011.

———. "Cognitive Science and the Naturalness of Religion." *Philosophy Compass* 5, no. 9 (2010): 779–792. doi:10.1111/j.1747-9991.2010.00326.x.

———. *Mind and Religion: Cognitive and Psychological Foundations of Religiosity*, edited by Harvey Whitehouse. Lanham, MD: Alta Mira Press, 2005.

McCauley, Robert. and Harvey Whitehouse. "Introduction: New Frontiers in the Cognitive Science of Religion." *Journal of Cognition and Culture* 5, no. 1–2 (2005): 1–13.

McDonough, Richard. "Religious Fundamentalism: A Conceptual Critique." *Religious Studies* 49, no. 4 (2013): 561–579.

McKay, Ryan T., and Daniel C. Dennett. "The Evolution of Misbelief." *Behavioral and Brain Sciences* 32, no. 6 (2009): 493–510.

McKim, Robert. *Religious Ambiguity and Religious Diversity.* Oxford: Oxford University Press, 2015.

———. *On Religious Diversity.* Oxford: Oxford University Press, 2012.

Medin, Douglas and Sandra Waxman. "Interpreting Asymmetries of Projection in Children's Inductive Reasoning." In *Inductive Reasoning: Experimental, Developmental, and Computational Approaches*, edited by A. Feeney and E. Heit, 55–80. Cambridge: Cambridge University Press, 2007.

Michel, Christoph and Albert Newen. "Self-Deception as Pseudo-Rational Regulation of Belief." *Consciousness and Cognition* 19, no. 3 (2010): 731–744.

Mill, John S. *On Liberty.* BLTC Research. https://www.utilitarianism.com/ol/three.html (accessed October 30, 2017).

Miller, Richard. "Chance and Providence in Early Christianity." In *Abraham's Dice: Chance and Providence in the Monotheistic Traditions*, edited by Karl W. Giberson. Oxford: Oxford University Press, 2016.

Mitchell, Basil. *The Justification of Religious Belief*. London: Palgrave Macmillan, 1973.

Mogensen, Andreas L. "Contingency Anxiety and the Epistemology of Disagreement." *Pacific Philosophical Quarterly* 98, no. 1 (2017a): 590–611.

———. "Moral Testimony Pessimism and the Uncertain Value of Authenticity." *Pacific Philosophical Quarterly* 95, no. 2 (2017b): 261–284.

Molinini, Daniele, Fabrice Pataut, and Andrea Sereni. "Indispensability and Explanation: An Overview and Introduction." *Synthese* 193, no. 2 (2016): 317–332. https://doi.org/10.1007/s11229-015-0998-4.

Molinini, Daniele. "A Symmetry in the Asymmetry: How Explanatory Asymmetries Might Shed Light on Explanations (in science and in society)." Unpublished long abstract (2012). https://sps2012.sciencesconf.org/3538/document (accessed July 4, 2018).

Montaigne, Michel de. *Essays of Montaigne, Book III*. Translated by John Florio (1553–1625). Renascence Editions. http://www.luminarium.org/renascence-editions/ren.htm.

———. *The Essays of Montaigne*, translated by Charles Cotton, edited by William C. Hazlitt. e-books@Adelaide. https://ebooks.adelaide.edu.au/m/montaigne/michel/essays/contents.html.

———. *The Complete Essays of Montaigne,* translated by Donald Frame. Redwood City, CA: Stanford University Press, 1958.

———. *Apology for Raymond Sebond*, translated by Roger Ariew and Marjorie Grene. Indianapolis, IN: Hackett Publishing, 2003.

Moore, Brooke N. and Richard Parker. *Critical Thinking*, 11th ed. New York, NY: McGraw-Hill, 2014.

Mühlebach, Deborah. "Reflective Equilibrium as an Ameliorative Framework for Feminist Epistemology." *Hypatia* 31, no. 4 (2016): 874–889.

Munevar, Gonzalo. "Fiction in the Brain." In *Questions of Character*, edited by Iskra Fileva, 415–432. Oxford: Oxford University Press, 2017.

Muscat, Robert. "The Contingency of Belief: Present Beliefs Stem from Past Happenstance." *Free Inquiry* 35, no. 6 (2015): 40–42.

Myers, David B. "Exclusivism, Eternal Damnation, and the Problem of Evil: A Critique of Craig's Molinist Soteriological Theodicy." *Religious Studies* 39, no. 4 (2003): 407–419.

Nagel, Thomas. "Moral Luck." In *Mortal Questions*. Cambridge: Cambridge University Press, 2013.

Nagasawa, Yujin. (ed.) *Scientific Approaches to the Study of Religion*. London: Palgrave-Macmillan, 2012.

Nelkin, Dana. "Moral Luck." In *Stanford Encyclopedia of Philosophy*, edited by Edward N. Zalta. Stanford, CT: Metaphysics Research Lab at Stanford University, 2013. https://plato.stanford.edu/entries/moral-luck/.

Nemes, Steven. "Ilaria Ramelli, *The Christian Doctrine of Apokatastasis: A Critical Assessment from the New Testament to Eriugena*." (Book review) *Journal of Analytic Theology* 3 (2015): 226–233.

Neville, Robert C. *Defining Religion: Essays in Philosophy of Religion.* Albany, NY: SUNY Press, 2018.

Nietzsche, Friedrich. *On the Advantage and Disadvantage of History for Life,* translated by Peter Preuss. Indianapolis, IN: Hackett Publishing, 1980.

Nola, Robert. "Do Naturalistic Explanations of Religious Beliefs Debunk Religion?" In *A New Science of Religion,* edited by Greg Dawes and James Maclaurin, 162–189. London: Routledge, 2013.

Paine, Thomas. *The Age of Reason: Being an Investigation of True and Fabulous Theology.* London: Forgotten Books, 1967.

Pascal, Blaise. *Pensees,* translated by A. J. Krailsheimer. London: Penguin Classics, 1995.

Peacock, James L. and Tim Pettyjohn. "Fundamentalisms Narrated: Muslim, Christian, and Mystical." In *Fundamentalisms Comprehended,* edited by Martin, E. Marty and R. Scott Appleby, 115–134. Chicago, IL: Chicago University Press, 1995.

Peels, Rik. *Responsible Belief: A Theory in Ethics and Epistemology.* Oxford: Oxford University Press, 2016.

Penelhum, Terence. *God and Skepticism: A Study in Skepticism and Fideism.* Dordrecht, Holland: D. Reidel Publishing Company, 1983.

———. "Fideism." In *Blackwell Companion to Philosophy of Religion,* edited by Philip L. Quinn and Charles Taliaferro, 376–382. Hoboken, NJ: Wiley-Blackwell, 1999.

Perszyk, Ken. (ed.) *Molinism: The Contemporary Debate.* Oxford: Oxford University Press, 2012.

PEW Forum on Religion and Public Life. "Faith in Flux: Changes in Religious Affiliation in the U.S." *PEW Research Center.* www.pewforum.org/2009/04/27/faith-in-flux/ (accessed September 2017).

Philips, Michael. *The Undercover Philosopher: A Guide to Detecting Shams, Lies, and Delusions.* London: Oneworld Publications, 2009.

Pigden, Charles. "Subversive Explanations." In *A New Science of Religion,* edited by Gregory Dawes and James Maclaurin, 147–161. London: Routledge, 2013.

Plant, Bob. "Religion, Relativism, and Wittgenstein's Naturalism." *International Journal of Philosophical Studies* 19, no. 2 (2011): 177–209.

Plantinga, Alvin. "Pluralism: A Defense of Religious Exclusivism." In *The Rationality of Belief and the Plurality of Faith,* edited by T.D. Senor. Ithaca, NY: Cornell University Press, 1995.

Plantinga, Alvin, Michael Sudduth, Stephen Wykstra, and Linda Zagzebski. "Warranted Christian Belief." *Philosophical Books* 43 (2002): 81–135.

Pojman, Louis. *Religious Belief and the Will.* London: Routledge, 1986.

Popkin, Richard. *The History of Scepticism: From Erasmus to Descartes.* Assen, Netherlands: Van Gorcum Publishers, 1960.

Potts, Richard. "The Religious Sense." In *Human Origins and the Image of God: Essays in Honor of J. Wentzel van Huyssteen,* edited by Christopher Lilley and Daniel J. Pedersen, 95–111. Grand Rapids, MI: William B. Eerdmans Publishing Co., 2017.

Pouivet, Roger. "Religious Imagination and Virtue Epistemology." *Ars Disputandi* 2, no. 1 (2002): 78–88.

Pritchard, Duncan and Lee J. Whittington. (eds.) *Philosophy of Luck*. Hoboken, NJ: Wiley-Blackwell, 2015.

Pritchard, Duncan. "Reforming Reformed Epistemology." *International Philosophical Quarterly* 43, no. 1 (2003): 43–66. doi:10.5840/ipq200343156.

———. *Epistemic Luck*. Oxford: Oxford University Press, 2005.

———. "Knowledge and Understanding." In *The Nature and Value of Knowledge: Three Investigations*, edited by Duncan Pritchard, Alan Millar, and Adrian Haddock, 1–88. Oxford: Oxford University Press, 2010.

———. "Risk." *Metaphilosophy* 46, no. 3 (2015): 436–461.

———. "The Modal Account of Luck." In *The Philosophy of Luck*, edited by Duncan Pritchard and Lee J. Whittington, 143–168. Hoboken, NJ: Wiley Blackwell, 2015.

———. "Epistemic Risk." *Journal of Philosophy* 113, no. 11 (2016): 550–571.

———. "Anti-Luck Virtue Epistemology and Epistemic Defeat." *Synthese* 195, no. 7 (2016): 3065–3077. https://doi.org/10.1007/s11229-016-1074-4.

———. "Faith and Reason." *Royal Institute of Philosophy Supplement* 81 (2017): 101–118.

Pronin, Emily. "Perception and Misperception of Bias in Human Judgment." *Trends in Cognitive Science* 11, no. 1 (2007): 37–43.

Pronin, Emily, Thomas Gilovich, and Lee Ross. "Objectivity in the Eye of the Beholder: Divergent Perceptions of Bias in Self Versus Others." *Psychological Review* 111, no. 3 (2004): 781–799.

Pronin Emily, Justin Kruger, Kenneth Savitsky, and Lee Ross. "You Don't Know Me, But I Know You: The Illusion of Asymmetric Insight." *Journal of Personality and Social Psychology* 81, no. 4 (2001): 639–656.

Pronin, Emily, Daniel Y. Lin, and Lee Ross. "The Bias Blind Spot: Perceptions of Bias in Self Versus Others." *Personality and Social Psychology Bulletin* 28, no. 3 (2002): 369–381.

Quinn, Philip. "Fideism." In *Oxford Companion to Philosophy*, 2nd ed., edited by Ted Honderich. Oxford: Oxford University Press, 2007.

———. "Epistemic Parity and Religious Argument." *Philosophical Perspectives* 5 (1991): 317–341.

Ramelli, Ilaria. *The Christian Doctrine of Apokatastasis: A Critical Assessment from the New Testament to Eriugena*. Leiden, Netherlands: Brill Publishing, 2013.

Rawls, John. *Political Liberalism*. New York: Columbia University Press, 1993.

Rees, Clea F. and Jonathan Webber. "Automaticity in Virtuous Action." In *The Philosophy and Psychology of Character and Happiness*, edited by N. E. Snow and F.V. Trivigno, 75–90. London: Routledge, 2014.

Rehder, Bob. "Property Generalization as Causal Reasoning." In *Inductive Reasoning: Experimental, Developmental, and Computational Approaches*, edited by A. Feeny and E. Heit, 81–113. Cambridge: Cambridge University Press, 2008.

Rescher, Nicholas. *Luck: The Brilliant Randomness of Everyday Life*. Pittsburg, PA: Pittsburg University Press, 2001.

Rettler, Bradley. "Analysis of Faith." *Philosophy Compass*. Hoboken, NJ: John Wiley & Sons Ltd., 2018. https://doi.org/10.1111/phc3.12517.

Ridder, Jeroen de. "Why Only Externalists Can Be Steadfast." *Erkenntnis* 79, no. 1 (2014): 185–199.

———. "Religious Exclusivism Unlimited." *Religious Studies* 47, no. 4 (2011): 449–463.

Riggs, Wayne. "Epistemic Risk and Relativism." *Acta Analytica* 23, no. 1 (2008): 1–8.

Rinard, Susanna. "Believing for Practical Reasons." *Noûs* (2018a): 1–22.

———. "Pragmatic Skepticism." *Philosophy and Phenomenological Research*, forthcoming (2018b).

Ruthven, Malise. *Fundamentalism: The Search for Meaning.* Oxford: Oxford University Press, 2004.

———. "Religion and Politics in the Age of Fundamentalisms." In *The Oxford Handbook of the Abrahamic Religions*, edited by Adam Silverstein and Guy Stroumsa. Oxford: Oxford University Press, 2015.

Sands, Paul. *The Justification of Religious Faith in Soren Kierkegaard, John Henry Newman, and William James.* Piscataway, NJ: Gorgias Press, 2014.

Samuelson, Peter and Ian Church. (2014). "When Cognition Turns Vicious: Heuristics and Biases in Light of Virtue Epistemology." *Philosophical Psychology* 28, no. 8 (2015): 1095–1113. doi:10.1080/09515089.2014.904197.

Sartorio, Carolina. "Resultant Luck." *Philosophy and Phenomenological Research* 84, no. 1 (2011): 63–86.

Savage, Sara. "Four Lessons from the Study of Fundamentalism and Psychology of Religion." *Journal of Strategic Security* 4, no. 4 (2012): 131–150.

Schellenberg, J. L. *Divine Hiddenness and Human Reason.* Ithaca, NY: Cornell University Press, 1993.

———. *The Wisdom to Doubt: A Justification of Religious Skepticism.* Ithaca, NY: Cornell University Press, 2007.

Schoenfield, Miriam. "Permission to Believe: Why Permissivism Is True and What It Tells Us about Irrelevant Influences on Belief." *Noûs* 48, no. 2 (2014): 193–218.

Schönbaumsfeld, Genia. "'Objectively There is No Truth' – Wittgenstein and Kierkegaard on Religious Belief." In *In Search of Meaning: Ludwig Wittgenstein on Ethics, Mysticism and Religion*, edited by Arnswald, Ulrich, 131–148. Karlsruhe, Germany: Universitätsverlag Karlsruhe, 2009.

Schouten, Maurice and Huib Looren de Jong. (eds.) *The Matter of the Mind: Philosophical Essays on Psychology, Neuroscience and Reduction.* Hoboken, NJ: Wiley-Blackwell, 2012.

Sessions, William L. *The Concept of Faith: A Philosophical Investigation.* Ithaca, NY: Cornell University Press, 1994.

Shaw, Kegan. "Faith as Extended Knowledge." *Religious Studies* (2017). doi: 10.1017/S0034412517000336.

Sher, George. "But I Could be Wrong." *Social Philosophy and Policy* 18, no. 2 (2001): 64–78.

Sider, Theodore. "Hell and Vagueness." *Faith and Philosophy* 19, no. 1 (2002): 58–68.

Silverstein, Adam J. and Guy G. Stroumsa. (eds.) *The Oxford Handbook of the Abrahamic Religions.* Oxford: Oxford University Press, 2015.

Simon, Dick. "The Most Dangerous Four-Letter Word." HuffPost. http://www.huffingtonpost.com/dick-simon/the-most-dangerous-fourle_b_4555551.html.

Simpson, Robert M. "Permissivism and the Arbitrariness Objection." *Episteme* 14, no. 4 (2017): 519–538.

Singal, Jesse. "The Bad Things That Happen When People Can't Deal With Ambiguous Situations." The Cut. http://nymag.com/scienceofus/2015/10/importance-of -dealing-with-ambiguity.html.

Slone, Jason. *Theological Incorrectness: Why Religious People Believe What They Shouldn't.* Oxford: Oxford University Press, 2004.

Smart, Ninian. *Worldviews: Crosscultural Explorations of Human Beliefs.* Englewood Cliffs, NJ: Prentice-Hall, 1995.

Smith, Holly M. "Dual-Process Theory and Moral Responsibility." In *The Nature of Moral Responsibility*, edited by Michael McKenna, Angela Smith, and Randolph Clarke. Oxford: Oxford University Press, 2014.

Smith, Tom. "Spiritual and Religious Transformations in America: The National Spiritual Transformation Study." National Opinion Research Center. Chicago, IL: University of Chicago, 2005.

Snow, Nancy. *Virtue as Social Intelligence: An Empirically Grounded Theory.* London: Routledge, 2009.

———. "Habitual Virtuous Actions and Automaticity." *Ethical Theory and Moral Practice* 9, no. 5 (2006): 545–561.

Sorensen, Jesper. "Religion in Mind: A Review Article of the Cognitive Science of Religion." *Numen* 56, no. 4 (2005): 465–494.

Spears, R. "Ingroup-Outgroup Bias." In *Encyclopedia of Social Psychology*, edited by Roy F. Baumeister and Kathleen D. Vohs. Thousand Oaks, CA: SAGE Publications, 2007. http://dx.doi.org/10.4135/9781412956253.

Srinivasan, A. "The Archimedean Urge," *Philosophical Perspectives* 29 (2015): 325–362.

Stanovich, Keith E. *Rationality and the Reflective Mind.* Oxford: Oxford University Press, 2011.

Stanovich, Keith E., Richard F. West, and Maggie E. Toplak. "Myside Bias, Rational Thinking, and Intelligence." *Current Directions in Psychological Science* 22, no. 4 (2013): 259–264.

———. "Heuristics and Biases as Measures of Critical Thinking," *Journal of Educational Psychology* 100, no. 4 (2008): 930–941.

Stenros, Jaakko. "In Defence of a Magic Circle: The Social, Mental, and Cultural Boundaries of Play." DiGRA. *Transactions of the Digital Games Research Association* 1, no. 2 (2014): 147–185.

Sudduth, Michael. "Defeaters in Epistemology." Internet Encyclopedia of Philosophy (n.d.). http://www.iep.utm.edu/ep-defea/.

Sylvan, Kurt and Errol Lord. *Well-Founded Belief: New Essays on the Epistemic Basing Relation*, edited by P. Bondy and J.A. Carter. London: Routledge, forthcoming, 2019.

Thagard, Paul. "Critical Thinking and Informal Logic: Neuropsychological Perspectives." *Informal Logic* 31, no. 3 (2011): 152–170.

Thune, Michael. "Religious Belief and the Epistemology of Disagreement." *Philosophy Compass* 5, no. 8 (2010): 712–724.

Tremlin, Todd. *Minds and Gods: The Cognitive Foundations of Religion.* Oxford: Oxford University Press, 2010.

Tucker, Chris. (ed.) *Seemings and Justification: New Essays on Dogmatism and Phenomenal Conservatism.* Oxford: Oxford University Press, 2013.

Vainio, Olli-Pekka. *Disagreeing Virtuously: Religious Conflict in Interdisciplinary Perspective.* Grand Rapids, MI: Wm. B. Eerdmans Publishing, 2017.

———. *Beyond Fideism: Negotiable Religious Identities.* London: Routledge, 2010.

Van Vugt, Mark. "Averting the Tragedy of the Commons." *Current Directions in Psychological Science* 18, no. 3 (2008): 169–173.

Vavova, Katia. "Irrelevant Influences." *Philosophy and Phenomenological Research* 96, no. 1 (2018): 134–152.

———. "Confidence, Evidence, and Disagreement." *Erkenntnis* 79, no. S1 (2014): 173–183.

Visala, Aku and David Leech. "How Relevant is the Cognitive Science of Religion to Philosophy of Religion?" *Scientific Approaches to the Philosophy of Religion* (2012): 165–183.

———. "Naturalistic Explanation for Religious Belief." *Philosophy Compass* 6, no. 8 (2011): 552–563.

Vorster, Jakobus M. "Core Characteristics of Religious Fundamentalism Today." *Journal for the Study of Religions and Ideologies* 7, no. 21 (2008): 44–65.

Welchman, Jennifer. "William James's 'The Will to Believe' and the Ethics of Self-experimentation." *Transactions of the Charles S. Peirce Society* 42, no. 2 (2006): 229–241.

Weltecke, Dorothea. "Beyond Exclusivism in the Middle Ages: On the Three Rings, the Three Imposters, and the Discourse of Multiplicity." In *The Oxford Handbook of the Abrahamic Religions*, edited by Adam J. Silverstein and Guy G. Stroumsa. Oxford: Oxford University Press, 2015.

Wernham, James C. S. *James's Will-To-Believe Doctrine: A Heretical View.* Montreal, Quebec: McGill-Queen's University Press, 1987.

Wessling, Jordan. "Theology and Luck." In *The Routledge Handbook of the Philosophy and Psychology of Luck*, edited by Ian Church and R. Hartman. London: Routledge, 2019.

Whitehouse, Harvey and Brian McQuinn. "Divergent Modes of Religiosity and Armed Struggle." In *The Oxford Handbook of Religion and Violence*, edited by Mark Juergensmeyer, Margo Kitts, and Michael Jerryson. Oxford: Oxford University Press, 2013.

Williams, Bernard. "Tolerance: An Impossible Virtue?" In *Toleration: An Elusive Virtue*, edited by David Heyd, 18–27. Princeton, NJ: Princeton University Press, 1996.

———. "Moral Luck." In *Moral Luck: Philosophical Papers 1973–1980*, 20–39. Cambridge: Cambridge University Press, 1981.

Wittgenstein, Ludwig. "Lectures on Religious Belief." In *Wittgenstein: Lectures and Conversations on Aesthetics, Psychology and Religious* Belief, edited by C. Barrett. Berkeley, CA: University of California Press, 2007.

Wood, Graham. "Cognitive Science and Religious Belief." *Philosophy Compass* 6, no. 10 (2011): 734–745.

Wright, Larry. *Critical Thinking*, 2nd ed. Oxford: Oxford University Press, 2012.

Xygalatas, Dimitris and Ryan McKay. "Announcing the Journal for the Cognitive Science of Religion." *Journal of the Cognitive Science of Religion* 1, no. 1 (2013): 1–4.

Yandell, Keith E. (ed.) *Faith and Narrative*. Oxford: Oxford University Press, 2001.

Yurak, Tricia J. "False Consensus Effect." In *Encyclopedia of Social Psychology, Volume 1*, edited by Roy F. Baumeister and Kathleen D. Vohs. Thousand Oaks, CA: SAGE Publications, 2007.

Zagzebski, Linda. "Religious Luck." *Faith and Philosophy* 11, no. 3 (1994): 397–413.

Index

Abrahamic religions, 175, 194n60, 211, 231, 238n27; predetermination teachings in, 18; religious fundamentalism and, 87–88, 102n9, 130, 166; teleological suspension of the ethical and, 97–98, 222–23

Abrams, Dominic, 157

actor–observer asymmetry, 118, 135n26

actual luckiness, 41n26

Adamo, Christopher, 169

Adams, Robert M., 156–57

adequacy of conception/model of religious faith: conceptions vs. models and, 158–67; epistemic/intellectual, 131, 139n60, 164; ethical, 131, 139n60, 164; theological, 131, 140n60, 151, 164

Advice-Focused Dilemma, 173–79, 185

Aijaz, Imran, 39n10, 146, 217, 233, 242n46

Aikin, Scott, 104n22, 140n64, 199n95

aleatory luck, 14, 41n25

ambiguity: evidential, 56, 137n45, 143, 147, 155–56; religious, 21, 44n42, 146–48

amodal processing, 136n33

anti-luck virtue epistemologies, 40n15

Aquinas, Thomas, 23, 44n39, 137n40

Armstrong, Karen, 45n45, 154

AS. *See* testimonial authority assumption

asymmetric religious luck attributions: CSR and, 3, 206, 211, 213–15, 225, 240n38; degrees of inductive risk operationalizing, 33–34, 57, 67, 74, 230; exclusivist responses to religious multiplicity and, 35, 51n73, 59–60, 66, 70, 80n33, 132, 143–44, 180, 188n19, 210–11, 223, 231; focus on, 35, 56; inductive risk account and, 3, 35, 73, 230; multisided interest in, 3–7; in New Problem, 62–70, *63–64*; as open to psychological study, 74, 110; study of personal biases and, 56, 93, 100, 110, *228*; study of social biases and, 56, 93, 100, 110, *113–15*, 117, 119, 225, *228*

asymmetric religious luck attributions, inductive risk account operationalizing: by degrees of inductive risk, 33–34, 57, 67, 74, 230; degrees of risk as scalable, 74; high risk as marker of fundamentalist orientation, 85, 100, 112, 131; high risk as measure of strong fideism, 85, 100, 131, 158; overview of, 85; source-monitoring failures and, 120–23

About the Author

Guy Axtell is Professor of Philosophy in the Philosophy & Religious Studies Department at Radford University, Virginia. He is author of the wide-ranging monograph, *Objectivity* (2015, Polity Press/Wiley), and of over 30 articles in the areas of epistemology, virtue theory, philosophy of religion, pragmatism, philosophy of science, and critical thinking pedagogy. He has served as a faculty fellow in the Radford Honors College, and as a research fellow at *Institute for Advanced Studies in the Humanities,* housed at University of Edinburgh, Scotland.